Memory Lake

ORIGINAL PHOTO OF THE NINE MAIN CHARACTERS:

Victoria, Lori, Nancy, Susie, Cindy, Christie, Sarah, Me, Mary

Memory Lake

[THE FOREVER FRIENDSHIPS OF SUMMER]

Nancy S. Kyme

vantage
POINT

This work remains faithful to actual events and real people, although some details have been altered to protect the privacy of individuals and the sanctity of locations.

Cover design by Michael Fusco

Vantage Point Books and the Vantage Point Books colophon are registered trademarks of Vantage Press, Inc.

FIRST EDITION: July 2011

Published by Vantage Point Books, an imprint of Vantage Press, Inc.

419 Park Ave. South, New York, NY 10016

Manufactured in the United States of America ISBN: 978-1-936467-05-1
Library of Congress Cataloging-in-Publication data are on file.

0 9 8 7 6 5 4 3 2 1

For Nancy, so she'll remember
For Christie, so she won't forget
For Misty, so she'll know

Heaven gives our years of fading strength indemnifying
  fleetness

And those of youth, a seeming length, proportioned to
  their sweetness.

—Thomas Campbell

ONE

A CAPTIVE AUDIENCE

"WILL THERE BE critters in this lake?" Angela asked. She shifted around in the backseat unfolding her long legs. Her morning voice, scratchy from a late night, nudged my concentration from the outside road.

Katie sat beside her and rummaged through the dividing heap of pillows, fashion magazines, purses, and snacks. "Yeah, I can't stand jellyfish, crabs, or seaweed." Her sleepy voice drifted through the car.

My daughter recognized the rustle of candy wrappers and turned from the front seat. She stretched a hand toward her two best friends.

"This is not a healthy breakfast," Angela playfully admonished.

"So, here's an orange." Katie smirked, setting a brightly wrapped confection into my daughter's open palm.

"No critters!" I answered from the driver's seat. At seventy miles per hour we sped across the smooth, reddish asphalt cutting a wide swath over Keyser Pass, so named by West Virginia's green information sign. This barren summit, high above the tree line, boasted a truck stop and panoramic views. A strong wind buffeted the car, and cool rain pelted the windshield from low-hanging clouds. I gripped the steering wheel and squinted into the blurry freeway. Suddenly, it didn't seem like summer. Up ahead, a tractor-trailer merged into my lane. I flicked my turn signal and switched to the left. My skin prickled from a flush of adrenaline as this giant hunk of metal gained speed, forcing its entry. I floored the accelerator to clear well ahead.

"There's a wide sandy beach." My daughter sounded indifferent, though her green eyes danced excitedly. "And . . . you cannot see the other side," she added before plopping the candy into her mouth.

"It's that big?" Katie marveled from behind my headrest. She leaned into the front as if able to see it from three states over. "I've never been west of Pennsylvania."

"Me either." Angela bounced next to her, raising her arms in a yawn. Her lively brown eyes scanned the instrument panel. "It is eight o'clock," she announced. "We've slept three hours."

"I could sleep eight more," my daughter groaned.

Speeding well ahead of the truck's downhill charge, I settled into the right lane, cleared my windshield, and posed the question I'd been waiting to ask for hours, "Did you stay up all night?"

Their gritty laughter confirmed it, and explained why they had promptly fallen asleep after boarding the car in early darkness.

"We watched some movies and talked to our friends on the phone," my daughter said.

I nodded at these benign activities.

"Angela had to spend every last minute with her boyfriend," Katie said.

I stiffened at the prospect of late-night visitors.

"On the phone," my daughter clarified.

"And we packed," Angela said, sending sharp accusing looks at both her friends for revealing anything about her love life to an adult.

"Don't you mean repacked?" I hinted. Again, their chuckles reinforced my assumption.

"How long have you had my light-blue hoodie?" Angela asked her backseat companion. "It was a birthday present sophomore year. We're going to be seniors and I haven't worn it once."

"Well, it's in your bag now," Katie said. "You should be happy because it got a lot of compliments. People said it matches my eyes."

"You guys." I shook my head, recalling Sunday-night deliveries of neatly folded tops, skirts, or pants. My daughter, KT, as everyone calls her, using first and last initials to set her apart from all other Katies in her class, often coerced her older brother into running out for ice cream so she could make a similar drop. I imagined a nightlong swap-fest had occurred to redistribute the mutually favored clothing among the respective owners.

Then again, maybe they had slipped out during the midnight hours of my innocent slumber to join a party somewhere, drinking and smoking until dawn, so Angela could say good-bye to her boyfriend in person.

I sized them up, especially my daughter, and sniffed the air for a whiff of fermentation or the scent of nicotine. I searched their faces for discomfort from nausea and headaches. I had a notion they might be as wild and troublesome as I had been at their age. The idea gripped me at times, tainting my perspective, and jarring me from the role of trusting parent. However, this time I could not verify my suspicions. Their tired eyes and hoarse voices justified either scenario. So I decided against a confrontation.

"About this lake . . ." Katie's voice rose from the backseat, prompting a return to Angela's original question.

"Lake Michigan is one of the Great Lakes," I broke in. "KT, why don't you show them the atlas?" I cast my daughter a curious look, wondering if she would brush me off. She knew our travel plans but Angela and Katie hadn't cared until now. They had tagged along at the last minute, eager to go anywhere, to escape their summer jobs. I rushed to enlighten them before the moment waned.

KT rolled her eyes and sighed. She would make the effort, I knew from experience, though not enthusiastically. So I envisioned a compromise. "Hold out your right hand," I said. To my delight she raised her hand like a traffic cop. I brushed my finger against her pinkie. "We are going there!"

Angela's ribald laughter and Katie's embarrassed snicker proved they misunderstood my attempt to use KT's hand as a map. Anyone from Michigan would have known exactly what I meant.

"And we live here?" Angela struggled to be serious as she jabbed KT's palm. My daughter wrapped her hand around Angela's finger and pulled. They giggled heartily at my expense.

"If you could see a map," I said, "you'd understand it looks like a hand."

"Hang on," my daughter kindly rescued me. She reached under her seat and retrieved the atlas. After fumbling through each state, pausing momentarily on our home state of Virginia, she turned it vertically and displayed the two-page spread. "Now pay attention, children," she mocked.

"See how Lower Michigan resembles a giant mitten surrounded by blue?" I coaxed. "You have to look past the detail of roads, cities, and inland lakes." I pointed to a coastal area where chocolate brown met royal blue. "We are going here, along the pinkie."

"Mom, I got it," KT said, shifting from me. She placed a finger where I had pointed. "This is where we are going."

My eyes returned to the road, and I scowled at the map's limitations. A bunch of geographic lines and bold colors could never depict the shoreline's simple beauty. Not even a well-crafted painting, a photograph, or an eloquent poem would do. One had to see it in person. And I, who had spent five youthful summers along that chart of blue and brown, wanted my companions to understand how profoundly it had impacted my life. It was there I had learned to soar beyond limitations, dream the future, and gain the strength to carry it out.

Now, thirty years later, it seemed I had come to the end of those dreams. My mom had died, and I faced the future from a precipice of fear and grief. Same as then, ripples of change invaded my complacent life, forcing me to grow without her. Somehow, I believed this trip would get me around it, through it, or over it, by showing me what I had lost.

I could never say this aloud. So, I held quiet, remaining grateful to have my daughter and her friends along. They emboldened me, giving me the courage to make this journey.

"What's that big piece of land up there?" Angela pointed. She bent toward KT, thoughtfully cupping her chin. "Is that Canada?"

"No, it's Michigan," KT said, taking a closer look for herself. "It's the Upper Peninsula. Everyone calls it the 'U.P.' Right, Mom?" She flashed the map in my direction.

"Right," I said. "And it looks like a glove." I turned my hand on its side to demonstrate.

"The Great Lakes have freshwater, no salt," my daughter proudly emphasized. "No shells either. That's one thing I miss from the ocean.

But there are really cool fossils to find along the beach." A melancholy expression darkened her youthful face, and I wondered at its meaning, for she also had spent a fair amount of time along the shores of Lake Michigan.

She closed the atlas and dropped it to the floor. She whirled to face her friends. Shining brown hair fell across her cheek as she flourished a palm, expecting another piece of candy.

"The Great Lakes are unique," I said. "They are the longest freshwater shoreline in the world. I've seen plenty of man-made lakes, but they are not the same. Even the ocean, amazing as it is, can't stack up. The salt gets in your mouth, and the sand sticks to your skin and clothing. Plus, it has jellyfish, barracudas, and sharks!"

"How do they make a man-made lake?" Katie asked.

"The Army Corps of Engineers builds a dam," I replied, peeking through my rearview mirror. Seeing her perplexed expression, I added, "They divert the flow of rivers and streams, creating one huge flood that turns into a permanent lake. Entire towns are lost forever. Think of it, old farmhouses entombed in the deep like ghostly sunken ships, their treasured memories lost forever. Fish swim through dilapidated doors and windows as layers of silt gather on a kitchen counter, once tenderly cared for, where a family used to gather."

"That's creepy," Angela said as she snatched the bag of candy from Katie.

"Once the lake is formed, its shorelines are abrupt drop-offs. Mature trees crowd the bank. You rarely find a sandy beach, mostly dirt, and the bottoms are mucky. Besides, who knows what you might step on!" I sneered. "The Great Lakes were formed by glaciers. They have firm clear bottoms. You'll see the difference when we get to Ohio this afternoon. If we beat the rain, Chip will take us out on his boat. He lives on a man-made lake." I clamped my mouth shut, determined to say no more; hoping my answer had not been too long.

"Day after tomorrow we'll see Lake Michigan." My daughter bestowed an alluring smile upon the backseat.

"Class dismissed," Angela concluded, and I caught sight of the other Katie knuckling her arm for more candy. "You pig!" Angela chided, though she offered a yellow square.

We rounded another curve, steeper than the last, and I braked in slow, cautious spurts. Already the outside air felt warmer as we descended back into summer.

My daughter impatiently slapped her bare feet along the dashboard. "How much longer?" she asked.

"Five hours left for today." I rotated my shoulders into my backrest, mentally coaching myself to sit up straight. Days of driving lay ahead, and I couldn't afford any strained muscles. Neither could I allow my passengers a turn at the wheel given such high speeds, large trucks, and abrupt guardrails, though they all had licenses. One wrong move could be deadly. My mother's accident had proved it.

"Mrs. Taylor," Katie garbled from behind me, her mouth full of goo. "Why are we going? Is this some kind of reunion for you?"

"Yes it is!" I exclaimed. My daughter's horrified expression caused me to regret such an overzealous reply. I was learning this was not cool and could turn a teenager away from the very thing one wanted to promote. I took a deep breath, lowered my voice, and said, "I used to go to camp in northern Michigan for seven weeks at a time."

"Seven weeks!" Both girls chimed from the backseat.

"I had best friends from all over. We were as close as you three, but there were nine of us."

"Nine!" they repeated. Even my daughter joined their surprise.

"How could you be best friends with that many girls?" Angela demanded. "Didn't you fight?"

"No. There was a counselor I didn't get along with," I laughed. "But my friends and I never fought. Maybe it was the combination of our personalities and the atmosphere."

"I just can't picture it," Angela said, shrugging into her seat, resting an elbow on a stack of magazines and the near-naked body of a teenage model. The catchy headlines referred to pages of advice on how to gain sex appeal and win boys. They made the idea of guileless female friendship implausible. But I knew it was possible as the photographic image of nine fresh faces popped into my mind and came alive beneath a bright sky. Outfitted in a mix of pajamas and street clothes, our arms flung haphazardly around each other, we perched on a driftwood log and hammed it up for the camera. Cindy towered in the middle, smiling secretively beneath a floppy hat, while Nancy directed us to "be serious" as she held peace signs behind our heads. Lori's ginger bangs peaked from beneath a baby-doll hat, and Susie whooped wildly, waving a towel. Tori held a coquettish dance pose, spouting witty remarks and cracking us up, while Christie anchored our stance and cheered for us to "hold the pose." Sandwiched between Sarah, the heart of our group, and Mary, sensibly perched on the end, a younger image of me spouted a nonstop narrative for the campers who eagerly snapped our picture.

All we ever needed to know about each other we had learned in our first welcoming smiles, and years of laughter cemented the bonds. Camp had let us become our true selves, without pretense. For me, it set the course of my life.

TWO

TWO CAMPS

"ARE ALL NINE of you coming to the reunion?" KT asked.

"I've been in touch with only two of them," I said. "So, probably not. It's been a long time."

"Will you recognize them?" Katie wondered.

"I hope so!" I laughed. "A few of us have written over the years and sent pictures."

"This is the same camp you went to for a few years, right, KT?" Angela said.

"Deena-hahna," my daughter breathed, her voice dropping into a whisper of sound. "Same place as my mom's reunion," she added. "But when my mom went to camp it had a different name and was in a different place."

The place had felt strange and unfamiliar when taking KT and her brother to half-sessions over nonconsecutive summers. Some cabins bore the old names, and many of our traditions remained, but it was not my camp.

KT faced the backseat and her voice descended into a metered pitch as if relating an ancient legend. "Resting high on a bluff, overlooking the Big Lake, Deena-hahna carries on its noble purpose of over eighty years to instill spiritual qualities in young women through an atmosphere of love."

"That was good." I averted my eyes from the road for a quick nod of approval.

Her friends chuckled at the performance, and I warmed to the sound of it.

"The boys' camp is there, too, but they have a different name," she said. "It's called Shenahwau."

"Do you miss it?" Angela asked, lightly pinching KT's arm as it draped over the armrest.

"I could be a CT this year," she said, pulling away. "But I don't think I'd like it for the full seven weeks. None of my camp friends is returning, either. They have cheerleading camps, family vacations, you know, stuff like that. Besides, we don't even get out of school until after the first session starts."

"East Coast schools end later than the Midwest," I interjected.

"What's a CT?" Katie asked from behind me.

"A counselor in training," my daughter said.

"Don't we feel special!" Angela tilted her head and regarded KT through a mischievous smile. "You chose us and your lifeguard job instead of camp!"

"It was never an easy choice," I qualified. "Every spring when the camp's enrollment came in the mail, she would agonize about leaving, and missing anything at home. When I was her age, I had to go. Not that anyone made me. I just couldn't imagine spending my summers anywhere else."

We fell silent, hearing the road beneath the wheels, the wind pressing through the vents, and I sought a deeper reason. Taking a distant, almost clinical view of the past, I realized academics had come easy to me at their age. I was bored and unchallenged in the classroom, and at home. I craved adventure and found it by skirting the edge of legal and illegal, moral and immoral, just to see what I could get away with. When summers rolled around, thanks to my clueless, devoted parents, I found myself in a completely different environment. The challenges were meaningful. Success did not come easy. And I discovered for the first time I was not good at everything. Luckily, camp's philosophy had resonated with me enough to stick it out so a healthier form of peer pressure could take root and hold sway.

A cherry-red Mustang roared past. "Oh! I want a car like that!" Angela exclaimed, seeing fun and thrills where I now saw peril. Its engine revved a crescendo of noise, then curved from view. The road twisted and climbed toward another summit. Deep woods crowded the shoulder, and my thoughts wandered back to a time before such fears had occurred to me. I could almost feel a breeze brushing my cheek, carrying the prickly scent of cedar as it blustered from shadowy woods and mingled into hot sunshine baking on golden sand. In the back of my mind I heard the distinct sound of a wooden door banging loudly from a recoiling spring. I ran behind a pair of long legs and bare feet. I chased her across a dune, and we splashed into the shallows of a crisp, blue lake. "My first friend at camp had the same name as me," I said.

"Wow! That was really random, Mom!" KT's tone sliced right through me.

"Aha!" The other Katie laughed from the backseat.

"What's that for?" Angela sharply rebuked.

"I don't know," Katie said, cowering away. "It seemed like a triumph for the two Katies."

My daughter spun around. "And don't you forget it!"

Angela's brown eyes calculated revenge as she stretched a tanned leg into the front seat and wiggled her toes into KT's ribs. My daughter laughed, pushed her away, and reached for the radio. Loud static filled the car. She pressed button after button searching for music.

"You won't find a station," I said. "The mountains block the signals."

Disgruntled, and resigned, she ended the annoying static. She rested an elbow on the armrest and placed her chin in her hand. I felt her staring at me. "Tell us what made you want to go in the first place. And don't say, 'because Gramsy signed you up.'"

"Well," I began, setting the cruise control for a safe speed, "at first I wanted to go because I loved the lake." I paused, suspicious of them using me to torment each other. But my daughter's eyes entreated me to say more. "Seven years ago," I said, speaking mostly to her, yet loud enough for the backseat to hear, "I packed you and your brother off to camp for the first time. You didn't know anything about Lake Michigan. However, as a kid from Indiana, for as long as I can remember, my family would visit the lake just to see what it looked like in different weather. The southern tip was only an hour from our house."

I envisioned it in summer, reaching out toward Chicago smooth as glass. "Sometimes the water raged." I recalled rows of whitecaps marching toward shore under layers of puffy clouds. "In winter, the waves can freeze over in mid-motion. We have photos," I added, a bit defensively, knowing how fantastic it sounded. "My sister and I are sitting on the edge of one frozen in the act of spilling over. All around us, they rise four feet or more, capped in snow, like curved fingers of a mythical giant clawing up through the ice. The air has to be really cold for the lake to freeze over, but it can, since it is fresh water. The entire surface, as far as the eye can see, changes into a wonderfully sculpted obstacle course. It's probably dangerous." I shrugged sheepishly.

"That sounds tight," Angela breathed.

"I have also seen waves almost as big as the north shore of Maui. They could knock you over when they hit the shore, ten feet at their peak. They came after the tornadoes." I squinted, trying to focus the hazy memory of two twisters cutting a path of destruction for camp. "Who was I with?" I muttered, struggling to see the beach through a misty fog from a bird's-eye view. "I swear I stood on that shore and watched."

"Yeah, the waves can get pretty big," KT spoke over me, launching a dubious scowl in my direction, as if I grossly exaggerated.

"The point is," I said, "even in bad weather, the lake has a calming effect on me. And from the very first I wanted to go to this camp because it was on Lake Michigan. I wanted to see picturesque clouds, vibrant sunsets, and exciting thunderstorms. You know, the lake is so large it can have its own weather patterns."

A triple tractor-trailer rumbled past on my left, dangerously close, picking up speed as we descended into a valley. It appeared more frightening to me than any act of nature and dispersed my inner calm. Heavy responsibility for my passengers pressed down upon me. I pumped the brakes and fought the truck's back draft, intensified by the winding curve.

"What about this other Nancy?" Angela prompted.

The road straightened. I held back from the triple and loosened my grip. I saw the image of another face smiling at me through soulful eyes and coaxing me to persevere. Her influence had been gradual, and my awakening took time, for the essence of camp lay in its details.

"I met her in the seventies." I laughed, knowing this sounded like an ancient decade.

THREE

A DAD'S DECISION

"WE NEED YOU to take a swim test." The counselor stared at a list on her clipboard.

My dad chuckled under his breath while my mom, my sister, and I tried to glimpse the water through a forest of evergreens. I couldn't wait to see the lake after having spent long hours in the Rambler, heading the furthest north I had ever been in my life, enduring slow traffic on two-lane roads trapped behind pop-up campers and motorboats. Dad had grumbled the entire time about this driver or another until the countryside turned to cornfields and cows. Then he cranked up his speed and left our stomachs in the air as we flew over the rolling countryside. Eventually the road darkened, encroached by shady cedars, and the air turned cool. We knew the lake drew near.

A wooden signpost read, "Shenahwau." Its burned letters marked an otherwise hidden entrance. The dirt road's narrow, winding course lasted an eternity. Finally, we entered a secluded gravel lot, and the sun shone brightly upon cars and station wagons from Michigan, Illinois, Ohio, Kentucky, Indiana, Wisconsin, and even as far away as New York and Missouri. Young men and women milled about wearing white shorts and white T-shirts. Shenahwau was stenciled across their chests in green script.

When Dad lowered the Rambler's hatch, they surrounded us and we became the targets of their interest. A sea of young women introduced a flurry of names, and two young men hoisted our gear and disappeared with it into the woods. Since our footlockers and duffels had been labeled, as required, I decided not to become too concerned about this unexpected separation.

The counselor with the clipboard led us into the forest of cedars. Crinkled, reddish bark bore a thick canopy of spiked branches. We crossed their carpet of rusty needles and spoke in hushed whispers as if we stood on holy ground. The smallest noise, even the crack of a buried stick, echoed loudly. Then, my dad sneezed. The musky air had inevitably affected his allergies. He reached into his trousers for his handkerchief and to my horror he blew his nose like a stag elephant leading a charge. The sound lasted interminably as he alternated swiftly between nostrils. Finally, he put an end to my mortification and stuffed the white linen handkerchief into his trousers.

At the edge of the woods we stood on the threshold of a wooden bridge. This storybook invention arched over a modest river whose overgrown bank teamed with life, evidenced by a cacophony of summertime insects and frogs. Their humming chorus reverberated from thick weeds, completely undisturbed by the thud of our feet as we trudged across the bridge.

Beneath us flowed a ponderous current. Beams of sunlight danced between dark shadows and revealed the clarity of the water and the pebbled riverbed.

"Ah, that's nice." Dad breathed deeply. A refreshing breeze cut through the river's muddled aroma of hidden life and decay. It ruffled our clothes and drew our attention outward. A flock of pure white seagulls flew overhead spouting random cries, and I squinted into the sudden brightness. The opposite riverbank had been cleared of all growth. It opened into a bowl, sweeping upward to a peak and held in place by tufts of grass, wildflowers, and junipers. Two small cabins perched inside this rise of dunes. Their wooden signs read Puccoon and Stardust. Opposite this, and partially obscured by the riverbank, I glimpsed the outline of a more solid structure. Painted logs, stacked horizontally, rose from a cement foundation into a stand of pines.

Beyond this, we saw the lake. Golden sand, filtered by ages of freshwater waves, sloped into a panorama of infinite blue sparkles blending perfectly into the sky. At the end of the bridge we paused, captivated and entranced by its natural beauty.

The counselor took this moment to study her clipboard. "Nancy is in Sandpiper," she read aloud. "And Susan is in Driftwood."

"I'm Susan," my older sister clarified.

"We have a lot of Susans this summer." She smiled, stepping sideways and inviting us to follow. She diverted our attention from the enticing water to a slim boardwalk crossing the sand like a railroad track. "Some of the planks are curled and warped on their outer edges. Be careful," she warned.

It felt sturdy enough, but I studied it suspiciously. "That's all I need," I muttered, "another stubbed toe." We turned the corner and followed a real cement sidewalk along the back of the lodge.

"You can change into your suits here." She pointed to a striped green and yellow fiberglass hut leaning against the lodge as an afterthought of necessity. The boardwalk picked up again, and we circled a tight ring of cabins, nestled comfortably on the outskirts of a mounded courtyard with a flagpole in the middle.

"There's your trunk and duffel," Mom directed across the sandy clearing.

They had been deposited on a cement stoop outside Sandpiper. I cringed to see my stenciled name broadcasting for all to see like a pair of underwear on a clothesline. I cut into the sand, running ahead, intent upon remedying its conspicuous presence.

Mom held to the boardwalk, walking dutifully around the circle while I tried to drag my footlocker and duffel through Sandpiper's doorway. The counselor, my sister, and Dad gathered Susan's belongings in one try and entered Driftwood. Mom soon caught up and raised the other end of my trunk. Once inside the dark cabin, the door banged shut. Two trunks and a few duffels took up space in the middle of the dimly lit floor. I placed mine among them.

Dad's voice carried across the clearing and through the open screens as he badgered the counselor with embarrassing questions, mostly about the weather. "I suppose it can get pretty cool up here at night," he said. "Does it get down into the forties?"

"Why does he keep asking her about the weather?" I whispered irritably, seeking an outlet for my rising apprehension about this new home for the next three weeks.

"It can get chilly," Mom explained, trying to calm me. We squinted into a continuous row of screens spanning the cabin's midriff. Heavy shutters hung from the outside eaves, propped on wooden poles. They sheltered the cabin from direct sunlight while allowing a view outside. Despite the close growth of untamed shrubs, we could see the lake.

"You will love this," Mom concluded.

Our eyes adjusted to the inner darkness, and we studied the beds. Three singles lined the back wall. Two appeared occupied, by a towel on one and a pair of shoes on the other. The counselor's slightly larger cot was positioned near the door and displayed a bright calico quilt. An empty bunk bed towered in the opposite corner.

"This is a nice spot." Mom indicated the lower bunk.

"Okay," I said, sitting along the edge of the thick cotton mattress. Its cool, metal buttons touched my bare legs. The top rails just cleared my head. "It's cozy," I decided.

We wrapped sheets and blankets around the institutional mattress, vaguely aware of other campers filling the surrounding cabins.

"Here are your tank suit and towel," Mom said. I had been peering about, wondering if I would find a friend among the four remaining beds.

Susan and I entered the bathhouse to change. A wooden tub spanned an entire wall like a horse trough. Painted gunmetal gray, it housed four chrome spigots at marked intervals. A conspicuous slant meant the spillage from these faucets would flow to a solitary drain on the far right. Already my mind pictured a murky river of toothpaste and spit making its disgusting way down the long communal tub. I decided to avoid the thing, if possible, or at least claim a spot on the far left.

An adjoining room held four wooden stalls. Susan braved the wet cement barefoot while I clung to my pink rubber thongs, curling my toes over the soft edges, avoiding the wet patches, suspicious of their content. She opened a door. It creaked loudly. I chose the one beside it. My arms and hips banged the painted plywood in a contortion of balance as I struggled into my Speedo, wrapped my towel around my waist, and gathered my clothes to my chest.

On the way out, a colorful message taped inside the door caught my eye. "After relinquishing all save Love, 'In Thy presence is fullness of joy. . . .' Psalm 16:11."

Susan's door creaked open. "Wait," I said. "What does yours say?" She cleared her throat, and I beat her to it, "And now shall mine head be lifted up above mine enemies round about me: therefore will I offer in his tabernacle sacrifices of joy. . . . Psalm 27:6."

I balked at the word enemies and pictured armies wielding swords, facing unbeatable odds, and prayed this had nothing to do with summer camp.

Susan's lips moved at a silent, laborious pace. At the end we shrugged our shoulders, unable to fathom its meaning.

"Yuck," I declared, pointing to a dingy shower tucked in the windowless corner. "I'm going to do all my bathing in the lake!"

Susan rolled her eyes. "It doesn't look that bad!"

"It does to me!" I said, and we headed outside to meet our parents.

"Would you like to take your test in the lake or the river?" the counselor asked. We spied a few heads bobbing in the river's deep current. Their parents stood on the shore, and a handful of male counselors paused from their duties to watch from the bridge.

Susan shifted her clothes over her ample chest, uncomfortable with her new figure, while I shifted to cover my lack of one.

"Oh, they'll take their test in the lake," Dad insisted, grinning confidently. Like mute zombies we agreed.

"To the lake, then," the counselor said, leading the way.

My heart pounded excitedly to leave the boardwalk and strike into the sand. We assumed the cautious march of beachcombers, raising our legs high, trying to keep the grains from flying into our shoes. After a short while of this unbearable nonsense, I hung back from the group to remove my thongs and burrowed each step, feeling the sun's radiant warmth upon my heels and toes.

We aimed for the dock extending over the water in the shape of a backward, upside-down L. Its whitewashed planks rested on a frame of birch logs with amputated branches and white curling bark, as if newly chopped from the surrounding forest. A metal slide resided nearby, half-in and half-out of the water. This grade-school relic perched forward, as if weary from whisking too many children into the shallow water. It seemed juvenile and insulting. I decided at once I'd never go down the thing.

The sand turned to cold, wet cement at the lake's edge. I leapt from the chill to quickly mount the dock. Thankfully, its planks held warmth from the steady sunshine. Our footsteps created a rolling thunder along the dock's underside. At the base of the L a ladder presented the means for our descent into the lake.

The counselor announced, "You need to tread water for seven minutes. Then, you can have full access to the lake and the river."

Instantly, I wondered how full that access might be. It had been a few years since my first camp experience; a one-week stay at Camp Tannahdoonah, near home. I shuddered at the memory of that swampy lake full of reeds, mud, mosquitoes, and its annoying "buddy system." It had been the longest week of my life.

I searched the shore for a giant board covered in hooks and round markers, dreading the burden of choosing a "buddy," or worse, having one chosen for me. I asked, "Is there a buddy system?"

"No. However, we do ask that you not swim alone."

I nodded, feeling a glimmer of freedom inside the configuration of cabins, metal beds, unfinished walls and rafters, and the grim bathhouse.

Mom took our bundles, and we dropped our towels.

"Jump," Susan dared. The water's surface lay about two feet below the dock.

"Let's take the ladder," I suggested.

"Go together on three!" Dad urged. "One, two, three," he counted and then reached out to push us.

Naturally, we jumped. My feet broke the surface, and I squeezed my eyes shut. Down I sank, spreading my arms wide, wishing I had entered by the ladder to keep my head above water. My breathing stopped, and I reeled from the shock as if someone had punched me in the stomach. My entire being disappeared into numbing cold. I had to force my cumbersome, detached limbs to move, harnessing all my concentration just to stay afloat.

"How cold do you suppose that water is?" Dad asked the counselor, staring down at us through fiendish amusement. "I imagine," he ventured, "the lake is much warmer down by Chicago."

Susan and I glared up at him. He'd known all along we were about to jump into the equivalent of newly melted arctic slush.

"Your lips are turning blue," Mom observed.

"How long has it been?" My sister ground through her teeth. Her face contorted in agony.

"Ten seconds," the counselor announced, staring at her round-faced stopwatch.

We moaned through the slow, lamentable passage of time, struggling against paralyzed body parts and labored breathing. Years later, Dad admitted to thinking we would drown right there in front of him, quietly freezing to death.

I kicked and swirled my arms in a slow, stationary dog paddle, forcing an inhale now and then as I worried about everything. Had I packed the right clothes and brought enough blankets? Would I make friends? Would I have to hang out with my sister? Would I fit in? As I watched my disconnected arms fight for survival, the next 410 seconds stretched into four million.

"You did it!" the counselor announced suddenly.

Susan reached for the ladder, beating me to it. I climbed behind her, stiff and clumsy. Every inch of my skin felt taut and deadened as I huddled beneath my towel.

"Now you can sign up for any of the water sports: canoeing, sailing, waterskiing . . ." the counselor began listing.

"Waterskiing!" Mom interrupted, smiling at us. We had to smile back. "You can pick up where you left off before Papa sold the cottage!"

"I can drop a ski!" my sister boasted.

"You could four years ago," I corrected.

"Maybe you'll finally get up on two," she shot back, alluding to my past failures and her nefarious delight in seeing the boat drag me through the water like a hooked trout.

"I got up twice," I sneered.

A group of unsuspecting campers mounted the dock. The counselor beckoned them forward, remaining close to the ladder to administer more tests. Our teeth chattered as we scooted past.

At the boardwalk, Dad pulled keys from his pocket and announced their departure. Mom hugged us, and we stared incredulously at both of them.

"So soon?" my sister asked.

"What good would it do if we lingered about?" Dad reasoned.

"Susan and Nancy!" Mom announced, using her rare tone of authority. "I want you to make the most of this wonderful opportunity! And don't worry about writing." Her smile became a rigid line of red lipstick as she struggled against an emotional outburst. In the blazing sunshine, I detected a halo of crimson along her crown of auburn hair. "I want to hear every song you learn," she mandated, "especially some good ones for the preschool."

"Go on," Dad urged more severely, pointing toward the cabins.

"Meet some new friends!" Mom implored. "This place is really coming alive now." They strode for the bridge, and Mom waved as they crossed the river.

Susan and I watched until they disappeared. We turned to face each other. Susan stood a few inches taller, but our green eyes, freckled noses, and wet strands of light-brown hair could have been mirror images. I considered our physical similarities a cruel illusion designed to torment me by shielding the brazen differences in our personalities from the rest of the world.

"I'm headed for a nice, seething shower," she said through clenched teeth.

"You mean soothing?" I tentatively corrected, having my usual conflicting emotions of pride and embarrassment. This was not the first time a battle raged inside me concerning my sister. Even our mother, having a degree in early childhood development, could not define dyslexia or recommend treatment. Year after year, the befuddled school system placed Susan in the same classroom as every troublemaker and outcast in our district. I loved this because she knew all the cool, fast guys. When they were around I didn't mind our striking resemblance. It allowed me to gain notice from these intriguing characters, especially since I was only one grade behind her. However, she resisted their attentions and the unruliness around her—by choosing instead to be a teacher's pet and tattletale. This humiliated me more than her predictably odd choice of words. And try as I might, I could not figure out why all the cool guys still liked her. I was beginning to think it had something to do with her bust line.

"Oh yeah, soothing, I guess," Susan laughed, shrugging it off. "Coming?"

"No." I shook my head. If she hadn't reminded me of our differences I might have clung to her side. But I refused to need her, never considering she might need me. "I don't want a shower. The air is warming me up. My skin feels tingly and refreshed," I added, actually meaning it.

"Suit yourself," she said, taking the opposite boardwalk to the bathhouse.

FOUR

A DIFFERENT SORT OF COOL

I ELBOWED SANDPIPER'S door, mindful of pinching tender skin in the outer spring. It creaked in protest while rubbing a small groove along the middle of the door. I slipped through, and it banged loudly. I flinched. My eyes adjusted, and I searched about to see if anyone else had moved in. The bunk above mine wore a colorfully striped woolen blanket tucked neatly into every corner.

"Hi, I'm Nancy," a voice said.

I saw her silhouette against the screened window, mirroring my height. She stepped into a golden ray of afternoon sun. Her hair hung twice my length, with bangs, and traces of red among strands of black and brown. Her smile boasted perfectly white teeth.

I exclaimed, "My name is Nancy, too! I've never met another Nancy my age! Not in my entire junior high."

"This is my first time at camp. I'm only staying three weeks," she said.

I understood her hopeful undertone. "Me, too," I gushed, equally relieved to know she would not be running off with some long-missed friends from a previous summer.

"Have you taken the swim test yet?" I shivered at the memory. "The lake is freezing!"

When knowing laughter erupted from her chest, I laughed along, believing I had found a friend in this strange place.

"It is cold," she said. "I did the test in the river."

"Did you get dressed in the cabin?" I searched through the screens for stray fathers or more guys carrying trunks.

"Yeah," she said. "If you hurry, the coast is clear."

She watched the boardwalk while I changed into dry clothes. I also ditched the rubber thongs in favor of my hip leather sandals. "We drove up from South Bend, Indiana," I said, hoping for more things in common. "Where are you from?"

"Dryden, New York," she proudly stated. "We live in the country. There is a small lake in front of our house. We have ducks, and geese. Our Main Street has one stop sign, and we have no mail delivery."

"How do you get mail, then?" I gasped.

"We take a trip to the post office!"

"Oh," I said, picturing the sense of it all. "Do you have any brothers or sisters?"

"No brothers, only sisters."

"Me, too!" I exclaimed, astounded by our similarities. "I have one sister in Driftwood."

"Mine didn't come. I have two sisters." She spoke of Theresa, a few years older, and Amy, equally younger. I admired her genuine affection for them as she listed their virtues without brag or shame.

The other beds in the cabin filled up. Their faces have grown vague over the years, as well as their names, but I still remember our counselor, Leslie. She coordinated introductions then herded us out the door to assemble with the rest of the campers around the flagpole.

A creosote log, more of a telephone pole than an actual flagpole, anchored a thick cotton version of the Stars and Stripes. It flapped noisily in the ever-present breeze. Our other cabin mates dispersed to find friends from different cabins. Nancy and I stuck together like glue. I counted roughly forty girls in our circle, some as young as eight and others as old as seventeen. Without warning, a handful of them started singing. They punched each note wildly and loudly.

The Cannibal KING with the big nose RING fell in love with the dusky maaaaid.

And every NIGHT by the pale moon LIGHT across the lake he'd
waaaade. . . .

"Who makes this stuff up?" I whispered to Nancy.

My sister waved from across the circle. She stood near the oldest girls.
I couldn't take my eyes off them. They whispered among themselves,
casually at ease in their dangling wire earrings, painted nails, low hip-
huggers, wide macramé belts, skimpy triangle halters, bare tanned
midriffs, and full figures. I would be entering high school in a year and
envisioned halls full of such girls. I wanted to be one of them. I imagined
they protested the immature song. So I held my silence and protested it,
too. I loved music, all kinds, and had been told my voice was nice, but
I didn't believe anyone older than I would want to sing this blather. It
belonged in my mom's preschool.

The pandemonium expanded as more campers joined in. Eventually
my newly anointed idols added their voices, carrying on and having fun.
A couple of them actually dispersed through the circle to teach others!
Even Nancy joined in! Amazed, I tried to sing along.

When the song reached its long, unnatural end it dawned on me—
camp required a different sort of cool.

Bess stepped into the clearing. Everyone fell silent. Neither her age, somewhere beyond fifty, nor her petite stature, less than five-foot, could deflect
from her vitality and authority. She planted a wide stance and made visual
contact with the full circle, conveying a no-nonsense manner of fairness and
respect. Her dark, cropped hair framed a round face, piercing brown eyes,
and bronzed skin. She wore white dungarees reaching mid-calf. When she
spoke, she jammed her fingertips into her pockets, palms flat against her
hips, and leaned forward to engage us.

"Welcome! This is our second summer in this location." She punched
her words in a nasal Michigan clip, void of any "ums," "you knows," or
languorous vowels of the South, to form a swift version of news-anchor
English. "We share a dining facility, an athletic field, and a theatre owned
by the year-round boys' school. To the outside world we are known as

'Camp Shenahwau for Boys and Girls.' But here among us we are Wild-wood. Our numbers are small compared to the boys, but together we can accomplish big things."

A bell chimed in the distance, mesmerizing us with its deep, mellow tone.

"That's the boy's bell," she said. "It tells them they have fifteen minutes until dinner. It tells us we should be at dinner."

As if on cue another bell clanged loudly above our heads. It hung from a second-story window of the lodge. Its shrill, rapid clatter startled the birds from the trees.

Bess smirked at its tardiness. "This is your signal to head for the dining hall. After dinner, return to camp. Change into sneakers if you are not already wearing them. Grab a sweater and gather as quickly as possible along our bridge; the one you crossed to get here. Now, follow me to the dining hall." She marched in the opposite direction of the lodge.

We cut between Driftwood and Gull's Nest and took the boardwalk past Whitecap. This cabin faced the lake, rested partially in the woods, and was the only structure to have a verandah. It housed the oldest girls among us, who were no longer campers but not yet counselors. They were the CTs, the counselors in training.

The boardwalk ended at the woods' edge. Our path tapered up to a sandy mound before dipping toward the riverbank. Upon this mound two knotty logs dangled a wooden sign on a rusty chain. Burned letters proclaimed, Wildwood, and marked the boundary between our land and the boys.'

Nancy and I glanced upward, already feeling a sense of pride as we passed beneath this magical portal. When the sand gave way to black dirt we knew we'd vacated sanctuary and entered common ground. Our trail skirted the river and its tangle of vines to the base of an arched bridge. For all we cared the woodsy path ended here, though in reality it circled back to the lake and entered the hazy netherworld of the boys' camp.

We crossed the bridge and moved seamlessly up three flights of steps. Rising into the trees, we climbed four abreast and landed on a wraparound deck. An impressive A-frame jutted from the center, poised in its mantle of overhanging branches. Windows encompassed most of the structure and faced the distant lake, now obscured by summer foliage.

We funneled through a glass entrance into a wide vestibule. The deck continued on the other side, effectively linking this facility to the winter school's dormitories. We veered to the right and entered the great hall of windows. Cooks served up food cafeteria-style across the back wall and overflowed our plates in portions of fried chicken, mashed potatoes, and buttery green beans. We helped ourselves to an open case of salads and desserts, and dispensers of cold milk, water, and soft-serve ice cream. Bess directed us through a maze of tables to settle near the windows where eight designated tables awaited. Naturally, we sat among our cabin mates. However, each table held a number to be assigned the next morning at random so we could meet others.

Midway through our meal the boys spilled in. With three times as many campers their deep voices and sweaty energy saturated the great hall. Given a fifteen-minute head start, and second helpings, they still finished before us. When their plates were empty, the director of the boys' camp stood from his table. This rugged man, having permanent creases around his eyes, commanded instant quiet. "I'm Hutch," the man said, turning to face us girls. He nodded to our director and politely gave her the floor.

Bess rose from her seat and addressed the boys. "I'm Bess." She took a deep breath and a small, quirky grin lifted the corner of her mouth as she hollered, "If you can't sing well; sing loud! Let's hear it for the cooks!"

Everyone pounded fists upon the tables and feet upon the floor while chanting, "We want a cook's parade! We want a cook's parade! Hi, Ho, the Derry O, we want a cook's parade!"

Nancy and I exchanged startled looks then joined the racket. Eventually the cooks appeared at the rounded windows of two swinging doors. A tall man and two large women in white aprons and puffy hats waved and smiled. They disappeared from view and our clamor ceased, turned off like a spigot.

"Carry your trays to the back," Bess instructed. "Trash goes in the can. Glasses in the partitioned crates. Silverware in the buckets. Dishes at the window. Trays stacked on the side."

"Girls first!" Hutch warned when the nearest table of boys made a move. "Boys remain for announcements!"

We meandered between the boys' tables. I stacked my tray, accidentally leaving my silverware on top.

"Silverware in the bucket!" the male cook rebuked. His long arm reached out and plucked the utensils from my tray, launching them into the bucket.

I skittered away, stunned and embarrassed.

"Don't worry," Nancy said, grabbing my arm. "You won't be the only one!"

"Trash in the can!" The cook rumbled for the next forgetful camper. We giggled and fled the cafeteria, running all the way back to camp. We took a detour by the lake to toss a few pebbles off the end of the dock then returned to the cabin.

"What do you think we're doing tonight?" I asked between ragged breaths. We hurriedly changed from sandals to sneakers inside the dark, empty cabin. Everyone else had already left for the bridge.

"Council Fire," she replied.

Deeply impressed by her inside knowledge, I wondered, "How do you know?"

"My mom went to camp. That's why she sent me."

"Here?" I muttered, thoroughly confused by her inexplicable connection and my own good luck in gaining such a friend. "But," I stammered, "this camp only started last year!"

"No." She shook her head, scattering her bangs. "It was in another place. It was called Deena-hahna. They had Council Fires and lots of other stuff."

"My mom never went to any kind of camp." I tried to picture her as a camper, but the image wouldn't come. "She grew up really afraid of the water." I paused as other phobias came to mind. "And bicycles, and heights, and boats, even shopping!" I laughed uncomfortably.

"Shopping!" Nancy exclaimed. "How can someone be afraid of shopping?"

"I don't know," I whispered, suddenly embarrassed. I had just revealed a family secret. "I suppose you'd have to know my grandmother. I'm thinking maybe Nanny put these fears into my mom. And Mom is sending us to camp because she does not want to pass them along to us the same way they were passed to her!"

"And here we are," Nancy concluded. She pulled a sweater over her head, thrust her arms through the sleeves, and flipped her hair out the collar. "Ready, Schmidty?"

I nodded, approving her friendly addition of a 'y' to my last name. "Lead the way . . . Romany?" I tested hers in the same fashion. Shaking my head, I decided against it. "Roman," I corrected, but she had already crossed the threshold and leapt off the stoop. As I ran behind her, my thoughts of home retreated to a safe quarter of my mind, lost behind leafy foliage, sunny dunes, the cool breeze from an open lake, and the warm sound of a new friend's laughter.

FIVE

THE PROMISE OF POSSIBILITIES

WE REACHED THE bridge just in time to be counted by Bess. Satisfied of a full attendance, she led us into the woods. We hiked through the gravel parking lot, across the dirt road, and climbed a grassy knoll to the edge of a playing field. Our line jumbled into a messy hive as we crossed the spacious gap between two netted goal posts. Bess aimed for another set of woods on the opposite side. Here, we formed a tight line and entered the trees single file to follow a winding path up the tree-covered dune.

Distant singing reached our ears as those in front began to sing. Others joined in, staggering their entry to create a dark, sober chant. Our counselor walked backward, motioning for us to begin, and it became a three-way round, unfolding into a complex harmony from the circular pattern of our voices.

"We climb, we climb, to the Council Fire with open amenable hearts, to light the fire of living hope, to light the fire of Wildwood, Wildwood."

This haunting melody accompanied our steep hike. With more than an hour before sunset the woods had already captured the darkness of early night. Branches masked the sky, shrouding our presence, and stifling any wayward breeze. Sweat beaded across my forehead and dripped down my back. My dad had told me the trees in these parts were still young and not particularly tall because of extensive logging in the last century. But it didn't seem that way as white pines, stately birch trees, cottonwoods, and sugar maples crowded close.

We entered a clearing sheltered by a web of leaves. Everyone found seats among a circle of giant logs. Their smooth surfaces had been worn and polished long before us by decades of young men from the boys' camp. The fire pit held fist-sized timbers stacked into a tall teepee. One of the counselors, Robyn, ignited the kindling. It burst into a blazing inferno of pungent smoke and crackling bark. She stepped back, and we sang more somber songs until the flames settled.

Bess praised the beauty around us, extolling the woods' peacefulness and the lake's blessings. She explained how each of us, as campers, could express these same qualities during the coming weeks. We could earn proficiency levels in each of the offered sports and crafts by passing through Beginner, Intermediate, Advanced, and perhaps Expert. We could also earn recognition by expressing special Wildwood qualities: cooperation, persistence, joy, consideration, resiliency, cleanliness, and enthusiasm.

Many of the campers wore feathers on their clothing and beads around their wrists. Nancy whispered, "Awards from last year." I nodded to show my appreciation of her intuitive answer, no longer surprised by her ability to supply it. At once, I wished to earn some beads in the coming weeks.

"Now we will assign teams," Bess announced. "Either Dune or Cedar, this affiliation will be yours for life unless you become a counselor. During competitions, each team earns points. At the end of the seven weeks we will declare a winner. That name will be sewn on the banner to be proudly displayed for generations to come. When I call you, step forward and draw your name." She indicated a grouping of popsicle sticks impaled in the sand.

"Susan Schmidt!" Bess announced my sister's name. My insides bolted as if she'd just called my name.

Susan rushed over. Her wavy ponytail flopped along as she swooped down and plucked a protruding stick from the assortment. "Cedar!" she shouted, holding it up and giving a winning smile. Bright green letters beneath her name confirmed the assignment. About half the camp erupted into cheers and howls.

A few more names were called and then Bess said, "Nancy Roman." She rose from the log and crossed the circle in a cautious, athletic stride. Her hair fell forward as she studied the collection of names. She knelt to draw one from the sand. Straightening, very slowly, she shook her bangs into place. Her hazel eyes toured the circle, drawing out the suspense. "Dune," she pronounced evenly, then spun around and headed for our log amid cheers from the other half of the camp.

"Dunes will win again this year!" one of the older campers called above the din. She teasingly elbowed her cabin mate. "No, Cedars will win!" the cabin mate disagreed. Their easy bravado and close proximity led me to believe team rivalries didn't run too deep. Even so, when Nancy rested her popsicle stick on the ground, near the tip of her shoe, I chanted its bold brown letters over and over, mentally supplicating, "Dune, Dune, Dune."

By the time Bess called me, only three sticks remained. Aware of many eyes watching, I walked into the clearing and extracted my name from the soil. Cedar, it read. Somehow I managed to call it out, as required, faking my delight and then glaring at my sister in accusation. Clearly, this dubious assignment followed family lines. She flashed a supportive smile as I returned to my seat and Cedars cheered loudly. I gazed into the flames while Bess summoned the final two names. More than ever, I hoped team rivalries were only superficial! I didn't want anything, or anyone, to get in the way of my new friendship.

"Everyone must pick morning and afternoon activities for the next three weeks," Bess said. Counselors passed out papers and circulated coffee cans full of broken pencils capped by old, shiny erasers. "Place your name on the top, then your cabin name," she continued. "Choose six in order of preference from the list on the bottom."

We made hurried, stressful choices, knowing our dried erasers and the narrow spaces between lines would not accommodate a change of mind.

"If all of you want to take waterskiing on Glen Lake as a first choice, obviously we can't fit everyone into the first week," Bess instructed in answer to a question. "Some of you seven-weekers may have to wait until the second session."

"Take waterskiing," Nancy said.

"Can you slalom?" I asked.

"No," she laughed. "I can barely get up on two!"

"Me either," I gushed. "What else are you taking? I've got riding and archery."

"Take sailing. We can learn together."

I checked that box just before Leslie snatched the papers away and handed them to Robyn.

A serious mood returned to the circle. Bess reached into a heap of pine trimmings and shook a small bough free. She held the cluster of needles at eye level, saying, "I hope each camper strives to achieve her goals this summer. And if the way becomes difficult, she should look around at God's beauty in this place and know that such power is near, as near as your own hand and ready to help when needed." She placed the bough on smoldering coals. It sparked a tiny show of fireworks.

One by one the counselors adhered to some secret order, as if their goal, or hope for the summer, could stick to the needles where the flames would transform it into smoky air for us to breathe and absorb, making it our own.

It was a feast of sentiment, but soon I'd had my fill. After hearing three counselors verbalize painfully similar versions to Bess's finer original, I tuned them out. Propping my elbows on my knees, my chin in my hands, I felt less and less inspired, even disappointed. I had expected more details about camp itself, its inner workings, or a specific guide on how-to-earn-those-beads.

Instead they spoke of intangibles like gratefulness, patience, diligence, charity, and the need to reflect and demonstrate God's limitless blessings. These vague concepts floated about the campfire, seemingly untethered to reality and inapplicable to me. I failed to glean any wisdom and simply stared at the fire. Bright orange and red petals gnawed on each pine bough. The supple needles fought hard to stay green, wafting their essence of pine, hissing in defiance. I rooted for each bough; fight harder, I thought, resist.

Eventually the rhythm of voices ceased. Everyone stood up, including Nancy. I imitated her movements, trusting she knew what to do. We gathered into a tight circle and joined hands. Bess smiled at everyone, apparently delighted by the new faces of Wildwood for the next three weeks. "We will sing the camp song," she concluded.

I prepared for a peppy chant or a rousing fight song. Instead, we sang a mournful dirge.

"Shenahwau, Shenahwau, can we tell you how we feel? You have given us your riches. We love you so."

I was transfixed. A handful of others sang a completely different version and the two melodies blended into a duet of harmony. I fiercely discerned who among the circle sang this secondary part. After picking Leslie, I relaxed, knowing I'd have plenty of time in the cabin to learn it before the next Council Fire.

A sweet melancholy took hold of me and I felt the stirrings of something new and special. The song had aroused in me what the counselors' words could not. All around, my tentative smile met eager, sincere returns, even among the older girls, as if to say, we are in this together. Here you can risk expressing yourself free from ridicule. The air crackled with the promise of possibilities.

SIX

A SIMPLE WISH

THE OLDEST CAMPERS shoveled sand and dumped water from a plastic bladder to douse the flames. Bess indicated who among the circle should be the first to leave, having noted the last to arrive. Since Nancy and I had been near the end, we found ourselves at the head. Following one other cabin, we proceeded in regal silence.

When the trail doglegged to the right, Nancy gripped my arm. "Let's run! So we can see the sunset!" My insides leapt at her rebellious charge. I glanced behind hoping not to see our counselor. Unable to detect her wavy dark hair, I agreed, "Let's go!"

We tore straight down the hill, avoiding the trail's winding switchback. We had become wild foundlings crashing through the forest, leaping over brambles and logs, dodging saplings. When we reached the front of the line, we rejoined the trail. Laughter rose from my chest and exploded repeatedly to match the rhythm of our stride. The grassy field spread before us, and we ran faster, out of control. Our legs gained a life of their own. We pounded over the bridge, down the length of boardwalk, and into the sand. We kicked off our sneakers and catapulted them into the air. Without breaking stride, we caught them midair and sped past the dock and down the shore. Nancy plopped into a rift where sand swept upward and blended into a copse of dune grass. My sides heaved, and I fell beside her. The sun's lower edge touched water. Vaporous stripes of purple fanned outward, resembling floating pieces of land. The lake's fresh scent cooled us.

The sun faded. In the distance we heard Bess on her megaphone. "Five minutes until 'Taps'!"

We hopped to our feet.

"Wait," I said, dropping my shoes. I headed for the shore and rolled up my pant legs. "Let's wash here." I smiled as Nancy joined me, and we stood in the clear water, warmed from the day's sun. Splashing our faces, I said, "We can brush our teeth in the cabin with a cup of water!"

"I still have to hit the Murphy," Nancy said.

"The what?"

"That's the name of the bathhouse. And the lodge is called the Hylton."

"The Hylton?" I repeated.

"Yeah, named after the man who built it. Mr. Hylton has something to do with the boys' year-round school. At least that's what my mom told me." She shrugged. "I don't know who Murphy is."

Again, I marveled at her vast knowledge.

On the run back to the cabin, we rounded the corner of Sunblazer, another cabin outside the main circle, and Nancy intentionally strayed from the boardwalk. I followed her leap over a mound, and on to the bouncy surface of an embedded trampoline. Its spongy fabric lay at ground level while its skeletal support was hidden inside a deep, snug pit. The white checkerboard of crisp woven bands softened upon impact, feeling new and tight against our bare feet. On impact, it flung us high into the air. Before anyone could register the telltale creak of recoiling springs, our feet had landed on the cushioning sand, propelling our stride toward the cabin. It seemed we had taken a shortcut and then flown part of the way.

"Nancy and Nancy!" Leslie yelled as we burst inside. She sounded relieved and annoyed.

We tossed our clothes aside, donned our flannel nightgowns, brushed our teeth with dry toothpaste, and slipped between cool sheets as Leslie hit the light. This solitary bulb suspended from the rafters proved barely effective in daylight. But, moments earlier, it had filled the cabin in a cheery glow. Now we lay under our blankets in darkness.

A distant bugle hit the first note of "Taps." I pictured flag-draped coffins emerging from the bellies of airplanes returning from Vietnam.

During the evening news, a bugler always played "Taps" while the anchorman narrated our national sorrow. I felt sadder and sadder as each note pierced the night, bouncing off the surrounding woods, evoking solitary loneliness and signaling finality.

When it ended, Leslie brushed against my bedding as she left the cabin. She joined a tight circle of peers by the flagpole. Nancy and I rolled to our stomachs and peeked through the screen. The counselors wore flowery flannels and oversized slippers. Bess had not joined them! Her glaring absence smudged the thick line of authority separating them from us, making the moment seem less serious, as if a substitute teacher had entered the classroom. Nancy leaned over the edge of the bunk, and we shared muffled laughter until the counselors began to sing.

Their choice of a familiar hymn generated a measure of respect and drained the last bit of spunk right out of us. Nancy's head disappeared from view. I nestled into my pillow, pleasantly snug in my blankets from home. I closed my eyes and lay still, hearing the rustling breeze and the soothing waves. The counselors paused after their second hymn and my mind felt wiped clean, like a fresh palette.

They sang "Taps" in a two-part harmony voicing words I never knew existed, creating a memory so indelible its clarity will never diminish.

> Day is done. . . .
> Gone the sun. . . .
> From the lake, from the hills, from the sky.
> All is well. . . .
> Safely rest. . . .
> God is nigh.

They replicated the bugler's melody, but every last trace of loneliness and sadness had melted away, producing instead a sense of safety and comfort among stately pines, sculpted sand, and tranquil waves. I anticipated tomorrow and cherished the thought of twenty more days at Wildwood.

Leslie whispered, "Goodnight, girls," and grazed her fingers across the metal screen. She turned her flashlight inward, shedding a warning against possible mischief before disappearing along the boardwalk. Soon, we heard them singing to the older cabins. After that, we heard only the rhythm of lapping waves.

In the darkness, I made a simple wish to sing among them one evening, to stand in their circle around the flagpole, to blend my voice into theirs to create an outpouring so beautiful it would complement the lake and sky. This desire lived in my mind long after that evening. It never changed, and never diminished. I always pictured myself among the counselors exactly as I was then, not of their age, not of their rank, not of their equal. In short, I visualized the honor but not the requirements to attain it.

SEVEN

ENHANCING THE ROUTINE

IT SEEMED MY eyes had just closed when the bugle announced its brash cry of Reveille. Nancy grumbled above me, "I hate to get up, I hate to get up, I hate to get up in the mooorniiiing."

The northern air had chilled the wooden floor and the bed frame, making it painful to leave the warm cocoon of blankets. I slipped on my rubber thongs and shivered in line at the Murphy. I hadn't yet found a way to circumvent this necessity, though I peered longingly into the woods beyond Driftwood. I held my breath when shuffling past the communal sink and its pungent mix of Ivory soap, globs of Crest, and the metallic tang of iron-rich water.

After breakfast we had twenty minutes of Bible study. I pretended to follow along while sneaking in a few pages of the Agatha Christie novel I'd brought from home. After this, we cleaned the cabin for inspection. I never witnessed an actual inspection, but we knew they happened because a banner would be tacked on the winning cabin's door, and a summary report would be left on our counselor's bed full of checkmarks and little comments.

"No way!" I peered over Nancy's shoulder to study the piece of paper. "I really thought we had it this time." I squinted to decipher the cramped writing at the bottom. "We're supposed to sweep the boardwalk! I knew we had to sweep the stoop, but the boardwalk? It's always something! The beds are never tight enough, the towels on the line are never straight enough. We fix the one thing, and they add another!"

"We'll get it next time," Nancy reassured, dropping the paper on Leslie's bed. "Let's go see the lake."

"Mindy shot a stray arrow and killed a turtle at archery!" I exclaimed as we ran along the boardwalk. "It went right through its head."

"Turtle soup for lunch!" she said.

"Gross!" I chuckled. "And she feels horrible about it! Leslie told her when we speak unkind words about someone they have the same effect. But that seems a little drastic to me."

A white fog rolled in from the lake, and the end of the dock all but disappeared. "No sailing this afternoon," Nancy said.

"Yeah, there's not a stitch of wind."

Tiny waves curled ashore and invisible seagulls squawked overhead, gathering their ranks to take advantage of the confused fish that would rise higher than normal to the surface.

"After canoeing on the river I was really looking forward to an afternoon on the lake," Nancy sighed. "Come on." she headed for the dock. Our toes scuffed the gritty surface. Looking back from the base of the L, only one cabin, Beacon, remained visible.

"Far out!" My voice echoed loudly through the silent mist. Then, I exerted the long drone of a foghorn.

"Spooky!" Nancy said. I grinned at the compliment. "Look at that," she breathed excitedly, pointing into the low clouds.

"What?" I murmured. She tugged me off the dock and along the shore. "What?" I protested.

"There!" she whispered when our toes touched the water's edge.

I had seen the lake in all sorts of moods, but I had never seen it shrink to the semblance of a decorative pond with two plump swans. They glided in from the mist, having white feathers and curved downy necks. I could almost reach out and touch the bigger of the two, who regarded me through one black regal eye.

"Hey! There are swans on the lake!" my sister announced from the rise of dunes. A small group of campers ran toward us.

"Come slowly," Nancy advised.

We noticed their fresh clothes and neatly combed hair. "We better get changed," I advised, seeing Nancy wore her swimsuit and the front of my shirt had a large, dark stain. We ran for Sandpiper.

The bell clanged as we sashayed around our trunks, the bed, and the window to access toiletries, hunt down a missing shoe, and clean the stain from my shirt. As usual, our choreographed routine lasted well past the exodus of campers. "Ready?" I asked when the camp had deserted.

"Let's go by Sunblazer," she suggested. We took the long way around, walking and talking, then ogling the banner on their door.

"They always get it," I moaned.

"We'll beat them tomorrow," she said.

We ran along the boardwalk to remedy our tardiness. Almost at once, my big toe caught between planks, painfully stubbing. "Darn it!" I cried, hopping into the sand.

"You okay?" Nancy asked, supporting my arm. She studied the boardwalk. "There must be a loose board."

"It's my foot," I said, hobbling along. "I had to wear a brace when I was a baby 'cause it turns in. It doesn't do it anymore unless I'm tired or in a hurry. Then it drags me down and trips me up."

"Bummer," Nancy said, staring at my foot.

"Okay, I'm better," I said, and we ran the rest of the way.

Leslie waited at the double doors. The boys thundered across the bridge behind us. "Why is it," she began, crossing her arms and frowning, "everyone heads for the dining hall when the bell rings? But you two start getting ready for the dining hall when the bell rings?"

We giggled, unable to provide any real answer. Flushed with illumination Nancy exclaimed, "Schmidty fell!"

"Baloney," Leslie accused, waving us through the line. "She wouldn't fall if you weren't running late!"

We laughed knowing the truth of it.

EIGHT

A NOTORIOUS COMPETITION

QUIET TIME FOLLOWED lunch. Everyone used these forty-five minutes to write letters or take a nap. Afternoon activities followed. Nancy and I usually met up for Beach Time just before dinner. We liked to swim out to the floating dock and share highlights from our day or read letters from home, if we were lucky enough to get some. This was tricky, because we had to swim holding the letter above water. Sometimes we chanced a towel. I usually carried a book. Always, the risk was worth it. This wooden platform on barrels could lull us into a pleasant stupor or rock us asleep beneath an intense sun masked by a prevalent breeze.

The bell would ring for dinner, and we'd race for shore. After the meal, Bess would announce the evening activity. This ensured our entire camp was busy all the way up to bedtime.

On Saturdays, we took short trips in the company of our cabin mates. We never tired of Cabin Day, having a wide variety of places to visit and the luxury of our own schedule once we got there. On Sunday mornings, we slept-in an extra hour. The counselors brought trays of sweet rolls and paper cups of juice from the dining hall, and we ate in bed. After cleanup, we dressed in white shorts and white shirts for Sunday School in the Hylton. Having only one set to wear, we worked very hard to keep them spotless. After the hour-long service we moved directly into our swimsuits and headed for the beach to play games or run relays in competitions between Dunes and Cedars.

"Can you do it?" my sister urged at the onset of our final competition for the session. She and Maggie stared at me, practically begging, since everyone else on our team had declined this leg of the relay.

"Who will be racing against me?" I asked, biting my lower lip. Nancy and the other Dunes gathered in the distance, divvying up events for their team.

"That really doesn't matter," Maggie said. Her warm brown eyes soothed away such concerns. I readily accepted her wisdom and found it difficult to believe she was my sister's age. "The question is do you want to?"

. I sized up the bridge, gauging its extreme drop to the river. "Well, it's taller than a starting block but shorter than a high dive. I could take a shallow racing dive."

"Then, you'll do it?" Maggie prompted.

"Okay," I agreed, primed full of optimism from three weeks of races in the lake, races up and down sand dunes at the state park, and competitions on the grassy field. We had played dodge ball, touch football, field hockey, baseball, and a foreign game we strove to master called soccer. If I could do all this, I certainly could dive from the bridge, swim downriver to the buoy on the right, grab the green ring and swim to shore, passing it off to the next camper.

"Good," Maggie and Susan replied as one.

Bess blew her whistle to signal an end to the planning phase. Switching to her megaphone she announced, "Everyone take your places along the relay course."

Both teams dispersed. Everyone had a mission. I walked toward the bridge, wondering who would be joining me from the other team.

"Hiya," Joanna said. Same as Maggie she shared my sister's cabin. I studied her dark muscular legs and bulging quads, amazingly defined. No doubt, she could kick. Her bare feet slapped against the bridge, and her athletic jaw snapped a wad of gum.

"So, you live in Florida all the time?" I asked stupidly, trying to make conversation.

"Yup," she said between snaps, her eyes focused straight ahead. Then she sized up my apparel. "Sure you want to dive in that two-piece suit?"

I sized up her Speedo, stretching tautly along her torso, and knew I'd messed up.

A starting gun went off by the lake.

"Don't let the current carry you into the weeds. There are leeches," she warned.

My target buoy bobbed near the overgrown bank while hers floated in the middle. Mine was closer to the bridge but hers was closer to shore. Supposedly this evened things out.

Girls cheered. A flurry of activity spread from the beach, through camp, toward the dining hall and into the woods. Joanna and I perched on the edge of the rail. The cheering drew near, and I saw Beth and Annie running toward us. Their little faces were tightly flushed, and they sprinted mightily, kicking sand from each whirling step. They appeared evenly matched as two of the youngest campers that summer. By an arm length, Beth tagged me first.

I dove from the bridge. My stomach flipped from the sudden drop. I thrust my arms over my head and slapped my thumbs together. The rest of my body turned rigid and I cut through the water in a sleek racing dive learned from years of practice on the swim team back home. The familiar rush of water spewed over my backside. It flooded under my bottoms and wrenched them to my ankles. I clamped my feet together, desperately clutching the bulge of fabric to prevent it from slipping away entirely. The dive carried me through a long underwater glide. I could see the buoy through the golden water and started using my arms. But without my legs, the river's strong current carried me into the weeds. My skin grazed the slimy foliage, and I shuddered at the prospect of leeches. Groaning through bubbles of frustration, I planted both feet into the muck, haphazardly tugged the suit up to my thighs, and pushed off. Pulling crosscurrent, I finally surfaced near the buoy.

Howling laughter greeted my ears. The river's clear flow had allowed no cover for my embarrassment. Joanna yanked the Dune's ring and darted for shore. I grabbed our ring and placed it in my mouth. Swimming the crawl, with a bunch between my legs, I furiously tried to catch up. By the time I reached the shore the Dune team had moved toward the lake.

Shane grabbed my ring and tore off. The crowd followed. Susan waited on the bank. She struggled not to laugh while I put myself together under cover of stirred-up silt.

Joanna stood bent at the waist, dripping water and heaving for air. "What happened?" she asked.

"Nancy lost her bottoms!" Beth jeered, gripping her ribs, trying to contain her amusement as she ran off to see the final leg of the race.

"That's why you beat me," I accused, glaring at Joanna.

"Don't take it so seriously," she replied.

"Yeah, it's not like it happened in front of the guys or anything," Susan added.

Joanna shrugged. "Should've worn a one-piece."

"At least you gave it the old cottage try," Susan said.

"Oh, Sue!" Joanna said, shaking her head and walking away.

"College try," I hissed, even more embarrassed, hoping Joanna didn't think us both idiots.

"Really?" Susan said, wrinkling her brow. "I like mine better," she decided, jogging away, saying, "Just laugh it off. Who cares? It was funny!"

I fumed inside, glad to be alone.

"Schmidty!" Nancy yelled, running from the lake. "I heard your suit fell off!"

At once, her adoring laughter diffused all the emotions raging inside me. "Yeah," I grinned. "I have a new claim to fame."

"Come on," she urged. "When this is over we're having dinner on the beach. Hot dogs cooked on sticks, corn roasted in their husks, bowls of coleslaw, and s'mores for dessert. And, it's Sandpiper's turn to build the fire!"

NINE

PROMISES MADE

WE HIKED THE Point for our last Council Fire. I perched beside Nancy, breathing in the smoky fire while counselors handed out certificates from our chosen activities.

"How did you find time to do everything?" I whispered. She won Beginner awards for waterskiing, sailing, arts and crafts, gymnastics, and riding. Plus she earned Intermediate in land sports, archery, riflery, swimming, and trips. She earned Advanced in canoeing.

She smiled modestly and shrugged her shoulders.

Bess awarded beads to those campers who displayed Wildwood qualities consistently throughout the session. Nancy won a bead for every one of them, plus a special bonus bead to prove that she'd won all the others, in case we couldn't see them on her wrist.

Bess and the counselors each placed pine boughs on the fire. They expressed gratitude for camp and thanked the three-weekers for a great summer. We gathered into a tight circle and linked arms for the final song.

True to form, Nancy tugged me into the trees. We carried our rolled-up awards like relay batons, dodging campers and saplings, not daring to look back. We broke free of the dark woods and landed in the sunny field. Drops of water lingered from an earlier shower, lying heavily on the grass and surrounding trees. Like small magnifying glasses they amplified the setting sun and tinted all the browns and greens of nature in a warm, honey glow.

Even the bridge radiated a golden sheen. We dashed across, smiling wondrously, and cleared the boardwalk. The sand winked flecks of gold upon its rain-encrusted surface. Our feet sank through the wet layer and into the dry grains below, leaving deep holes as we churned past Puccoon and Stardust, through the hollowed path created by summer upon summer of foot traffic. Purple, pink, and yellow wildflowers fringed the upper edge of dune grass.

We ran to our usual place and plopped out of breath. Creamy blue clouds outlined in orange filled the horizon. The sun blazed behind them, dipping into the lake, spreading across the water and upon the shore.

"Let me see those beads," I said, grabbing her wrist. "I've decided you are the perfect camper because you will try any activity, take any trip, and help with the most awful chores. Plus, you are always happy about it."

Nancy exhaled a puff of breath, scattering her bangs. "I'm not always happy," she disagreed.

"I know," I said, dropping her wrist. We watched the sun's swift and final plummet. The lake's sparkling surface deepened to navy blue. "That's how you have them all fooled," I concluded. "You keep it well hidden."

"And so they think I'm the perfect camper," she said.

"But you are!"

She smiled and tilted her head, as if needing to be further convinced.

"Have you ever seen me keep it all in?" I tested, treading on new ground as I regarded myself from an outside perspective away from family and childhood friends. She giggled in response. My insides sank to have my suspicions confirmed.

"But, ya know," she said, "I have my moments."

"It's not the same!" I laughed. "You bottle it up and save it for later, in private. Like, I'm sure everyone saw I didn't want to be a Cedar at that first Council Fire, especially my sister."

"Naw," she said, flopping a hand on the sand.

I sat cross-legged to face her. "Remember when the flies were biting us to death on the soccer field?"

She nodded hesitantly.

"I complained and complained. You just grinned that patient grimace of yours and made the best of it. I made such a scene that Robyn finally called it off. She must have been really mad at me. But I couldn't help it. I was so miserable."

"We were all miserable. You were right."

I wrapped my arms around my knees, digging my toes into the sand, scooping a little hole, wishing I could go back and do some things over again. "Oh! What about that nature hike with old Mr. Chinn?" I grimaced to recall. "He wouldn't let us stand in the shade while he goes on and on about Puccoon and Trefoil both having yellow flowers. And how the Colorado Puccoon has fringed petals, but Michigan's does not. He gave me nasty looks every time I interrupted to ask if we could move out of the hot sun."

"It was a good idea," she said. "You're too hard on yourself."

"Cleanliness and persistence," I said, holding up my two beads.

We howled in laughter, lying on our bellies, cupping our chins in our hands.

"I thought riding would be fun," I said. "Who knew it would get so hot? Or that they'd make us wear long sleeves and long pants? Then, mucking stalls! I was covered in sweat, and dust, and manure. All I could think of was jumping in the lake." My voice rose from melodramatic anguish. "After two days I begged for something closer to the water. That left more mucking for the others, which wasn't very considerate. But I had to switch. Linda worked a deal so I didn't have to talk to Bess. That put me into arts and crafts. Talk about boring! I suppose I should have helped others with their projects, to get that cooperation bead after I rushed through mine. Instead, I read my book in the sun. But Linda didn't seem to mind. She actually sat with me a few times, and we talked. She's kind of hard to understand sometimes, but I really like her."

"Then you did archery," Nancy prompted.

"Ugh! The mosquitoes! The range is too close to the river with hardly any breeze. What a downer. I was eaten alive. I never passed Beginner! Look," I groaned, holding out my arm, instantly wanting to scratch it. "I still have the bites after two weeks!"

"Same here." She displayed a tanned arm dotted by tiny white mounds.

Feigning exasperation, I buried my hands in the sand and lightly tossed grains on her legs. "But you got Intermediate!"

She laughed, genuinely entertained. "What else? We did land sports together?"

"That was the hottest week ever, with no shade and no breeze! I couldn't wait for it to end."

"But you like soccer," she disagreed. "Ya know we're getting pretty good at playing forwards, especially for just learning. We scored 'em high." She sighed, rolling on her side, appreciating the moment through objective humility.

"But, we didn't get anything for it."

"Who cares?" she scoffed. "Oh! You liked canoeing."

"It's all right. But the paddling gets monotonous, and the river gets claustrophobic." I reached out and gently shoved her. "Waterskiing is a riot! I like the signals. 'Speed up!' with a thumb in the air, and 'slow down!' with a thumb down. Or, 'one more time.'" I circled the air above my head. "Then, 'Cut!'" I sliced my throat. "I love sinking into the water like a statue."

"Yeah," she lazily agreed, watching the horizon. "There's nothing like that wooden Chris-Craft speeding across Glen Lake when the water is calm and glassy."

"I love it when everyone in the boat is staring at you, waiting for those two little words. You're all tucked into a ball." I pantomimed floating in the water with ski tips in front. "You grip the spongy bar. The nylon rope floats in a tangle between your legs. And you can't say it, not until everything feels just right. The moment builds; the boat stretches the rope taut, your arms lock. Water flows between your legs and the skis begin to resist. And then you say 'Hit it!'" I shouted dramatically. "Was there ever a more powerful set of words?" I called out to the lake, imagining the boat lifting me up and away. "I always panic, afraid I'll fall. Who knew the secret is to hold still and let the boat pull you up? It amazes me every time. I gaze at the lake and realize I'm standing on it! I look at the sky and think of Papa, my grandfather. He made me keep trying."

"Did you ski in Michigan?"

"Yeah, Papa and Nanny had a cottage on Lake St. Helen in the middle of the state, near Houghton Lake. Ever hear of it?"

"Nope," she said, shaking her head.

"Lots of people in Michigan have cottages 'cause there are so many lakes! Susan and I, and our three cousins, Paula, Marie, and Julia, used to spend summers there. They all got the knack of skiing long before I. At twilight, when the lake would turn smooth as silk they'd start pestering Papa to take them out. Just before docking for the night he'd make me try. The boat would yank me into a belly flop, and I'd give up." My voice lightened, and I spoke through bland indifference. "Then one day I just stood up. And my skis skimmed across the water."

"And now you can tell your cousins you learned to drop a ski." She leaned back, staring at the darkening lake. "Next summer we'll learn to ski double."

"Sailing is nice," I mused, reclining against the bluff, glancing down shore at our small fleet of tublike skiffs. "I didn't even mind memorizing all those sailing terms."

"I love shoving off, when wind fills the sail. It is such a rush." she smiled wistfully. "And staging fake rescues."

"You mean falling overboard and capsizing the boat?"

She chuckled. "It is tough lifting the sail after it fills up with water."

"Yeah," I agreed. "But none of that bothers me 'cause it's great to be on the lake." I stared up at the North Star winking above. We listened to the lonely wash of waves.

"Well, Schmidty," she said, standing suddenly. "It's dark, and we haven't heard Bess on the megaphone."

"Yeah," I said, still sitting.

"Chicky, you better come back for seven weeks!" She presented a look of mock severity.

"Oh, I will." I took her hand, and she pulled me up. We brushed sand from our shorts, gathered our shoes and certificates, and climbed the bank to our cabin.

TEN

SUSAN'S PERSPECTIVE

THE NEXT DAY, my parents returned, and we loaded our duffels and trunks for the trip back to Indiana. I piled into the backseat of the Rambler, our family's only car, and opened the triangular window. Staring out, I felt blanketed in the aftermath of a long, pleasant dream.

"You are so quiet!" Mom said. We had left the lake country far behind and entered rolling farmland. "Did you have fun?"

"Yes!" I grinned. "And I want to go back."

"I worried a little after you called home," she said, staring at Susan. "You called home?"

Susan glared back at me.

"I told her we weren't driving all the way Up-North to get her!" Mom added, growing perturbed all over again.

Susan squirmed. "I was so homesick. I couldn't stop crying. On the third day I begged Bess to let me call home. I just had to. She let me use the phone in her upstairs office."

For a split second I wondered about this private office and if Bess slept in a cot or a real bed. Then I blurted my greatest fear of all. "You want to go back, right?"

Susan had the power to keep me from returning. As sisters, we either did a thing together or not at all. This was the one area in which Mom replicated my grandmother's view of parenting. Thankfully, it only applied to big things like tickets to the Ice Capades or Saturday matinees at the River Park Theatre because Susan liked to be home, even if it meant being alone. I chose to be at my friends' houses all the time, especially the ones having very little supervision. Since Mom and Dad preferred peace and quiet to a house full of visitors, they never complained as long as I made it home for dinner at five and returned again before dark. Naturally, I took full advantage of the freedom.

"Of course Susan wants to go back," Mom assured. "Why would you want to be in South Bend all summer with nothing to do except swim team?"

"I had fun," Susan admitted. "Bobbi, Maggie, and Joanna want me to come back. They are going for seven weeks."

"Oh, can we?" I begged.

"Seven weeks!" Our dad whistled as if impressed and doubtful at the same time.

I bent forward to gauge their interaction. When I saw Mom's determined resolve I knew she would make it happen.

Years later I discovered it had taken all her profits from the Woodard Preschool to foot the bill each summer. Not because camp had been so outrageously expensive but rather because preschool paid so little. Mom and a savvy business partner, who also happened to be her best friend, personally directed a substantial enrollment at the church on the corner. However, neither of them could have lived on this income alone. Dad held two jobs during the seventies' recession to keep our modest household running and food on the table. Ultimately, if he hadn't approved, and Mom hadn't pulled the money together, it wouldn't have happened.

"What songs did you learn?" She turned to face us.

"There's this cute one about a little frog. The kids would like it," Susan suggested. "Do you want to hear it?"

"I'd rather have a poke in the eye with a sharp stick," Dad countered, peering at us through the rearview mirror.

"Do you know 'Taps'?" I solicited, eager to relive the experience. "The counselors sang it every night around the flagpole, under the stars. If you can hold the melody, I know the harmony. It goes, 'Day is done. . . .'"

I plowed ahead, not giving Dad a chance to interrupt. I wisely skipped the harmony and stuck to the melody so Mom could learn it. The second time around, she sang with me, and I hit the high notes to offset her lower ones in a resonating chord at the end of each stanza. Susan jumped in, too, struggling to hold the melody by plugging her ears. Near the end, she wandered fully into my part, and we completely drowned out Mom. "Well, you get the idea," I said, a bit apologetically.

"That was wonderful." Mom sighed. Her face beamed. "I've never heard anything so lovely," she insisted. "It is perfect. I can picture the lake at night, the setting sun, the wind in the pine trees. It must have been beautiful." It seemed she yearned for the same experience. "I'll sing it any time you want," she promised.

Winter and spring passed quickly. Nancy and I wrote tomes to each other in sprawling cursive on neon-colored notebook paper. Doodles covered every inch of the margins. We barely mentioned our lives at home. Mostly, we planned what to take next summer. My list included bugspray for the archery range, a poncho for rainy days, and a high-beam portable lantern from L.L. Bean for trips to the Murphy. Nancy's list included, first and foremost, a heavy-duty sleeping bag for camping trips. We joked about those cold, dark trips to the Murphy, sitting on the freezing toilet while bugs whisked around the yellow bulb suspended from the ceiling. We made fun of the silly songs. But always, we cemented our promise of returning.

ELEVEN

LEAPING AHEAD

"Soooo," Angela said, leaning forward, slyly regarding me. "What about this family secret? I can't imagine anyone being afraid of shopping."

"I don't mind telling you," I decided, speeding up to pass a white car. "But I'd rather wait until we reach Flint, after you meet my nanny."

"I already know." My daughter waved a hand in dismissal. She promptly hesitated, "Do I?"

"Maybe," I said. "Actually, it was more my mom's secret. But she is gone now and we live far away from Nanny, so whom could it hurt?"

"By the way," KT said. "When I went to camp, we called the bathhouse The Ritz."

"I remember you telling me that," I said. "Kind of funny, like the hotel."

"Seriously, Mom," she said, "we had to climb higher than you to reach our Council Fires. My legs would burn!"

"But our climb started from the beach. Yours started about a hundred feet above the lake. So if both dunes are the same height, you had a head start."

"Wait," Katie said, stretching forward. "Wasn't KT's camp right on the beach? Like yours?"

"No," my daughter corrected. "Deena-hahna sits on the top of a really steep bluff. It overlooks the lake. You have to go down a hundred steps to get to the beach."

"That's a killer," Katie agreed.

"I wish you could have gone to the old camp," I yearned, "and passed beneath the wildwood sign, adding your memories to the same stretch of beach. Maybe carved your name in one of the cabins beside mine. It was so amazing to fall asleep to the sound of the waves."

"Some nights we heard the lake," she said. "And I liked it that way."

"Now, tell the truth," Angela demanded, fluffing her pillow against the window. "With so many girls living in close company there must have been some fights over clothes or makeup. Somebody must have made up something that wasn't true. Or, there were some guys you all liked and fought over."

"I really can't think of any. You have to consider how busy they kept us. We practically fell into bed each night, exhausted. Plus, we were surrounded by the most breathtaking natural beauty. It's hard to be grumpy in paradise."

"Come on, you must have been jealous some of the time?"

"I fought with my sister," I admitted.

"That doesn't count," Angela said.

"I wouldn't know," KT teased, poking me in the arm. "My mom only had two kids and made the other a boy."

"If you had a sister, you'd want a brother," I deconstructed. "But, you have the best of both worlds. You have a brother and friends who are like sisters." I turned to smile at Angela and Katie.

"Better than sisters," Angela scoffed as the oldest in her family. "My younger sister can really go at it."

"Not as bad as my older sister," Katie whispered more softly, as the youngest in hers.

"Honestly, we didn't fight," I said. "And we never put pressure on each other to be someone we weren't."

"No, the camp did it for you, with all those beads and stuff," Angela said.

I winced at the steely bluntness of her remark, and searched for its thread of truth. "Sure," I agreed. "However, the pressure wasn't to change, but to grow." Small goose bumps sputtered down my forearms in response to a time when I could not see the distinction, or understand the difference. "The beads were a positive thing," I decided. "Not so we'd compare ourselves to others, and feel inadequate, but so we'd gain sight of our own worth." I paused as this adult perspective finally brought clarity to a system I had once struggled against.

"What about Dunes and Cedars competitions?" my daughter said. "We cared about winning."

"Yeah, but once a race was over, it was really over. We tried to be good losers and good winners, especially when we returned to our cabins, even though Cedars suffered so many humiliating defeats," I recalled, lowering my voice to a disgruntled tone. "We only won the banner two times in the seventies. And both years we had the most unlikely captains leading us to victory. One of them was my sister, and the other, well I haven't told you about her yet." I laughed, still not believing it. "She was very unsure of herself. But when she found her resolve, look out!"

"What team did you get, KT?" Angela asked.

"Cedars," she said, turning to face her. "Remember, it stays in the family, unless you become a counselor. Then you aren't a Cedar or Dune anymore, you become a Sky."

"If a Cedar becomes a counselor," I said, reaching out to swat my daughter's arm in a burst of camaraderie, "then you're a Cedar in the Sky!"

KT gave a disingenuous laugh and backed away. Her embarrassment slammed down like a curtain between us. "Is that a Beatles' song?" she said, making a sour face.

Angela's commanding voice cleared the air, "So, who won the most when you went to camp, KT?"

"Cedars ruled the nineties," she said, raising her thumb in solidarity. "So, don't worry, Mom. We had it covered."

"Really?" I smiled, happy to have her back.

"Sure. Cedars won every year I went to camp. They also won two years before I went, and the year after. My camp friends e-mailed me the news."

I grinned admiringly for as long as the road would allow, and wondered why I had not picked up on this before now. "Well, thanks," I said, "for making it even."

"So," she yawned. "Tell us about your next year at camp."

"Go ahead, Mrs. Taylor," Angela reassured.

"I'll have to jump ahead to my third year. It was the summer before we became CTs. All of us, except Mary, were together in Sunblazer." I glanced back at Angela. "We didn't argue, but there were a few pranks. Some were not very nice. Nothing cruel or destructive like these TV reality shows," I said, shooting a contrite glance at my daughter, knowing she liked to watch them.

"They can be pretty mean," she admitted. Her friends agreed.

Pleased by their response, I turned reflective. "It would be our last year as campers. Every summer before this had been a blur of fun for me. I floated along, loving the lake and my camp friends, caring more about being away from home than actually accomplishing something while I was there. During the school year, my mom's health had deteriorated, and my dad's stress mounted as he juggled work and trips to the hospital. I didn't know how sick she was, or how worried he was, until years later. Susan helped by staying home. I helped by getting out of the way."

I was home only to eat, sleep, and sort through the destructive choices I was making inside the fast crowd. "Camp was the most positive influence in my life," I said for my passengers' benefit. "Thankfully my parents made sure I continued to go."

TWELVE

A DISCOVERY

I ENTERED THE senior cabin of Sunblazer. Two empty bunks and four singles remained unclaimed. I easily recognized Christie, Lori, and Nancy's blankets. Their familiar bedding erased all memory of the older girls who had been here before us.

I breathed in the familiar scents of summer; dry heat from the rafters, a whiff of pine, a fresh breeze, and tried to gain a feel from this perspective of camp. The flagpole seemed very far away, and only one other cabin, Beacon, stood nearby. From the clarity of the waves, and the view of open blue, I could have been standing on the beach. Three sides of the cabin overlooked it. A row of junipers hemmed in the fourth. And the southernmost corner commanded the best view of it. Lucky for me, an empty bed awaited. I crossed over, my leather sandals scraping grains of sand. The noise bounced off the walls and rafters to emphasize the cabin's near-empty state and forced me to wonder if my trunk had arrived. Not seeing it, my heart leapt in a moment of panic.

This year we had shipped it ahead. Dad had traded in the Rambler wagon for a Cadillac Calais and no trunk room. This made arrivals easier and the good-byes shorter. I had hiked in alone, eager to meet my friends, while Susan, a brand-new CT, hung around the gravel lot greeting campers. I hadn't run into anyone, but I trusted they would find me.

At last, I spied the black steamer trunk in shadow against the wall of junipers. Dad had bought it at an estate sale for one of us to use. Susan shunned it right away, saying it was too big, too old, and too different.

I fell in love immediately. Made of solid wood panels and thick metal corners, this indestructible monstrosity held everything I needed for camp, including my bedding.

I pushed its weight across the floor to the base of my chosen bed. After digging through my homespun denim purse, sewn from an old pair of overalls, I found the ancient-looking key. It turned easily in the newly oiled lock. The lid magically arose as layers of bedding expanded. My pastel-flowered sleeping bag, my grandmother's down quilt, and two plump pillows eased out the sides. Along with my tie-dyed sheets, they covered the cotton institutional mattress. I set cosmetics along the window ledge. My toiletries went into a plastic pail for easy transport to the Murphy, and a tiny framed photo of my boyfriend fit nicely on an old nail.

His charming smile and startling blue eyes leapt out at me, sending his flare of insistent desire. For an infinitesimal second, an unbidden tremor of desire answered through me. Then, I considered his shallow expectations, pawing hands, and failure to heed my rebuffs. He teased me constantly about camp. He hadn't wanted me to come. He didn't really know me. How could he? I didn't fully know myself. I snatched him off the nail and tossed him into my trunk. I buried him deep at the bottom, under a stack of shorts, along with intoxicated memories of smoke-filled basements and cars, and morning hangovers. I slammed the lid on my high school, mindful of the metal edge, completely relieved to know he and so many others were hundreds of miles away. I stretched out on my bed and gazed through the screens to enjoy the waves and the breeze. At once, everything from home slipped away into peaceful oblivion, and the present moment held a brilliant intensity of life-affirming clarity.

The door creaked, and I bolted from the bed.

"Hey, you got a perm." Nancy smiled, flinging the door ahead of her.

I smiled back, noticing her short layers. "You got yours cut."

Christie and Lori streamed in after her and the door banged.

"Hey, fellow Indiana girl," Christie greeted in a deep, raspy voice. She reached out to give me a hug. I carefully wrapped my arms around her long, blonde hair and hugged back. I could almost feel the cheerleader vaulting inside of her. Even her thick hair performed as a team to create a perfect curtain; always unified, always in place.

She turned stiffly from her waist, not to disturb it, and glanced at Nancy and Lori to gain their attention. Her eyes glistened mysteriously. "Our high schools actually played each other in basketball this year. I saw Schmidty at the game."

"How far away do you two live?" Nancy asked, as if we were next-door neighbors and had never mentioned it.

Christie and I stared at each other. Our brows furrowed. Finally, Christie said, "Oh, I guess about two hours?"

"I've never really been in The South," I said, meaning I lived on the northern side of an imaginary line running east to west from South Bend to Chicago. Everything below this line was The South, or so I believed, and I took great pride in having never ventured down there. Indianapolis may have been our state capital, but when we went to the city, it was Chicago. This left only one logical explanation for our meeting. "Christie's school came up to ours."

"Oh, and Nancy," Christie addressed me, whispering confidentially. "I can finally do that roundoff back handspring."

"Couldn't you always?" I asked.

"Remember?" she groaned. "That night during the game? I was in the bathroom agonizing over the halftime performance? I had messed it all up! I was so mad at myself. I was practically crying when I said to you, 'Nancy, I can't do a roundoff back handspring!' You were so sweet. You gave me a hug and said, 'Don't worry, Christie, I can't do one either.'" She laughed a deep, husky rumble. "It was just what I needed!"

"Oh, yeah," I said uncomfortably, not really remembering. I had been drunk out of my mind. One of my friends had been vomiting in the furthest stall. Even the shock of seeing Christie hadn't sobered me up. She meant more to me than nearly everyone in high school, and I hadn't been able to carry on a conversation. I quickly changed the subject, not wanting that noxious world to come crashing into this wholesome sanctuary. "Guys," I said, trying to hide my embarrassment, "we made it to Sunblazer."

"It's about time," Lori agreed.

"We missed you last year," I said.

Lori's ginger, silky hair fell in front of her face. She brushed it away, and I was surprised by her pale skin, recalling it tanned and golden at summer's end. "Couldn't afford it," she replied. "But this year my sister and two brothers are counselors. So, I'm the only one paying. But I had to come early." She wrinkled her freckled nose as if digesting something rotten. "At the crack of dawn my sister put me to work cleaning cabins. Just once I would like to arrive leisurely, taking a slow drive from Detroit. But you know what?" she added, placing a hand on her hip.

"What?" we chimed together.

"I had a date this year." She proudly tilted her head as if this had been some kind of milestone.

We held expectant, ready to be amused.

"When he came to my house to pick me up, my younger brother placed a water balloon in each of his hands." She held out her palms and cupped them in demonstration. "He goes, 'Better take these. It's the closest thing you'll get to touching a pair of boobs tonight.'" She stared down at her modest chest.

"Jerks!" Christie said.

Nancy shook her head and smiled. "Oh, Lori."

"Wow," I exhaled, trying not to laugh. "First of all, you have a great figure." I ticked my fingers. "Second, you're a great catch. And third, I'm soooo glad I don't have brothers!"

"Our mothers met in the parking lot," Christie interrupted, affecting a reverent tone as she looked at Nancy. "We just found out they went to camp together. Nancy's mom had my mom as a counselor at Deena-hahna."

"Deena-hahna?" I whispered, mimicking her exact timbre, as if the name alone held a forbidden taboo.

Christie leaned near. "Remember, the other camp before this, at a different location?" She straightened, pulling away. "We aren't allowed to use its name because it's copyrighted, and the landowner won't let us. But we can carry on its traditions" She spoke sternly, as if repeating her mother's exact words.

"Oh," I remarked, vaguely recalling its mention years earlier.

"Now it's called Innistock." Nancy shuddered. "All sorts of free-love, hippie druggy things go on there."

"Really?" I gasped, unable to believe people would pay for a hippie experience when it could be had for free, even in my school's bathroom, if you knew the right people.

"They do it on the old campsite," Christie added. "The founder passed ownership to her son, who passed it to his daughter, and she sold out. So, we had to move here."

I looked from Nancy to Christie. "So, your mothers went to camp together, and you guys never knew it?"

Christie bobbed her head. Her eyes penetrated mine while she shared a tight smile. The combination always fascinated me—reducing me to blubbering laughter or rendering me mute, depending on the situation.

"That's right. But this is our camp. The old camp is gone." She paused for emphasis, and this time I was rendered mute. Her unwavering gaze dared any of us to deny it. We didn't. We cared little about the past, especially if it wasn't ours. Neither did we comprehend the resources and commitment needed to keep such a place in existence. The concepts of prime real estate, land title, copyrights, and eminent domain held no meaning for us. Only our youthful energy mattered, and it formed a bond of tensile memories whose strength, I would discover, could outlast even the most significant events of adulthood.

"Wildwood is not our mothers' camp," Nancy concluded.

"There will be eight of us in here for the full seven weeks," Lori said.

This had never happened before. We gazed about the peaceful cabin, listening to the waves, wondering who would fill the remaining four beds.

"Who is our counselor?" I asked.

"Jenny," Nancy said. "She's Maggie's older sister, newly hired this summer."

"Oh, she's really nice," Lori said. "We shouldn't have any problems doing what we want."

"Come on," Christie declared. "Let's go jump on the tramp before it gets crowded." Instantly, we scrambled out the door, past Beacon, and over the mound of sand, landing together on the fabric in a slow-motion parade like astronauts walking on the moon.

"I declare a seat war," Nancy announced, "with Lori."

"You're going down, Roman," Lori warned, lowering her voice to rough it up.

"I get the winner," Christie called, carefully positioning her bottom in the sand, mindful of sitting on her hair. I eased beside her. We didn't worry about spotting for wayward bounces, or injury, since the worst that could happen was a spill in the sand. Repeatedly, they rebounded from seat-drops, with straight legs and stiff backs. About fifty drops later, Lori took an illegal double bounce and Nancy became the winner.

"You're dead meat next time, Roman," Lori threatened. But her voice rose too sweetly for any of us to think she really held a grudge.

Christie stepped across the woven canvas and warded Nancy away. "Give me some room to limber up," she said.

Nancy straddled the springs, keeping one foot on the tramp and the other in the sand while Christie performed a neat, compact backflip. Her hair flowed along, dutifully precise.

"Oh brother, don't make me puke my guts out," Lori said, rolling her eyes.

"What?" Christie asked.

"She's impressed," I translated.

"Ready!" Nancy said, undaunted by this display of prowess. She jumped aggressively while reciting the litany, "One, two, three, four, I declare a seat war!"

Christie fired three drops in rapid succession. She barely grazed the surface between them. On the final one, she successfully stole Nancy's bounce.

Nancy sputtered, displaying good-natured defeat as she sat beside Lori. "At least she's a Dune."

"Dunes are going to win this summer," Lori said.

I snorted at the inevitable prospect of another losing season. "Here goes," I said, trying not to laugh as I started to bounce.

Nancy said, "Too bad you're not a Dune, Schmidty."

"Yeah," I glumly replied, shooting high into the air.

"One, two, three, four, I declare a seat war!" Christie chanted.

I landed in a sitting position, tilted forward to rise up, expecting a rebound in my favor. Instantly, the bouncy fabric steeled against me. "So soon!" I accused, unable to spring up. Christie's quiet rumble of delight was so infectious I couldn't be angry.

"Free for all!" Lori called. She and Nancy leapt between us.

"I brought my cassette player!" Christie announced as our faces flew up and down. "I taped all my Beach Boy albums!"

"That'll be fun," I said, eager for a break from heavy metal.

"And this summer I am going to get Expert in gymnastics," she added.

"I want to learn how to spray in waterskiing," I said. "So I can send a wall of water into the boat to wet down the passengers."

"Hey!" Nancy reached out to swat my arm. "Let's sign up for that canoe trip."

"I'll go," Lori said.

"Not me," Christie said. "I'm signed up for gymnastics all week, and I don't want to miss it."

Nancy and Lori stared at me and our bouncing slowed. Their eyebrows rose expectantly.

"No!" I shook my head for emphasis.

"It's your loss," Lori said.

"This summer," Nancy vowed, "you are going on a camping trip."

The possibility filled me with dread. "Maybe," I lied. "But why leave a perfectly good camp to sleep in the wilderness?"

"For the fun of it," Lori said, lying down on the woven surface to gaze up at the sky. She flopped around until we joined her. "I've spent every summer of my life Up-North, either at camp, or with my family, and I'm always finding new places. I'm not psyched about going primitive and carrying our own water. But canoeing is cool. And rivers are so much better than lakes. Just paddling down a lazy current, having the river do all the work, taking you someplace new, that's my idea of heaven. Then, stopping for the night, building a fire. We can be as messy and grungy as we want, which, for my brothers, is pretty disgusting."

Nancy chuckled, and I stared at Lori, fascinated by her point of view. I vastly preferred the lake to any river.

"Can we have a turn?" a group of younger campers interrupted from the side.

"Sure," we replied, jumping off.

"You know," Christie said, as we walked toward the beach, "the guys' camp still resents us for being here. Even after five years."

"Hey, they offered," Lori said.

"Didn't they have a junior camp here?" I asked.

"Yup. Then, they rescued us from extinction," Nancy said.

Christie reached around to poke Lori in the shoulder. "We both have brothers over there this year."

"I didn't even know you had a brother!" I interrupted, suddenly curious about the occurrences downshore. "Do they really take morning dips in the nude?"

Christie's impish laugh confirmed the rumor.

"Big deal," Lori sneered. "I have four brothers. They tell me enough to sour the mystery."

"We could get up in the morning before Reveille and have our own dips," Nancy suggested, half-teasing.

"Then we can see if it's true," I played along.

Christie's expression turned doubtful. "They get up really early. Much earlier than we do."

"We can do it," Nancy said, taking the challenge in stride.

"My clock has an alarm," Lori said. "But I'd rather sleep in. Got a couple of trips coming up."

"Mine has an alarm, too," Christie said.

"Look!" I exclaimed. "Another camper." A brightly flowered footlocker was being carried into Sunblazer upon the back of a CT from the boy's camp.

Lori led the way, "Let's go meet her."

THIRTEEN

UNITING

ACTUALLY, TWO CAMPERS arrived simultaneously, and the guys who delivered their trunks announced they were heading back to their camp. They had hung around for the airport arrivals and now considered their duty complete.

Susie and Victoria had flown directly from Chicago. This fact alone aroused our interest. Only a handful of kids flew to camp from faraway places like Florida or Arizona. They tended to show up late in the day, exhausted and cranky. If their plane arrived early in the morning, they had to wait all day for the last arrival because Mr. Chinn would only make one trip. But Chicago was not far away. Many of us had arrived by car from even greater distances. Thus, flying from Chicago seemed an impersonal ordeal for the camper and an unheard-of luxury for the parents.

This fact hovered among us, affecting our initial impression as we surrounded their beds and introduced ourselves.

Susie struggled to find places for her cosmetics, clothing, shoes, hair dryer, and curling iron. During her dilemma, she rambled busily to herself. "Maybe this can go here. Oh no. That won't fit. I'll need that to be handy. This ledge is too crowded. This can go away for later . . ." She paused often to stare at us. Then she'd shake her long brunette layers and start up again.

Victoria, refined and stately, wore her chestnut hair in a classic chin-length bob. Undistracted by our presence, her regimen seemed to follow a boarding-school routine. Upon the completion of her neatly made bed, she laid out a black velvet helmet, riding crop, tall leather boots, and a pair of beige jodhpurs.

"You ride English!" I realized. When she did not immediately respond, I plowed ahead, "I ride western, that is when I ride. I wore cowboy boots once, and my feet got so hot I thought they were on fire. I bet those boots would get even hotter!"

"I wouldn't know," she said. "I've never worn cowboy boots."

I felt like a poor serf gawking over the aristocrat's finery.

"Could someone please put up a nail for me?" Susie asked. "To hang my shoe bag." Her sandals, tennis shoes, slippers, and colorful rubber thongs now resided in the generous pockets of a pink plastic holder. She had chosen a bed opposite the lake with a view of the junipers. We sauntered over to stare at her collection. I'd never seen so many shoes belonging to one camper.

"Where do you want it?" Lori muttered, grabbing the hammer and tucking the last nail between her lips.

"I don't know." Susie frowned, a damsel in distress. "There aren't any walls."

Lori couldn't wait. She bounded on the bed, pounded the nail into a narrow strip of wood between the screens, and leapt off.

"Thanks," Susie said, standing beneath it. "I guess that will work." On tipped-toes, she stretched the heavy contraption as far as she could reach, trying to hook the metal grommet on the nail. When she fell off balance, the pink plastic swung around in front, and we lost sight of her altogether. Silently fascinated, we watched her struggle until Nancy broke the spell by shuffling over to make the connection.

Victoria snapped her riding crop on the base of her cot. "Perfect," she announced, offering a wry smile for the nail protruding from her window ledge. She sauntered over and hung it in place.

Even when the entire camp truncated "Victoria" to "Tori," she remained glamorous and intimidating. With eight varieties of Susan, four Debbys, three Jennys, and every other name imaginable that ended in y, or its phonetic equivalent thereof, a shortened version of her name proved inevitable. However, she must have permitted its usage or no one would have dared.

The door swung open, and two more campers arrived dragging their trunks and duffels. The afternoon had become early evening, and an air of urgency permeated the cabin.

Sarah and Cindy, both from Saint Louis, appeared windblown and exhausted after two days of hard driving. Sarah smiled openly, and I recognized our physical similarities right away. She could have been my long-lost cousin. We stood eye to eye, had turned-up noses, scattered freckles, and short brown hair.

Cindy's secretive smile, wispy blonde hair, and sharp blue eyes captured ready notice. But when she straightened from unpacking, her long legs gained the real attention. A head taller than the rest of us, I imagined her running fast, jumping high, and spiking a volley no one could return. If only the Cedars could gain her as a teammate!

"There's not enough room for Cindy to open her trunk. Let's move my bed," Christie said.

"How 'bout those rafters?" Tori held a blue suitcase. This glaring reminder of the outside world begged to be hidden. Nancy immediately hopped on my steamer trunk; the tallest, sturdiest perch available. She slid the suitcase into a small gap along the beam. The row of sleeping bags shifted slightly. When she hopped down, they all fell like dominoes except the suitcase. We broke into relaxed laughter, pouring levity into awkwardness. All lingering tension and apprehension shattered. From that moment on, the frequency of this mirth would be our measuring stick of expectation.

"Figures!" Lori exclaimed. Her rolled-up sleeping bag had unfurled on impact, and its contents flew across the floor. "There's my suntan lotion, my deodorant, and oops . . ." She tucked a box of sanitary pads under her sweatshirt, and we laughed some more.

"Can we fit my duffel up there?" Sarah asked.

"Sure, there's room for everything," Nancy said. "We just have to think about this for a minute."

"This beam is empty." Christie pointed. She walked the length of the cabin.

"If we store everything we don't need on a daily basis, it will be less cluttered for inspections," I suggested.

"Inspections?" Susie giggled. "We have to be neat?"

"Only if we want to win," Nancy said.

"I can make a bed as tight as my Latin teacher's derrière," Tori remarked. This took a moment to digest. But, after a gasp of recognition, we chuckled appreciatively.

"Step aside, buster!" Cindy directed, waving her long arms at Nancy. She stood on my trunk and easily touched the rafters.

"Now we're talking," Nancy admired, handing up duffels and sleeping bags for Cindy to align. We rearranged our beds and trunks for efficient access. By the time our counselor entered the cabin, we had become a cohesive blend of diverse personalities.

"Welcome, Sunblazer!" Jenny announced, clapping her hands together. She addressed each of us, one at a time, deliberately pronouncing our names as if we comprised a kindergarten class.

We stared, our mouths agape. Her authoritative manner didn't match her petite physique. Plus, she could have been the prototype for Skipper, Barbie's little sister, having long blonde hair, perfect teeth, and unblemished skin tanned to a golden brown. This stunning likeness to a doll shocked us into speechless wonder as she ushered us out the door for welcoming announcements around the flagpole.

We joined the circle, standing close together, making an early statement of identity. We were Sunblazer, and we would be Sunblazer for the entire summer. I felt the eyes of the younger girls staring at us, appraising our dangling earrings, embroidered cutoffs, smock tops with puffed-sleeves, daring triangle halter tops, and puca shell necklaces. I still felt like a kid, brimming excitedly to be back at camp, but when I gazed at the girls in front of Sandpiper it really dawned on me. Not only had we taken up residency in the largest cabin, but we had become the oldest campers.

Bess stood by the flagpole, completely unchanged, and introduced the CTs assigned to Whitecap. All four were rising seniors in high school. Joanna's dark eyes attacked anyone who dared look at her. And if they proved brave enough to stare back, she cracked a tight grin. Behind her, Bobbi offered a sweet, complacent smile. Her rounded shoulders sloped into a comfortable slouch. Maggie shared a warm smile at random, framed by her luxurious brown hair and doe-like eyes. My sister grinned at everyone.

"Bobbi will be our piano player this summer," Bess said, giving Bobbi a curt nod. We applauded politely. She moved on to explain our daily routine for the newcomers. Her white sneakers reflected the bright sun in stark contrast to her tanned calves. She stuffed her palms into the front of her white pedal pushers and her T-shirt displayed the Shenahwau name in green script. She bent slightly from her waist and spoke rapidly. "The CTs are starting an early-morning dippers. Be up at 5:45 if you want to join them. If you don't have an alarm, they will tap on your door. Raise your hands if you want to join so they can see who you are."

"It was our idea," Christie whispered.

"We were talking about this before you guys came," I informed our new arrivals.

"It's okay," Nancy whispered back.

Lori shrugged. "The more the merrier."

I narrowed my eyes at Susan. As much as I loved the lake, I still wondered why she and her friends wanted to jump into freezing cold water at the crack of dawn. For that matter, why did I? Suddenly, I didn't care that much about spying on the boys.

Nancy nudged me. "Come on, let's do it." She raised her hand, and Lori followed.

"Don't come naked!" my sister interrupted. Shocked laughter followed. She smiled along, more than happy to be laughed at while I cringed, wishing she had said, "Wear your suits." That would have been subtle and witty. Since my bustline had caught up to hers, though not as generously, I had discovered it was an achievement lacking merit. I craved more substantial traits to admire in my older sister. But nearly everything about her fell short in my mind and embarrassed me to the core. I tried to set us apart, to not blurt whatever sprung to mind, barring any kind of filter. But lately it seemed the harder I tried, the worse I felt. Not from shame or remorse, but because it didn't seem to be working.

Christie raised her hand and cheered, "Come on, you guys. It will be fun." Cindy and Sarah raised their hands. More campers decided to join.

"I'll go," Mary said, coaxing others from Beacon, the next oldest cabin.

Nancy raised my hand for me. Grudgingly, I went along. Since she had two sisters, rather than one, or maybe because they were further apart in age, she still had no inkling of why I chose activities apart from mine.

"Stardust will go, too," Linda said. Four young campers, still in grade school, gathered where she sat in the sand. Their limbs entwined hers, filling her lap and clinging about her shoulders. I marveled at these young girls and their courage to leave home for three weeks at such tender ages. But Linda was the perfect solution to any possible home-sickness. Having blonde curls, startling blue eyes, and a pixie-like nose, she presented the living image of a full-grown fairy princess. Obviously, she sprung from a long line of Scandinavian ancestry and only needed a round metal cap with horns to become a Norse goddess of legend. Understandably, the youngest campers adored her. The rest of us sensed something different about her, as if she chose to be with us but not one of us. Every summer, she maintained a permanent position as the arts and crafts counselor assigned to Stardust.

The little ones whispered their woeful protests. "You don't have to go in the water." Linda smiled consolingly. "But if you are up before Reveille, we may as well do this."

Nancy brushed against Tori and said, "The water is really refreshing in the morning. You should join us."

"Negatory there, Big Nance," Tori calmly stated, close to boredom. Her undertone of absolute certainty ensured no one dare awaken her. "I may be new to camp but I am not new to Lake Michigan."

I found this exchange to be deliciously amusing and reveled in Tori's candor. She could not be baited or coerced into any camp activity that did not readily appeal to her, despite the lure of a Council Fire award. She would never start an activity, like me, then learn she hated it and have to quit. Guilt always seemed to follow. She knew better than to sign up in the first place.

Nancy met her gaze and nodded, as if granting Tori permanent leeway for the rest of the summer.

"Well," Susie said, "I'll go. But only if I'm awake." Through a tremor of laughter, she added, "And I don't want anyone to wake me."

FOURTEEN

DIPS

SNUGGLED BENEATH LAYERS of blankets, I dreaded a trip to the Murphy or the sound of Reveille. However, when Christie shook my shoulder that chilly morning I hopped out of bed, already wearing a two-piece suit. I had made this choice the night before, deeming it more comfortable than sleeping in my damp Speedo.

I danced around the painfully cold floor donning my rubbery thongs, wishing I had a nice fluffy rug like Tori's. Christie rounded the cabin and slipped outside while Lori, Cindy, and Sarah discretely changed into their suits. Nancy had fallen back to sleep beneath her mound of quilts.

I wrapped a towel around my shoulders and watched her sleep, fretting about whether or not to disturb her. Cindy crossed over. Appearing especially tall, her long arms swooped down on Nancy's blankets to gouge her ribs with ferocious accuracy.

Nancy bolted awake. "Wha . . . ?" she gasped, rising from her blankets. Her gaze landed on me. Cindy had darted away.

"Dips," I said quietly.

Cindy flung her towel across Susie's face and tiptoed toward the door, dragging the heavy cloth. Susie clawed at the suffocating intrusion until her eyes fluttered open. Cindy held the door for Sarah, and they left under Nancy's sleepy glare. "Cindy," she growled from a thoughtful trance.

I couldn't find any real fault. Cindy had simply followed through on a plan Nancy had promoted. Her clever actions had given both Nancy and Susie a chance to come along. Susie grunted drowsily, rolled over, and fell back to sleep. Nancy flung off her quilts, shimmied out of her nightgown, and revealed a purple-flowered two-piece suit. She grabbed a towel and one sneaker.

Instinctively, I helped look for the other.

But she didn't bother with it. She went to Cindy's bed, turned the sneaker upside down, and sprinkled sand inside the sheets. She tossed the shoe under her own bed and headed for the door. Barefoot and smiling, she chirped, "Ready?"

"I didn't see that," I said.

Linda met us on the boardwalk. She whispered lightheartedly, "For once, I have four little campers who decided to sleep until the bugle blows."

"You could be sleeping, too!" I quietly protested on her behalf.

"Oh no, I always wake early. But those little ones need their sleep, or they barely make it through the evening activity. So I'm testing the notion this summer that if they have to get up early, they won't."

"Pretty smart," Nancy nodded.

"Yes," she said. "I never would have thought of morning dips as the answer. It is nice how prayer always delivers better than you could plan."

I nodded, half-agreeing, thinking random chance had more to do with it.

"Wait, Linda!" a small voice called over the clatter of ill-fitting Dr. Scholl's sandals. "You forgot to wake me!" Bonnie wore a giant sweatshirt three times her size. It fit like a dress. She clutched a towel, a pink flowered bathing cap, and nose plugs. Her short black hair bore the tangled signs of a restless night.

"Oh, bonny Bonnie," Linda sighed, shaking her head. "My little joiner, good for you."

"Why do you always say my name twice?" Bonnie cheerily wondered, boasting a smile of giant front teeth, not yet framed by permanent eyeteeth.

"It's because you're doubly cute," Linda whispered.

Bonnie pressed against Linda, who wrapped a comfortable arm around her.

Other campers emerged from Beacon, waving silently and cutting in front of us. We ventured after them, straying from the boardwalk to cross the sand.

My sister and her fellow CTs lined the shore between our floating dock and the L-shaped dock. The sun climbed over the trees and blanketed our backs in golden warmth. I fought the impulse to burrow my feet, knowing the sand would only reveal the night's chill and the water's temperature. An off-shore breeze wafted a heavy aroma of bacon and oatmeal from the dining hall. My stomach growled.

Little by little, we dropped our towels. I tried to see the boys' camp. As always, a jutting dune blocked the view.

"You'll be able to see them from the sandbar," Mary commented dryly, as if discussing the weather.

"See who?" I asked innocently.

"You know who," she said. "It should really rattle them to see us out here."

"What about your brother?"

"Oh, David won't care. He'll think we're a bunch of nuts for dipping voluntarily."

"He's really cute," I added impartially. I glanced at Nancy, trying to include her in the conversation. She stood apart from us. I spoke louder, "He always says, 'How's it goin'.'" I lowered my voice, imitating a guy at odds with his towering height and manly voice. Then I laughed at myself, thinking I did it pretty well. "Now he would be a nice older brother!"

"Oh, yeah," Mary dripped, rolling her eyes.

"Don't you think David's cute?" I turned toward Nancy. She focused on the water, strangely quiet. Lifting one leg at a time, she stretched a knee to her chest, breathing briskly. I considered how she smiled more and talked less when David came around on the deck after dinner. Perhaps he was not really saying hi to his sister after all. Perhaps it was a ruse in order to say hi to Nancy! I nodded to myself, thinking it made perfect sense.

Cindy skipped a rock. It leapt three times over the smooth water. The lake's glassy surface carried the expanding circles to eternity.

"Come on! We can do this, you guys!" Christie said, inching closer to the edge.

Nancy bolted into a sprint. Her toes skimmed the water. She lunged past the natural drop-off in a sleek dive. Her fingers parted the way like an arrow and she disappeared.

"Oh my God!" I screamed. "She went under!"

"You can't take the lake slowly in the morning!" my sister said, dramatically flinging her towel. She breathed deeply and jogged in place, bending her elbows and flopping her wrists. Her ample bosom heaved against the stretchy fabric of her one-piece suit. She resembled a squirrel perched on a fence, paws in front, tail waving for balance. Gradually, she ambled forward. After making a splash she sank past the drop-off. The water dragged her down to a slow trudge. When the lake reached her shoulders, she thrust her arms forward one at a time, holding her elbows above water, running in slow motion. Her sharp hissing breath could be heard from shore. Upon reaching the sandbar, the water fell away to her knees. She appeared childishly delighted and waved in grand gyrations to capture our attention. She pointed down shore with exaggerated discretion and mouthed, "I see them!"

I recoiled at her display. "I'm not going under," I vowed, watching Nancy swim around the perimeter of the sandbar, performing a stiff crawl, completely unaware of my sister's blatant actions.

Christie announced, "I'm going to run in before my mind catches up to the shock!" She inhaled and sprinted forward, splashing wildly. Her strategy inspired most everyone to follow. Shrieks filled the air.

Only two of us remained onshore.

"Nan," Linda sighed, peering at me. Her voice cascaded high to low, performing a lyrical aria as she amputated my name and breathed new life into it by drawing the "a" into two long syllables. If anyone else had tried this, no matter their age, I would have snarled my displeasure. "Nance" was okay, but never "Nan"! Nance lived in a chic French city. Nan was a backwoods spinster having bad teeth and greasy hair. However, when Linda said Nan she evoked the image of a noble Tudor maiden from the old English court, outfitted in pearls and brocade.

"Yes?" I responded, equally formal and regal, deciding then and there that Linda would be the only person who could ever call me Nan.

"Shall we?" she invited.

"Yes, we shall," I replied. She laughed softly, bending her knees and pointing her toes. Pale skin, void of freckles, perfectly offset her bright pink bikini. "I have so many freckles," I groaned, wishing mine looked like hers. "And I'd much rather have curly hair instead of straight."

"Nonsense." She smiled. "Like what you have, and learn to enhance it."

"Whoa!" I breathed. My feet had entered numbing chill and I knew only a raw, mindless urge to get to the sandbar. The bank fell off. Icy cold spread from my ankles to my thighs, creeping to my hips. Beneath the surface my toes skimmed small rocks, scrambling for a foothold so I could run. When my feet dug into hard sand, I scurried, stiff as a plank with a rigid back and extended arms. Water licked my chest. It was the slow-motion nightmare, the dreaded hallway that elongates unnaturally as you try to run down it. Any progress is completely forestalled by some hidden force. My stride became giant leaps of survival. When my chest broke the surface, I catapulted forward, trying to use the brief, friction-less momentum to my advantage. I hissed in small controlled breaths, realizing I sounded exactly like Susan.

The water subsided to my calves, and I began to run. I reached the sandbar just ahead of Linda. Goose bumps covered my skin but the air felt warm from the rising sun. We had stepped from Iceland to the Caribbean.

Our small group gathered in the middle of the sandbar, trying not to appear obvious as we stole clandestine glimpses of the boys' camp. Nancy alone swam a wide circle around us, alternating between back-stroke and crawl.

A quarter mile away, boys' heads bobbed in the water like ship-wrecked victims. A shrill whistle pierced the air, and the water boiled as the guys stampeded for shore, hitting the beach and diving for their colorful towels.

"Did you get a load of those bare backsides?" Joanna chortled.

"I feel sorry for them," Christie said. "Imagine being forced to do that every morning."

"It's the only way to keep them clean," Lori replied as if stating a tried and true fact. "My brothers don't mind it."

A spray of icy water blasted my face as Joanna leaned down and chopped the surface. "You're still dry above the shoulders!"

"So are you," I protested, trying to return the favor. Instead, I got Mary. She gasped a wordless sputter. Her eyes fluttered while drops fell from her nose. "I am so sorry," I blubbered.

But Mary knew I hadn't meant it. With both arms she scooped the glassy surface and hurled a geyser toward Joanna.

"I have to pee," Joanna snapped, shaking water from her face. "Everyone steer clear," she announced, dropping down, placing the lake at shoulder level. Instantly, we shoved off the bar, seeking wide individual paths toward shore.

"That was exhibiting!" Susan exclaimed. We trudged into dry sand, allowing its warmth to cling to our feet and ankles.

I laughed, unable to control myself. "You mean exhilarating?" I suggested.

"I mean exhilarating!" she quickly corrected, looking about to see who had heard.

"I liked the first one better," I said, knowing she would never intentionally say something so suggestive.

"So who's up for this tomorrow?" she asked more loudly.

"I am," Linda said, rubbing a towel over her wet hair that still held loose ringlets. "Bonnie?" she asked. "Will you be joining us again?"

Bonnie nodded a wide grin of honest enthusiasm; an attribute highly cherished at camp. Her innocence shone from implacable optimism and a desire to join and do everything, plus a whispered connection to the old camp, as if her genealogy sprung from a secret lineage of royalty. Even if she hadn't been so energetic and cheerful, her presence alone would have earned recognition for bravery as she held the distinction of being the youngest camper in our short history at Wildwood. I felt lacking beside this sprite, for she represented the type of girl I never was and could never be.

Susan's roving gaze solicited the group for future participation. Most of us committed as we walked up the sandy bank, but I wasn't so willing. "Are you headed for a hot shower?" I asked.

"No!" she proudly proclaimed. "I feel great! My skin is all tingly and warm. Isn't this a great way to start the day?"

I agreed, though something in me wanted to disagree, especially since I'd been trying to tell her this for years. "I suppose," I mumbled, "but I'd rather be sleeping."

"What are you signed up for this week?" she asked.

"Sailing in the morning. I'm refreshing from last year, trying for Expert. Then, water safety in the afternoon. I'm trying for water safety instructor."

"It's tough." She insinuated I couldn't handle it. "You have to rescue one of the guy counselors and get them on top of the floating dock during storm conditions."

"What?" I staggered backward, envisioning my scrawny arms trying to hold someone like Eric or Luke. Built of solid muscle, they each weighed at least two hundred pounds. Luke was the head counselor of the boys' camp and seemed taller than our rafters. Eric was shorter, built like a heavyweight boxer, and so handsome and intimidating even our counselors barely spoke to him. "You've got to be kidding!" I snarled, realizing I would have to place an arm around Eric's bare chest! "He'll sink me. I can't possibly chest-carry one of those guys and get them on that floating dock!" A four-rung ladder was the only way to the top. In storm conditions it could spike three feet in the air.

"You can do it," Susan said. Her tone carried an edge of impatience as Reveille sounded in the distance.

Her glibness set me on edge. "Wait," I said, growing suspicious. "Didn't you take your test on Glen Lake?"

"That's right, on Big Glen, not Little Glen."

"How is that the same?" I challenged her lame reference. She knew, as well as I, that neither of these glacial lakes, separated by a narrow bridge, could ever match Lake Michigan's turbulence in rough weather.

"And I had to rescue Robyn," she added, as if that made up for it. "She fights like a mountain lion!"

"You don't think Eric or Luke will struggle?"

She grunted noncommittally.

"So why did they change it?" I snapped.

"Don't know. Ask Robyn." Then she laughed. It sounded like a witch's cackle to me. My insides boiled. I wanted to say, you always get the good deals. But then I stopped short. I knew she didn't, not really.

FIFTEEN

THE SETUP

"WE'RE LATE AGAIN, Schmidty," Nancy said, showing no distress or anxiety as we scrambled around before dinner. "Cindy hid my favorite earrings, I'm sure of it. You know, the ones with the blue beads?"

I shunned her accusation, "Why would she do that?"

"To be ornery." She laughed in a way that said, "Isn't it obvious," and I read a hint of admiration in her lingering smile. "Oh, here it is, poked into the screen. There's no way I put it here!" she declared, plucking it free. Tilting her head, she threaded the wire through her earlobe while shuffling over to Cindy's bed. She thrust a hand under the mattress, between the tucked sheets, and withdrew a stash of candy. She climbed on Sarah's bed and hid it in the rafters.

I shook my head, unable to fathom this apparent feud. Except for the way she had awakened Nancy that first morning, Cindy was quiet, almost shy, even a bit corny. Sarah called her our gentle giant.

Nancy chuckled and smoothed the bedding.

"So one time she goofed with you," I exclaimed, rolling my eyes.

"Uh-huh," Nancy grunted, her mouth half-opened. One eyebrow rose higher than the other as if I didn't know the half of it.

I held the door. "Ready?"

She darted past. The door slammed behind us as we raced along the boardwalk behind Sunblazer, toward Whitecap. "Not again!" I screamed, banging my toe on a warped piece. I hopped in place. "Why do I always do that?"

Nancy placed an arm around my waist, wincing compassionately, and

I hobbled along. The pain subsided quickly, and I gained a lopsided skip as we passed beneath the Wildwood sign.

"You need to follow Jenny's beauty tip number twelve," she grinned.

"Wow," I droned, truly amazed. "We have them numbered?"

She snickered while I seriously reviewed our counselor's many words of advice, tapping my chin in reflection.

"Come on, you know," she insisted.

On field trips, people often mistook Jenny for another camper. This amused us in a perverse, unspoken way because she never let us forget her true age. Despite her thin, girlish figure, she maintained a quiet authority on every subject. But mostly, she spouted an endless supply of obscure beauty hints. "Girls," she'd say before bed, "be sure to sleep on your backs so you don't get wrinkles on your faces." Or when we were about to go swimming, "Wear your two pieces! Your one-piece will smash down your breasts. You don't want them sagging to your knees when you are in your thirties!" Suddenly I recalled the tip most relevant to my situation. "Lift your legs when you walk!" I declared, marching.

"It will shape your thighs," Nancy said.

"Who cares if you look foolish?"

"Think of the benefits!" Nancy extolled, stumbling on a tree root.

We doubled over in laughter, gripping each other's arms. We sprinted across the bridge and hustled up the steps, taking them two at a time. At the top we jettisoned apart and slowed our gait, just in time to pass the dining hall's plate-glass windows.

I couldn't see the faces within and pretended not to look. However, if I had turned my head, I would have seen a few of them looking back. And they were not just the annoyed glares of Robyn or Jenny at our persistent tardiness. This year, the guys ate dinner before us.

A new crop of teenagers had appeared that summer, perhaps also leading up to CTs. They stood out in the sea of faces as my acute teenage sensors noticed them noticing me. However, my hardened life back home put a chip on my shoulder, making me believe I was either too fast, too clever, too good, or not good enough for any of these church guys. So I paid them little heed.

Nancy's situation proved entirely different. Not only had she grown keenly aware of these staring eyes, but she cared very much for one particular set. She flipped her hair, scattered her feathered bangs, and straightened her spine while sucking in her breath, as if her insides were not heaving same as mine.

I smiled at our transparency, for I, too, had modified my appearance. Mainly out of fear. I did not want to trip. I lifted my thighs, more than usual, while planting a wide, fluid step. I would try anything, even Jenny's little tip, if it could solve my problem once and for all. I also vowed for the millionth time not to be so late.

The chefs filled our plates, and we peered about to gauge our tardiness. I noticed a few girls at the milk machine, and Robyn was choosing a salad. "Perfect timing," I declared. "We didn't have to wait in line!"

"Now isn't that the excuse of all chronically late people!" Robyn snapped.

I blushed. Nancy chuckled.

"Seconds!" the male chef boomed. Our trays cleared the metal track and a frenzy of boys queued for more. Nancy and I skirted around them, fully accustomed to this ensuing chaos in the wake of our entry. We expertly navigated the flow and took our assigned seats at opposite tables, sliding into the molded plastic chairs just as our presiding counselor offered a brief, meaningful grace.

Before taking a bite, Nancy called across her table, "Cindy!" I perked up to listen, glancing over my shoulder.

"Yes?" Cindy replied, assuming a look of angelic wonder.

"I need to talk to you after dinner," she insisted, very businesslike, placing her napkin in her lap.

"Would that be on the deck outside while you visit with David, or would that be back at the cabin?"

"On the beach," Nancy said. "Before our evening activity."

"Super-duper," she agreed, flashing an amused grin.

"What's up?" Christie whispered at my side, gripping my arm.

"I'm not sure," I said. Christie's shoulders rose, as did the corners of her mouth, as if she knew something but wouldn't tell. When I asked, she only leaned away, holding a stiff back and a secretive dimple.

After clearing our trays, we returned to our tables for announcements. Mary slid the saltshaker toward me. Plastic against plastic, it moved like a hockey puck on ice. I cupped my hands where the Formica ended. If it balanced perfectly along the edge, we would admire it, even clap for a few seconds. Mary might say, "That's one," as if an actual point had been scored. Instead, the shaker stalled, tipped, and fell into my cupped hands. "Oooh," everyone moaned.

"Tonight is the horse show," Bess announced. We halted our game and shifted in our chairs. "Riders from both camps will meet at the North Bridge in one halfhour. We can only take one busload of spectators. Wildwood campers not attending will play Capture the Flag. This is not a Dunes and Cedars competition," she said, facing Hutch.

"Team leaders gather Spokes and Hubs for Operation Skeleton," he said. "If you are a rider follow Procedure Alpha." He bent low to hear a private word from one of his counselors, which everyone took as a signal for dismissal. Urgency spread through the hall, and we flocked for the doors. There would be no lingering on the deck this evening.

"Let's be on the same team," Christie said.

"Yeah!" I agreed. My gut churned excitedly. In all my accumulated weeks at camp, over so many summers, I had never played Capture the Flag on the same team as my Dune friends.

SIXTEEN

A MEETING OF MINDS

I CHANGED INTO dark clothes and tucked a tube sock into my waist-band so that its green and yellow stripes dangled near the hem of my shorts. I faced the lake and held a steady eye on Nancy and Cindy where they stood together on the beach. I couldn't hear them, or decipher any meaning from their neutral body language, so I imagined all sorts of scenarios. Was there an underlying friction to all the pranks? Did they both like David? Had something happened during one of their activities?

I dipped below the bed to grab my sneakers. When I rose, Cindy had fallen back on her heels, knees in the sand, and was hugging her stomach. Nancy stood over her. I believed the worst until I noticed their spasms of laughter. Cindy straightened, took a deep breath, and ran toward the cabin. Her long legs stretched effortlessly and a serene smile lit her face. Upon entering, she darted for her footlocker.

Had they called it even? Had they reached a truce? Greatly relieved, I felt certain of this and happily anticipated losing my role as witness to Nancy's secret retaliations.

Crack! Tori snapped her riding crop on the base of my bed. "You," she paused ever so slightly to relish my startled look, "have fun capturing that flag."

I froze, entranced by her lazy lack of interest. She patted the velvet hat, tucked the strap under her chin, and sashayed out the door.

"Cheerio!" I called after, figuring this to be the proper send-off.

Cindy kicked into cowboy boots. "Time to giddy-up," she said, shoving the tails of an orange-checked western-style shirt into her jeans.

She threaded her belt while scooting toward the door. Lori held it open, and Cindy darted past, saying, "Muchly obliged."

"Sarah and I are going to watch," Susie announced. They wore short shorts and tight tops, and Susie had touched up her curls.

"Both of you?" I asked, incredulous to learn they'd want to.

"I love watching the animals prance around," Susie defended their choice. She wrinkled her nose. "I just don't want to be the one on the horse!"

"Gonna drool over the boys?" Lori accused.

"Har, har." Sarah protectively hugged Susie's arm.

"I'm so glad you're going!" Christie was genuinely relieved. "I was feeling bad about not offering them some cheers of support."

"Never fear!" Sarah soothed. Tossing her chin-length tresses, she focused on the rafters. "We will represent Sunblazer!" She placed a hand on her hip and struck a Wonder Woman pose. Then, she propelled Susie out the door.

"So it's only the four of us," Lori concluded, as we followed after.

Roughly half the camp gathered in the sandy bowl between the Hylton and the two younger cabins, Stardust and Puccoon. Maggie judiciously appointed Nancy and Bobbi as opposing captains. Bobbi picked fellow CTs as commanding officers, and Nancy picked us. In order to avoid the painful ordeal of someone being chosen last, we let the remaining campers decide on their own. Somehow, it always worked out.

We blindfolded Bobbi and spun her around. "Point! Point!" we chanted until she raised her finger and indicated the general direction of the river. This became their land. By default, we claimed the beach. The wide area in the middle, including our cabins, extending to the border of the boys' camp, became No Man's Land. We separated from the enemy and headed for the beach.

Nancy's first command put Mary in charge of our Base Camp and Debbie in charge of guarding the flag. This left her free for raiding and reconnaissance. These initial decisions ran contrary to how our Cedar captain usually ordered things, and I would have mentioned it, if I'd had a winning record to support me.

Debbie chose a secure, somewhat hidden spot along the beach to mount our flag and to post guards. Nancy and Lori disappeared to scout for the enemy's flag. It didn't take long for them to return and announce, "It's on the bridge."

A raiding party was formed. Moments later, and before I could fully digest it, Christie, Lori, Nancy, and I were climbing the dunes behind Puccoon and Stardust. I had never walked this stretch of land because it belonged to the Resort. It was as though we had entered a forbidden yard that we had studied and gazed upon for years from a bedroom window across the street. Apparently, it held no novelty for them. I gaped at our cabins.

"Get down," Lori whispered. "Past this tree, they can see us from the bridge." She waddled like a primate. I followed her hunched lead, and we skirted the untamed riverbank.

"This is very ambitious." Christie's low voice penetrated the rustle of underbrush. We picked our way through berry bushes, horse nettles, sand cherry, burr marigolds, and spindly bloodroot.

"Are we going in the river?" I asked. To me, the river was only good for canoeing. Beyond this I didn't care to get to know it.

Nancy's reply carried a tone of obscure honesty. "It's the only way."

"Aren't there bloodsuckers?" I worried aloud, using the slang term from Papa's cottage.

She chuckled confidently. "Has anyone ever gotten leeches before?"

"Well, no," I admitted, sizing up my sneakers, deciding it would be okay to get them wet. They were dirty and a bit big, anyway. One afternoon on the dock in full sun would dry them, shrink them, and bleach them all at once.

"Far enough," Lori announced, cutting straight for the water. Clearly, she knew the plan.

Thorny vines attacked our bare legs as we trampled zigzag down the steep bank. At the very last we slid into the river's warm current up to our necks.

"We'll have to cross over." Nancy trained a cautious eye on me.

I was about to object. No one ever visited the woodsy side of the river. We swam in the middle and used the lake side where a nice beach had been cleared and no critters could hide. The other side was dark and dense, completely in shadow, except for a sunny section that was even more overgrown! It flourished under the late-afternoon rays and was so thick it could hide a beaver dam.

"It won't be so bad," Nancy addressed my look of disgust. Lori struck crosscurrent. We prowled after, single file, exposing our heads above the current as we dug our feet to walk along the riverbed. On the other side, we huddled near the bank.

Nancy whispered, "Around that curve we'll see the bridge."

I scrutinized the mucky shore and its slick tendrils. They sprouted in and over the water. Who knew what creatures lay hidden in those moist layers of accumulated decay!

"Schmidty," Nancy whispered. I bristled at her notice, wondering how she knew I was considering heading back to the beach. "Do this," she demonstrated, wiping mud on her cheeks and forehead. "We can't let the guards see us. We have to stay in the weeds. And when we get near the beach, where the sun is shining, we have to swim underwater all the way to the bridge. Are you up for it?" She sank low until the water covered her chin. Her eyes implored me to play along, to get into the game.

She handed me a fistful of mud. Reluctantly, I slathered my cheeks and forehead, mirroring Lori and Christie.

My body had stiffened into a permanent cringe as we pressed deeper into the muck. Our limbs slicked across layers of soggy sediment and masses of roots so compacted we barely disturbed the leaves above. This gnarled growth pulsated against our scalps as busy inhabitants transmitted waves of vibration into the air. Thousands, perhaps millions of cicadas and crickets insulated us in a cloud of noise.

When thirty feet separated us from the bridge, we gained sight of the enemy. Despite our heavy camouflage, as we huddled beneath a woven canopy amid the deafening song of insects, I felt exposed to anyone having the sense to look. I hardly breathed, and my heart beat wildly at the prospect of detection.

"Yuck!" Lori hissed. She pulled a thin, slimy object from her shoulder. It could have been a snail without a shell.

Nancy registered a glimmer of concern, then returned her focus to the bridge.

Underwater, I rubbed my legs, just in case. On the back of my thigh I felt a slippery piece of slime. Hoping for a worm, I pinched my short fingernails around it and flung it away. I shuddered, trying to convince myself it was too large to be a bloodsucker.

"Four on the bridge," Nancy whispered.

"Check the woods," Lori spoke into my ear.

I parted the tangled vines to gain a tunnel view of cedars, too slim and bare for anyone to hide behind. The carpet of needles remained undisturbed. "Clear," I mouthed.

"Roman, what's the plan?" Christie hissed.

"We'll swim for the bridge when shadows cover more of the water," Nancy advised. " After that, we'll scale the outside to get their flag."

I rolled my eyes and tried to envision such a scheme. "Like trolls?" I whispered.

For a split second, rumbles of laughter formed in Christie's chest. I strangled an answering chirp. She gained control and held her breath. "Roman," she grilled, through a pinched nose, "are you strong enough to go hand to hand?"

"Sure. The water will float me half the way."

"You might splash your legs," Lori considered. "Could be noisy. We need a distraction."

"Look." Christie's wet finger jutted from beneath her chin. Mary stood waving behind Puccoon, well hidden from the bridge on the opposite shore.

"Can she see us?" I gasped.

"No, but she knows we're here," Christie reassured.

"Mary, what do you have planned?" Nancy whispered as if Mary could hear. Unbelievably, Mary answered through a series of hand gestures. Nancy translated, "She'll rush the bridge when we're in place."

"You guys have done this before," I breathed, thinking Cedars could use some sign language.

"Roman," Lori whispered, "remember the last time?"

"Lori, I can do it this time." Nancy cryptically referred to some Dune secret. "The river is much higher. They won't see us coming."

"Us?" Lori's melodic voice poked fun at Nancy's presumption. "All right," Lori conceded. "I'll help you get your hands on that rag hanging from a stick, propped along the middle of the bridge."

"How is it you always make things seem so unimportant?" Nancy whispered.

"Not unimportant," Lori said, pleasantly detached, "just not as important."

"Because you don't care about winning or losing," Nancy teased, showing no rancor.

"I'm happy either way," Lori sighed.

"That doesn't make sense," I quibbled. "If you don't care, why try? And if you do care, why not put everything you have into it?"

Nancy tilted her head, thoughtfully considering me. We stared at each other for what seemed a long time. Then, she tightened her lips and shrugged her shoulders. I wondered if I'd missed something profound, or worse, something obvious, unable to name it or grasp it. "What?" I whispered.

She shook her head and looked away.

SEVENTEEN

COLLATERAL DAMAGE

"LET'S GET MOVING," Christie's gravelly whisper interrupted. We had slime between our legs, tendrils wrapped around us, water up to our necks, and critters vying for a piece of us. We gathered a few well-spaced breaths. On the final count, we puffed our cheeks and dipped below the rippling current.

We pressed our torsos into the weeds, swimming with our arms and digging our feet into the silted riverbed, walking horizontally. We grabbed a few underwater roots along the way, keeping below the shadowy overhang. I cracked my eyes to hold sight of Christie through the churned-up sediment and rationed bubbles until my chest ached. Then I felt a darkness deeper than the overgrowth. Christie gripped my arm in warning, and I knew we had reached the cover of the bridge. I wanted to spring above water, splashing and gasping for air. I fought the impulse and surfaced to my chin, feasting on muffled breaths.

We stood shoulder to shoulder, trying not to disrupt the river's flow. A green, luminescent dragonfly lit on the surface and claimed a patch of sun. It held motionless on the current and floated past. A cricket chirped noisily in my ear, and the enemy walked above us. Their footfalls thudded loudly as they changed guards and warned each other to keep a lookout for runners from shore, or swimmers in the middle of the river. They foolishly discounted the possibility of someone venturing into the wild, sinister bank.

"Now what?" Christie mouthed. She glanced at me, and together we faced Nancy.

She tapped her chest, jabbed Lori, and pointed up at the bridge. They would now scale the upriver side. Christie and I would do the same, only in full sun on the downriver side.

Christie shook her head, refusing the plan. Her long blonde hair floated from its thick ponytail and surrounded her submerged shoulders like a delicately spun web. Wearing a devilish grin, she pointed up the bank.

Nancy and Lori thoughtfully considered this.

"Go!" Christie mouthed, adding a sprinkle of water from her fingertips.

Nancy reached up and gripped the outer braces. Her hands remained hidden from the guards by a series of raised two-by-fours. Holding a stiff torso, she cut into the water, moving hand over hand toward the middle.

Christie and I sank into underwater isolation and pushed off the weeds. Our stomachs grazed the riverbed, and little bubbles escaped the side of my mouth as I swam in the surging wake of her violent scissors kick.

We surfaced upriver, gulping for air. Nancy's silhouette hung from the peak of the arched bridge. Her legs kicked the air to raise the rest of her body. Her long tube sock hung from her waist like a soggy tail. An arm's length away, Lori dangled from her fingertips. Her ankles dragged in the current, and she hung limp. Her freckled shoulders quivered in silent laughter.

Mary and her raiding party invaded from the lake side, aiming for the bridge, whooping and hollering.

Christie and I mounted the bank, charging through the tangled brush. We ducked low, dripping across the carpet of pine needles. In breathless terror, I watched Joanna and Maggie confront our teammates attacking from the opposite end. They pulled their socks and made them prisoners. The flag stood unguarded.

We ran. Our shoes squished loudly when we landed on the first planks of the bridge.

"Gotcha!" my sister shouted. She emerged from a nearby tree.

I jumped in place, frightened beyond words, feeling the sock ripped from my waistband. I prickled in loathing at the sound of her laughter. She darted for Christie's sock. I whirled and held my arms wide, blocking her reach.

Susan yelled, "Guard the flag! Jo, Maggie, Shane, guard the flag!"

Christie sprinted past. Shane pursued from the woods. Maggie and Joanna abandoned our raiding party and darted for the flag.

Christie lunged for the green triangle of fabric tied to a stick, wedged into the decking. Her stomach slid across the planks. She gripped the stick, yanked it loose, and thrust it between the rail posts.

"That doesn't count!" Joanna declared, standing over her.

"You can't drop it in the river," Maggie explained, sounding almost apologetic.

Shane knelt against Christie's wet, sprawled body and plucked the dripping sock from her waist.

Christie's laughter caused me to chuckle, for I knew she had made contact. Mary and the others from our team began to giggle.

"What's so funny?" Shane demanded, drawing her dark eyebrows together. This plucky camper had wisely suspected another trick.

Christie displayed her empty hand. The flag hung in midair, outside the railing, propped inside someone's fist.

"No!" Shane protested.

The flag disappeared, and we heard a loud splash in the river. A secondary splash mimicked the first. We scrambled to our feet and leaned over the edge. The flag drooped from Nancy's mouth as she plowed her arms into a smooth backstroke, moving upriver against the current. Lori swam toward her and rolled on her back. Both of them grinned from ear to ear, kicking toward No Man's Land.

"We have the flag!" Beth crowed.

"Thank you," I said, taking my sock from Susan.

"No," Susan said, snatching it back. "They have to reach the beach."

"They only have to reach the shore," Mary objected. "It's No Man's Land."

"They have to cross over and not get captured," Susan corrected. She called to her teammates at the top of her lungs, hoping they waited in ambush. "Get Lori and Roman!"

"They have the flag!" a voice replied from the woods, and we heard sticks snapping among the underbrush.

Susan gripped my arm and would not let go. Everyone else ran off to view the chase. She tugged me across the bridge, behind the Hylton, around the flagpole, and into the grassy dunes near Whitecap. All the while, she shouted for reinforcements to stop Nancy and Lori from reaching the beach.

"The Lake team wins!" A chorus rose from the west. Screaming laughter echoed, "We won! We won!"

"Ha!" I crowed to my sister. "You guys never saw us coming! We were in the river, right in front of you!"

"You have leeches on your calves," she observed. "They are bigger than I remember."

"Ew!" I gagged, peering over my shoulder and down my legs. Dark amoebas, the size of baby carrots, dotted my skin, tenaciously feasting. They clung so tightly I hadn't felt their numbing tendrils sucking my blood. "They are huge!" I screeched, frantically stomping my feet. I twisted sideways to see if any had fallen off. When they had not, I instinctively tried to pinch them away as I had done in the river.

"No!" Susan warned, drawing a crowd.

"Yuck!" a younger camper exclaimed. "I'm never going in the river again!"

"Me either," a few others agreed.

"You won't get them in the current," Susan chastised, sounding like a counselor. "Just stay away from the bank. It's silly to let a few leeches spoil all the fun."

She had learned this at Papa's cottage when a tiny bloodsucker, the size of a pea, had taken root under her little toe. She had entered the lake too early in the morning, before the sun had driven them into the reeds. She had carried on, crying and blubbering. Uncle Dean had caused further hysterics by insisting her toe would fall off. Of course, a few salt crystals later, it dropped off leaving her toe intact. So, I glanced about, wildly desperate, wondering where in the world I would find a shaker of salt. Perhaps I could run to the dining hall. Maybe they'd forgotten to lock it!

"Come to my cabin," Susan said. "We have salt for popcorn."

"Popcorn," I repeated. "Why do you get popcorn?" I asked, jogging after.

We reached Whitecap's porch, trailing an entourage of thrill seekers, and I became an object of curious inspection. I presented my legs while Susan shook a plastic shaker pilfered from the dining hall. "We're only borrowing it," she sheepishly offered.

The slimy parasites foamed and frothed. One by one, they lost their grip and fell. A handful of campers squatted down, poking sticks.

"Toss them off the porch," Susan directed.

"Flying leeches!" they hollered, flinging them high into the air.

Josie galloped by, sweeping the sand with a broom between her legs, still wearing her English riding finery. Her chinstrap dangled and her jodhpurs bore streaks of dust. She neighed like a horse and pivoted toward the Hylton. A large, fancy blue ribbon bounced across her bottom like a tail.

"Way to go, Josie!" we called.

I pried off my shoes and rolled my waistband. Susan checked my spine and I felt inside my armpits and the crease of my thighs. "All gone," I sighed.

"Take it." Susan handed me the shaker. "Go help the others. I think Nancy has them the worst. I could see them from the bridge."

That calm, safe feeling came over me, and a measure of pride. Susan was acting the wise, dependable older sister. Suddenly, I didn't care if she wasn't cool, or bad, or crazy—all the traits my teenage mentality admired and longed for her to be. She would always take care of me. Plus, she'd been chosen Cedar's captain that summer and had actually led us to a few victories.

"One time I got about ten bloodsuckers at my grandfather's cottage!" she proclaimed to the assembled campers, and the feeling left. Her transparent boast had shattered the moment. Once again, she faded in my estimation. The girls begged for the gory details, and she embellished the tale. I snorted at her exaggeration and ran away to help my friends.

Nancy and Lori stood at the water's edge trying to rub away the dark splotches with sand. Christie patiently waited to see if this had any effect.

"We get the flag and they carry it off!" Lori summarized through a bemused smile and a face still flushed from the effort. "Like we're some sort of creatures from the Black Lagoon."

I presented the shaker like a prized elixir. Christie had two on her forearm, one on her thigh, and another clinging to her ankle. We cupped our hands to localize the distribution. They fizzled into a bubbly froth. After an eternity of dangling, they dropped squirming and foaming on the wet sand.

"We'd better wash off so the salt can stick," Nancy decided. She and Lori plowed into the lake.

"What's up?" Tori strolled from Sunblazer, battle worn and sweaty. Her helmet had left creases on her forehead, her jodhpurs bore streaks, and her boots no longer held a shine.

"Leeches," I said. "We got them in the river."

"Sooooo," Tori's beguiling expression lit into a congratulatory smile, "you captured more than just that flag!"

"We did," Lori droned, cutting splayed fingers through her hair in search of slimy irregularities.

"How'd it go?" Christie asked.

"Josie's jumping dazzled everyone," Tori replied. "I did precisely as expected."

"And Cindy?" Nancy asked from the lake. A sunset formed beyond us, blazing red and orange.

"She is pleased by her performance."

"Good." Christie nodded, putting a cap on our mutual interest. Tori would no more stand to hear the details of our underwater strategy than we would listen to her nuances of dressage. We were water-persons and she was a horse-person. Perhaps the lines had been drawn at birth, like one's innate fear of snakes or spiders. Regardless, once established, few crossed over, and we all benefited from an economy of words.

"We're ready!" Nancy said. "Make them die."

I tipped the shaker and discovered the air's moisture had caked the opening. I unscrewed the top and used my fingers to coat the dark, grotesque shapes. They gradually fell on the beach to be washed away by the lake.

"Was it worth it?" Nancy asked under the sky's burnish glow.

"Yes," I agreed, shuddering from the repugnant task, but actually meaning it.

"Well, remember that," she stated, as if in warning.

I puzzled at her reply, eventually deciding she had meant this advice for Cedar-Dune competitions, to help us win more often. Her fearless determination surely explained why our adversaries accumulated so many wins. I wouldn't realize until much later; she meant this for me alone.

EIGHTEEN

THE STING

WE AWOKE TO a drizzling patter and the low cover of gray clouds. After a week of continuous sunshine, our cabins felt dark and cozy, making it difficult to head out. Regardless, our routine carried on. We gathered around the flagpole wearing ponchos and holding umbrellas as the trees dripped upon us. Moist, warm air swirled about, ineffectual in its attempt to disturb the water-laden sand. Annie and Mary stepped forward, somberly presenting the folded flag to perform their assigned duty.

"Not today," Bess corrected, taking the flag and tucking it under her green poncho.

A few unseemly giggles spread among the circle. Annie and Mary peered about, perplexed by the laughter.

"Archers will join arts and crafts," Bess said. "Water-skiers will join swimming."

"What about sailing?" one of the newcomers queried. More sporadic giggles dashed about.

"Sailing will meet in the Hylton to review terms and tacking," Bess answered, ignoring the disturbance as she outlined the rainy day routine we seasoned campers knew so well. "Swimming, canoeing, and land sports will continue in the rain unless we hear thunder. Riders will go to the stables as scheduled. Gymnastics will share the guys' covered facilities. In the afternoon Robyn will be holding tryouts for a new play. If it hasn't cleared, the rest of us will watch a Don Knotts movie in the Hylton."

Bess paused. Her eyes darted around the circle trying to locate the source of continued interruption. I gauged the thickness of the socked-in clouds

and anticipated the clippity-clip of the projection reel in the darkened lodge
as rain splattered the windows and black-and-white images filled the blank
wall. Maybe the CTs could make popcorn . . .

"That's mine!" Susie uttered a squeal of horrified accusation, thrusting
a finger toward the top of the flagpole. All heads craned skyward. A
pink, frilly brassiere blared immodestly.

I tried not to laugh for Susie's sake while everyone cracked up at its
unlikely appearance. Pretentious and intimate, it was not the kind of bra
anyone ever expected to find at camp, and I suspected an undertone of
mocking, though Susie seemed not to care. She only wanted her bra back.

Bess stated crisply, "That is quite the bra."

I looked over at Nancy to share a smile, but she and Cindy stood stiff,
wearing bland expressions.

"The boys raided last night!" one of the younger girls speculated. All
eyes zoomed to our head counselor for confirmation.

"I don't think so," Robyn said slowly and definitively. She stepped
up to the pole and uncleated the line. Hand over hand, she lowered the
damp bra. After unhooking it, she tossed it to Susie.

Nancy and Cindy piqued my curiosity. They held too still, too quiet,
too uninterested, and I suspected a gross misjudgment on my part. Instead
of ending their pranks against each other, what if they had joined forces
to unleash their quirky humor on the rest of the cabin? Or worse, the rest
of the camp! I decided to keep an eye on them.

The next morning on our way to breakfast we passed beneath the
Wildwood sign and observed its wood-burned letters completely cloaked
by a bra. This generous double-D of stark, institutional design was tied
across the back with twine. Its pointy cups had been stuffed full of tissue.

Days later, a driftwood log landed on Driftwood's front stoop,
blocking their exit, as if some giant wave had washed it there overnight.
It surprised everyone at Reveille and required three campers and one
counselor to carry it away. Then, Sandpiper flunked inspection because
they had neglected to sweep away a mountain of sand from their front
stoop. Sandpiper lamented their innocence to everyone who would listen,

insisting this gargantuan pile of sand, practically a baby dune, had originated through sabotage. Of course, we all believed them, but no one claimed responsibility. And when they won practically every inspection after that, I suspected it had been a sort of motivational prank.

Near the end of this peculiar week, Whitecap awoke to find their verandah woven from post to post in white toilet paper. Its grand beauty provided a great distraction on the way to breakfast.

On the way back, Christie and I paused for one last view of this spectacle before the CTs tore it down. I pondered these accumulated pranks and my inability to catch Nancy and Cindy sneaking around, or moving about at night. Either they were very clever, or they had inspired some copycats.

"Did you hear?" Christie said. "Bess is letting us have Cabin Day on Friday because it's the Fourth of July." We headed for the trampoline under a cloudless sky and blaring sun, planning to steal a few jumps before cleanup. Christie remained determined to teach me how to do a backflip.

"What will we do on Saturday?" I wondered, craning my neck for signs of jumpers.

"The whole camp is going into Traverse City for the Cherry Festival!"

"Yummmm!" I pictured dark, ripe cherries dripping sweet black juice.

"It's empty!" Christie declared, and we ran for the final leap into the air.

A chorus of invisible campers shrieked, "Don't jump!" Mary's voice rose above the others. "We're down here!" A handful of girls hunkered inside the pit, beneath the woven straps. They struggled against gravity and the narrow gap, straining to raise a shiny blue footlocker.

"How did it get down there?" I asked, kneeling down.

They presented tight disenchanted smiles. "If we only knew," Debbie answered for the group.

"You could unhook the springs," Christie advised. "It should be easy. The fabric is pretty worn."

"In fact," I spoke to the faces below, but my words were meant for Christie, "a person's legs could slip between the bands right smack in the middle of a jump to get straddled like a giant wedgie!" I could barely get the words out. Christie's shoulders quivered, and her husky laughter converged upon me. We gripped our chests and writhed on the sand, lost in the raw, uncontrollable spasms we had not been able to release the night before when it happened to Joanna because she had been glaring at us.

"Yeah, Bess ordered new fabric last week," Mary spoke over us. "It hasn't come in yet."

"I think we should unhook the springs," Debbie sighed, dropping her end of the trunk. "Then we won't ruin the pit. How 'bout some help?" she asked, smiling expectantly.

We wiped our eyes and sobered up. After dislodging five industrial springs, they pushed and we pulled until the trunk slid through. Replacing the coils proved a bit trickier. It took all six of us and a few pinched fingers to stretch the trampoline into place. "Thanks," they mumbled, one at a time, and lugged the trunk away. At the very last, Mary cast me a sly, inexplicable grin.

"I hope she doesn't think we put it there!" I fished for what Christie knew as we began to bounce. "Who do you think did it?"

"Who knows?" She plunged forward to augment my bounce. We stuck to the outer edges, avoiding the worn middle.

I flew high into the air, circling my arms and flexing my knees for balance, mentally wondering when Nancy and Cindy could have done such a thing without being seen.

"Hey, guys!" Nancy called from the edge. "Jenny told us we're going camping on Friday for our Cabin Day."

"Camping?" I flinched. Despite all my years at Wildwood I had never slept outside under the stars. A group always gathered on the beach after a bonfire, but I always ended up hauling my sleeping bag to the cabin and crawling into my bed. The night sky proved too big, too distracting, and too unsettling for me to fall asleep.

"Where?" Christie asked.

"On the lake," Nancy said.

"Which lake?" I suspected the narrow, mucky shores of Bar Lake, where Susan's cabin had gone the week before and been eaten up by mosquitoes.

"This lake," Nancy laughed.

"Lake Michigan?" I brightened a little.

"The one and only. We're camping in the Sleeping Bear Dunes. Jenny's borrowing a tent from the boys' camp, large enough to sleep us all."

"A tent?" I reconsidered, bringing to mind the red pup tent my dad had won in a sales contest. Five nylon stakes ran through sleeves on its outer edges and gathered at the top into a metal grommet. When set, the tent popped into a five-sided dome for hours of fun inside a cocoon of red canvas and piles of blankets. "I could do that," I decided suddenly.

The next day, Susie's blow dryer disappeared.

"Who took it?" she openly accused us. Layers of hair plastered her eyes like a wet show dog. She stomped her foot and thrust her glossy lip into an annoyed pout. Wet strands stuck to it.

"I haven't seen it," I said, wishing I could help. Everyone hustled about, shuffling along the wooden floor, efficiently dressing for lunch. A breeze pushed through the row of screens. My eyes flew to the lake, and my thoughts wandered in dreamy appreciation as I absently looped a white macramé belt across the hips of my cutoffs.

"Go brush it in the sun," Christie suggested. "That's what I just did." Her thick blanket of hair lay dried and obedient across her back.

"That won't leave any time for me to curl it!" she balked.

"Use mine," Tori offered. She sat on her bed, lazily brushing her thick chestnut waves.

"Thanks," Susie exclaimed, parting her bangs to see. She skittered over and plugged the dryer into our sole electrical outlet. "Oh!" she shrieked a few moments later, stomping her foot. "Where is my curling iron?"

This got our attention. It couldn't be a coincidence. We paused to consider her predicament because it felt like the culmination of an orchestrated scheme. The pranks had begun with her bra, and now perhaps they would end with her hair, because this had been the ultimate target all along. Suddenly, it seemed like the rest of the pranks had been merely a subterfuge of disguise.

It could be argued she spent far too much time on her hair, especially for camp. She raced to the cabin upon the completion of every activity, slavishly curling it before meals. She missed out on Beach Time and waterskiing because these activities left her barely enough time to change clothes, let alone a blow-dry and curl.

"Can't help you there," Tori yawned. "Don't use one."

"What good is a blow dryer without a curling iron?" she pouted. "My hair is falling in my face!"

"Here, use these." Christie presented a set of bright yellow barrettes.

"Yuck," Susie sneered. Surprised by her own impulsive outburst, she inched near Christie's outstretched hand to be polite. Closer scrutiny only confirmed her initial displeasure. "Have you had these since the first grade!" she shrilly accused.

"You could let me cut your bangs," Lori suggested. "I'm pretty good at it."

"No offense, Lori." I grimaced to cushion the blow. "But your cuts have been dubbed a visit to the 'Snip, Snip, Oops' Salon."

"Sometimes I have to cut off more than planned," she said.

Sarah sat up from a secretive huddle on her bed where she'd been deciphering her boyfriend's scrawling penmanship. "Theresa gives the best cuts," she interjected, speaking of Nancy's sister. She tousled her own short layers, proudly displaying Theresa's latest work. "I can run and get her, if you like?"

"I'll take the barrettes," Susie grunted, snatching Christie's clips. She clamped them on both sides of her forehead. "I look like a five-year-old!" she screeched upon peering into her hand mirror.

"Susie, we're going camping tomorrow," Nancy entreated. "What will you do with your hair then?"

"I don't know," she snarled. "Wear a bandanna, I guess!"

"Wear one now," Cindy suggested.

"Here!" I snatched a yellow bandana, rolled and tied, from a nail by my bed. "It will go with your peasant top."

"Okay," she agreed, removing the barrettes and throwing them at Christie. She pushed the bandanna along her forehead. Instantly, we offered a deluge of compliments.

The curling iron and blow dryer returned the next morning, after breakfast, just before we left on our camping trip. Susie squealed her delight, positively tickled as she hugged them to her chest before hiding them in her trunk. Still, they would disappear and reappear, again and again, like roaming feral felines daring her to live without them. Her flabbergasted explosions became part of our routine. Then, one day she wore a bandanna even when she didn't have to. She started joining us for Beach Time, relaxing in the sun right up until the bell clanged. And during our last week, she chose waterskiing for an afternoon activity. By then, her tirades seemed less sincere and more dramatic as she dared the culprit to come forth. No one ever did. And through it all, I gave daily thanks for my wash-and-wear perm.

NINETEEN

MAKING OUR MARK

WE CLEANED THE cabin and rolled our sleeping bags, stuffing clothes and a pillow inside. Beneath a promising blue sky we hiked across the bridge, hearing the van idling in place long before seeing it. Jenny sat in the front. She had remained in the dining hall since breakfast, personally overseeing our supplies. "Hop in!" she called as we emerged from the woods. "Mr. Chinn has a busy day!" Her slight figure left a sizeable gap across the front bench between our gruff, grandfatherly driver.

We crammed into three bench seats and hugged our sleeping bags across our laps. Mr. Chinn peeled from the gravel lot. This armchair botanist who kept a sluggish pace on his nature hikes wasted no time when taking us places in the van or bus. We sped along the dirt road through a blur of green, and his sudden turn into the highway's smooth pavement sent us sprawling. The radio had been tinkling in the background, and now he cranked it up, filling the van with the kind of music he knew we liked.

"Satur . . . Satur . . ." we stuttered, as Chicago's brassy intro teased us. At last we exploded on cue, "Saturday in the Park! You'd think it was the Fourth of July!"

A few songs later, Mr. Chinn swerved from the two-lane highway onto a narrow dirt road. We ground to a halt inside a small turnaround. Keeping the van running, he helped us unload and then roared away to deliver another cabin someplace else. He left us standing in a cloud of dust beside an insurmountable heap.

We slung our sleeping bags over our shoulders and dove into the pile. Among the nine of us, we carried two containers of water, four unwieldy boxes of food and utensils, a huge rolled-up tent, and five bamboo poles.

I chose a container of water and hugged it while stepping over a smattering of orange lilies. We picked our way through yellow puccoons, purple thistle, and blue sailors, whose small delicate blooms tracked the sun's path across the sky. Dwarf junipers cropped up now and then, forcing us to go around them, and a light breeze carried the scent of the lake. Eventually, the mounded terrain expanded into near barrenness.

"Don't step on the dune grass," Jenny cautioned. We steered clear of the sporadic clumps swaying in the wind like bouquets of bright green ribbon. "This grass built these dunes," she urged us to notice. "They trap the blowing sand and hold it still long enough for a juniper to sprout alongside. The shrub takes over catching sand, until a poplar takes root. And so it goes, until a forest is formed."

We splayed our feet, trudging along, trying to gain traction along the loose, shifting sand.

"Imagine," Jenny continued. "The first explorers to this region would have crossed miles of dunes, sensing water, but not seeing it. They had no idea what they were to come upon."

"Aching arms," Susie whispered. I snorted my agreement. Our sleeping bags had not been designed to be carried like backpacks. The little straps cut into my skin while the thirty-two pounds of hermetically sealed water sloshed and jostled. I desperately hoped we hadn't miles to walk.

"And then," Jenny said, climbing the crest of a dune, "they would see a body of water with no end in sight!"

Lake Michigan took our breath away. We paused in that moment of wonder, letting down our burdens to gaze upon the sparkling water meshing seamlessly into a vibrant sky. A passing gull, a skittish sandpiper, and an occasional beetle were our only companions in this pristine world.

"Perhaps they thought it was the ocean," Jenny said.

"What are those two islands?" Sarah pointed.

"The Manitous," half of us spoke as one.

"We can see the South Manitou from camp," Tori said.

"Oh yeah." Sarah and Susie nodded, making the connection.

"They used to have dune-buggy rides all over here," Lori said. "The state shut it down last year 'cause it was tearing away the sand."

"It was fun, and noisy," Christie smiled. "Like a roller coaster."

"According to Chippewa legend the Manitous are baby bears," Jenny said. "Their mama led them across the lake to escape a forest fire on the Wisconsin side. A storm came up, and she lost sight of them. Exhausted and nearly dead, she waded ashore to watch and wait." She pointed beyond the graduated dunes and bowled-out craters to a peak of shaggy trees. "There she is," she whispered dramatically. "She's fallen asleep and will wait as long as it takes for her babies to reach the shore."

We quietly contemplated a hold so great it could tie the mother to the shore forever.

"The Great Spirit Manitou placed the islands on the spot where the cubs disappeared and turned the grieving mother to sand to honor her faithfulness. So that's why it's called the Sleeping Bear Dune."

"Let's camp in that bowl!" Lori announced, leading the way. We stumbled downhill after her, trying to run. At the chosen spot my cube of water slipped and skidded across the sand. Tori's landed like a meteor at my feet and Sarah slid by, laughing merrily as her box split open. Christie kicked her sleeping bag the rest of the way, then dropped the tent poles in a clatter.

"First thing!" Jenny announced. "We must raise the tent!"

We paused to watch Nancy and Cindy's labored approach. They plodded into the clearing, panting and grunting to maintain their grip on the log of fabric. Susie skittered out of their way. When they let go, the green canvas thudded on impact.

"Jeeze!" Cindy guffawed. "That was like lugging a dead body!"

"I'll say!" Nancy exhaled.

"This is a great spot," Christie said. We surveyed the basin of a sweeping dune. High walls of sand sheltered us from crosswinds yet provided easy access to the lake and a scenic view of the monolithic dunes.

"Do you know how to set this thing up?" Nancy asked. She kicked her sneaker against the dark mound.

"Nope," Jenny declared, tying her silky blonde hair into a ponytail. "Let's spread it out on this level area. We'll put the cooking supplies over there. We'll make a fire pit there."

Our shoes came off, and we milled about, arranging the supplies and tugging at the twenty-by-twelve rectangle of stiff fabric. Eventually we located four lumpy corners. Jenny decided we needed to flip it over to find the door. We folded it like an omelet, grabbed hold, and lifted. All hands awkwardly rotated the bulky mass, reopened it midair, then set it back down.

"That was really heavy!" Susie exclaimed.

"I can't believe only two of you carried this!" My stunned admiration focused on Cindy and Nancy. They never complained, so I did it for them. "You know, those supply boxes were not packed very well. We could have fit everything into two boxes instead of four. Then more of us could have helped carry the tent."

They both shrugged. It had been no big deal. "It's okay," Nancy said. Her warm eyes met my indignant expression. "We got it done."

I wished for the same underlying fortitude so I could perform a similar act of selfless rigor, yet I never saw the need, or the benefit, until it had passed. "Well," I huffed, "I can help on the way back because the water jug will be empty."

The open seam presented itself, and we glimpsed the inside, now full of sand. We tried to brush it away using our palms.

"We have to shake it out," Jenny said. "It will be easier to do it now."

Tori sighed heavily, and I sensed further reluctance from the others. "I don't mind the sand," I boldly announced, thinking I spoke for everyone. It was an inevitable companion; as innocuous as the air and as clean as the water.

"I mind." Jenny's severe tone held a note of petulance.

"Okay," I whispered, instantly embarrassed.

Christie and Tori sent me commiserating smirks.

We repeated the process of suspending it midair and turning it over. Some of us shook the bottom and scooped sand out the opening. After flipping it back, we spread it flat so the door would face the lake.

We stood around it, panting from the effort, and Nancy took a census. "What about the poles? Inside, or outside?"

"Inside," a few of us guessed at random. The remainder said, "Outside."

Jenny's perfect brow wrinkled into a scowl. She bent to inspect an outside corner. The fabric was knotted into a tight bulge. "There is nothing to slide them into."

I searched the nearest corner for a sleeve like the red pup tent of memory.

"They must go inside." Nancy sprang to action. She and Cindy grabbed the bamboo poles and forced an opening through the flap.

"Lift the edges," Jenny ordered.

We grappled to support the unruly blob. From inside the musty folds, they fumbled about until four points emerged at the corners. Nancy's muted voice instructed, "Hold steady while we set the middle!"

The center towered into shape, transforming the squat hut to a regal temple. Nancy staggered out, her eyes wide and uncertain. The flap fell, and Cindy's muffled voice called, "Let go! I got it!"

We hesitated to obey, having scant faith in the contraption. Jenny hovered about, biting her lip, sizing it up. "Okay, try it," she said. "Go ahead," she encouraged, since none of us had moved.

It felt unstable. I gripped the pole through the stiff cloth and attempted to anchor it. Susie did the same on her corner. We shared tense, wary smiles, and slowly backed away.

A breeze whipped around the bowl, carving an infinitesimal layer of sand. It whipped the flap aside and pushed aggressively into the tent. The green canvas yawned and moaned, swaggering into a billowing swell. We watched it sway. My hands went to my mouth. My insides bubbled from anticipation. A chorus of screams pierced the air when it toppled. Cindy crawled out wearing a ruffled grin.

We dove on top of it, claiming a free-for-all, rolling against each other. Someone said, "Let's just sleep on it."

"No! We have to try again!" a lone, demanding voice heralded.

We froze, as if awkwardly posed in a giant game of Twister. Jenny stood above us, greatly distressed. Truly, I felt sorry for her as I gazed upward. She looked as if she would burst into tears.

"I really want us to do this!" she implored. "The guys said we would never figure it out. When I asked for this tent, they told me, 'You'll end up sleeping on top of it like everyone else from the girls' camp who has ever borrowed it!'"

A great intake of indignation spread among us. Cindy rose to her knees and blustered, "Them's fightin' words!"

"Yeah, if the guys can do it, we can do it," Susie declared. "Right?" she added, searching our faces for encouragement.

"We can do anything we set our minds to," Christie guaranteed.

"Maybe the poles go on the outside," I suggested, trying to think of an alternative, though it made no sense.

"Hold up." Lori sat cross-legged and picked at a corner where the tent folded into itself, forming a tight-fisted bulge. She pinched and pulled the wrinkled cloth until the corner was exposed. A gnarled loop of scratchy rope fell out. It was sewn into the seam.

We darted for the remaining corners and found similar loops.

Jenny's eyes widened gleefully. "That makes sense! The poles go on the inside, but we need stakes to hold the shape."

"Did they give you any stakes?" Sarah asked.

Our fair counselor bit her lip, then shook her head. In the next three seconds of silence we registered suspicion toward the guys, followed by outrage, on to resolve, then back to self-reliant optimism. In one fluid motion our eyes shifted to the distant woods.

"Might as well get firewood while we're at it," Lori said.

"Yes," Jenny agreed. "We'll need some thick green branches for the stakes. We can whittle them to a point. I'll look for the knife. Cindy and Nancy Roman, can you make a fire pit?"

The rest of us took tentative steps, each considering which direction to bolt for scavenging. Nancy pondered where to lay the fire, based on the direction of the wind and the placement of the tent. Cindy directed a slender finger our way, sternly mocking, "Now, don't go too far. There's more work to do!"

Everyone darted for the woods. Christie and I aimed for the beach to scrounge for driftwood. We straddled the shore, wading lopsided in the shallow waves, staring out at the Sleeping Bear Dune. We found scant pickings. It had been a long shot anyway, but it provided an excuse to bond with this new corner of the lake. Eventually, we struck into the sand and headed for the woods. Christie climbed while I paused to inspect a half-buried piece of gray, weathered wood. I shoved it into my pocket for kindling. When I looked up, Christie's footprints had carved an arch across the untouched sand.

"You made a giant C!" I observed. The darker sand underneath contrasted nicely against the pale outer. Christie leapt sideways to form a block letter H. I tried to help. We fell over, scrambled to recover, and soon it resembled a messy slop of unintelligible lines.

"Let's start again and stick to cursive," she decided. We ran to the base of the next pristine wall of sand. It stretched parallel to the coast, rising higher and higher until it grew into the head of the Sleeping Bear. We visualized our spacing then cut into it sideways. I became the caboose to Christie's locomotive, and we churned out her name. At the end of her track, we changed positions, and I led to write mine.

"I bet a low, flying aircraft could read this," I said, when we stood side by side in the water, appreciating our creation.

Christie stated quite simply, "It won't last."

The natural state of a dune was change. Mr. Chinn had told us that many times. Our work would be smoothed away by the persistent wind as it swept the malleable, shifting sand. Every summer, the dunes reshaped around us but in such gently creeping degrees we hardly noticed. By tomorrow this exact landscape would be only a memory.

"We just carried one full load of firewood!" Susie accused. She and Tori approached from the beach.

"We came looking for driftwood," I explained, "and got a little distracted."

Tori appraised our masterpiece. "Names and faces should never be seen in public places," she recited, then added, "Nice graffiti."

"Uh-oh!" Christie pointed at Sarah and Lori, poised to leap into our work.

"Go around!" we shouted and waved.

"I'm adding my name next!" Sarah declared, charging through the bowl we'd already messed up.

"It has to be cursive," Christie cautioned.

Under advisory comments of "go higher" or "widen it out," they added their names. Our chain stretched the length of a football field. It ascended three times our height and employed only a fraction of the dune. Then, having a pang of conscience, we jogged back to the campsite. Christie and I charged for the woods so we wouldn't return empty-handed.

TWENTY

SOARING TO NEW HEIGHTS

CHRISTIE AND I descended into the campsite clutching dead branches and birch bark. Jenny eyed us suspiciously, and I wondered if she was keeping track. Did she tally everything we did, even on our Cabin Day? I shed my load on the pile and arranged its sprawling chaos while considering this fantastic possibility.

Nancy sat in the sand, a craftsman at work, meticulously shaving flakes from the end of a green limb. "Let's see if these will work." She nudged her toe against a finished pile of pointed stakes.

We stretched the tent floor while Lori and Nancy pounded stakes at deep angles using cans of beans. When it slung tautly over the sand like a low hammock, Cindy clawed the depths of musty fabric to venture inside. "If I don't come back," she said, her voice wavering melodramatically, "I give my bandana to Susie, my share of the food to Sarah, and my sleeping bag to Roman, so she can carry it back to the van."

"Cindy," Nancy breathed, exasperated, "I'm coming in with you."

"Same here," Christie said, inching behind them. Jenny and Lori followed. They each brandished a pole and pushed upward as they went. The rest of us clawed the rough fabric, trying to shape its outside edges.

"Everyone let go!" Jenny's muffled voice demanded when the middle formed a sloping peak above four square corners.

I eased back from my post, as did Susie. "It's holding," she whispered. We tiptoed toward the entrance, wary of the slightest shift of sand. Sarah and Tori met us, moving like cartoon characters stepping away from a time bomb. We held the flaps for the others to emerge. Then we stretched these triangles across the slanting roof to transform its length into a huge doorway.

We waited for the breeze to arrive. It blustered through, pummeling the sides and swirling about. Despite its vigorous assault, our fortress held firm. We shouted triumphantly and ran for the pile of sleeping bags.

Mindful of the middle pole, we spread into a row and plopped on our bellies. We rested chins in our hands, kicked our feet, and presented gleeful faces toward the lake.

"I'm very proud of us," Jenny announced, standing over us. "Aren't you?" Our replies staggered a medley of groans and laughter. Some of us had done more work than others, but in that moment we were unified in our accomplishment. The need to earn beads seemed as distant and irrelevant as the rest of the world.

"There is plenty of time to start a fire," Jenny declared. "Let's take a hike."

We left everything behind and migrated for the shore, aiming for the Sleeping Bear.

"So this is what took you so long," Nancy said at the glaring presence of our names. She and Cindy charged ahead to make their mark. Under our loud and bossy directives, even Jenny wrote her name. When complete, we stood on the beach and admired the monumental chain of script. For this day, in this moment, we owned it all.

Christie pointed to the Mother Bear, high above us. "Guys," she said, "let's see what it looks like from up there!"

"That's pretty steep," Sarah objected.

"What if we fall off?" Susie worried.

"It's sand!" Lori exclaimed. "You'll fall in before you fall off."

"I don't know." Sarah persisted, "It looks pretty tough from down here."

"Babes," Nancy derided, striking upward.

We laughed at the challenge and lumbered after her. Vegetation had not yet taken hold on this monstrous accumulation of golden flecks. We bounded directly up its face, cutting through encrusted ripples, taking generous strides. However, our feet sank deeply into the loose grains and collapsed our effort to baby steps. We nearly toppled backward on the vertical slope. Our thighs and backs ached, so we changed tactics and angled our ascent, cutting sideways and spreading out to give each other room.

At the crest, my body felt as if I'd been running an all-out sprint. Nevertheless, we hardly paused. The dune beckoned us onward. We walked single file along its backbone, aiming for the tree-covered summit. Our feet pressed into the sand, whittling its crown, and the strong wind lifted the grains to build elsewhere. It also pushed against us, adding suspense to the dizzying height.

A forest unfolded to the east. In an isolated meadow, a dairy barn captured the sun upon its metallic roof. Big Glen and Little Glen formed blue holes on the shaggy carpet of cedars, pines, maples, beech, and poplar.

Looking west, the Great Lake dominated. It seemed we circum-navigated the top of the globe. Never-ending blue surrounded us and spanned the horizon. Whitecaps appeared as wispy stripes on a blue plate, and the sun cast luminous sparkles across the sand. We did not cower from this brightness by squinting and cringing into downward stares. We joined it.

We held our heads high, smiling serenely, absorbing the sun into our hair and faces. Each step held an element of profound contentment and silent significance. My insides swelled from pure happiness to be with my friends in this place, at this moment, and I wanted it to last forever.

The crest widened until it became relatively flat. A copse of cottonwoods and dense pines anchored the peak. We foraged through this scruffy knob of vegetation, no longer needing to walk single file. We hiked a more gradual slope, then aimed for the edge.

Wind and rain had compacted pebbles and sand into a slippery, vertical grade. Its treacherous incline dropped toward the steely water, and the wind roared up it.

We hurled rocks, foot-sized or larger, into the air, gripping each other for a measure of safety. We leaned over the precipice, into a bolstering airstream, and watched them skid down the face. They tumbled end over end, shooting outward at intervals, dislodging and crashing into larger embedded rocks along the way. After shrinking to pebbles we glimpsed only a faint cloud of dust as the avalanche plummeted into the lake.

"This is like being on the roof of a skyscraper," Tori hollered over the wind's whipping force.

"It looks hard and unforgiving. Let's head back to the softer sand," Jenny cautioned, peering about as if a menacing foe might spring from the woods to shove us off the edge.

We retraced our path through stubby saplings and evergreen shrubs. When we emerged from the Sleeping Bear's head, our footsteps on the ridgeline resembled the spine of an ancient sea serpent. Both glaring and fleeting, it signaled our presence.

"I wish we could see our names!" Christie declared from the head of our single file. "Look!" She jutted a finger across the vista. Lone and statuesque, our dark green tent stood out upon the miles of sand as a solitary symbol of civilization, though not quite our civilization. Its tallest peak, surrounded by four lesser peaks, presented a foreign and exotic display.

"Looks like it belongs in the desert," Lori whispered. Her ginger hair whipped about, partially blinding Sarah, who pressed forward to see.

"An Arabian sheik's tent," Christie gasped.

"Awrence . . ." I gripped my throat as if dying of thirst. I staggered forward closing the gap between Cindy and me, stooping as if I would collapse. "Awrence," I repeated.

"What are you doing?" Cindy reproached.

I gazed up at her. She appeared taller than ever.

"It's from the movie *Lawrence of Arabia*," Tori answered for me. Her tone suggested I did it badly, though well enough for even a dimwit to recognize.

"It's like we crossed the desert and finally reached the ocean," Christie said, shielding her eyes in salute.

"But thank goodness we're not in Arabia," Jenny said. "Our sisters over there are still in bondage."

We paused to consider her meaning, staring out at the endless lake, mirroring the endless possibilities inherent in each of our young lives.

"Imagine having to wear all those robes and veils," Susie said.

"In the heat," I added.

"I guess you could never go outside and just run," Cindy mused.

"And would they have cheerleaders?" Christie wondered.

"As women," Jenny said, placing special emphasis on each word, "because of what happened in this land almost two hundred years ago, we have more freedom than any other time or place in the history of the world."

We felt wrapped in blessings. Standing high above the earth, we bore this gift like the wings of a dove. In my short lifetime I had seen dress codes lifted, colleges granting admittance, and new fields of study cracking open every day for women. I knew I could become anything my heart desired.

"Next Fourth of July will be the bicentennial," Nancy said. "We'll never see another one. Not for our entire lives."

"For sure, they'll go overboard on the fireworks," Lori said.

Sensing an end to our reflective pause, Christie resumed our hike. Then, she spun around to say something. Susie bumped full force into her immovable, athletic stance. Her squeak of surprise hung midair as she tipped over the edge. We watched, helpless and amazed, as Susie flayed her arms and legs trying to gain her balance. But the momentum was too strong to overcome. She had to go along; sliding, shrieking, and running the rest of the way to the distant shore.

"Thank goodness she didn't fall back there!" Jenny gasped, shaking her head.

"I'll save you!" Christie catapulted into a forward flip. She planted her feet at an angle about fifteen feet below us, cutting through the outer crust and sinking into the base. She arched her back and flung her arms like an Olympian sticking to her landing.

We clapped our approval. The sound echoed all around for a split second until the wind carried it off.

"Let's go!" Nancy said. She could have fired a gun the way we took off. Each forward step became an outward leap. Rather than running out of control as one might descend a hill of grass, we bounced, cheating gravity as the sand slowed our descent and cushioned our steps. At the bottom, we splashed into the water and peered up at the mountain we had just run down.

Lori summed it up, "What a riot."

"Well, I'm not doing it again!" Susie gasped.

"Chicken Little," Tori said.

Susie sputtered, pointing up, perplexed that her statement would need defending.

"It might be worth it." Sarah wrinkled her nose at Susie. "You know, to run back down again instead of falling."

"It's like flying." I smiled, wondrously elated.

"Let's do it," Nancy said. And Jenny capped our decision by declaring, "It's great exercise."

The thrill of running down proved worth the effort, and we spent the rest of the day climbing, jumping, rolling, and leaping over the dunes, usually within sight of our tent as we admired it from every angle.

TWENTY-ONE

A STICKY SITUATION

OUR STOMACHS GROWLED from hunger as we built a fire and assembled the meal. We opened the dented cans of precooked northern beans and set them in the coals, leaving their metal lids partially connected to keep ash from flying inside. After soaking corn cobs in the lake, we laid them on the embers, still in their husks. We boiled water in a banged-up aluminum pot after discussing exactly how much water, since we lacked a proper measuring cup. To this, we added packets of Minute Rice. When the rice looked fluffy, we drained the beans and mixed them together in individual bowls. We sprinkled shredded cheese on top and devoured "a complete protein" as Jenny classified it. Next, we attacked the ears of corn, stripping away their strands of burnt silk, to roll them in a slab of creamery butter. Our fingers, lips, and chins dripped from the sweet, salty nectar.

"Banana boats!" Jenny announced, handing out large yellow bananas.

Still ravenously hungry and forsaking all sanitary preparation, we passed the knife between our greasy, charcoal-encrusted fingers. We slit the peel lengthwise and mashed the insides to make room for squares of chocolate, globs of peanut butter, and pieces of marshmallows. After tightly wrapping them in foil, we positioned them on the coals. It melted into a gooey, delicious mess that burned our tongues, ran down our chins, over our hands, and dripped onto our bare feet. Every sticky spot became a sand magnet.

After consuming all except the peel, to include licking the foil, we dipped into the jar of peanut butter. Christie grabbed a handful of marshmallows and squished them to resemble cottage cheese. She pulled repeatedly until the mash smoothed into lustrous taffy. "Yum!" she announced, stretching the gleaming band. She leaned forward, grinning deviously, and bit the middle. The ends fell away like trapeze artists. She lowered the satiny ribbons into her mouth.

The rest of us scrambled for handfuls to do the same.

"Girls!" Jenny announced. "Did you know if you stand up straight, you can cut two inches off your waistline?" I considered this new tip and wondered what had prompted it. Testing the notion, I stiffened my spine and thrust my chest until my shoulder blades touched in back. It felt entirely unnatural and uncomfortable.

"Nancy," Jenny said, greatly pleased to see me try. "Straighten from the small of your back then rotate your shoulders."

"Okaaaay," I breathed, contorting into an awkward pose. Extending my arms for balance, I took a few steps, working diligently to lift my thighs. I'd never seen a crane in action, but this had to be it.

Nancy recommended, "Give it up, Schmidty."

"No way," Lori said, forcibly distending her lean belly. "If you have a layer of fat around your middle, standing up straight would make it show more!"

"How would any of you toothpicks ever know?" Tori said.

"I suppose this meal was not very healthy," Jenny critiqued, rubbing her stomach, as if for once in her life she'd eaten too much and needed this beauty tip as a personal reminder. "But it was the best I could do without bringing freeze-dried packages," she apologized. "I wanted us to have fresh ingredients. But I had to pick things that wouldn't spoil."

"It's protein and fruit," I defended her choice, sensing a lecture on nutrition.

"Too much white food," she said.

"Better not talk that way in Chicago!" Susie spoke through a mouthful of marshmallows.

"As opposed to dark food," Jenny clarified.

"Still racy," Tori said.

"Use your intellect and not your emotions," Jenny chastised, dipping her fingers into a plastic bowl of water. "I'm talking about the actual color of different foods. Pasta, potatoes, northern beans, rice, bleached flour, cheese, and bananas are not nearly as nutritious as dark foods like raisins, spinach, beef, black beans, dark lettuce, and dark chocolate, which are high in iron. Something we young women need plenty of. Even a small glass of dark beer, like Guinness, can be beneficial."

"Beer!" We laughed hysterically to hear her say it. Some of us had never tried it while others had tried too much, though I'll never know who fell into which category because we dared not talk about it.

"Hush," Cindy interrupted, pointing to the sun as it fell behind the lake. "It's sizzling." We paused to listen, wanting to believe our boiling sun could actually touch the lake and cause it to steam. "Gullible!" she sniped.

"Har, har," Nancy said, pulling her taffy into a satiny ribbon. A piece of it plopped into the sand, instantly coated as if swarmed by miniature brown ants.

"Yuck it up, Roman," Cindy said. She swooped down and pinched Nancy, leaving two sticky globs along her arm.

"I could get you back," Nancy said, "but you already have so much on your face it hardly seems worth it."

"Where?" Cindy's tongue swept to the corners of her mouth to investigate.

Nancy inched near, feigning great interest in something on her forehead. "Here," she said, laying gluey marshmallow hands across Cindy's cheeks to squeeze her mouth into the likeness of a fish.

Taffy oozed from Cindy's mouth. "Oh!" she squeaked through her fish lips. "Gross!" we answered, backing off. Nancy pulled away, leaving sticky handprints.

"Tori, there's some on your leg," Susie spoke rapidly, slapping taffy across Tori's tanned thigh.

"Susala darling," Tori said. "Was that wise?"

"Don't anyone touch me," Sarah warned, defensively raising her hands. Christie swiped her arm and left a glob.

For the next thirty seconds our gummy hands swatted, pinched, and hailed a blur of destruction. Everyone's arms, legs, and faces proved fair game, except Jenny's. She had been one of us all day, but no one would touch her. When it ended, we stood like shell-shocked soldiers, stonily assessing the damage, amazed at how utterly thorough our efforts had been. Sand clung to every inch of our bare skin.

Jenny tossed a garbage bag, and we gathered our litter. Armed with biodegradable soap, we waded fullyclothed into the lake and scrubbed the aluminum pot, the grimy cooking utensils, and our bodies until the sky turned pitch black. By the amber light of smoldering coals, we changed into dry apparel. Completely exhausted, we claimed our places in the tent and waited for the fireworks. We rested on our backs and gazed at the sky through the tent's opening. We had been promised a meteor shower.

TWENTY-TWO

PROMISES IN THE DARK

"TEN O'CLOCK," NANCY said. "That's when it's supposed to start."

"Sunset was at quarter till," Jenny announced into the darkness.

"Then it's about time," Christie said.

"Let's sing 'Taps' while we watch," I whispered, eager to stimulate the counselor's hymn sing. "I'll do the harmony." I took a deep breath, "Day is done . . ."

"The Cannibal King with the big nose ring!" Lori interrupted.

"Good grief, no!" Cindy said, covering her ears.

"Fell in love with the dusky maaaaiiid . . ." the rest of us blustered, unable to resist. "And every night by the pale moonlight across the lake he'd waaaaaade. To hug and kiss his pretty little miss, under the bamboo treeeeeee. And every night by the pale moonlight, it sounds like this to meeeeeeee. Ah rump! Smack, Smack. Ah rump! Smack, smack. Ah rump diddle-ah-eeee-ay . . . Oh, we'll build a bungalow big enough for two! Big enough for two! My honeeeey. Big enough for two! Waddle, waddle, waddle. And when we're marriiiiied, happy we'll be. Under the bamboo, under the bamboo tree!"

It ended as abruptly as it had begun, and we absorbed the quiet, staring at the star-studded sky. I blinked at the mass of lights, unable to decipher the few constellations I knew.

"Try not to focus too closely on any single cluster," Jenny advised. "Let your eyes roam."

"There!" Nancy said. Her arm ascended like a black cannon aiming for the multidimensional heavens.

"I saw it!" Susie blurted. "My first shooting star."

"Quick," Tori said. "Make your wish."

"These are the best kind of fireworks," Christie said.

"There is Cassiopeia." Nancy drew a flat W in the air to match the dots.

"Good one," Jenny lauded. "In Greek mythology she was queen of Ethiopia. And would have been considered beautiful if she had not been so boastful. The Romans believed the Gods chained her to her throne as punishment then placed her in the heavens upside down for all eternity. But," she added through a heavy, yawn, "the Arabs think that constellation is a kneeling camel."

We pondered the boastful queen and the dark eternity of space while Jenny's breathing slowed, perfectly matching the cadence of lapping water.

"There's the Big Dipper," Cindy whispered.

"And the North Star," Sarah added, barely making a sound.

My shoulder ached from a clump of sand. I gently pounded the musty cloth until the grains beneath shifted into submission.

Christie exhaled through a breathy whisper, "This is my favorite camping trip."

"This is my first camping trip," Susie said.

"Me, too," Sarah said.

I thought hard, guessing the same, though it didn't seem possible after all the nights spent in the little red pup tent, or the summers at Papa's cottage, and my years at camp, plus late-night parties back home involving kegs of beer in cornfields.

"I've spent plenty of nights out," Tori clarified. "But never on a camping trip."

I nodded along thinking this best described my experience as well.

"It's tough to get better than this," Nancy said. She leaned over to swat my arm. "But we can always try." I stared at her silhouette, wondering what she meant. "How 'bout coming on the canoe trip with us Thursday?"

"There's another one?" I stammered.

"I'll go," Susie said.

"You like canoeing," Nancy insisted.

"It's just for one night," Lori said, refusing to whisper. "If Susie goes, she'll need a partner."

"Doesn't anyone else want to go?" I pleaded for a volunteer.

"Negatory there, Big Nance," Tori uniquely declined. "I have an aversion to rivers."

I wanted to say, "Me, too!" But I knew they'd never let me off so easily. "I'll be missing land sports," I said.

"Big whoop!" Lori shunned my best excuse.

"Soccer is fun." I turned defensive, though I had only signed up because I'd already taken everything around the lake for the first session.

"We're trippin' down the Crystal River," Lori said. "No portages. Perfect for first-timers. Why, last week we had nine portages, ended in a small lake, and carried our canoes along the same route once used by the Indians. It was fun, but grueling."

"Truth is," I said, gaining courage from Tori's declaration. But my voice erupted far too loudly. Clamping my mouth shut, I glanced at Jenny. She lay undisturbed. I pressed on, more softly, while staring at the reflective water. "I like being near the lake. There is always a nice breeze and there are no mosquitoes."

"It's okay to feel that way," Christie said. "The lake makes you happy." I faced her just as she turned to face me. Her steady gaze and certain tone added weight to an otherwise simplistic statement. "Gymnastics make me happy," she added.

I nodded along, sensing the glimmer of something wise and meaningful.

We heard Jenny's sleepy voice paraphrasing a mish-mash of things we'd learned in Sunday School. "If you find yourself in an unhappy situation, offer sacrifices of joy and soon you'll dwell in the house of the Lord."

"Heaveee," Lori sighed. We grew silent. The wisp of a bat or the wings of a moth brushed the outside of the tent. In the distance an owl hooted.

"That beats sacrificing a goat," Tori whispered and we started to giggle.

"Does sacrifice mean we have to give up some happiness?" Sarah asked.

We waited patiently in case Jenny was thinking. We heard only the deep sound of her breathing.

"It's about acting joyful even when you don't feel like it," Nancy said.

"Which is freaking hard to do!" I snorted.

"We dwell in our thoughts," Nancy said. "Good thoughts are like dwelling in the house of the Lord. When we're angry or sad we leave it. So, offering up some joy gets you back. It's all mental, you know."

"You're mental," Cindy said, and the rest of us snickered.

"Guys," Christie implored, "have any of us faced any real hardships?"

"If having brothers is a hardship, I have plenty," Lori said.

"So maybe it's only the little things that matter right now," Christie insisted. "Like that basketball game when I couldn't do a roundoff back handspring. Schmidty, you made me realize it wasn't worth being unhappy about."

I shrugged, unwilling to take any sort of credit.

Lori gasped, "Like the time my mom made a pass at my date. Who knew I should have fought back with joy?"

Our mirth spilled over. Gripping our sides and covering our mouths, we laughed at nothing and everything, even each other, until tears filled our eyes. We could only go so far into the philosophical before the prospect of life's deeper meanings thrust us into absurdity. It took a while to exhaust ourselves, but we eventually did.

"Schmidty," Nancy whispered. "Why don't you bottle up some of that joy from dwelling around the lake and offer it as a sacrifice on the canoe trip."

"Wow," I breathed, stunned by her argument. The idyllic weather and the coziness of the tent had won me over. It seemed nothing could go wrong. "Okay," I agreed, snuggling further into my cotton-flowered sleeping bag, away from the open flap. I wiggled into a trough in the underlying sand and closed my eyes, anticipating a restful night.

I woke into daylight, thoroughly confused about my surroundings. Sarah and Susie slept alongside me. The others had already rolled up their bags, made a small fire, and gathered for toasted bread on forked sticks.

"What time is it?" I croaked, hobbling toward the fire. The sun had never seemed so bright and obnoxious.

"Quarter to six," Jenny announced. "Mr. Chinn is picking us up at seven-thirty. We'll get back to camp in time for hot showers and cleanup before leaving for Traverse. The bus loads in the parking lot at ten."

"What are you eating?" I scowled, watching Nancy stab a fork into a giant can of peaches. She pulled out a rounded half and plopped it on her toast, to resemble a monstrous undercooked egg. She sprinkled brown sugar and shoved it into her mouth. "Yuck!" I sneered.

"It's peach surprise!" She grinned. Juice ran down her chin.

"It's good," Cindy exclaimed, similarly dripping.

I remained unconvinced, and I stumbled off to find a secluded place to relieve myself. After that, I rolled my sleeping bag. Sarah and Susie hustled around me, equally grumpy, equally rushed. The others had let the fire die so we used our fingers to spread peanut butter on soft bread while they collapsed the tent. Jenny redistributed the supplies. Since we had eaten most of our original load and drunk all the water, four more of us were free to carry the tent. We hoisted our gear and trudged off. Despite the prevalent uphill course, I shouldered my share of the green canvas without complaint. And thanks to Jenny's Timex watch, we arrived on schedule to meet the white van.

I positively swaggered across our bridge into Wildwood feeling proud and aloof. I had become a trips taker. I bore my dirty clothes, crusty fingernails, unwashed face, and smoky scent like a prize I had won. I couldn't imagine why I had been so afraid. Camping was easy!

TWENTY-THREE

GOING WITH THE FLOW

FIVE DAYS LATER, after morning cleanup, we stood on the bank of the
Crystal River surrounded by supplies and canoes. The white van sped
away in a noisy rattle towing an empty trailer. I experienced a hollow
sense of abandonment and a pang of regret.

"Mr. Chinn will pick us up tomorrow morning at the culverts,"
Robyn, our trip's counselor, instructed.

A whole day of canoeing! I dreaded the prospect of aching shoulders.
Already the strap of my two-piece suit cut into my neck and I wished I'd worn
my Speedo. I glanced down at my least-favorite sandals and felt good about
that decision. I wouldn't mind too much if I lost them to the current.

"Put your sleeping bags, spare clothes, and towels inside garbage bags.
The food goes into bags as well." Robyn laid a direct eye on Susie and
me. "Tie them tightly," she advised, since we were the only ones who
had never done this before.

Susie bore an expression of even greater reserve than me. Recalling
Nancy's initial advice upon drafting me for this adventure, I put on a smile
and hoped for the best. Instantly, I felt better. What could go wrong in
the company of friends, on a nice day, cruising down a clean, sparkling
river? Susie and I copied the way everyone packed their garbage bags and
loaded them in the canoes.

Lori and Nancy had entered the river ahead of us, expertly sculling in
place against the current on the edge of visibility. They wore their bikinis,
no doubt hoping to get wet. "Stay put!" Robyn barked with obvious
affection for these capable campers and potential trip counselors.

"Can I steer?" Susie said to me.

"Sure," I replied, noticing that Robyn and the others had not stripped down to their suits, so I stayed in my clothes and climbed into the bow. Juggling my oar, I settled into the smooth hollow of my wooden seat. Susie sat in the stern, and Robyn shoved us from shore. After the initial jolt, we glided over the calm river and cut a shallow wake. I paddled in smooth strokes, digging deeply on the right side, trying to catch up to Nancy and Lori. I assumed Susie would match this pace on our left. Instead, she had dipped her oar on my side and held it rigidly against the current. The canoe swung a wide arc from the lopsided thrust and we darted for the opposite shore. I stopped paddling and placed the oar on my lap, anticipating Susie's correction.

Her effort plowed us headlong into a thicket of low-hanging branches. I ducked. A cluster of leaves grazed my scalp, and something fell from within. It landed heavily, then wiggled a slow course through my hair, down my neck and beneath my collar. A zigzag of moistness rolled over my bare shoulders. Too stunned to scream, I scooted to the edge of my seat and stretched the hem of my shirt so the critter would find a way out. The oar clattered from my lap and the landscape blurred as Susie successfully turned the bow toward the middle of the river. Slapping a hand over my waistband so it wouldn't get into my shorts, I felt it slither down my back for a final wiggling roll. It plopped upon my seat. I glimpsed a thin black snake and pictured it lurching into the canoe, becoming impossible to discern from our black garbage bags. Impulsively, I grabbed it. My fist closed on a cool rope of twisting, turning muscle. The tail and head dipped and looped in opposite directions as it struggled against my palm. Its sharp tongue jabbed repeatedly, and its black eyes glistened. I shuddered in revulsion and flung my arm, letting it go. The snake straightened midair and bounced off Susie's shoulder.

She screamed and stood in a burst of terror. The canoe ejected her. She fell on her back, splashing into the cool water. The snake jackknifed away, skimming across the rippling surface toward shore. My rear hit the bench from Susie's backlash, and I hunkered down, holding the sides, waiting for it to stabilize.

"I can't believe you threw a snake at me!" Susie's scream echoed from the treetops. She stood in the waist-high water, bombastically waving her arms.

"It was in my shirt!" I fired back, loading up to say, "because you pushed me into the trees!" But I couldn't say it. She waded toward me, taking leaping strides, her nicely curled hair ruined for the entire trip. She wrapped her fingers around the rim of the canoe. I gripped the sides and leaned for counterbalance as she flung a leg over and spilled inside, bringing a trail of sparkling liquid. We sat in silence for a few moments trying to recover from the shock.

"What is going on?" Robyn demanded. She sat on a box of supplies, perched in the middle of a canoe paddled by Mary and Debbie. They deftly hovered alongside us.

"A snake went down my shirt!" I retorted, reliving the slimy sensation through one giant shudder. I slapped the tail of my shirt and was comforted to find it empty. Then, my frustration seized on Robyn, wondering if she had orchestrated the episode as some sort of test.

"What color?" she demanded from her middle throne.

"Black," Susie gasped.

"Any markings?"

"No," I replied, after thinking a moment.

"Harmless," Robyn said, handing Susie her paddle that had been floating in the river. "Now, let's get moving!"

When their stern passed us, Mary playfully mouthed, "Get moving!" Her warm energy softened Robyn's demand.

Luckily Susie had brought a bandanna to tie her hair, and the episode was forgiven. We found our stride and fell into a rhythm. The sun reflected hotly off the river, feeling unusually warm and humid for northern Michigan, without a hint of a breeze. We stripped down to our suits. I noticed Nancy and Lori traveled in the shade when they found it by steering close to the bank and ducking repeatedly beneath the trees. For obvious reasons Susie and I remained in the middle, enduring the heat, and falling into a glazed stupor.

Robyn called a rest for lunch. We aligned our canoes like a Polynesian raft, propping our feet across each other's gunnels. We floated downriver eating from soggy boxed lunches, sipping sodas and swapping food.

"A boy took a girl in a little canoe and the moon was shining all around," Lori sang and we joined in. It spilled out of us, like all camp songs, on a purely physical level requiring only an expansion of the diaphragm.

"And as he plied his paddle, you couldn't even hear a sound!" We shouted, frightening the birds from the trees. "So they talked and they talked until the moon grew dim! He said you better kiss me or get out and swim! So whatcha gonna do in a little canoe when the moon is shining all ah, boys are paddling all ah, girls are swimming all a-round. Oh yeah?" We shrugged at the end, flinging our hands in disbelief, decrying the injustice of the girl's expulsion from the canoe just because she didn't want to kiss the boy.

Susie and I successfully traded places after lunch. This involved hunched postures, careful footing, delicate balance, and a narrative of our every move. By late afternoon we complained to each other about aching arms and cramped backs. Thankfully, the river narrowed, and the trees linked branches to provide shade and gave us one less thing to grumble about. The water also deepened, and the current accelerated, revealing sharp, winding turns. Our speed created a refreshing breeze, and we paddled less strenuously while concentrating on steering. Eventually, we lagged further behind the others, peering suspiciously around each bend, leery of more surprises.

Robyn's distinctive whistle pierced the air. I pictured her cramming her index finger and pinkie into the sides of her mouth, making the sound we had learned to respond to over previous summers. We sat tall in our seats, craning to find her canoe. But she had already quit the river and stood on the bank. She became a blur of red hair as we sped past.

"Great!" Susie gasped from the bow, straining to paddle backwards. I plowed my oar, trying to shift us. We rounded a curve. A bridge spanned the river ahead, though it looked more like a wall of rock with a road on top. Two metal tubes channeled the river into foaming chutes of rapids.

"You're headed for the culverts!" Lori shouted from shore. Out of the corner of my eye, I saw her and Nancy crashing through the trees, trying to keep up. "Steer toward the bank!" they hollered. We paddled harder but the current had taken control. Seeing no alternatives, they rapidly recapitulated in loud demand, "Pull in your oars and DUCK!"

"Duck!" Susie and I repeated to each other. I plopped my paddle on the garbage bags in front of me, leaned forward, and placed my head between my knees just before we funneled into a giant metal tube only slightly larger than our vessel. Cool darkness enveloped us. We rocked and scraped amid the deafening render of metal as the water carried us through at a tumultuous speed.

We shot out the other side. Bright sunlight blinded us. The current slowed. We rose from our hunched positions and glided lazily toward shore.

TWENTY-FOUR

IT COULD BE WORSE

NANCY AND LORI stood waiting. "Was it fun?" they asked, helping us bank the canoe.

"It would have been fun if you guys hadn't freaked us out!" I exclaimed.

"I thought we were going over a waterfall!" Susie gasped.

"It's not good for the canoe," Nancy said. "That's why we aren't allowed. But we can swim through the culverts. It's a riot! That's why we like this trip."

"Oh, I've heard about culverts," Susie said.

Of course I had, too. But until now the uninspired term had only meant, "utilitarian aqueducts made of rusty, corrugated metal." Now I understood and rightly envisioned a waterslide, infinitely more enticing than the schoolyard slide at camp.

We took hold of the canoe and carried it through another culvert, dry as a bone, used for spillage during spring rains. This returned us to the opposite side of the elevated road and the campsite. Robyn rushed to meet us, mainly to inspect the canoe. She ran a hand along its layers of shellac, red cedar hull, and basswood inlays. "I suppose it's no worse for the mishap," she sighed, rapping her knuckles against the mahogany gunwales.

We set it near the other canoes and sized up the place we would be spending the night. It consisted of a fire pit and a picnic table inside a dirt clearing, surrounded by a thin forest. A solitary patch of grass thrived nearby, and I wondered if camping etiquette would allow me to claim it. I couldn't bear the thought of placing my flowered, cotton-quilted sleeping bag in the dirt. It was made for sleeping on shag carpet or inside a tent.

"Now that everyone is here . . ." Robyn smirked at Susie and me, "We have two logs in the canoe so we need kindling and branches."

"Firewood is hard to find here," Nancy offered for our benefit. "This is a popular site on weekends."

We foraged the undergrowth picked clean of fallen branches. I peered into the trees, searching for a dead limb that might be pried loose. I found gray clouds gathering beyond the leafy cover, expanding rapidly and covering the patches of blue. By the time I returned with a few sticks the clouds had diminished the sun's brightness, making the time seem later. But no one seemed concerned. Robyn was more interested in the hefty branch Mary and Debbie had found. They jumped on it, snapped manageable pieces, and stacked them in the fire pit.

High above our heads the treetops swayed from a gust of wind. It dispersed the stale, moist heat and brightened my mood as we unpacked the food.

"Now we can go swimming," Robyn concluded. "We'll start the fire when we get back."

"All right!" Lori hooted, walking briskly to the river's edge.

"Let's shoot some culverts!" Mary exclaimed. She and Lori dove in, each aiming for a different tunnel. In synchronized precision, they rolled on their backs, feetfirst, and flung their arms over their heads. "Woo-hoo!" they yelled, before disappearing into the rushing water.

My heart pounded excitedly when my chance came. I pointed my toes downstream and held my breath when the foaming rapids took control, buoying and whisking me into the culvert. The churning force sucked me under and smothered my face until daylight disappeared. After five seconds of exhilarating speed it spit me out the other side. The current slowed, and I immediately wanted to do it again.

Trees rustled above from advancing winds, and the air increasingly cooled, making the river feel like bathwater. Over and over, we rode a variety of combinations; hands up, hands down, feetfirst, headfirst.

Robyn's shrill whistle brought us to a stop. I planted my feet on the rocky riverbed and shook water from my ears. "Thunder!" she yelled. "Everyone out of the water!"

Mary shot from the tube, and I repeated the warning. We ran back to the campsite during the first bolt of lightning. Robyn placed a tarp over the firewood, and Lori weighted the edges with rocks.

The sky darkened, and the wind thrashed a haphazard frenzy so violent I imagined the trees would snap. We heard another deep roar of thunder, saw a startling crack of lightning, and the sky let loose thick drops. I stood in the middle of the clearing, paralyzed and stunned. I had never been without shelter during such an event. What were the rules? Was it every woman for herself? Did Robyn have a grand plan? Should I crawl under the tarp and join the firewood?

"We call the table!" Lori said, and I watched the protocol unfold. She and Nancy lifted their canoe, empty of gear, and angled it against the picnic table. They crawled under and lounged beside their bags.

"Come on," Nancy encouraged, "bring yours over."

"We call the other side of the table!" I announced, making the declaration official. Raindrops spun from the trees. They stung our skin and popped on the tabletop as Susie and I positioned our canoe to match theirs. The entire configuration resembled an upside-down seaplane. We huddled in the dirt beneath, watching Debbie and Mary wedge their canoe inside a triangle of trees and spongy underbrush.

Thunder and lightning heralded swaths of cascading rain. It swept across the clearing and drove sideways to ensure our bathing suits remained thoroughly wet. Groundwater pooled beneath us then flowed in little rivulets. Nancy and Lori cracked wry jokes about mud, raw food, and pruney skin. The storm passed through, but thick clouds remained, leaking a steady pour.

"We're done for the night!" Robyn announced. The tarp had blown off the fire pit. The kindling and logs were saturated. The cardboard boxes fell apart, and Robyn doled out their contents. We received a few garbage bags, some Hershey bars, a bag of marshmallows, a package of Graham Crackers, hot dogs, and a can of peas. "I have the opener," she muttered, walking back to her canoe, hugging an equal quantity for their shelter.

"Will Mr. Chinn come for us?" I shouted. But Robyn did not answer and proceeded to improvise with the tarp. She looped the ends on some saplings to create a generous awning above their canoe and an effective means of water drainage. Tearing open two garbage bags, she spread them over some trampled weeds, half under the canoe and half under the tarp. She unzipped her green military-style sleeping bag, plopped a marshmallow in her mouth, and crawled inside. "Not till morning," she answered before zipping up to her nose.

"Is she going to sleep?" I muttered. Robyn's motionless cocoon confirmed it. I decided she must be sleep deprived. Since she and Bess practically ran the entire camp, it was the only explanation that made sense.

"Give me a break!" Susie hissed at their ingenious layout. Mary had produced a deck of cards. She and Debbie lounged beneath their shelter and engaged in a game of War. "Why do they get the tarp?" she griped.

"Because we have the table," Lori proudly stated.

Susie did not see this as the superior option, and neither did I. "But the ground is going to mud," she whispered disgustedly. We crouched on our feet, unwilling to sit.

"It's a warm rain, though," Lori said, shrugging her shoulders and kneeling on a garbage bag. She took a bite from a cold hot dog and shook it toward me. It wiggled grotesquely like a dead, amputated finger. "Could be worse." She grinned. "It could be snowing."

"Do this," Nancy said, taking a sharp rock. She drew lines in the dirt, creating a trough to divert the runoff.

"Can we eat raw hot dogs?" Susie asked.

"It's like bologna," Lori said, offering one from the pack.

Susie took a tentative bite, decided it was okay, and nibbled away.

Lori opened her sleeping bag, and her clothes spilled out. "There goes that," she said, leaning into the rain to don some farmer jeans and a sweatshirt. She slit the side of a garbage bag, stretched it out, and set her sleeping bag on top, keeping most of her torso under the bench. "See you in the morning," she said.

"You can do that?" I asked.

"For sure," Lori mumbled, zipping up.

Something crawled up my leg, and I brushed it away. A big black ant rolled to the ground, then washed away in the narrow flow. Another ant sped up my other leg. Nancy brushed one from her arm. Susie rose up and squealed as they found her ankles.

"You know what!" she proposed through dramatic ire, backing out and brushing them away. "I'm exhausted from paddling that canoe for eight hours! I am going to crawl into my sleeping bag and tie the top closed. No ants will get in, and it's supposed to be water resistant."

"Is that the same as waterproof?" I asked.

"Who cares," she sniffed. After assembling a place under the other picnic bench, she disappeared inside her bag.

I studied Susie, Lori, and Robyn, completely amazed! My back ached, as well as my shoulders and neck, but I felt wretchedly out of sorts. I could never relax enough to sleep. Facing the prospect of a long, wet night, I wondered how our soldiers in the jungles of Vietnam ever endured it.

TWENTY-FIVE

A CRUCIAL DECISION

"WHAT ARE YOU going to do, Schmidty?" Nancy asked. Her hazel eyes appeared especially large.

"My sleeping bag isn't cut out for this. It will get muddy and drenched."

She nodded along. "There's no way around it."

"I don't want to ruin it," I added defensively. "I've had it a long time."

"We can wash it when we get back. And dry it in the sun on the dock."

"What's the use?" I sighed, brushing another ant. "I won't be able to sleep anyway."

"If you're tired enough, you'll sleep." She stifled a yawn through an apologetic smile.

"I'll never be tired enough for this." I gawked at the water pooling around my feet. "Why do you keep going on these trips?"

She shrugged. "At least I don't have poison ivy," she said through a rueful laugh.

Her plight from the previous summer had become legendary. On a different canoe trip, she had chosen an unlucky place to pee. The rash had spread along her entire backside. For days and weeks afterward she had endured the healing process, having to scratch for relief in delicate areas at unlikely times. But everyone understood and admired her fortitude. She never complained and always displayed a brave, modest smile, endearing everyone to her plight.

"You amaze me," I whispered. We listened to the rain. "It's letting up," I decided, making a move to crawl out.

"Wait." Nancy gripped my arm. "Feel that?" An aura of prickly static tingled my scalp. The soft hairs on my arms and legs bristled on end, as if a million rubber balloons rubbed against us. CRACK! Lightning and thunder burst simultaneously, casting a blinding strobe of bluish light. We leapt in place. The raindrops resumed their loud plopping.

"At least sit down," Nancy advised, loosening the knot on my garbage bag until its contents flattened like a bean bag chair.

"I don't know why I came," I moaned, sliding against it. The weight of my world pressed dismally upon me. I wished to be back in the cozy, dry cabin. I even wondered if I'd rather be home. Promptly, I shook my head in denial. "My high school sucks," I whispered confidentially.

"I really like mine," Nancy remarked, scooting closer, inviting me to say more.

"My boyfriend . . ." I paused, fearful of saying his name, as if uttering it here might cause him to appear. "He only wants sex. And my best friend smokes too much pot, and drinks too much." I paused, realizing this might be sharing too much from home. But the two worlds were colliding in this stripped-down moment of raw truth, and the words poured out of me in a torrent to match the rain. "Sometimes we go to class completely wasted." I sputtered a cynical laugh. "The teachers don't notice, and I get really good grades. I've been shoved around in gym class, and if I told anyone it would start a riot. A real one, because we have some angry kids, you know, poverty, bad homes, and it all boils down to a fifty-fifty split of racial tension. Getting wasted together is our only common ground. We can't have a homecoming queen because if she's white, half the school will riot. If she's black, the other half will. Our hall guards are trained in the martial arts. One morning, I showed up for swim team, and we found a dead kid at the bottom of the pool! We never heard why." I took a deep breath, and sighed, "Everything feels out of control. My mom is real sick. She may need surgery. Food goes right through her, and she's always in pain. Dad is stressed from work and taking care of her. Our little family is falling apart, and I don't know how to help." I pushed my hair from my face. "I'm sorry. I just feel so mad all of a sudden. It's like I'm a different person back home than I am here."

"Why?" Nancy prodded.

"I don't know. Maybe because nothing around me is the same." Lightning flared on the other side of the river. "Or maybe this miserable trip reminds me of it all." Nancy's brow furrowed, trying to understand. "It's like," I ventured, testing the notion as I spoke, "nothing bothered me on that other trip with Jenny. There were no flies, mosquitoes, ants, or mud. It was idyllic, uncomplicated, like camp. Then there is this trip." I slapped an ant racing up the back of my thigh. "This mud," I groaned, shaking my hand, flinging a glob of dirt. "The river is dark, out of control, overwhelming, but also boring and monotonous. I hate it. And I hate myself for hating it. But why would anyone want to be here when they could be at the lake? I'm happiest there. And if I could bottle up that feeling, and take it with me, to be that person all the time, I would. But I can't. So, I just want to find a way out. My dad wants me to graduate early from high school," I whispered, leaning toward her.

"We're not really talking about the river. Are we?" She smiled gently.

"I have enough credits since I tested out of two classes my freshman year. I can even graduate on the college-track." I desperately wanted to convince her, and myself.

"Then you should do it." Her tone mandated I follow through.

I nodded without speaking, looking down at the small gorge between my feet. An ant crossed the top of my foot. I also wanted to tell her I shoplifted clothes in the mall even when I had the money, wishing someone would catch me because a family secret was too big for me to handle alone. But I couldn't bear the look on her face. Her disapproval would crush me, and I knew it was wrong. "This is going to be a long night," I sighed, glancing at the road, wishing for the white van to pull up. "But I'll keep quiet so you can sleep."

"Don't worry about me," she said. "We can play cards, or keep talking. I have a flashlight somewhere."

"I bet you get Pioneer Camper at the end of the summer," I decided suddenly.

"Ya think?" she said, reaching for the Graham Crackers.

"Sure, you deserve it. You're a natural leader at camp. I don't want to lead. I want to rest. The school year tears me down. Camp builds me up again. Just being around you guys is enough for me."

"I know," she said. "I have plenty of friends at home, but I trust you guys more."

"Me, too. Back there, friendships get muddled by looks, clothes, boyfriends, and who can party the hardest. I have so much trouble getting back into it when camp is over. Everyone always asks, 'Why are you so quiet?' which is really strange for me. But all I can do is smile. It's too big a feeling to explain."

"I leave here feeling so jazzed," she thoughtfully disagreed. "I can't wait to start school. And next year we will be CTs."

"And after that, some of us will be counselors."

"Why not all of us," she said, ripping open the Hershey Bars.

"Nine of us? I doubt it. If they allow Mary to jump ahead into our group, which you know they will, there is no way they'll need nine new counselors the year after. And what would I be the counselor of? I haven't passed my Water Safety Instructor. That eliminates everything around the lake! I have to be around the lake."

"Didn't you take the test?"

"Yeah. Robyn made me rescue Eric. The resort was flying a yellow flag, but I swear it had to be red flag conditions. Those whitecaps were rocking that ladder to at least twice my height!" I reached up and banged my hand on the bottom of the table. "Ouch." I cringed, shaking it off. "I couldn't get my arm around his chest, let alone haul him up the ladder. He kept sinking, and I swallowed so much water. Why wouldn't Robyn let me drag him to shore? Isn't that what a real lifeguard would do?"

Nancy handed me a cold s'more. "Here, this will give the ants something to eat besides us." She had smashed the marshmallows into little pancakes over the chocolate bar and covered them with graham crackers.

I continued my harangue through a mouthful of food. "Then I had to rescue Robyn. She dug her fingernails into my arm, and pulled my hair and bit me! I gave up and said, 'You deserve to drown! Only a complete idiot would go out in such dangerous conditions without a life vest!'"

Her ripples of laughter washed over me like a tonic. I felt her adoring approval, void of judgment, as if she saw good things brewing inside of me, things I couldn't see, and waited patiently for me to find them. And even if I never found them, she would care for me just the same.

"You know," I said, "I would be happy staying a camper forever around the lake."

"You have goals," she countered. "And you can be determined when you make up your mind. You only have to put the two together."

"Why is it, I watch you and everyone else rake in awards and never feel a twinge of jealousy?"

She paused to consider this confession. "It's like, when a person is jealous, they fear that good things can't happen to them. As if there isn't enough good to go around. But, you know there is enough, only it shows up in different ways for different people."

We fell silent, both of us thinking. "Hey," she realized, after I'd actually closed my eyes, "my sister Theresa is going to be our counselor next session."

"I love your sister. She's fair and levelheaded."

She chuckled. "Are we talking about my sister?"

"You know, she won't pick favorites or treat us like little kids."

Susie snored loudly, having attained sleep, and we giggled from punchy fatigue. We changed into dry clothes and relaxed against our plastic-clad sleeping bags. Our conversation slowed, and Nancy suggested we close our eyes for a while. When the rain stopped, the air felt warm and steamy. I probably slept a little though I shifted relentlessly against numbing limbs and occasional mosquitoes. I nearly kissed Mr. Chinn when he arrived the next morning, long before the sun and way ahead of schedule. The rain had started up again, and he took pity on us after all.

This time, when I strode into camp beneath a drizzling sky I didn't feel so proud of myself. I didn't wear my damp clothes and dirt-covered limbs like a prize I'd won. Instead, I vowed "never again." And when anyone asked me about it, I rolled my eyes, eager to share my miserable ordeal.

TWENTY-SIX

A VERY LONG DAY

AFTER BREAKFAST, WE witnessed the impending departure of our three-week friends. Cabin mates exchanged addresses and promises to write, some growing tearful, because parents would filter in all morning to take pieces of us away. Shaken up and stirred about, the camp would dwindle to half its size by lunchtime while trunks, duffels, and occasional beds switched cabins for the second half. After lunch there would be a stream of activities to distract us until a new assortment of campers arrived the next day to fill the empty beds, making the cabins whole again, so we could plunge headlong into a new session.

However, Sunblazer felt insulated from the imminent commotion. Nothing would change except our counselor. Far from sad, because Jenny had only moved across camp to Puccoon, and far from unsettled, for the disruption only meant a morning free of cleanup, we desired a normal Saturday. We gathered Theresa's belongings from Beacon and piled them inside the cabin, then ran to see Bess.

We found her on Whitecap's verandah giving assignments to the CTs. They would be leaving Whitecap for in-cabin training. Luckily, Sunblazer was not on the list. My sister, Bobbi, Joanna, and Maggie would be moving into cabins around the flagpole. If Robyn thought we needed extra supervision, Bess had overruled the idea, thus delivering me from the nightmarish scenario of sharing a cabin with my sister.

Bess glided along the boardwalk, and we hovered like a ring of bumbling gnats.

"Please," Lori said. "Can we have a Cabin Day?"

Bess peered straight ahead, deep in thought, ostensibly unaware of us.

"No one in Sunblazer is leaving. And no one new is coming." I stated the obvious, just in case she didn't already know.

The boardwalk passed narrowly between Driftwood and Gull's Nest. We ducked below the shutters, pressing into the screens, so Bess could round the turn. She gripped her clipboard, swinging her arms, heading for her office. Our opportunity dwindled with each successive step. Once she mounted the stairwell we could not follow.

"Please," Nancy implored, hopping sideways in the sand. "This is our last summer as campers, and we want to make the most of it."

Just outside the Murphy, a mere stride from sanctuary, Bess paused. We halted in our tracks and swallowed our breath.

Focused and alert, no longer in a hurry, she parked her gaze on each of us. This interlude ended with a short intake of breath pushed out through her nose. I heard it as a sigh of resignation. "Where would you campers go?" she asked.

This question may have inspired hope in others, but I felt certain we'd be heading to the dunes with the rest of the camp. We'd asked for something out of the ordinary. During the transition, campers always stuck together to preserve Wildwood's unity. And Bess rarely broke tradition. Steady as a pine tree, she focused her energies on upward growth and never sprouted superfluous sideways branches like a deciduous tree.

"To Fishtown!" Christie offered.

"With your new counselor, of course," Bess said. We nodded energetically. "Regardless of what I decide, you'll need to ask Mr. Chinn to drive you," she concluded.

This sounded easy, but I had no idea how to find Mr. Chinn. He didn't exist other than to lead a nature hike as a last-choice option because our speedboat needed repair or the boys' camp needed full use of the playing field. Mostly, he sprang to life in the parking lot at the wheel of the bus or the white van.

"Can you call him?" Nancy asked.

I slapped my forehead against my own stupidity. Of course, Bess had a telephone. How easily I had forgotten the ways of the outside world.

"Please." Nancy donned a winning smile.

For a moment Bess appeared weary and introspective, as if she knew our time and her time at Shenahwau was slipping away at an ever-increasing rate through the natural progression of life. For the land was indeed valuable. And while we frolicked, others planned.

"If Mr. Chinn is busy, maybe Thaddeus can drive us," Tori suggested.

"Who's that?" I whispered, tugging on the hem of her haltertop. I faltered behind her, scraping my leg against Whippoorwill's cement stoop.

"You girls!" Bess laughed. Her gaze toured the lot of us, delving into our youthful souls as if foreseeing grand accomplishments, future leaders, and trailblazers. This loving regard emanated mostly from her dark eyes, and I always felt better inside from the contact. I returned her gaze, respectfully awed. Few adults drew this type of response from me. They always seemed to be judging and condemning. So, it made an impression every time, no matter how brief.

At last she promised, "We'll see," then bounded into her stride.

My mouth fell open as she entered the Hylton. Obviously, Bess had decided this outing would foster our upward growth.

Tori poked my collarbone. "You space cadet! Thaddeus is a driver and a camping guide for the guys' camp. How could you not know him? He's not a counselor, but you've seen him a hundred times at meals!"

"Oh!" I exclaimed. My sight roamed to the rustling treetops. Lush poplars danced beneath a bright blue sky as I conjured the image of an attractive man, rugged and quiet. He'd emanated a reclusive aura, so extreme, I'd never really noticed him.

"Mr. Petrovich," Sarah censured, raising a dubious eyebrow at Tori.

"Is that Russian?" I wondered.

"Beats me," Susie said. "But he does have lovely eyes and a really sweet smile."

"He tries to hide his accent," Tori said. "He defected from the Soviet Union. He is a writer, you know, and needed asylum here in the U.S."

More than willing to believe this, since everything Russian had been swallowed up by the U.S.S.R. during peak days of the Cold War, only one of us protested.

"Wouldn't it be on the news, or something?" Lori batted her golden lashes.

"No," Tori said. "Only famous people make it on the news."

"Because only famous people defect," Lori countered.

"Guys," Nancy entreated, "Bess practically gave us the go-ahead."

We gathered our street purses and Theresa. She smiled at our organized energy, breaking free to visit the Murphy, while we lingered in the Hylton, awaiting final approval. At the base of the paneled stairwell, we quietly debated whether or not Bess had already left for the parking lot to greet parents. Alternately, we stooped low and peered high. None of us would dare mount the steps. In all my summers I'd never been past the first three. Finally, the floorboards creaked. We bumped each other, the screen door, and the knotty pine walls just to get a glimpse of her bobby socks and white sneakers.

"Hush," Cindy breathed as a cognitive warning, sensing our Bess would now speak.

"He'll be 'round the parking lot in ten minutes," her succinct, nasally voice proclaimed.

"Thank you!" we shouted, bolting through the door. We grabbed Theresa and crammed along the narrow sidewalk behind the Hylton, passing between its cinderblock foundation and the overgrown riverbank. We pounded across the bridge and entered the woods. Upon hearing the crunch of gravel from an approaching vehicle, we started to run.

Instead of the white van, we found a stationwagon with Minnesota plates arriving slightly ahead of schedule to kick off the morning's onslaught.

"You must be Missy's parents," Theresa greeted. We formed a protective circle around her, claiming her as our leader now, instead of Jenny. We never once thought of her as Nancy's sister.

"We adore Missy," Theresa prompted, glancing at each of us. We added comments like, "We'll really miss her," or, "She's so funny," while scanning the parents for a resemblance, as well as their car and clothing for clues into Missy's outside life. However, same as at the sun, we dared not look too long. None of us wanted to risk losing sight of Missy as a camper first and foremost, who loved archery and delivered lofty spikes at beach volleyball. Picturing her in any other way risked tearing the protective lining to our mirage world of endless summer days.

"You can head into camp if you like," Theresa said. "Just follow the path to the bridge. She's in Gull's Nest by the flagpole. Some guys should be arriving to help carry her trunk."

My insides dipped into homesickness at this mention; not for home, but for camp, as if our day of departure had arrived as well. We all felt it. We stared at the entrance of the parking lot, willing the van to appear. Before long it churned into view.

"It's Mr. Chinn." Tori sounded disappointed.

"Big whoop who drives us!" Lori exclaimed.

"Yeah," we agreed. She had nailed it. We needed to escape all signs of camp's fragile longevity by any means.

"Let's blow this pop stand!" Christie rallied, as if cabin unity alone could sustain the illusion. We eagerly spilled into the three bench seats, politely muttering over and over, "Thanks, Mr. Chinn." If we had known a tear to our mirage world awaited us in Fishtown, one not easily mended nor long concealed, we would never have stepped into that van.

We avoided the pariah front bench, but Theresa energetically scooted in. "You look really nice in that blue shirt," she said to Mr. Chinn, entirely at ease. Her curls framed a heart-shaped face and glossy lips, likening her to a beauty from the roaring twenties. "Did Mrs. Chinn buy that for you?" she added.

Our eyes darted between them, enthralled by Theresa's familiarity. We expected his cranky rebuff because, according to rumor, some very sensitive parts of his body had been blown away in battle during World War I. The very idea brought shivers of pity. We had trouble thinking of anything else, and allowed him permanent leeway to be grumpy. So, when he smiled we nearly fainted. He never smiled, not even when extolling the virtues of some obscure plant or insect. It transformed his grouchy countenance into a boyish likeness that only added to our fascination upon learning of a Mrs. Chinn!

He gunned the gas pedal, still smiling, and made a hairpin getaway. He roared along the dirt road, straddling the shoulder to accommodate a steady stream of arriving cars. When we hit the highway's pavement, he cranked up the radio. Perhaps he endured rock 'n' roll to avoid conversation and awkward silence. Or he welcomed a break from the corny songs we screeched on the bus. Either way, he allowed it and we sang along.

"Lazy day in bed. Music in my head. Crazy music playing in the morniiiing light. Ho, ho, ho, It's ma-gic. You knoooow. Never believe it's not so. It's ma-gic. . . ."

Nancy wore a grin of remorse and her eyes begged us to hold back. We typically sang, "Ho, ho, ho, It's ma-dick . . ." over and over, gaining volume. "Never believe it's not so. It's MY-DICK!" The song spoke of little else. And after a while, the word "magic" really sounded like the words "my dick," especially on Christie's little portable radio inside the cabin.

Luckily, she caught us in time. We couldn't sing it this way in front of Mr. Chinn, not if the rumor was true. He was the happiest we'd ever seen him, patiently playing the music we liked. So we silenced our parody and waited for the next chance to drown out the radio.

TWENTY-SEVEN

THE FIRST SIGN OF A TEAR

"RIGHT HERE, FOUR o'clock sharp," Mr. Chinn said after dropping us in front of Merdick's Fudge Shoppe on Main Street, surrounded by other establishments with shake roofs, paned windows, flower boxes full of color, and French doors standing open in ready welcome.

"We won't be late," Theresa promised.

"No, no, we won't be late," Cindy agreed, punctuated by Lori and Sarah's emphatic nods. The rest of us mumbled obediently while I snickered at the idea of time meaning anything at camp, or even back home in school. We simply listened for bells.

As the van circled away, Theresa asked, "Who has a watch?"

We giggled in response.

"I do." Tori raised her arm like Lady Liberty. A golden wristband glinted brilliantly from the morning sun. We stared agog for a few seconds. I envisioned her shopping for designer labels at Water Tower Place in downtown Chicago, then shook it off.

"Me, too, but it doesn't work." Susie's wrist displayed a red and yellow acrylic timepiece.

"Then, why wear it?" Lori said.

"It goes really well with this top," Susie reasoned, refusing to meet any of our stares, believing she had to hurry or we'd interrupt. "It kept really good time until it fell off the window ledge after the door slammed and sand got inside so now the windy-thingy feels gritty when I try to turn it."

We paused to abridge her words.

"What a drag," Theresa concluded, genuinely concerned. "Then we'll stick together." She reached into her blue suede purse for a roll-top container and applied rosy goo all over her lips. "Let's start at the wharf shops," she suggested. "Then, we'll walk over to The Blue Bird for homemade pie." She pointed down Main Street, past a wooden bridge, where the road curved out of sight. "It's over that way," she explained, since none of us had been there. "Remember, we're ending at Merdick's. So don't buy any fudge at the wharf. It's not fresh."

We struck poses of wonder at her highly agreeable leadership style. Jenny would have established a strict timetable, given a lecture on the fat content of fudge, and never would have suggested pie!

The pungent odors of salty fish and charred wood blasted our olfactory senses. Although Michigan maps placed a different name on this small town, we called it Fishtown in honor of this overwhelming scent. It wafted from the wharf and permeated every aspect of town.

As we turned off Main Street, a blustery wind carried fresh air from the lake. We gazed down at the marina, grudgingly noting the increased number of pleasure crafts from distant places. Tall cabin cruisers, double-masted schooners, and outboard runabouts floated inside a maze of docks. A rock barrier rose from the water like a giant moat to encircle them. Beyond it, the lake's blinding ripples joined the sky for an imperceptible horizon of blue.

"Hard to believe the Ottowans once called this Mishi-me-go-bing, 'the place where canoes run up into the river to land because they have no harbor.'" I spoke over the melodic clang of rigging, feeling Nancy's wondrous smirk. "Someone told us, maybe Leslie?" I said.

"And you remember?" she chortled.

"Well, there's a harbor here now," Lori droned.

We passed The Fish Hook and Fishtown, both prominent retailers. One sold smoked fish, and the other bait and tackle. We crossed the street and descended a hill of wood chips to the river's edge where fishermen slopped and chopped trout amid the billowing fumes of a stone smokehouse.

Stepping clear of their busy activity, we headed for the gray, weathered shacks selling beaded earrings, fragrant candles in twisted shapes, peasant tops imported from India, driftwood art, saltwater taffy, and Michigan cherries. Next to every cash register, sandalwood incense burned a slim torch of resistance against the fishy odor, creating its own unique scent that clung to every piece of clothing.

We made a few purchases then returned to the more substantial shops on Main Street. Half of us aimed for the pharmacy to buy candy, lotion, and flashcubes. The rest of us entered a gift shop selling greeting cards, artwork, and crystal. Christie needed to find a present for her mother's birthday.

At once, we lowered our voices, slowed our steps, and hugged our purses in fear of the valuable inventory. I combed the greeting cards for funny lines.

"Dear!" An imperative voice startled us into eavesdropping. "Don't you think Maaary would like this crystal bowl?" A woman in the far corner shimmered in a red jumpsuit splattered in silver anchors. A golden zipper stretched from her crotch to her chin, ending in a giant ring pull.

"Yes, Maaary would like it!" a man in the opposite corner loudly agreed. His voice rang familiar, though uncharacteristically irritated. He wore a royal navy, double-breasted jacket with brass buttons. A frosty-white skipper's cap sat atop his graying sideburns.

I vigorously sought Nancy on the opposite side of the card display. "Look," I whispered. "Is that Murray from the *Mary Tyler Moore Show?*"

"Could be," she allowed. Christie and Lori also paused to notice as the couple debated the merits of two different bowls. We had never seen such costumes outside the variety shows on television.

The woman's long fingers, tipped in red paint, closed about the neck of a crystal vase and she emphatically declared, "Maybe Maaary would like this better."

We studied them like exotic animals in a zoo. Then, on a renegade impulse I sidled over. "Are you Murray from the *Mary Tyler Moore Show?*"

I asked, having the odd feeling I had just entered stage right, on cue, to deliver a line.

"Why yes," he replied, bending to my height. His annoyed, edgy manner melted away, and his TV personality took over. In a snap, he had transformed from a snobby tourist to an earthy newsroom editor.

Aha, I thought to myself, I was right. His smile lingered, just waiting for me to remember my next line. But I had nothing else to say. I had merely wanted to vindicate my curiosity. I hadn't thought about what would come next. I crossed my arms and wondered if I should make small talk. Should I praise his acting ability, inquire about his boat, discuss the weather, or just run away?

Thankfully, Nancy saved me. She thrust a white envelope between us, and said, "Can we have an autograph?"

Very pleased, he stood tall.

I heaved a sigh of relief. This was his desire all along! Why else would they wear such outlandish clothes, speak so loudly, and drop the name "Mary" over and over?

He reached into his perfectly pressed coat, fiddled behind the anchor buttons, and pulled out a golden pen. Taking the envelope from Nancy's fingers, he held it against the palm of his hand and scribbled a grand flourishing message. Handing the envelope back, he offered a charismatic flash of teeth. "Keep watching the show!" he cheered, using his TV character's northeastern accent.

The woman in the jumpsuit had chosen a vase. He stepped up to pay, and the salesclerk fawned all over them. I glanced at the purloined envelope, still in Nancy's hand, and then at the salesclerk to see if she cared. Obviously, the sale of the vase meant more than one missing envelope. Christie held the door and we raced away like thieves fleeing authority. Eventually it would all make sense, years later, when this same actor played Captain on a television show called *The Love Boat*, eerily resembling this real-life persona. But for the moment, we could only offer our sincere pity at his transparent need to be recognized.

"I'm going to make my mother a card and buy her a candle!" Christie decided. This strange little episode had cemented her choice. "And I'm getting it from the wharf!" She led a stiff-necked charge for native territory. Nancy stuffed the envelope in a back pocket, and the three of us sat outside the bait shop to wait for her.

"Some of those boats are really big," Nancy observed. Cockpits rose to the height of two-story buildings. Teak decks, polished to a shine, held elaborate furniture. "Imagine sailing to Chicago," Nancy breathed.

"Yeah, it would be great to own one someday," Lori sighed.

I usually ruminated along with them, envisioning myself lounging about in an opulent, luxurious cabin. Yet today conflicting emotions darkened my mood. Part of me wanted to run for the pharmacy to tell the others we'd seen a famous person. Maybe they'd decipher his real name. The other part of me wanted to pretend it hadn't happened, because it meant outsiders had discovered northern Michigan's unique beauty.

"Which boat do you suppose belongs to that guy?" Lori said. We stared more intently at the marina until she reached for the autograph. "Let's see that thing." She studied it through a skeptical scowl, turning it different angles to interpret the scrawl of letters. "Beats me," she concluded, holding it out for Nancy. She shook her head, unwilling to take it.

"Here, Schmidty." Lori passed it to me. "You talked to him." So, I stuffed it into my pocket where it would disintegrate before the week's end in the camp laundry. Christie returned bearing a little package and a contented smile.

TWENTY-EIGHT

THE SECOND SIGN

THE PHARMACY'S MUSTY wood and medicinal compounds actually succeeded in defeating the smell of fish. High ceilings, dark wooden floors, and long aisles packed full of merchandise ran parallel to the soda fountain. Large ceiling mirrors reflected the entire store, making it seem there were two chrome-rimmed counters flanked by red barstools.

Theresa and the others had already paid for their purchases and crossed the street to the Mercantile. We fetched paper bags and dug into wooden barrels for caramels, root beer kegs, jellies, sour drops, aqua mints, and imported fruit confections. A loud, canned voice announced, "Timex. It takes a licking and keeps on ticking!"

We shared confused recognition, then shuffled over to the soda fountain to investigate. A small black-and-white TV, perched on the counter, picked up one of three channels from Chicago. We stood transfixed as if we'd never seen one before, instead of having only gone without for three weeks. Stranger still, we'd never watched television inside a store, except for a TV store. Its glaring, incongruous presence befuddled us. We thought people came to the soda fountain to visit Bob and Betty behind the counter, to see other customers, and to twirl on the barstools while fifties tunes blared from the jukebox. Instead, an elderly gentleman and two small boys watched *The Wide World of Sports* while their ice cream melted! And Bob from behind the counter, in his spotless apron, with his spectacles pushed down his nose, was equally absorbed.

I heard a voice just like mine hotly accuse, "Why do you want a television here?" Bob and the customers barely flinched. Their eyes never strayed from the action.

"You goober!" Lori hissed, drawing me into the next aisle. Christie tried to contain a mirthful chuckle. Nancy's serious consternation equaled mine.

We paid for our candy and drifted from the cash register to make room for two businessmen pressing into line. Nancy and Lori exited the screen doors while I hung back for Christie. She clenched the candy bag in her teeth and held her mother's present under her arm while sliding coins into her beaded change purse. I started eating my candy.

One of the men placed a day-old *Chicago Tribune* and a can of shaving cream on the counter. "Yup, this sure is pretty country," he said, staring at the paper's headlines while reaching into a side pocket for his money clip.

"Loads of opportunities," the other commented. "And nothing in the way. They've approved the expansion and the camp's lease runs out next fall." He rocked on his heels, hooked his thumbs in his belt loops, and assumed a thoughtful manner. "We can put a lot of condominiums on that stretch of beach."

"Which stretch of beach?" Christie inquired, stepping forward, speaking through the bag in her teeth. She hastily stuffed the coin purse in her pocket. "Which camp?" she demanded more loudly, now holding the lumpy bag in her hand.

Both men glanced at her white T-shirt, turned red in the face, and discreetly turned their backs on us. Christie stepped away, shocked by their reaction, and whipped from the store. "Guys!" she hollered. Everyone had wandered over to the wooden bridge to lean over and watch the river as it rushed to the wharf.

I trailed after her, wishing we had gone to the dunes with everyone else. Better still, I wished Christie hadn't been wearing "Shenahwau" stenciled across her chest. "They couldn't mean us," I argued, finally catching up to her. "We aren't the only camp around here. Those two geezers were probably talking about some other place." My voice shrank to a whisper. I wasn't even convincing myself.

Christie relayed the encounter through a cool reserve and deep mono-tone on our way to The Blue Bird. I could barely hold my excitement in check. I would have spilled the news in a jumble of shrill, exhaustive emotion. She simply repeated the conversation. Whether a loud cheer, a funny story, or tragic news, Christie's tone always stayed the same. Only her eyes ever betrayed the difference. And just now a fire smoldered within.

"We'll ask Bess about this," Theresa concluded, putting a lid on any rumor as we entered the busy restaurant. Though I suspected she really didn't want to know, or even to ask. None of us did. Like kids playing outside on a summer night we didn't care to know how much time remained before adults would put an end to the fun. Instead, we ordered pie. The waitress tapped her foot at our indecisive selections, all the while keeping an eye on her more important adult clientele. When our slices of cherry, blueberry, apple crumb, and lemon meringue arrived, they were left on a giant tray for us to sort. Forks and napkins came later. When we had finished, she ripped our tickets from her pad and dropped them in a heap. It was the perfect arrangement designed to save her time and save us money, both of which we had little. This is why, when all around dads and grandfathers were tossing folded bills across their tables as tips, and women were securing crisp new bills under sugar shakers, we headed straight for the cash register, made exact change, and departed without leaving a dime.

TWENTY-NINE

THADDEUS TO THE RESCUE

"IT'S BEEN A halfhour. Did we miss him?" Theresa's brow wrinkled into a map of concern.

"We've been here since four," Cindy reminded her. From the outer fringes of our circle of worry, she peered down at the numbers on Tori's watch.

"Can you read the hands from up there?" Sarah teased.

Cindy stood even taller. "Yes, I can. And the air is better up here, too, shrimp."

"Don't call me that!" Sarah snatched Cindy's candy and passed it to Lori. They flitted about Merdick's parking lot, evading Cindy.

Theresa flung her arms in weary dismissal of the matter and sat on the steps, keeping an eye on the street. The rest of us congregated around her until the white van turned the corner and scattered the game of keep-away.

"Here he is!" Theresa announced.

"Thaddeus is driving," Tori cooed.

I closed my box of fudge and squinted into the sun's glare on the windshield.

"So, what happened to Mr. Chinn?" Susie worried.

"I hope nothing bad. He's pretty old," I decided.

"Maybe he's tired," Nancy said, stuffing candy wrappers in the trash can. "Anyway, there's nothing we can do about it." Same as rain, ants, poison ivy, and the camp losing its land, she would not make it a problem.

"He's never late," Christie said.

Lori wagged a finger at us. "It's like my granny always warns. Don't take a strange dog by the ears."

"What dog?" I sputtered, searching the parking lot for a stray canine. My insides lightened at the illogical premise of her remark.

Lori frowned impatiently. Her freckles seemed to jump out, appearing more pronounced than ever. "It means, don't make trouble where there is none."

"I don't get it," Christie said.

"Because that dog might bite," Lori sneered at our ineptitude.

"Worrying makes a dog bite?" I puzzled, having never had a dog, or been bitten by one. Christie started to laugh, which was reason enough for me to do the same as we settled into the rear of the van. Lori's baffled looks only escalated our spasms until we basically lost consciousness. Encapsulated by an intoxicating forgetfulness, my eyes watered, and my chest hurt.

Somehow, we heard Theresa over the radio, "Mr. Chinn fetched the rest of the camp an hour early. Bess asked Thaddeus to pick us up."

"No catastrophe." Lori rested her chin on the back of her seat and gloated at us.

"That dog didn't bite," Christie said, gripping my arm and quivering while I tried to breathe. When we finally settled down, we noticed Tori sat in the pariah front bench. Theresa filled the middle and someone much taller than Mr. Chinn, having a shock of black hair and a tanned neck, commanded the driver's seat. His unexpected presence, so radically different from Mr. Chinn's thinning white hair and red blotchy neck, knocked the laughter right out of us.

We started singing with the radio, expecting our friends to join us. Instead, they played it cool for our new driver. Feeling betrayed, but unable to blame them, we clamped our mouths shut and glared at Thaddeus Petrovich. He had invaded our cabin unity right here in the white van, a sacrosanct extension of Wildwood. We mouthed the words instead, singing into our fists, refusing to change for any man, no matter how mysterious or attractive; even if he had just rescued us from the outside world.

He drove us straight to the A-frame dining hall. We stashed our shopping bags and purses behind the potted plants and bolted inside. Seating rules had been suspended since half the camp was missing. We dispersed among them, sitting at different tables, openly amused by their lively chatter, as if we'd been gone for weeks. Fishtown was a million miles away along with all the political machinations threatening to invade us. We were home. And like members of a large family returning to the fold, we instantly belonged. They needed us, same as we needed them, because our fragile connection depended on every camper, not just cabin mates.

Bess smiled serenely from the far corner as if she'd known our break from tradition would allow us to realize this.

"We missed you guys!" Mary said, carrying two cones from the ice cream machine. A fresh layer of sunburn lit her cheeks and shoulders.

"The flies were biting," Debbie remarked, openly disgusted by the rare phenomenon. Usually the flies left us alone by keeping to the woods and shadows.

"They weren't so bad," Joanna interjected from two tables over.

Shane disagreed. "I was sweating like a pig, and they wouldn't leave me alone!"

"Not sweating," Jenny corrected. "Horses sweat. Men perspire. Women glow."

"Then, I was glowing buckets," Shane said.

"Why were they biting?" Bonnie asked Linda. I sat beside them, awaiting Linda's reply.

"Because we need rain," she said to her only camper remaining for seven weeks. "All flies bite during their last two weeks of life. Without rain, they die sooner and in greater numbers. So, we notice them more."

The boys gorged on seconds and thirds, taking full advantage, since the cooks had not scaled down in quantity. Their bottomless appetites and undying enthusiasm for flank steak amused us. I showed the autograph to my sister. Someone at her table deciphered the handwriting, which made little difference because it went into my pocket for the last time.

"The evening activity is a soccer game," Bess announced for the girls.

"Counselors rally for Eagle Talon and resume Sand Storm! Forces double up!" Hutch commanded in a life-or-death manner.

"What the heck does that mean?" I implored anyone who would listen as we stood to leave.

"These guys," Mary said, offering wry agreement. "Everything is so secretive. They're probably playing dodge ball."

THIRTY

ANOTHER ENCROACHING FORCE

A HANDFUL OF us lingered on the deck, gathering around Robyn and Luke, our head counselors, as they resumed an ongoing battle of wits.

"What would you have done?" Luke leaned down from his lanky six-and-a-half-foot frame, hovering intimately.

"I would have stretched it out, as you did," Robyn continued the enigmatic dialogue, her voice seductively inviting. "But when they appeared out of nowhere, I would have owned up to it."

"So, how are they going to learn?" he countered.

"Are you qualified to teach the lesson? You've never learned it." Robyn delivered the insult so confidently it belied her diminutive five-foot stature.

"Oh, he's learned it," Eric reassured, coming to Luke's rescue, insinuating hardships in the field of which Robyn could only imagine. He stood nearly as tall as Luke, having the physique of a quarterback and the face of a movie star. But this did not intimidate Robyn like it did the rest of us.

"Then he should lead by example," she shot back.

Eric paused to consider, gave a painful smile, and moved back into the circle.

"And are you always so exemplary?" Luke said.

Robyn's chuckle could have been a culpable reply, though I decided it was the winning blow if a victory could be had. Even if we didn't understand the topic (which on this evening involved forgotten matches on a trip that were planted by Luke at the campsite, then passed off as a miracle when the campers found them after a moment of prayer), we still drew pleasure from them, feeling safe and connected like children watching their parents. But we weren't children. And to confirm it, the summer air felt electrified by adolescent tension. The circle dispersed into couples. Nancy stood slightly apart from David. Susie gravitated toward one of David's friends, tilting her head in order to hear his low voice. Theresa touched shoulders with a counselor named Jay, who would eventually tell her about the planted matches, and she would tell us. My sister, Joanna, and Maggie stood near the potted plants and lined the deck's rail. A row of guy CTs hemmed them in.

I now felt conspicuous, having lingered too long past the main event, and aimed for a quiet exit. I retrieved my purse and shopping bags, then paused when Joanna blurted the one question that would hold me.

"Guys! Tell us about Eagle Nest and Sand Storm."

"Eagle Talon," a deep voice corrected, laughing derisively.

"Wouldn't you like to know?" another teased. And the guy on the end crowed provocatively, "What do you think it means?"

Apparently, they weren't giving up any secrets! Not even to impress some girls. For the millionth time I wondered what went on at the guys' camp. Their taunts fueled my desire for revenge because I detested their ability to arouse my curiosity. I grabbed my purse, straightened my spine, and fired the most castigating remark I could think of. "You guys just cloak every stupid little thing in secret codes because you resent having to share your camp with girls!"

There, I said it. And after today I could have said much more.

Everyone heard. I felt Robyn and Luke's eyes boring into the back of my head. But I only cared about the guys in front of me. Their longish hair and scruffy chins resembled the upperclassmen in my high school. Normally, I would have been too intimidated to expose myself to their glaring scrutiny, especially stone-cold sober. But since I thought of them as harmless church guys, their wide-eyed surprise only emboldened me. I had learned quite a lot from the real world. Or so I thought for all my sixteen years. At least enough to launch my own battle of wits! Especially if it would gain some answers.

"Sure, that's part of it," the guy closest to me teased, leaning in with a broad, refreshing grin.

Sensing his interest and the nearness of victory, I unleashed a flirtatious smirk. "What's the rest?" I whispered, stepping closer, trying to remember his name.

"I can't say it here," he replied, his face mere inches from mine.

His attractive brown eyes and engaging smile activated my school-year personality. My resolve slipped a notch, and I knew he wished me to say, "Name the place." I contemplated breaking my self-imposed rule to say it.

"Time to head back!" Luke boomed loudly.

We jumped in place. I heaved a sigh of relief. He stiffened as if a drill sergeant had issued him an order. Then, he presented a façade of independent will and boredom. They all presumed to depart on their own terms. But Luke undeniably called the shots. Such regimental respect never occurred in the girls' camp. I was savagely entertained as they loped away, taking overly casual strides. Their bellbottoms dragged the ground, swishing along and showing only the rubber tips of their Converse shoes. This wasn't the inner glimpse I had expected. But I had my answer. Their secret codes were designed to sustain the illusion of a military camp.

"Let's go," Robyn commanded. Not to be outdone, she held her arms wide as if herding a pride of lionesses. We followed the guys down the steps and across the bridge. They veered to the left, and we took the wooded path along the river.

Nancy raced ahead, casting me a delighted grin. I gave chase, hugging my purse and parcels, easily matching her flurry of speed. Away from the dining hall we were twelve again and never walked anywhere. We ran through the woods, leapt over tree roots, sprinted across the sand, the boardwalk, and whisked past the lake. Through each carefree step I felt the protective lining of our mirage world weaving itself back into place. We landed on Sunblazer's front stoop in a grand finale. For the second time that day I had made a successful escape from encroaching forces.

THIRTY-ONE

GETTING SWEATY

NANCY BLASTED THE door. It smacked against the inside joists. The spring went to work, straining and creaking the door into place. Anticipating the Bang! to follow, we ran to our beds, dropped our packages, kicked off our sandals, and gathered socks and sneakers. We sought to accomplish as much as possible while the door closed, as if time hung suspended and we cheated the universe.

Susie slipped in at the last second to maximize the yield. Nancy lent her a ponytail holder, and we ran to the playing field.

Under long shadows of a warm evening, Robyn coached and refereed both sides toward holding positions and executing plays. The majority of us had never played a team sport because our high schools only offered individual sports for girls, like swimming and gymnastics. Maybe a couple of us had played softball. As a result, our lack of a team mentality and insufficient ball skills turned every match into a frenetic blur of cumbersome folly.

As our goalie, Susie screamed for assistance whenever the ball came near, like a sacrificial maiden chained to the dragon's cave. Cindy spent the entire game at her beck and call. Tori staked a defensive position near the opposite goal and attacked passing balls like a Broadway dancer in a kick line. She rarely made contact but we steered clear anyway, suitably afraid, because she wore authentic soccer spikes. This worked well for their goalie, who was more interested in searching for four-leaf clovers. Over and over, Lori tried to complete a midfield pass to Christie. Every time, Joanna would send it out of bounds, strutting as if she had achieved a great victory for her team. Robyn would yell for Joanna to use her ball skills to intercept, to keep it in play. Joanna would roll her eyes, retrieve the ball, and it would start all over again.

Those of us playing forwards simply gave up trying to pass and ran the entire field to score multiple goals. The evening ended with double-digit tallies more suitable to a basketball game.

Before sunset we straggled back to the cabin and helped Theresa move in. We tweaked our beds into a slightly different configuration, then relaxed into our new setting. "I'm so glad you're our counselor," Christie said, the image of angelic honesty. She sat on Theresa's bed, swinging her legs and stretching taffy between her fingers, flaunting a casual intimacy unimaginable around Jenny.

"Me, too," Theresa agreed, sending a pleasant smile around the cabin.

I garbled, "Me, too," through a mouth full of cherries. Nancy and I sat on my steamer trunk and flicked pits, aiming for a rusty coffee can in the middle of the floor. Most of hers hit the target. Most of mine did not. Yet I continued to try, craving the plinking sound on contact.

"Okay," Tori said, making a face of roiled disgust, "that one nearly landed inside." She closed her footlocker and pointed under her bed. "Don't expect me to pick that up."

"We'll sweep the pits in the morning," Nancy said.

"Go fish!" Sarah ordered from a card game on Susie's bed, squared against Lori and Cindy.

"I'm out," Cindy said, gathering the deck. Her opponents scattered for their toiletry buckets and aimed for the door.

"Too late," Theresa announced. She dashed her hand across the light switch. The bugle's drawn-out notes reached our ears. We paused in the shadowy darkness, staring at the placid lake and the golden remains of a cloudless sunset. Instinctively, I gave thanks for four more weeks in this idyllic setting.

"Time for hymn sing," Theresa announced when it had ended, breathlessly tugging a flannel nightgown over her clothes. She scooted into white tennis shoes, breaking their backs while dragging toward the door. A flashlight landed on her face. Her brown eyes sparkled, secretly amused. "Shine on my feet." She bent down and used her fingers like a shoe horn.

"I really have to pee," Sarah whispered nearby. The rogue flashlight revealed her silhouette bouncing up and down in a cross-legged stance.

"Sneak into the bushes," Theresa said.

"Here." Nancy tossed a white comet through the air. Sarah groaned in disgust, caught the roll, then followed Theresa outside.

The sky faded to inky black while we readied for bed, hearing the counselors singing near the flagpole. Sarah returned from the junipers just as they gathered on the boardwalk between Sunblazer and Beacon to sing for us.

"Goodnight, Beacon," Robyn crooned at the end, bestowing a sweet blessing upon our neighboring cabin. She paused to muster the energy to address us. "Goodnight, Sunblazer." Her voice dripped lethal warnings and preemptive disapproval.

"Goodnight," one of us squeaked in return, followed by smothered laughter, and coughs.

Instantly the door opened and Theresa stood on the threshold. "You have to be quiet," she said. Casting her nightgown across her bed, she promised, "I'll be back later." We assumed some mysterious duties as counselor required her participation.

"Hold up," Lori said, waving a washcloth, "I'm pitted-out from that soccer game.

"Me, too," Susie agreed.

"Yeah, and my hands are sticky," Christie said.

"Go skinny-dipping," Theresa remarked quite casually, as if naming a regular activity.

I recalled the delicious sensation of skinny-dipping at Papa's cottage on summer nights when the darkness lay so thick you could barely see your own feet. But I had been a little kid. Now I was a modest teenager, starkly and soberly aware of my body. The prospect seemed stressful and risky.

"You will be quiet?" she cautioned.

"Yes," we dutifully answered.

"Good." Theresa smiled cheerily before sliding out. We heard her skip along the boardwalk until she crossed into the sand. We stood like statues in the dark cabin.

"Let's go," Christie said. We all knew July's heat had worked its magic on the lake and turned it to bathwater.

"Do you skinny-dip in Indiyaaana?" Cindy said.

Christie snorted a throaty reply of secretive implications. "I do live on a small lake, you know."

The blaring flashlight reappeared at random. We shielded our eyes and ducked for cover. "Turn that off, Lori," Nancy said, naming the culprit.

The light went out. "Swimming sounds good," Lori yielded.

"But we should wear our suits," Susie decided.

"You guys," Christie cajoled. "Why struggle in and out of a suit? There's hardly anyone in camp. There's no moon." She stepped into the middle of the cabin where the starlight passed through the screens, faintly outlining her presence. "This is the night to do it." A palatable silence communicated our reluctance.

"I'd much rather skinny-dip than morning-dip," Tori said.

"You never take dips!" I accused.

"Exaaaaactly," she drawled.

"So, how do we do this?" Sarah asked, crossing her arms uncomfortably while glancing at the rest of us. Suddenly, the darkness didn't seem so dark.

"Wear your robe and drop it on the beach," Christie said, digging through her trunk. We all had bathrobes, a very necessary cover-up for late-night trips to the Murphy.

"Yeah, but what if someone sees us?" Susie challenged.

"No one is going to be looking," Christie stated. "Whitecap is empty. And we'll stay out of sight of Beacon."

Susie dogged in a worried plea, "How do we get out? You know, when we're done."

"Susala darling," Tori said. "You just show a little skin to the night. March up the shore and put on your robe."

"And stand up straight to shed ten pounds from your waist," I added.

"Cindy, are you in?" Nancy aptly solicited the only one of us who had abstained through silence.

"Oh, all right," Cindy laughed.

THIRTY-TWO

THE END OF A VERY LONG DAY

WE EXITED THE cabin on a level of solemnity reserved for Council Fires. The spring recoiled in a low groan. Attentive fingertips silenced its impact, and our eyes scurried about, fully alert. Endowed by the night air with the heightened senses of nocturnal creatures, we struck into the sand, single file, and hastened to the shore.

The water stretched out like glass, and the stars reached down in bright reflection.

I wedged my feet into the thick, wet sand. Tepid water lapped my ankles. To my right, Christie disappeared in a flurry of fabric and a tiny splash. Lori flew away on my left. I hesitated, feeling anxious and uncertain. Out of my periphery, I saw Nancy's sleek dive. Tori and Susie went next. I stepped a little deeper into the lake. Warmth spread up my calves. I gathered the robe above my thighs and extracted my arms while hugging the fabric to my chest in lingering reticence. My gut stirred from a sense of urgency. Once I ditched the robe there would be no turning back.

I took a deep breath, cast it away, and hurtled through the frictionless depths. Without a bathing suit to contain it, my body splintered into a million liquid droplets on contact and mingled into the lake. I pumped liquid arms and legs, coursing along an invisible current, dropping further into the dark cocoon of primordial privacy. In this silent isolation I hummed a song of monotone delight, sensing my voice along my unclad skin as the lake insulated its sound. My body felt intimately protected, but my lungs pressed for air. I surfaced into a free-float, feeling plastered to the earth's surface. Stars winked back.

The Big Dipper, Little Dipper, Cassiopeia, and Pegasus stood out among the sparkles. In the handle of the Little Dipper, a point of light methodically crossed the stationary heavens. I tilted my head to follow this relatively new phenomenon; a satellite. Water fell heavily into my ear. The pressure was unbearable. I touched bottom and jerked sideways to release the droplets. Through each violent thrust I saw a blur of Cindy and Sarah on the shore, still in their robes.

I floated near, completely underwater except for my head. I did this more for warmth than modesty because the night air now felt cooler than the water. "Aren't you coming in?" I whispered, grazing my elbows against the soft carpet of pebbles.

"This is too much like the opening scene in *Jaws*," Cindy's voice carried easily.

I glanced across the calm surface, recalling a lone beach and a teenage couple high from partying. "Oh yeah, the girl gets eaten while she's skinny-dipping."

"Ugh," Sarah moaned.

"Know the difference between freshwater and saltwater?" Lori's melodic voice issued from a trim body dwarfed by the shallow water. She glinted like a pale fish in the starlight.

Tori glided past, side-stroking elegantly, and said, "A shark would never survive the St. Lawrence Seaway."

"You guys," Susie whispered. "It's just really, really neat, better than any shower or bath could ever be. It feels so light and free. You have to get in here."

A solitary leg rose from the dark water like the chiseled limb of an alabaster statue. Christie surfaced beneath, adroitly treading in place. In the foreground, Nancy's toned muscular leg also rose to a perfect point.

"Oh," Susie lightly squealed, "teach me how."

"It's the Statue of Liberty move," Christie instructed, luring her to deeper water. "Hold your breath. Go below and stretch out flat. Raise your leg and let the water float you up. Hold stiff and scull your hands until your chest meets the surface."

"Supposin' a shark made it through the Seaway," Lori continued. "There's Lake Erie and Lake Huron before reaching Lake Michigan. Weeks of swimming! The darn thing would never last so long out of saltwater." She floated away from shore. Orange tendrils of wavy hair covered her torso in a horizontal likeness of Venus emerging from the shell.

"And what about Niagara Falls?" Nancy casually whispered the greatest barrier of all.

"It's warm," I coaxed, as a final entreaty before swimming away to give them privacy. Following Christie's instructions, I held stiff as a plank along the sandy bottom. I extended one leg, released some bubbles, and floated upward. My hands gyrated like propellers to keep level. When cool air hit my toes, I imagined a perfectly pointed leg rising into the night.

"Your knee is bent," Cindy critiqued, speaking directly in my ear. She and Sarah glided past, grinning mischievously.

"Guys!" Nancy hissed. We had drifted toward Beacon. In a flash, we submerged and vanished. Beneath the blanket of water we sighted a unified heading and surfaced near our cabin, bouncing on our toes to gauge our new proximity from shore.

Nancy studied the lake's onyx veneer. "You know, there is a lot of unexplored water out there."

"It's easy to imagine this could be the ocean," Christie whispered.

"Don't talk about it," Sarah said.

"Yeah," Cindy agreed, turning to face shore.

"Nothing is hidden out there but some sunken ships and toothless fish," Lori said.

Feeling perfectly at ease to poke fun, since I had never been in the ocean and could not take its threat seriously, I twitched and dunked, as if something had tugged on my leg. "What was that?" I pretended in a fearful, raspy voice.

Wicked laughter escaped from Christie's throat. She immersed her chin and encouraged me through an intense gaze.

I mimicked a stronger pull from below, groaning upon surfacing, as if a predator had really taken a bite out of me. Glancing about, turning wild, I strangled a shriek and plunged violently from right to left. I propelled backwards, kicking beneath the surface, holding a stiff torso, pretending the Great White had clenched me in its jaws and hauled me away. I gurgled a mouthful of water, my eyes wide in terror, as it pitched me below to devour me in the deep.

I doubled back toward them and tickled the first pair of legs I came upon. Thankfully they were Lori's and she only swatted me away as I came to the surface. "That was farout," she praised.

"An Academy Award performance, Nance," Tori said.

"Sorry," I grimaced at Sarah and Cindy. "You aren't mad, are you?"

"Cripes," Cindy said, sharing a terse dimpled grin. "We may never go in the water again." Sarah agreed, yet neither of them made a move for shore.

I glanced at Nancy, seeking her approval. She gazed upon the water's indefinable edge, lost in thought. I decided she hadn't been watching. "Truth is," she whispered, unexpectedly proving me wrong, "we can play around because we know nothing from this lake could ever harm us."

"Amen," Sarah exhaled, and we began to giggle.

"We should go in." Christie's deep voice bounced toward camp. She splashed a hand to cover her lips.

"SSShhh," Tori said. We sank low. Our crocodile eyes prowled the surface, searching for life upon the shore.

"We need to do this tomorrow night," Susie said. Her decisive tone startled us. "Maybe," she added, falling back into uncertainty, mistaking our surprise for disagreement.

"First, let's get in without anyone noticing us," Lori whispered.

We broke apart, skulking toward shore, and emerged from the shallows in hunched postures, groveling for our robes in ankle-deep water. The long sleeves stubbornly resisted our wet arms. After a seeming eternity of struggling, we struck fully wrapped into the dunes and aimed for Sunblazer. All of us had drenched the lower third of our robes, save Tori. She had strutted forth upon dry sand to retrieve her robe. Holding a straight posture, she had cloaked her body in one fluid motion by skipping the sleeves. We noted this superior technique for future outings.

THIRTY-THREE

RED AT MORNING . . .

THE LAKE HELD its warmth despite windy days and cool drizzles, allowing more skinny-dipping in the remaining weeks. Only the appearance of lightning could deter us. I repeated the shark routine on demand, and my audience grew to include water-skiers on Glen Lake.

As August neared, bringing hot days and still evenings, even the screens proved too much of a barrier for the scant breeze to penetrate. So we'd drag our sleeping bags and pillows to the lake's edge, unrolling mere inches from the wet shoreline, to feel the lake's refreshing presence. However, without a tent or a cabin to shelter my head I could never fall asleep. Staring up at the sky, I would grow suspicious of the night air, thinking it brewed trouble. By midnight, when the dew made its chilly descent, I would return to the cabin. Usually, a few others came with me. We'd ease into our beds right about the moment of Theresa's breathless return. She'd offer explanations of laundry and staff meetings or appear flushed from the excitement of a night off.

We took full advantage of our senior camper status, the secluded beach, and Theresa's leniency. Time passed faster than the stolen moments between the recoiling spring and the door's resounding slam and each day held more meaning than the remaining 316 at home. Busy as the sun's steady march across the sky, we filled every hour and didn't let up until our light switched off for the night. Even then, in those moments of repose, not a single reminder of the outside world penetrated the darkness apart from the moon, the stars, and the lake's clear reflection. We existed on an island of harmony, secure in our community, and constantly aware of our humble place in the universe by the lake's pivotal presence. More dependable than the sun and the moon, it anchored our existence and provided a subtle, lasting assurance of our insignificance. It melted petty annoyances, egotistical rants, and personal disappointments. We sought to be near it whenever possible, to stand upon its shore, to be soothed by its calm or empowered by its strength.

I slipped away to the beach on our final evening, knowing I would have to leave the lake in less than twelve hours. The counselors sang around the flagpole, soon followed by their serenade of Beacon and Sunblazer. I pressed into a low rise of sand, watching the lake, and drinking in the rich harmony of "Taps."

"Goodnight, Sunblazer," Robyn barked at the very end. A giggle, a comment, a stray flashlight, or a tumult of falling objects inevitably followed. Perhaps my friends had been sneaking around in the dark preparing a surprise for Theresa's return from hymn sing. A tower of soda cans might surround her bed. Or the fire-bucket was changed from sand to water and would be placed over the door waiting to spill. They may have short-sheeted her bed or placed pinecones under her pillow. Possibly they looped streamers of toilet paper from the rafters, covering her bed in a canopy of white. The list had become varied and endless. Theresa always laughed and never grew angry.

Nancy eased beside me, graceful as a shadow. We sat in silence, feeling the gathering wind and hearing the trees wrestle against it. The sun had been a vibrant ball of fire. A swath of crimson filled the western sky.

"Next summer we'll be CTs," I sighed, repeating the words my friends had been saying for days. Bess had asked all of Sunblazer to return as counselors in training. I knew my parents would be pleased for this honor meant half the cost, and with Susan returning as a counselor the financial burden all but disappeared.

"Did you hear?" Nancy whispered. "Bess told the counselors after dinner. The resort wants to develop this land."

"So it's really going to happen."

"Next summer will be our last. The boys can stay longer if they sleep in the school's dormitories and give up their cabins on the beach."

We leaned our shoulders against each other, relaxed and content. Even this devastating news could not shatter the lake's comforting effect. "Maybe they'll change their minds," she ventured. "And besides, we still have one whole summer."

Optimism coursed through me like a potion, restoring the promise of fun and excitement still to come. The air seemed to crackle in response, similarly charged, while streaks of red spread like bloody fingers across the sky. "Red at night," I prompted.

"Just a pretty sight." She recited our version of the old sailor's adage. After witnessing plenty of sunrises and sunsets, we felt perfectly qualified to alter it.

"Red at morning," I continued.

"Just a silly warning," she finished.

"Do you think it will change very much next year?" I wondered.

She declared quite emphatically, "Not if we don't let it."

THIRTY-FOUR

NOTING THE TIME

"MOM!" MY DAUGHTER'S voice swelled from enthusiastic recollection. "We sang that canoe song at camp, but it had a different ending. The girl pushes the boy out."

"Really?" I bristled from embarrassment at this blind spot in my generation's quest for equality. "I wish we'd thought of that. It always felt outdated and corny even when I was a camper."

"And, about these dips . . ." She waggled a finger at me. "You and Aunt Susan are the reason I had to take them every morning?"

"You couldn't have minded too much, you got the Perfect Dipper Award every summer!" She had assembled a wide collection of metal soup ladles, each inscribed with a year.

"That doesn't mean I liked it," she said. "I just wanted to join everything. I earned all the beads my first summer."

"That's right," I crooned. Those seven beads and the all-important eighth had been tied to her wrist when I picked her up. At ten years old, she had been one of the youngest campers that summer. Her messy curls, friendly disposition, and willingness to join must have been endearing to the counselors. Why else would they have gathered around to say good-bye? And, as a daughter of the old camp, not Deena-hahna, but Wildwood, she had become what I never could.

"Mrs. Taylor?" Katie's voice rose from the backseat. "When KT's brother went to this camp, did he know about the dips?"

"I kind of forgot to tell him. But I really thought the guys' camp would have made them optional by then."

"When we get to Michigan," Angela said, "are we staying on the lake?"

"No, we're staying at my grandpa's place," KT said. "He and Barbara have an A-frame in the woods."

"It's about a mile from the lake," I interjected, veering past a tractor-trailer straining uphill, hauling logs. "But, there is a campground nearby, right on the beach. My sister suggested it, so I packed a tent if you want to camp out one night."

"That would be fun," KT longed. She nodded encouragement at each of her friends. "And the car?" she asked, facing me. "You could let me drive, you know. Then, you could get a ride to the camp with your friends. I have been driving for over a year."

"On a permit," I said.

"Three months with a real license," she corrected.

"I suppose the roads Up-North will have fewer drivers, no merge lanes, or trucks."

"And I'll need to drive myself to swim practice when school starts," she said, glancing in the backseat.

"We're gonna rule the school and boss around the younger girls!" Angela imperiously took control of their future.

"Like you don't already!" my daughter accused. "What about that girl who wanted to go out with . . . ?"

"Shush!" Angela leaned forward and covered KT's mouth with her hand.

The other Katie pried her loose, and the two of them fell into the backseat. A wayward limb jarred the back of my seat, and a foot pressed the base of my seat belt, tightening it across my shoulder.

KT undid her seat belt and whipped around, cutting into the middle of these polar opposites like an equator, to patch them together and even them out. "We are going to have so much fun next year! We'll be the seniors!" Her declaration forced a pause in their ribaldry. They took a long moment to ingest it before sharing hums of anticipation.

"Just remember," the other Katie concluded, "we didn't like it when the seniors did it to us."

Angela's bold confidence turned self-mocking. "Like the younger girls would ever listen to me, anyway! My sister will be one of them. She's never obeyed me a day in her life."

"We'll figure it out," my daughter soothed as she refastened her seat belt.

I willed time to slow. Where had the years gone? My daughter had turned the same age I was my CT summer! It had been a pivotal time of dramatic and sudden change. Like a storm brewing over the lake, we could see it coming, and feel its effects, yet we could only watch as it sculpted and realigned the beach.

"Hey, Mrs. Taylor," Angela asked as she raised her arms in a long stretch. "Had anything changed when you went back to camp?"

"Well, yes and no. There was a lot of building going on. To this day, when I catch the scent of freshly cut cedar I think of that summer. And Bess had not returned. She started a camp of her own, downshore, and none of us had heard about it in time to attend. We probably wouldn't have gone anyway. We loved Bess and all, but we rarely thought about the people behind the scenes. I suppose she felt abandoned. Someone probably prevented her from notifying us, some kind of noncompeting clause.

"Then, our new director, Lou Ellen," I laughed at the memory, "was the complete opposite of Bess. She wore bright jewelry and fragile city shoes. She had platinum blonde hair, teased high, with loads of hairspray. She may have been told about our traditions, but we knew she had never lived them, so we felt perfectly entitled to run amok. We were the largest group of CTs ever in the history of Wildwood, especially since Mary had also joined our group, and we took over Whitecap. It was a great cabin. Tucked into the woods and hidden from the flagpole, with a nice view of the lake. And Robyn became our counselor."

"Poor Robyn." my daughter smiled sympathetically.

THIRTY-FIVE

THE MYTHICAL LAND OF NOD

"OUCH!" CINDY MOUTHED. Her hand was pinched between the doorjamb and the metal frame of our counselor's oversized bed. It took eight of us to lift it, one of us to hold the door, and a locomotive mentality prevented us from slowing down or altering course. Absolute stealth required Cindy to grin and bear it as her knuckles scraped the wood and her skin peeled. I cringed on her behalf then quickly adjusted my grip because the same thing was about to happen to me.

We cleared the threshold, crossed Whitecap's verandah, and prepared for three blind steps. All muscles attuned to holding the bed level, despite the awkward poses and scant light. Smoothly and evenly, the bed floated over the steps and landed on the sand, straddling the boardwalk.

We regrouped while Lori reattached the spring to secure the cabin against raccoons and possums. Cindy absently licked blood from her hand and Susie grinned at me from across the mattress. Her brown eyes sparkled in the moonlight beneath a short, pixielike hair cut. She had ditched the long layers this year and hadn't even brought a curling iron or a hair dryer to camp. She wore the style well; a subtle victory and silent jab against tormentors. I wanted to say, "That sure is a cute haircut." But I had already complimented her about a dozen times, and it was only two hours past midnight into our fifth day at camp.

A parley of nods indicated our readiness to move. Nancy mouthed, "One, two, three," and we raised the bed, standing shoulder to shoulder around its frame. Lumbering along the boardwalk, past Sunblazer, we moved like a fat centipede in the night. We were the legs, and Robyn was the body, lying sound asleep on the cotton mattress.

We churned across the sand and regulated a level keel over the drop toward shore. The fluffy sand caused a few missteps. The bed jostled. We metered our stride and pressed on to set the bed along the beach.

The confines of the narrow dock caused us to resume our positions at the foot and head, same as when we had cleared the cabin door. I gripped a corner and inched along, ever fearful of the abrupt edge and the cold water below. My shoulders burned, and I felt a kinship with all the litter-bearers through history.

The dock's extension had been designed as a gathering place and spanned wider than the base. We lowered her along this roomy platform and regrouped. Placing four of us on one side, and five on the other, we gripped the side rails and pivoted the bed forty-five degrees. The head swung out over the water until we aligned the bed on the dock and Robyn's feet pointed toward shore. It was a perfect fit, measured ahead of time, and regardless of which side of the bed she awoke on, she would assuredly step down on the dock.

We watched her sleep, making sure we had really pulled it off. I felt confident of our success because two nights before, at this approximate hour, Susie had returned from the Murphy to find a raccoon on our porch. She had shrieked, "Scram!" in a voice loud enough to wake us all, except Robyn. I had leapt from my bed to see the little bandit fleeing into the night with a candy wrapper in its mouth. Susie apologized for waking us, claiming her outburst had been necessary because the raccoon was barring the door. Half of us teased her, the other half defended her strategy, and during the entire commotion Robyn slept same as now, dead to the world.

Nancy, Mary, Cindy, Susie, and Tori backed away from the bed, preparing to leave the dock, silently guffawing at those of us on the opposite side. We returned their joviality with stunned expressions, begging to be let in on the little joke. Finally, we got it. We were trapped between the bed and the water.

We could climb over Robyn. Or scale the outer frame. Either way, the bed would jiggle and wake her up. There was no other way; we would have to swim for shore. Christie and Sarah tugged on Lori's arms and faked a launch into June's freezing waters. Lori retaliated by jerking back, threatening to take them along. And we all snorted softly, trying to contain our laughter.

At some point in our clowning around, Nancy and Mary communicated the obvious solution, which caused more smothered laughter. One by one, we dropped on our bellies and slithered across the damp, gritty dock to pass beneath the metal frame.

We ran back to Whitecap with the silence of expert skinny-dippers, though fully clothed against the night's chill in long pants, sneakers, and sweaters. After retrieving Robyn's footlocker, shoes, and personal effects, we paused on the bluff, completely entranced. Her solitary bed resided on the end of the dock under a full, circular moon, majestically enlarged by the earth's atmosphere. The lake's luminescence reflected a golden path of light toward this friendly face hovering over Robyn's slumbering head, resembling a picture postcard from the Land of Nod.

Our prank seemed divinely blessed. I felt a measure of sleepy pride because it had originally been my idea, though I would never say it. Our wild schemes belonged to every participant. And this had been a collaborative effort, right down to our arrangement of Robyn's trunk, toiletries, and shoes. For a final act of compassion we draped an extra quilt over her body. Then we dashed to the cabin, hoping to sleep the remaining hours until Reveille.

"I want to see her face when she wakes up," Christie decided as we entered Whitecap.

"Then, we'll have to sleep on the beach," Mary concluded.

"Not me," Tori said. "I'm setting my alarm for quarter-till when the dippers head out."

"Dips!" we echoed together, realizing they would see her first. My sister and Joanna continued to spearhead that early-morning activity, but we had become too lazy to join them, planning instead to resume our nightly dips when the lake turned warm.

"All the doubly more reason to hit the beach," Cindy said.

My cot appeared very inviting. Sarah and Tori settled euphorically into theirs.

"I'll go," Susie said, stretching into a bulky sweatshirt.

"Come on, Schmidty," Nancy said.

In the end, my desire to see Robyn's reaction proved stronger than my desire for a good night's sleep. I gathered my sleeping bag, pillow, and an extra sweatshirt, and followed them out the door keenly aware this was not like a camping trip. I could always return to my bed.

THIRTY-SIX

THE NIGHT WIND

WE REPOSED AT an angle below the bluff, to leisurely keep watch. Wedged between Christie and Susie, I adjusted my pillow and snuggled into my pastel-flowered sleeping bag until the sand conformed to the curve of my back. We touched shoulders and the sand gradually warmed beneath us.

Christie's breathing turned steady. But Susie continued to shift and wiggle. "I'm a little freaked out," she whispered when our eyes met.

"About sleeping down here without a tent?" I offered my most immediate concern.

"No, silly." She rolled her eyes as if we'd both already checked this off some list.

I needed to correct her. "You fell asleep on that canoe trip, in the ants and mud. But I never did."

"Forget that," she said. "I'm talking about the election."

"Oh," I sighed. Cedars had voted her Team Captain that very evening and we had kicked off the season by losing our first competition.

"I don't want to be captain!" she moaned.

"Don't hate me," I confessed, "but I voted for Cindy."

"Me, too," she said, smiling incredulously. "So how in the world did I get elected? I don't know how to be a leader."

"Just tell everyone what to do," I supposed.

"That's the problem!" she choked into a high-pitched whisper. "I can't tell them what to do when I don't know what to do!" She rocked forward and hugged her pillow. "The odds are stacked against us. Dunes have six CTs. We have three and practically all of Stardust. Why didn't Cindy get elected? She's a better athlete. Wait a second," she quietly reconsidered. "I'll put Cindy in every event. I can, because I'm the captain. I have to get organized, figure out who is good at what. I'll get everyone excited. Make them think we can win again. Oh, it would be so cool if Cedars could get the banner again this year. It would prove last year wasn't a fluke." She shimmied from her sleeping bag and stumbled to her feet wearing an inspired grin. "I can't sleep out here. I need a good night's rest. I have gobs of stuff to do tomorrow. Besides, it's cold."

She ambled away, shaking her sleeping bag and muttering a filibuster against her own doubts. I would have followed, but a sense of duty kept me. I eased closer to Christie to pool our warmth.

A breeze ruffled my hair and splayed the grassy tufts above our heads, voicing a low whistle. It spread like a wave of adulation over the trees behind our cabins. Every leaf seemed to welcome the intruder in generous, rustling applause.

Defenseless and alone, since my friends had abandoned me to their dreams, I listened acutely as the breeze prowled beyond my hearing. The night is clear, I admonished my rapid heart rate. The wind is not blustering any differently than it blustered all day. I spoke to my shoulders and neck, willing them to relax. Listen to the steady waves. I directed my eyes to shut and channeled my worries toward mundane matters. A necklace had knotted during the transport of my trunk. Would I be able to untangle it? My beach towel smelled musty when I hung it on the line. Should I fetch another from my duffle in the rafters?

A breeze blasted my cheek. Newly alarmed, I rose to my elbows and witnessed our tallest pine rustling laboriously. Its stiff branches, laden by stubby needles, moved up and down and side to side as if shadowboxing an invisible foe. The wind's leading edge swept through the woods, beyond the river, and roared up the tree-covered dune of Council Fire Point. Opalescent clouds, darkly edged, cast wispy tentacles across the pearly moon.

My attention revolved around the lake, the sky, and back to the trees, trying to find a pattern in the breeze. It grew eerily quiet. I forced my head into my pillow. I watched and listened. I waited. Then, it ginned up again, whooshing over my face. The trees creaked and the multitude of leaves clapped a raucous, sweeping ovation, as if paying tribute to a sinister and erratic ruler; the night wind.

I sat up. My senses sharpened. I knew a storm was brewing. I scrutinized the lake's surface for ripples. I watched the progression of patchy clouds as they masked the starlit heavens. Each gust erupted stronger than the last. Over and over, pine trees enlivened, the dune grass moaned, and millions of leaves rubbed against each other to turn an otherwise insignificant sound into the intensity of a band of locusts. It had to be the stirrings of rain. Soon the drops would fall in earnest. There would be a gathering tempest, an inevitable thunderhead. I searched the sky for sheets of rain and bolts of lightning.

I owed it to Robyn to keep watch. When the storm hit, her things would be ruined. Her footlocker was fabricated of little more than glorified cardboard. Unlike my sturdy steamer, hers would fall apart. Her blankets and sheets would soak through to the mattress.

Worse still, Robyn slept upon a metal frame! Her bed hung out over the water like a lightning rod. It stood ready to conduct deadly bolts of electricity! I dropped my head into my hands and gripped my hair. I had to wake everyone. We had to carry her back to the cabin. What could I have been thinking? I reached toward Christie, dreading my actions.

Things always seem worse at night.

I paused. My hand lingered near her shoulder. This random thought had popped into my head as if spoken aloud. I saw a clear mental picture of blue marker on red paper inside the Murphy's stall. "Shew forth thy loving kindness in the morning, and thy faithfulness every night."

Perhaps the spelling of "shew" had caused me to recall it so easily. Sequestered in the little stall, I had pondered the ancient conjugation of the verb "show." Could it be show, shew, showith? Now, I tilted my head and contemplated the word "faithfulness." I couldn't define it. It was too vague and insubstantial. Yet, I could probably name what it was not. It was not lying awake in alarmed panic, outlining danger and imagining disaster.

I withdrew from Christie and took an unbiased account of the night. Tiny waves licked the shore. A few transparent clouds veiled the stars. A greater portion of the sky sparkled clearly. The air felt cool, pleasant and dry. The wind did not brew a tempest. My friends slept undisturbed, and I wanted to be like them, to wake in the morning fully aware of "thy loving kindness."

When my raging thoughts quieted, I saw things more clearly. I had been surrendering to the night wind; not fighting it, or aiming to defeat it. After all, only an insane person would consider fighting the wind. Wasn't it far too powerful? Instead, I had been wrestling against the calm. I had been fighting a battle no sane person should want to win. For who wouldn't desire peace of mind?

In my anxious state, I had seen enemies everywhere. Fear had induced me to fight. Instinctively, I had chosen to battle the weaker foe, to better my chances of winning. But I had wrongly assumed the calm was weaker. By association, I had made the night wind more powerful. If I wanted to win I would have to switch sides.

So, I surrendered to the great, calm lake, knowing nothing from its vast expanse could ever harm me. At this beckoning, a gentle presence seemed to press my head into my pillow. My eyelids fell shut. My shoulders relaxed. Water lapped the beach in a soothing cadence, and I regulated my breathing to match. A light sensation of safety and peace filled my chest, expanding beyond my body, spreading among my friends and into the night. Without fanfare or triumphant awareness, I fell asleep. For the first time in my life I slept under the stars without a tent.

In the aftermath of sunrise, when the trees behind camp shielded an array of golden beams, I heard whispers and giggles. Stretching, I smiled to see my sister surrounded by her campers from Driftwood. Not only had Susan become a counselor that year; she had attained the status of waterskiing instructor in charge of driving the boat. Joanna, and her campers from Sandpiper, completed the gaggle of girls twittering at the unusual sight.

Sarah, Susie, and Tori stampeded the bluff, pouring sand over our heads. "She's still sleeping," Sarah whispered.

We shed our sleeping bags, leaving them like mangled corpses on the beach, and drew near the base of the dock. Instantly, as if sensing her audience's arrival, Robyn sat up, sightlessly composed. She raised her arms in a long stretch. Bright shafts of sun bathed her spiky red hair in light. She located her slippers from the row of shoes and stepped into them. Grabbing her toiletry bucket, she marched past. "I feel sooo refreshed," she said, cutting a path for the Murphy.

My mouth dropped open. "Did she know the whole time?" I gasped.

"No," Nancy decided, grinning commendably, "she's just playing it cool."

My sister waded into the freezing water and exclaimed, "That was a great prank!" Her excitement faded upon hearing her campers' hearty agreement. She jabbed a finger of stern warning. "Don't get any ideas!"

Josie skipped over. "I'll take your picture." Her bright green eyes peered from beneath a row of sandy red bangs.

"Thanks," I said, noticing she didn't have a camera.

"Here!" Susie tossed hers, and we assumed cheesy, proprietary poses near the base of the dock.

Robyn returned trailing a crowd of spectators. We backed off, forming a sentry for her ascension to the whitewashed planks. Nonchalantly, as if she dressed every morning on the dock, she chose items from her trunk. Under the cover of her Lanz flannel nightgown she donned a bra, slipped on shorts, and maneuvered into a shirt. After kicking into a pair of Dr. Scholl's sandals, she thudded down the dock, swinging her arms. "Be dressed and at the flagpole in ten minutes!" she commanded the open-air audience.

When she hit the beach, the crowd scattered.

After breakfast, we restored her belongings for morning cleanup. The empty bed felt heavier and the dock more treacherous. But no one complained. The prank had been worth it. And, whenever someone mentioned this particular episode, which they often did, along with everything else the nine of us did that summer, I felt a special pride. Not because I took personal credit. It didn't work that way. But because in the dark hours of the night I had reached out and found a comforting presence. It had abolished my worries and brought me peace. No longer would the night wind get the best of me and mask the lake's calming effect.

THIRTY-SEVEN

A WAKE-UP CALL

FOR DAYS I pondered why this comforting presence eluded me in the outside world. It had been a turbulent school year. In the fall, my sister had gained enough confidence from her victory as Cedar's captain to ask for help from her senior English teacher. For the first time ever, she confided how the letters jumbled together until they became so overwhelming the plot made no sense. The teacher suggested she read aloud while he waited on the bleachers for his track team to come back from their long-distance run. In this way, she sat alongside him, reading slowly, and after each page he explained the content. It took the entire track season to read *Great Expectations*. It became the first novel she'd ever read cover to cover.

My mom had endured experimental surgery and was recovering nicely. I had graduated a year early, joining Susan's class, and had received a letter of acceptance from Indiana University for fall enrollment. However, I still caved in to the wants of my boyfriend, hung out with a toxic group of friends, and worried about what my peers thought of me. Other voices guided my actions instead of my own convictions. But that night on the beach I had found a way to quiet them, to take control amid the veneer of chaos. If only I could tap this newfound source beyond the boundaries of camp! It was a fresh summer, full of possibilities. I had many weeks ahead to practice. I also vowed to make it to a few meals on time.

"You are late again!" Robyn accosted Nancy and me as we entered the double doors to the dining hall. Hands on her hips, she appeared the solid gymnast about to pull off a backflip. "You are holding up the guys." Her arm swept a crowd of young men and boys shuffling impatiently.

I wanted to disagree, because plenty of girls continued to file past the cooks, but Luke stood beside her. His formidable height suppressed my voice, despite his unconcerned slouch and hands casually stuffed inside baggy jeans. He leaned down and said something only Robyn heard. She smiled sweetly then scooted us inside.

I grabbed a tray, plate, and utensils, cynically amused to see Robyn in my usual place at the end of the line. The cooks piled on grilled cheese sandwiches, buttered peas, and Tater Tots. We passed an assortment of salads and desserts, and Robyn discreetly brushed against Nancy. "Luke has offered to sing for us tonight, after 'Taps.' It is such a treat! He plays the guitar and sings better than James Taylor."

Nancy nodded, properly impressed. I nodded, paying homage, knowing I should be excited when in reality I was shocked. Planned activities never happened for regular campers after "Taps!" But we were no longer regular campers, which continued to take me by surprise because I still felt like one.

After dinner, Lou Ellen distributed lists for a scavenger hunt. My team spent two hours puzzling the items hidden in riddle. A few could be satisfied by things brought from home. But mostly it was a test of who had been paying attention on Mr. Chinn's nature hikes. We rummaged through our cabins, then traipsed from the river to the lake and back again. When Robyn announced "Time's up!" on the megaphone, the sun was setting, and "Taps" loomed. We ran to the Hylton along with five other teams and presented our hulking paper bag to the judges. An early winner was declared, having returned well ahead of time with all twenty items. The rest of us vied for second and third places by defending our choices against disqualification. My team argued, a knot could come from wood as well as rope. A piece of deck could be a scrap of decking from the new construction, rather than a playing card. And Count Dracula's bouquet might be bloodroot, but thorny-pitcher's-thistle actually drew blood, and we had Shane's scratched-up hand to prove it. The judges relented, and we tied for second. Prizes were awarded in the form of full-sized candy bars, and everyone headed for bed.

When all the cabins had grown quiet, Robyn summoned us from Whitecap. Wearing jeans and cabled sweaters, we followed her across the boardwalk and toward the dining hall. We grew alert when she veered from the path and led us into No Man's Land. Apart from chasing someone down during Capture the Flag games, we rarely entered this stretch of beach separating our two camps.

A band of steely clouds buried the sun's afterglow creating an early darkness and leaving just enough light to show the way. We stepped over cedar saplings, dune grass, lady slipper, and puccoon. "Oooh," I gushed at the discovery of horsetail poking through the sand at intervals. This primitive plant had been our missing item in the scavenger hunt. Slender green stems, void of leaves or branches, resembled hollow bamboo and tapered to a cone-shaped tip. Near the Sleeping Bear Dunes we found them in abundance and often separated their joints, replacing them in a different order, even on different horsetails, and they would continue to grow and thrive. They also doubled nicely as pretend cigarettes when Mr. Chinn wasn't looking.

"Come on, Chicky." Nancy tugged me along, as if physically dragging me into our new role as CTs. Robyn parted a wall of junipers and led us over the border. Forbidden in an unspoken way, I had never passed this point. It never occurred to me that others did it regularly.

We descended into a natural bowl sheltered from both camps by a scruffy rim of foliage. A circle of logs lay at the bottom. Luke sat at the head, facing a blazing fire and a tunnel view of the lake. He strummed a couple chords, frowned at the sound, and adjusted his tuning.

Counselors and CTs from the boys' camp lounged at spaced intervals, not too near each other. We knitted tightly together and dropped on the nearest log. I wedged between Christie and Tori. Sarah, Lori, Cindy, and Mary completed the row. But Nancy crossed the circle toward Mary's brother and Susie bravely followed. They eased into the empty spaces.

I glanced at Christie, and our eyes widened. "I never knew the guys' camp was so close," I whispered, actually meaning I never knew Nancy and Susie were so close to the guys.

"I did." She tried to quiet her deep voice. "On rainy days we use their camp for gymnastics. They have parallel bars and a padded boxing ring that's covered and great for tumbling. But I didn't know about this fire pit. Robyn always steers us around it, which is how I knew where to find horsetail."

"You were on the winning team," I realized.

We heard rustling, and two silhouettes arrived from the beach. When firelight flickered off their faces we recognized Theresa and Maggie. They mixed among the guys. Theresa sat in the sand, casually leaning against Jay's knee. Her cheeks flushed, and the two of them shared a long, knowing smile.

A collective awareness spread among my fellow CTs. We turned smug, then appalled. Theresa hadn't been at staff meetings or doing laundry until midnight last summer. She'd been here!

"Did they watch us swim?" Sarah whispered. We shrank from the possibility.

"Naw," Lori said, "they were too busy doing other things."

"And I was afeared of sharks," Cindy said.

Mary chuckled. "We saw you guys from Beacon."

"You did?" Five of us hissed together.

Tori alone remained cool and collected. "Hope you had a good show."

"This doesn't change anything," Christie said. "We can still skinny-dip."

Luke strummed purposefully. His left hand formed a rapid succession of chords, and we quieted down.

"Personally, I don't get the attraction to these church guys," Tori spoke under her breath. "How 'bout you?"

I felt her staring at me, daring me to be honest. I knew nothing about Tori's home life; if she attended public school or private, lived in the city or the suburbs. I only knew I had lost even more of my innocence during the school year, and I speculated from her tone that she had, too. All at once I felt torn between these two friends like warring aspects of my personality. Christie's wholesomeness personified my longing to be virtuous. Tori's rebellious nature provoked my need to be anything but.

"You're so cute, you could get any one of them," she said.

My face heated from the insult. Nothing maddened me more than being called cute. Especially when my high school peers bitterly cited it as the reason I never got caught. It was like being called chicken at the onset of a dare. It ignited my need to be bad because, quite frankly, I just didn't look the part. But this was Tori, and she didn't mean to offend me. Her eyes broke free and toured the circle, perhaps searching for the one guy who would hold her interest. Thaddeus. "So, could you have a thing with one of them?" she pressed.

I almost said, "Why not? We're church girls," but her cynical half-smile prevented me, as if scorning my duplicity. I never imagined this half circle of guys might face similar challenges, or could relate to my inner struggle between rebellion and compliance. Instead, I faced Tori and squared my back so Christie wouldn't hear. "They couldn't handle me," I said through an air of worldly despondency.

Tori brazenly sized me up. I stared her down until she looked away. "Me, too," she whispered as Luke began to sing.

From across the campfire David smiled at Nancy. His greetings had moved beyond "How ya doin'?" into actual conversations. Nancy's shy, secretive smile, very different from the bold, confident one I had come to expect, made her seem unfamiliar, and I marveled at our inability to confide this aspect of our lives. It was another area having a boundary, same as every camper's life outside of camp. As we grew older, these boundaries would take over. But for now we ignored them, only vaguely aware of how they defined our personalities, determined our camp experience, and provided the reasons we returned each summer.

I returned because I craved the company of trustworthy friends. The beautiful setting didn't hurt. I did not want or need the complications of a boyfriend. I imagined Nancy came to challenge herself and to accomplish outdoor skills. If she met the perfect guy along the way, well, that would be fine because it would be a relationship founded on honesty. It could work because, unlike me, she felt free to be the same person at home as at camp.

I leaned forward resting my chin in my hands, watching Luke's expert fingering over the frets of his guitar. I should have been entranced by the fire and entertained by the music. But I was on edge. This outing had highlighted our differences, expanded my awareness, and shattered my sense of isolation. It might be a reward to Susie and Nancy as they glimpsed the freedom they would enjoy as counselors. To me it was a threat. It meant change and growth, the two things I feared most.

Inexplicably, my eyes strayed to Robyn. She returned my gaze, satisfied and victorious. For me there could be no other interpretation. This was her way of getting even for our prank. Since we had behaved like regular campers, she retaliated by treating us like counselors. I stiffened in my perch and crossed my arms, vowing never to return here, no matter how superb the music. I didn't want a wake-up call.

Christie nudged me, wearing an impish grin and ready dimples. Her deep voice echoed Luke's song and Carole King's lyrics. "When you're down and troubled . . . Soon I will be there . . . to brighten up even your darkest night."

I melted against her, our shoulders grazed. "You've got a friend . . ." I sang along, forgetting everything save the hiss of the logs, the crackling of thick sap, and the low, whipping sound of the flame punctuated by the honeyed notes of Luke's guitar.

THIRTY-EIGHT

CTS STRIKE BACK

LOU ELLEN'S VOICE crackled over the megaphone, "Whitecap come to the flagpole!"

"We slept through Reveille!" Mary screeched.

I blinked away my jumbled dreams of guitars and campfires. Morning had arrived far too quickly.

"Where's Robyn?" Cindy yawned.

"We need to get moving!" Mary insisted. She leapt about the cool wooden floor, kicking on shoes and throwing on clothes. Her vocal directives had become a welcome addition to the cabin. She would chuckle at our antics and usually joined in, but she also worked very hard to keep us out of trouble. We appreciated her mothering though it frequently sent us into hysterics because she was younger than us.

Susie crawled out of bed wearing pajamas and a bathrobe. She gazed unseeing into her open trunk. "Can't we just go in our PJs and robes?"

"Yes!" Lori decided. Flinging away her covers, she emerged in a flannel nightgown, a pink chenille bathrobe, and aqua-colored socks. She shoved her gingery flaxen hair into a pink shower cap, crammed a pillow along her chest, stuffed her backside with dirty clothes, and cinched the robe. She pivoted before us as a plump, matronly floozy.

The cabin enlivened into a flurry of inspired activity.

"You're all nuts," Mary said, backing toward the door, staring at Cindy who rolled curlers into her hair. "I'll tell Lou Ellen you're coming." She strangled a laugh then made her escape.

We padded the front and rear of our bathrobes. The sashes pulled it all together and accentuated our waists. We felt buxom and bold. A hideous pair of slippers I'd purchased at a thrift store completed my look. Nancy wore a stylish washcloth over her head. Cold cream highlighted Christie's cheeks, nose, and chin. A few hastily placed curlers boosted Susie's hair. We hooked arms and strutted around the cabin.

Tori hastened for the door wearing normal clothes. "I have to pee," she announced.

"Me, too," Sarah called. "Wait up."

Two by two, the six of us paraded to the flagpole wearing respectively pink, aqua, rose, blue, yellow, and purple robes. Mary had saved a space, and we bunched into it, pluming and posturing like anthropomorphic hens competing in a beauty contest.

With hands on their hearts, the camp mumbled to completion, "And liberty and justice for all." The flag whipped above, wrapping in and around its stripes.

Lou Ellen assessed us through a painful grimace. "You girls didn't get enough beauty sleep?"

We offered pinched faces in reply. She was hardly outfitted to complain, wearing red shorts embroidered in little daisies, a lime green top, and red scarf.

The assembly gaped at us while she outlined the day's activities. Seeking adoration from our audience, we fluffed our padded rears, fondled our bosoms, and exchanged arrogant, insolent glares while vying for prominence in the circle.

Robyn strolled from the Hylton reading a clipboard and savoring a mug of coffee. In the minds of camper and counselor alike, she was the real authority in Wildwood. So everyone awaited her reaction. The six of us perfected our poses as if the premier judge, talent scout, and movie producer of the world had arrived.

She crossed the boardwalk, reading as she went, and paused often to take a sip. She merged into the circle while Lou Ellen broadcast a weather report and shared cleaning tips for morning inspection.

At last, the public messages had concluded, and no one made a move for breakfast. Sensing an irregularity, Robyn peered around. When her gaze landed on us, she squeezed her eyes shut, lowered her mug, and struggled not to smile. Emitting a deep groan, she placed the clipboard under her arm and regained her composure. "Go change now," she choked through a briny scowl, pointing toward Whitecap, "and you better not be late for breakfast!"

Lori bumped into my heaving chest. "Excuuuse me," she trumpeted a high falsetto plea.

"No, no, excuuuse meee," I begged forgiveness, cascading from a piercing high to a bellowing low.

Lori leaned over to adjust a knee sock, and Christie bounced into her. "Well! I never!" Christie sputtered a crescendo of squawking protests and jabbed an elbow into Cindy's fortified stomach.

"The nerve!" Cindy harangued, though it sounded like 'noive.'"

Susie swooned against Nancy, overwhelmed by prim contempt. Nancy wobbled her head and fluttered her eyes in confused dismay.

The chuckles we sought finally burst forth. We promenaded along the boardwalk, spurred on by their laughter. "Oh dear, pardon me, my apologies, please excuse me," we caterwauled all the way to Whitecap. The entire camp followed, primarily because this boardwalk led to the dining hall.

We struck haughty poses on our porch, critiquing and condemning the inferior specimens as they passed. "Scrawny little girls!" Lori pompously disapproved. "Why, they have no shapes, no figures at all!"

"Are they all scullery maids?" I wondered aloud.

Christie supplicated to the heavens, "Are they poor? Have they no cake to eat?"

"Yes, yes," Nancy clucked, "they must put some meat on their bones!"

"And some roses in those cheeks!" Cindy said.

"Men prefer women who have shapely curves!" Susie pirouetted to flaunt her hourglass bulk.

Robyn walked past, trying not to express anything we might construe as encouragement. My sister and Joanna rushed their campers along.

Jenny appeared most amused, perhaps because she no longer bore any responsibility for us. Bobbi allowed her campers to snap pictures. Linda bit her lip, delighted by our dialogue. Her new crop of youngsters giggled merrily about her.

We arrived late for breakfast. Christie had cold cream encrusted along her scalp, and I wore my slippers. We didn't care because the guys breakfasted a full hour before us. This summer, we only saw them at lunch and dinner.

After morning cleanup we sat on our trunks, and Robyn lectured. "In just under two weeks the second session will begin. Each of you will be assigned a cabin. You will move into that cabin and be in charge of its campers whenever that counselor is not there."

"Like student teachers," I said.

"Like counselors in training," Robyn corrected. "You have had years of fun. Now it is your turn to ensure other girls have the same experience. They look to you for guidance and leadership. It is your duty to instill our traditions in a way that enhances their spiritual progress while allowing them to nurture friendships and develop new skills."

I half listened, wondering how this would work since I had to leave camp around that time for freshman orientation at Indiana University. My sister wasn't too happy about me taking the car for three days, since she'd be without wheels on her day off. But it was the only way I could visit my new school and choose a schedule of classes.

"Everything Wildwood stands for you must teach them: cooperation, persistence, joy, consideration, resiliency, cleanliness, and enthusiasm." She ticked them off on her fingers. "As counselors, you will lead by living these qualities every day. Listen," she pleaded in a passionate tone I had never heard. She focused mostly on Nancy, Mary, Cindy, and Lori, inching toward them. "This location will go away, and it is painful, but we have lost our grounds before."

My eyes widened. She spoke from the standpoint of having lived through it, which seemed impossible since the old camp belonged to our mothers' generation. Or so I believed.

She smiled sadly and relaxed, as if addressing colleagues. "But Council Fires, Dunes and Cedars, our sisterhood, and this atmosphere of unconditional love will live on. It's up to us to ensure it lives on. We will carry these traditions and our memories to a different piece of land."

I admired her loyalty and emotional attachment. I loved camp and would always turn dreamy-eyed at its mention, but I had always considered it something to outgrow, certainly not a career choice. This is why in that fleeting moment I felt grateful for Robyn's dedication. She and her kind kept Wildwood alive throughout the winter and through the years. For them, camp was more than a youthful pastime or a cushy summer job. For me, it wasn't even a summer job. It was a vacation.

"Will we spend Cabin Day together?" I interrupted.

"No," Robyn said. She crossed her arms and stared at me. Her face soured. "You will spend all your time with the cabin you are assigned, and with your campers, like real counselors."

"There goes skinny-dipping," I whispered, staring at the floorboards and a sprinkling of sand we'd missed with the broom.

"What about the CT trip?" Nancy's casual tone disarmed her, and she visibly softened.

"Yes, there is the CT trip."

"Just tell us where we are going," Lori begged.

We waited for an answer, hoping to gain a hint. Counselors never mentioned their past trips, and current CTs always returned cloaked in an aura of silent mystery. Susan had proved no exception. And my sister didn't believe in keeping secrets! So when she refused to share the slightest tidbit of her experience, even after returning home, I grew excited and suspicious. Either it was too painful to speak of, or such a triumph of fun and accomplishment that Susan had been cowed to silence.

My fellow CTs and I had speculated about this trip many times in the privacy of our cabin. Most of them could hardly believe it would be anything less than the adventure of a lifetime. I hoped they were right.

"It's a secret," Robyn said, pursing her lips. She had become our counselor once again. "But I will tell you one thing, if you promise to keep it quiet!"

"Yes!" we unanimously replied.

"We will be backpacking."

"Oh," I said, having no inkling of what this entailed. But Lori, Nancy, Cindy, and Mary seemed pleased. So I smiled along, happy to know we would have six days together like old times.

THIRTY-NINE

A STORM OF EMOTION

MY DAUGHTER LEANED across her armrest, appearing confused. "You were seventeen, our age, and you drove alone from northern Michigan to southern Indiana?"

"Round trip, it was about twenty-four hours of driving," I recollected. "I ate grapes and popcorn to stay awake."

"Didn't your mom worry?" Angela asked.

"I suppose she did." I glanced at my daughter, knowing I would worry.

"And you're afraid of letting me drive to some campground?" KT said.

"Oh," I breathed uneasily. My seat belt seemed to have tightened into a snare. She had exposed my hypocrisy and handed it to me on a plate. I could only squirm in silence as no one came to my rescue. Additionally, her correlation to my mother humbled me. How could I have overlooked the magnitude of her courage? Mom had been terrified of driving beyond the church on the corner. But somehow she had managed to keep her fears hidden, so I could succeed at something she'd never dare attempt.

"And you didn't have a cell phone?" Angela's amazed voice further drove the point home.

"You can't miss what you don't have," I quipped, sensing another underlying hypocrisy. I cast my daughter a sheepish look. She appeared lost in thought, staring out the window, oblivious to another failure on my part. So many times I had denigrated her camp experience because it wasn't the same as mine. But she may never have known if I hadn't repeatedly pointed it out.

Katie tapped my shoulder. "Weren't you afraid of getting a flat tire, or stopping alone at a gas station?"

"I never thought about it," I said, as we coasted along a country road. Rich chlorophyll from newly mown grass permeated the car, and velvet pastures unfolded for miles to the east. Opposite this, a housing development sprung from the prairie to be near the hidden lake. A row of distant clouds leaked gray streaks on the western edge of sunshine. "But I would now," I added.

"So does my mom," Katie said.

"You can call her from Chip's house."

The girls fumbled for their shoes while I searched for the correct entrance.

"Who is Chip, again?" Angela asked, struggling under KT's seat.

"He's my stepdad," I said, slowing for the turn. "My parents divorced when I was twenty-two. Chip moved to Ohio from Indiana soon after Mom died to be near his son."

"You'll love him." KT smiled. "He's like a big, sweet teddy bear."

"Tomorrow," I laid out the plan, "we'll drive to my grandmother's house in central Michigan, spend the night, and head for northern Michigan the next day."

The housing development confused me. Its man-made channels spread like watery blue fingers between houses and cul-de-sacs preventing passage between streets.

"Haven't you been here before?" KT asked.

"Nope," I replied. "I'm seeing this for the first time, same as you. I wonder if we're on the right street?"

"We're good," Angela said. "That's the address, over there."

A spacious driveway and three-car garage outweighed the attached home and its quaint covered porch. I aimed for the far edge and parked. We stretched from the car, and all three doors rose in a hum of machinery. Chip greeted us from the left bay, as if he'd been watching all day for our arrival. His foxlike canine raced toward us.

"Sammi!" My daughter knelt to rub the dog's thick coat and pointed ears. He rubbed against her and licked her hand.

"What kind of dog is that?" the other Katie said.

I looked upon her blonde hair and fair skin as if seeing her for the first time, since she had been little more than a voice behind my seat for the past eight hours. "It's a Pembroke Welsh Corgi." My tongue tripped over the pretentious name.

"Get a load of that long body and stubby legs!" Angela chuckled. "He's a cross between a brown fox and Donkey in *Shrek*."

"Ssshh," my daughter said. "You'll hurt his feelings!"

"So you finally made it here!" Chip held his arms wide from a six-foot-four-inch frame. KT and I accepted his hug, then introduced her friends.

Angela shared a forthright handshake, and Katie chimed, "Nice to meet you."

"I suggest you hurry and change into your suits," he said. "More rain is coming. As if we need more rain! Take the steps to the lower bedrooms. I'll have the fishing boat ready 'round back." He dropped his voice, replicating his days as a United Parcel Service trucker on CB. "We need to make hay while the sun shines!"

They hustled through a garage lined in workbenches and tools, clutching beach towels and overstuffed plastic duffels.

"After you." Chip held the inner door. I paused on the threshold. It should have been an unfamiliar house; new walls, new foundation, and a new location, but its furnishings and the scent of bayberry remained shockingly familiar. I imagined my mom bustling from a distant room, welcoming me to their new home through her big, happy smile. "My littlest is here," she'd crow, her voice overflowing in the sort of tangible love only a mother could give.

I descended a long flight of carpeted stairs. He remained at the top. "Take the room on the left," he directed. I stepped into a generous chamber, half underground. Bright daylight filtered through an oversized window-well crowned by lime-green grass. My throat tightened upon noticing the king size bed, side chests, and tall dresser. Mom had slept on the left side.

I wrenched forth a distressed protest. "Isn't this your bedroom furniture?"

"I bought new for the master bedroom up here. I couldn't bear the memories." Loneliness hung between every word. His pained voice strained to a lighthearted cadence. "It sure is great to have you here."

I dropped my bags and stood at the foot of the bed. Rampant emotions distorted Mom's side bureau until it loomed larger than the bed. The top drawer begged to be opened. Its floppy brass handle glinted from a bouncing ray of sun and taunted my curiosity and morbid dread. I hoped and feared it would be the same.

Like a patient agonizing over an encrusted Band-Aid, dreading its removal but wanting to see beneath, I tried to secure a sense of emotional detachment to lessen the blow. I gazed upon the squirrel's-eye view of the lawn. Birds chirped. A distant goose honked. I grasped the cool handle and slid the drawer open.

Her reading glasses, scraps of handwritten notes, and collection of hard candies remained exactly the same as the day she had run an errand and never returned. I dropped to my knees, simultaneously comforted and devastated by this intimate reminder of her presence and absence. I could hardly breathe. It had been almost two years but the sorrow of her passing hit me anew. In the hospital, only Susan had grasped the inevitable. Maybe the doctor had outlined the prognosis. But I hadn't understood, and neither had Chip, that everything the physicians tried had been as futile as a stewardess distributing peanuts before a crash. Even when Mom placed a weak hand on my wrist and asked me to sing "Taps," I sang without knowing, my voice alternating between the harmony and the melody because Susan was too choked up to join in. I still didn't get it when the morphine dulled her green sparkling eyes to glass. And when she released that final breath, my mind rejected the evidence.

I stared at her burgundy velvet rocker, motionless by the window, and finally accepted it. She would never sit there again. Desolation pressed upon my heart forcing me to crumble, urging me to cry.

Loud crescendos of rippling, boisterous laughter echoed down the hallway. I paused at the unexpected mental picture of all three girls crammed inside a tiny bathroom to change.

Get into your suit, a clear thought penetrated my gloom. Mom would have said this. How many times had she gently reminded me to focus on the task at hand? I shut the door and unzipped my bag. Rummaging through its contents I thought of the camping trip with Jenny and how we had discussed the meaning of sacrifice while looking up at the stars. Christie had been right. Back then, none of us had known any real hardships. I had tackled a few over the years, but this was the worst. After reaching my twenties, Mom had become my best friend. Her wisdom frequently guided me. So now it was a paradox of recovery; the one person who could lift me from this suffering was the reason for it.

I hadn't expected her to die so young, at sixty-four, when she'd appeared so healthy for most of my adult life and her mother, Nanny, was thriving at ninety-one. I didn't suppose I'd ever get over it, but I wanted to get through this moment. Their laughter neared my door. I shut my eyes and wiped the tears. Determined to beat back this wave of sorrow, my thoughts returned to camp and all the lessons I'd learned there. Could I act joyful now when I felt the furthest from it? I forced a grin. It felt macabre. Common sense told me this silly attempt fell just short of defeat.

But I didn't want the girls or Chip to know I'd been crying. It would sour the boat ride. And Mom would want me to swim and enjoy the day. Isn't this why she had hidden her fears behind a smile? So I could enjoy what she could not. I pictured her healthy and vibrant as she had been on that first day of camp, her red lipstick smile and auburn halo of sunshine. "Susan and Nancy!" she had announced in her rare tone of authority. "Make the most of this wonderful opportunity!"

This had been her send-off. She had cut the cord and relinquished her claim to the center of my universe for those summers. In many ways, the lake had filled her place. "Thank you for sending me to camp," I said aloud, as if speaking to her, "for encouraging me to try new things so I could learn to conquer fear." This had been the greatest lesson of Wildwood.

I tugged my suit into place, cinched the towel around my waist, and opened the door. The girls traipsed past. Their giddy anticipation for the boat ride affected me. They mounted the carpeted steps, and I followed, experiencing a surge of gratitude and a spontaneous smile.

FORTY

A SWIFT, SIMPLE REMEDY

"STOP." MY DAUGHTER halted in the middle of the stairs. "Turn around," she urged. "There's another way out."

"Where?" her friends objected.

"Follow me." She led us around the narrow hall, past their bedroom and the bathroom. Plush carpet hardened to concrete, and we instinctively paused before the vast emptiness of pitch darkness. KT brushed a switch and illuminated a cavernous basement dissected down the middle by a staircase. Boxes and plastic bins lined the walls from floor to ceiling. A black coffer, taller and wider than any other container, drew me like a magnet.

"That's my old trunk." I spoke as if mesmerized. Deep gouges marred the wood, and its dull brass corners bore dents, but it was unmistakably my old companion.

"It's huge!" KT observed while heading for the stairs. "I'm glad I didn't take that to camp."

"The guys hated carrying it. But it was a great trunk." My eyes narrowed suspiciously, "Until I moved into Whippoorwill as a CT." I ran a finger along its middle seam of cold, hard metal. My nerve endings tingled in response.

"What happened?" Angela asked, sensing another story.

"I'll tell you in the car, if you're still interested."

"This way." KT had opened the door at the top of the stairs. Sunlight streamed in from the garage. "There's a back door!" she exclaimed. "I see the boat!"

Self-consciously, I tightened the towel around my waist as we entered daylight and crossed the lawn. Angela glanced sideways. "You look pretty good in that hot pink bathing suit, Mrs. Taylor."

"Thanks," I responded, both flattered and pragmatic. My companions flung towels over their shoulders, completely at ease in their bikinis. "I suppose lifting weights and walking reduces the humiliation when summer comes," I said, mentally preparing for the moment I'd have to remove the towel.

"That's what you need to do, Angela," the other Katie taunted.

Angela raised her chin, ignoring the jab, but her smile betrayed foxy patience. "Ha!" She reached out, moments later, and lunged into an attack.

Katie tripped on her flip-flops to get away. But Angela had hit her mark. "Ow," Katie pouted, rubbing her arm. "You left a handprint!"

"I did not!" Angela said. She inched near to have a look.

My daughter wedged between them and wrapped her arms about their shoulders. They leaned into her, instantly reconciled, and I laughed at them, feeling light and free from my depths of despair.

At the end of a grassy slope, a slender dock stood nearly underwater. The boat hulked beside it, and we had to step up to climb aboard. "Is the water always this high?" I said.

"It's a record year," Chip stated. "Some districts are already flooded. But our neighborhood sits above all historic marks."

"So, they made the lake to prevent flooding." I frowned at the illogic. "Then everyone builds along the edge of the lake, and their houses flood!"

"You sound like your mother," Chip said. "You think I could have gotten her to move out here?" We traded wistful grins. Chip tossed the line. "I need someone to sit on the bow," he directed, turning the key.

"I will," Angela volunteered. She maneuvered past the steering wheel and settled into a captain's chair bolted to the frame.

Sammi paced the dock awaiting permission. "Come on," Chip invited and he leapt aboard.

"Some fishing boat," I commented dryly, having pictured a stripped-down runabout, not a brand-new powerboat, nearly as nice as the old wooden Chris-Craft of memory. "If you had equipment, we could water-ski."

"Let us not get ahead of ourselves." A fun-loving grin tugged at the corners of his mouth. "Next summer," he promised.

We churned through the channel, slowly navigating shallow water and submerged trees until the passage gave way to open blue. Chip throttled to full speed, and the girls whooped their exhilaration. We skimmed across the surface and pounded against occasional waves. Isolated by the rushing wind and roaring motor, I fell into a meditative trance. The tree-lined shore and cobalt water could have been Glen Lake. I easily imagined a Cabin Day as counselor in charge of three young teenagers. I wanted to protect them, to nurture their blossoming maturity, and to sustain their energetic smiles. Three decades had passed since Robyn's little speech, and I finally understood how she had wanted me to feel.

Chip cut the motor and dropped anchor. We stood in a row along the port side. I appraised the water's depth while the girls appraised each other's tans.

"I am so pale," Katie spoke of her fair, almost ethereal complexion.

My daughter held out her freckled arm to compare. "It's because you've been life-guarding inside."

Angela thrust her olive skin into the mix, and they instantly declared her the winner. "Now, let's jump!" she coaxed.

"Wait. How deep is this?" I asked, "We don't want to touch bottom. Who knows what's down there!"

"I'll check the doohickey." Chip cupped a minicomputer screen against the sun's glare. "Ten feet," he said.

"Deep enough," I decided, assessing the small pointed waves. "But let's jump shallow," I warned. "You know, a racing dive or a lifesaving jump." Both Katies nodded, being lifeguards, but Angela looked puzzled.

"Jump with your arms and legs out wide," KT translated.

"Let's go on three," I said.

Angela's deep brown eyes penetrated mine, narrowing skeptically. "You aren't one of those who say it then don't do it?"

"No, I will," I promised, feeling like a kid back in high school. I never could resist this sort of dare.

"One, two, three!" my daughter shouted. "Go!"

I leapt a split second before them, needing to prove myself adventurous. However, I stuck to the lifesaving jump, designed to keep an eye on a thrashing victim. My arms and legs slowed my speed and held my head above water. Both Katies shot past with pinprick entries and long horizontal glides. We shrieked at the all-encompassing water, despite its warmth. The girls splashed toward me, their smiles sparkling like the water.

"Ha, you did it!" Angela laughed.

"Told you I would. It's like riding a bike," I boasted, but the words rang hollow. If nothing had changed, I would have done a racing dive. I met Chip's gaze where he stood in the boat. Sammi paced the side as if preparing to join us. "What do you think of those clouds?" I treaded water, facing west. The sun blazed above us, but the distant shore had darkened.

"We're fine," he reassured. "That weather is miles away, just rain, no thunder."

The girls performed shallow porpoise dives, slapping their feet like mermaid tails. "Show us that Jaws thing," my daughter said, swimming on her side and crooking an elbow above water to create the facsimile of a shark's fin.

The prospect of a reenactment brought a twinge of real fear. Our tiny heads bobbed in a sea of bumpy water. I no longer felt invincible with an eye to the sky. My focus drifted below, and I envisioned our fleshy, vulnerable legs, kicking invitingly. In mere seconds, a row of teeth could bite them off, leaving us in a murky cloud of blood. Never mind the facts. I knew there were no sharks in Ohio. But I suddenly wanted us to get out of the water.

"The Statue of Liberty!" Katie announced, thrusting her leg in the air. But the lake was too turbulent. She gulped for air as the waves created choppy obstacles between us.

"We should go." I instinctively searched the sky for sheets of rain and bolts of lightning, though Chip seemed unconcerned. The boat rocked wildly, and the stern roamed freely against the anchor line off the bow. We swam a full circle before catching up to it. Taking turns, we gripped a handle near the motor and climbed over the stern. A blast of warm air whipped our towels, wrapping them around us, and Chip hauled anchor. We dropped to our seats as the motor came to life and the boat scuffed across rough water toward the channel.

The frontal winds moved east, and clouds had settled in by the time we reached the boat slip. A quiet spackle of rain dotted the boat cover while we tied it off. It spread to a warm, soaking mist as we crossed the yard and entered the kitchen through a sliding-glass door. We headed to the lower level for dry clothes. Upon entering my room I noticed a change had occurred. The chamber was now an impersonal guestroom, an area to move in and out of, no longer a theater of emotion. I dressed quickly then rapped on the girls' door. It swung open, and I noticed a change had occurred in this room as well. It was a mess. Hairbrushes, bottles of lotion, and makeup lined the dresser tops. Towels and suits formed wet piles. Mismatched shoes littered the carpet, and an array of clothing covered the queen-size bed. The girls circled it, discussing which Virginia college T-shirts to wear over their tank tops.

How I wanted to scurry about and straighten up! Instead, I haplessly suggested, "There are hooks in the closet to hang the suits and towels and . . ."

"Mom! We will," KT said.

"I'll go help Chip," I whispered, easing away.

We ate dinner on a red-checked tablecloth in the great room and watched the sky clear through a wall of windows facing the channel. "Chip, you can cook!" I complimented, knowing Mom had done it for him for the past twenty years.

"This has been a blast," KT managed to say through a mouth full of pasta and salad. "Yeah," Angela and Katie mumbled agreeably.

"Oh, you do make an old man's heart pitter-patter," Chip preened.

"Now, before I forget," he said, reaching into an antique desk. "Here's the route to Nanny's house." He presented handwritten directions, precise and detailed from years of professional driving. "Since there are only two seasons here, winter and construction, you will hit road work at the Michigan-Ohio border. It's best to pass through around one o'clock. That requires a departure time of eleven."

"Piece of cake," I said. "Nothing can be worse than the traffic in Virginia."

"I had to write directions for every place your mom went," he said. "Even the mall. She kept a little notebook." His eyes glazed over, recapturing some bittersweet memories. After a while, he added, "She would be proud of you. Though, I'm sure your Nanny will have plenty to say about you traveling alone."

"I'm not alone," I rebuffed his warning, smiling at my young comrades.

"You know what I mean," he cautioned and we shared a moment of grim agreement.

THE NEXT DAY, as predicted, two hours of productive speed came to a screeching halt in bumper-to-bumper traffic at the Ohio-Michigan border. KT found the perfect song on the radio. She grinned at the backseat and cranked up the volume. "Do you knooooow, do you knooooow . . ." they sang a heavy monotone, gliding their heads to the hip-hop beat.

When the song ended, I switched to the news. "My brain needs some exercise," I said. They grumbled about it, but three hours of formulaic pounding had cemented my decision.

"I'll find some oldies for you," KT said, perching forward to block my access. She hit the scan button.

A three-second snippet revealed a song I recognized from my son's music collection. "Wait, I like that one."

"There, some oldies!" She folded her arms and leaned into her seat as if she'd worked very hard to please me.

"It's from last summer!" I disagreed.

"That's old. And we are sick of it." She glanced into the backseat, trying not to giggle. "Right?"

I groaned at her impertinence, now feeling completely entitled to take control. "I can't listen to any more of those depressing lyrics in the songs you pick. You girls like being called whores?"

"We just like the music," Angela said. "We don't listen to the words."

"Oh, yeah," I said, "then why do you sing along?"

"Silence is better than the news," my daughter frowned, turning it off.

"Mrs. Taylor," Angela said after a long spell of inching along, listening to traffic through the open windows. "We don't mind you talking. You could tell us about your CT trip."

My daughter shifted backwards. Squeezing her head between the window and the headrest, she whispered, "Suck-up!"

Angela laughed, "I'm serious!"

"And your trunk," Katie prompted from behind me.

I felt warmed by their encouragement and realistic about my tactics. I had left them little choice, unless they wanted to sleep, because their collection of fashion magazines had made them carsick. "After my freshman orientation at I.U.," I said, "my trunk and duffel were moved to Whippoorwill. Whitecap was empty. It would never again hold campers or CTs."

"That's sad," Angela said.

"It was," I agreed. "But I liked the campers in Whippoorwill. They surprised me with their independent ideas. Then, after a few days, we left for the CT Trip."

"I wonder where I'd be going if I were a CT this year," KT said. Her question unsettled me. I sought her expression, to gain the measure of her longing. Then she smiled and asked, "Where did you go, Mom?"

"To the Porcupine Mountains," I sighed, picturing lush woods and protected miles of isolated footpaths. "In the Upper Peninsula, nearly to the Wisconsin border. We hiked for four days and carried everything we would need on our backs. No frills, no makeup, no multiple changes of clothing, and some pretty bad food."

FORTY-ONE

LOADED UP, AND MOVING OUT

"Now it weighs a ton!" I whispered to Christie after Robyn had distributed some necessary supplies among our backpacks. The weight crushed my shoulders, despite padded straps. Thanks to the guys' camp, everyone carried a high-tech sleeping bag, a metal plate, one fork, some mysterious items that would piece together for our food and shelter, plus our clothes and canteen. We assembled near the trailhead, in a dirt lot beside the van.

"Thaddeus says we'll get used to it," Christie whispered, trusting as a lamb.

I glanced at our driver, soon to be our guide. Supposedly we needed his expertise. Allegedly, he'd explored every lake, river, and piece of land in Michigan. But ten hours in a cramped van plus an overnight at the ranger's station had not made him any less mysterious or any more trustworthy in my estimation. I didn't think we needed him, nor did I care to follow his advice, as rarely as he deigned to offer it.

"Fasten your belt," Nancy said, pointing to the knotted masses on both sides of my pack. "It will take the pressure off your shoulders." Testing her fit, she jumped up and down. Apart from the dangling cook pot, her equipment barely moved. "The tighter you have it the better. But . . . you have to be able to breathe!" she self-critiqued, upon struggling to laugh and exhale at the same time.

I untangled the belt and fastened it around my waist. The pack hiked up. The shoulder straps floated near my chin. "Ah, that's nice," I said, as the circulation returned to my neck.

My shadow revealed a monstrous presence looming over my head.
Nancy tried to shove it down. "There's a problem," she said. "You have to
wear the belt across your hips, not your waist. You'll kill your back with
it up so high."

I assessed the status quo. Not that I didn't trust her, but the technique
ran contrary to my idea of comfort. Seeing how everyone else wore it
the same, I gave in and lowered the belt until it squeezed my hip bones.

"That looks better," Christie said.

"Does it feel better?" Nancy asked.

"Yeah," I lied. Not only did the contraption ride heavily on my shoulders, it also cut into my hips.

"Listen up," Robyn boomed. "Everyone gets one bag of Gorp. It will
be your lunch. But it's not just today's lunch, it is four days' worth."

"Yum," Christie said, taking the mix of M&M's, raisins, and peanuts.

"Make it last," Robyn cautioned, doling out the plastic bags. "We're
doing between six and eight miles a day over rough terrain, prepping
for breakfast and supper only." She glanced at Thaddeus, checking to
see if he wanted to add anything. He stood mute. His blue nylon pack
morphed sleekly against his rugged body.

I stashed my Gorp and decided six miles wouldn't be too awful.
During the school year I frequently walked home to clear my head. I
could easily cover a rambling course of 3.4 miles through neighborhoods
in an hour, even carrying a book or two. Twice as long seemed a reason-
able allotment for this. Maybe a bit longer with rest stops, of which I
hoped to have many.

We entered the woods single file on a well-marked trail. I placed my
mind in limbo, buoyed by a two-hour goal and the need to maintain
my interval in line. Our bright orange packs bobbed like safety vests
in a sea of green. Black squirrels, small and strange compared to the
plump brown ones further south, scampered in and out of shadow, and
around bare trunks to peer at us. Violets splattered the woodsy carpet,
and a recurring breeze parted the leafy canopy to bathe us in cool air
and spotty sunshine.

One by one, we crossed a sturdy footbridge over a small creek, then started to climb. Protruding tree roots cradled the earth in elongated, twisted staircases of pulverized leaves and spongy pine needles. The dry, dusty roots had been rubbed smooth by hikers.

"It's slippery!" Mary relayed from up ahead. We studied her technique as she embraced a youthful tree and pivoted up two sizeable steps. We all wore running shoes with very little traction. The slightest misstep could lead to an ungainly fall backwards. Even Robyn, our experienced trips counselor, wore the footgear of a nimble sprinter rather than a top-heavy hiker. Ounce for ounce I'd wager our thick, cotton tube socks, stretching up to our knees, weighed more than our airy equivalents to ballet slippers.

Tori alone had the sagacity to bring a pair of real hiking boots to camp. When the path doubled back on itself, I counted Thaddeus as the only other exception. His gusseted mountaineering boots and boiled wool socks sprung from the pages of an L.L. Bean catalog. His hiking shorts and collared shirt, both abundantly pocketed, completed his classic Nature Guide outfit. All together it created a mental quandary as my perception of him alternated between a respected expert and an enthusiastic nerd.

While the trail unfolded beneath the placement of my royal-blue Nikes and the jiggling of my thighs, the pack grew heavier and heavier.

"I love to go awandering along the mountain track," Robyn's scratchy voice invaded the peaceful wilderness. "And as I go I love to sing," we drearily joined in, "my knapsack on my back."

"Valdaree, Valderah. Valdaree . . ." Nancy and I sought eye contact through the palisade of trunks. "Valdarah, HA, HA, HA, HA, HA, HA, HA, HA," we pummeled the cheery phrasing into bawls of fake laughter as we had since our days in Sandpiper; though mine now sounded more like howls of pain.

At the end, Lori shouted, "Do your ears hang low?" We belted a unified discord, "Do they wobble to and fro? Can you tie them in a knot, can you tie them in a bow? Can you throw 'em o'er your shoulder like a Continental Soldier? Do your ears hang low?" We stomped our feet and shouted, "Ev-ery-bod-y in the crowd! If you can't sing good! Just sing loud!" and transitioned into, "Dooooo youuuur boobs hang low? Do they wobble to and fro? Can you tie them in a knot? Can you tie them in a bow? Can you throw 'em o'er your shoulder like a double-D boulder? Do your boobs hang low?" We cavorted along the path to show just how low and floppy those boobs might go.

Thaddeus laughed. His deep, unexpected chuckles had an enthralling carnal effect after so many days and hours of hearing only female voices. Instantly, he drew our hilarity to a close, and we hiked in silence. Which suited me fine, because I didn't want to sing anyway.

FORTY-TWO

AN ECHO OF ADVICE

ROBYN CALLED A rest, and I loosened my pack.

"Don't take it off," she said, seeing the straps drift down my arms. "We're not stopping that long."

"I was just giving my shoulders a break." I turned away and mumbled, "Besides, it wouldn't be worth the trouble since we're almost halfway done."

Lori and Cindy broke into their Gorp, placing one morsel at a time into their mouths. "This is the best," Cindy said, displaying an M&M like a crown jewel. Mary and Christie perched along a stump while everyone else found trees to lean against. I crouched in the dirt to stretch my calves.

Thaddeus stood straight as a plank, resting a hand on his hip near a pedometer hooked to his belt. A similar device had allowed me to clock the distance from school to home. I struggled to stand, eager to learn the outcome of our efforts and to have my calculations validated. "How far have we gone?" I asked, stumbling toward him.

He studied the numbers while reaching for his canteen. Silently and deliberately he unscrewed the metal cap to gorge on a swill. After a long swallow, he whispered, "One point two."

"One point two?" I repeated.

"And it's taken us just over an hour," Tori said, checking her watch.

I blinked back the horror. My pack enlivened into a deadly parasite screwing tentacles into my muscles and boring into my bones. "Barely a mile?" I gasped, my face turning hot. "At this rate we'll be hiking for another five hours!"

"Yes," he replied. His dark eyes appraised me, chilly and indifferent.

I slumped away from the group, hiding behind a large tree, thinking I would never make it through the first day. Frustration welled in my chest, and tears pooled in my eyes.

Nancy eased beside me, thoughtfully concerned. We stared at each other, and I blinked away the evidence of my distress. I thought she would speak. She opened her mouth to speak, then closed it.

"What?" I prodded.

"You said something once that I still remember."

A skeptical grunt escaped from my throat. "I said something worth remembering?"

"Sure, it bugged me at the time," she said. My eyebrows raised in question. "It was that Capture the Flag game, in the river, with the leeches. You said, 'If you don't care about a thing, why try? And if you do care, why not put everything into it?'" She waited for me to recollect.

"I care about this trip," I argued, blind to the responsibility of my words but mindful of others within hearing range. I quickly lowered my voice and seethed, "But I can't do it."

"We're all struggling."

I hung my head. Of course everyone shared the same lot. But none of them had plunged into self-pity. Their peppery banter from the other side of my tree proved it.

"Just in case you can't 'put everything into it,' here's a reason to try harder."

I stared at her.

"For growth," she whispered.

"For growth," I echoed, trying to fathom her reasoning.

"We don't grow by doing things that come easy. Growth happens when things are difficult." A bright encouraging smile lit her face. "We're going to have so much fun. If you feel bogged down, all you have to do is look up for strength."

"Okay," I played along. The confused pattern of overhead leaves wasn't a bit like the endless, beautiful lake where I had reached out and found a comforting presence. I'd never be able to tap into that newfound strength here, amid this smothering tangle of woods. Besides, I wasn't afraid. I was in pain. "I'll have fun when we're done," I decided.

"Why be in a hurry to get it over with?"

"Because my back hurts."

"We'll get used to it." She raised her chin.

"Ya think?" I sneered.

"Yeah." She gave a rueful laugh. "And you can't quit this one, like high school."

"Hey, I graduated. I completed all the required courses."

"But not the final year."

"No," I agreed. "I won't have a senior year."

"And that's the hardest part!" She added more lightly, "At least that's what I hear. I'm psyched to be a senior, you know, but at the same time I'm sure it will be boring. There is nothing left to look forward to except getting out. All the cool guys have graduated. Still, I'm going to find a way to make it fun."

Cindy plodded toward us. "Who wants my raisins?" She held out a palm of black dots.

"Not after you've had your fingers all over them!" Nancy said. She tugged me into the group, deliberately bumping Cindy's shoulder.

"Don't tangle with me, Roman," Cindy said.

Nancy jutted a hip against her pack.

"Okay, now you've done it," Cindy said, tossing a raisin into her face.

Nancy blinked. One after the other pelted her nose, eyes, and cheeks. "Cut it out!" she gushed through rippling laughter, ducking for cover.

"Someone has to loan me their toothbrush," Susie lamented, rubbing a stick against her front teeth. "I can't go five days without brushing!"

"Don't blame us because you forgot it," Tori said.

"I'll share," Christie said. "But we brought soap, right?"

"Biodegradable soap and shampoo," Robyn announced. "But not enough to lather in it," she huffed as a precaution.

I stared at Thaddeus, wishing I could go back in time and redo my reaction to be more like Cindy or Nancy. He hooked his canteen in his belt and sized up our circle, no doubt labeling me the most troublesome.

He swung around and continued on the path. "Let's go!" Robyn boomed, waving us along.

"The Cannibal KING with the big nose RING!" Mary chanted. Her outburst shattered an intolerable spell of silence. We grumbled against her choice but joined in, no longer caring how many birds or squirrels we frightened, if anyone heard us, or what Thaddeus thought. In essence, we owned the forest. This impression would last for the entire trip. Not a single hiker or park ranger would cross our path.

"Let's sing, 'You Can't Get to Heaven,'" Susie said. Her tentative nature prevented an autocratic outburst.

"You can't ask," Mary said.

This wasn't a rule. But as soon as she said it, it sure felt like one. Camp songs were irrational. They required no mental energy and only an expansion of the diaphragm. Asking permission put the matter up for choice, and choosing required thinking. Thinking required energy. Energy produced a rational decision, and rational decisions prohibited singing camp songs. Thus, asking became a means of prevention. The coarse melody had to burst forth spontaneously, driven by one person's demand and the group's robotic response from summers of conditioning. I nodded at Mary's wisdom. It made sense. Rather than asking my friends to sing "Taps," as I had on that camping trip with Jenny, I should have just sung it.

"In a cabin in the woods!" Christie belted out, and we joined in like trained monkeys. "A little old man by the window stood! Saw a rabbit hopping by! Knocking on my door! 'Help me, help me, HELP!' he cried. 'Fore the hunter shoots me dead! Come along and live with me! Oh how happy we will be!"

We sang it again, quieting the first phrase to a hand signal. By the eighth round we were humming a pantomime of gestures. When it ended, a ceremonious pause loomed above our meandering line. Would Susie stepup?

"Oh, you can't get to heaven," she shouted in a high falsetto.

"Oh you can't get to heaven," we echoed.

"In a rocking chair!" she sang, wearing a bemused smile of requited power.

"In a rocking chair," we sang.

"'Cause the gosh darn thing . . . won't go nowhere . . .'"

"Ohhhhh, you can't get to heaven in a rocking chair," we reprised. "'Cause the gosh darn thing won't go nowhere. I ain't a gonna grieve my Lord no more!"

We sang all the traditional verses, then ad-libbed a few more. I hollered, "Oh, you can't get to heaven . . . in my back pack."

"In my back pack," they answered.

"If you add more weight . . . My back will crack!"

"MY BACK WILL CRACK!" they wailed to the treetops, and I gloated to have found an acceptable expression of agony.

Christie and Lori exchanged hurried whispers then alighted into a duet. "Oh you can't get to heaven . . . In Susie's mouth."

"Hey!" Susie flared.

"In Susie's mouth!" we stormed.

"'Cause the gosh darn thing . . . will gross you out!"

"Hey, hey!" Susie sputtered, marching forward to punch Lori in the arm.

"Will gross you out . . ." we withered away.

"All right! All right!" Lori said. "We'll stop."

Susie had reached the point where despair outweighed her insecurities. Otherwise, she would have anxiously replied, "That's not nice," or, "Cut it out."

My misery now occupied the realm of resignation. My shoulders had gone completely numb. When we paused for another break, I didn't ask how far. Thaddeus didn't offer, and I didn't want to know. I retrieved my bag of Gorp and leaned against a tree, stretching my neck from side to side. Too soon, our column resumed its winding, narrow trek. I ate one M&M at a time, holding the candy shell on my tongue until the bumpy letters wore off and warm chocolate eased out the circular edges. Then, I smashed it against the roof of my mouth.

FORTY-THREE

A REVELATION OF FUTILITY

THE PATH UNFOLDED to level ground, offered a teasing descent here and there, then reestablished its excruciating uphill rise. After we'd climbed above the deciduous tree line, into a forest of white pines, the highest peak still eluded us. We navigated sharp rocks beneath spindly branches and a beating sun. Sweat dripped from our temples.

"How old do you think Thaddeus is?" Tori hung back to ask me. I squinted ahead, hoping he hadn't heard. "Oh, he's too far away," she dismissed my concern.

The adults in camp had never interested me, mainly because the line of authority separating us was firmly established in my mind. But she had asked, and I was bored. I searched his face for a clue. His tanned skin bore creases at his eyes and brow when he frowned, as he did just then, stepping off the path to wait for the end of the line.

"Maybe forty," I ventured.

Tori guffawed, "Oh, no. He's got to be in his late twenties. He's just weathered from spending winters in Siberia. "

I clamped my mouth shut, wishing Tori would do the same because we were about to catch up to him. I hurried the pace and raised my chin, not wishing to be the brunt of any stories carried back to the boys' camp.

My foot hit a rock embedded in the path. I careened forward, splintering into an abrupt dissection of mind and body. My mind held upright in irksome disbelief while my body spilled forward. Knees skidded across the carpet of pine needles, scraping over tree roots. Palms grated and crunched against tiny rocks. The pack's weight slammed down upon me, sending my stomach to the ground and my chin against a rock.

I laid facedown in the dirt for an extraordinary length of time. Or so it seemed. In reality, I scrambled forward, clumsily gaining my stride with the help of a firm grip upon my forearm. The fall replayed in my head as I brooded over stinging palms and knees. Gradually, sharp prickles of pain melted to warm surface burns, and I noticed Thaddeus standing beside me on the up side of the path.

"It drops off," he said, pointing into a row of brambles on the down side.

"Oh," I replied, not really understanding because I had just registered his hold on my arm. I wanted to shrink into the woods.

He watched as my breathing slowed. I gazed ahead, where Tori stood waiting. When I took a step he removed his grip. I plowed along the trail, lifting my thighs.

"Come see this." Robyn called, "We've reached the summit. Keep single file!"

A stone wall cantilevered over the edge like the turret of a castle. We gained a panoramic view of vertical crags, rolling forests, and sparkling patches of blue. "This is the highest point between the Mississippi River and the Appalachian Range," Robyn said.

I glimpsed the edge of the path we'd just covered. The ground fell into nothingness. "Whoa," I whispered, feeling faint.

"Nice save," Tori said, smiling at Thaddeus. He shrugged, and took a gulp from his canteen. "That was close," Sarah said, rubbing my arm. "And I thought you only tripped on boardwalks," Nancy teased.

"I'm such a klutz," I said, "I'll trip on anything."

"Same as those hippies at Innistock," Lori said.

"I hope not!" Robyn admonished.

"No!" I blurted, denying any commonality to the derelict campers overrunning Deena-hahna's land. We'd heard they dropped acid, guys and girls shared beds, and they nearly starved from trying to grow their own food. They also engaged in Roman-style orgies and their lodge

MEMORY LAKE

OUR WILD GALLOP cease...
barricade of log seating
The pack's slippery
Orange backpack...
mine sprawled

 "You can

the belt.

rose l...

absenc...

infirmity!

across the U.P. ...

the van.

 Tori laughed uproariou...
 Cindy wandered around the...
and Sarah, trying to unhook her b...
 "Hold still," Robyn said. "Mine just a...
the catch, and Thaddeus lifted the pack fro...
us with his act of chivalry.
 "Woman thou art loose!" we hollered. Cindy he...
taking springy steps around the clearing. Over the next ...
repeated this irreverent cry at the slightest inducement, gainin...
satisfaction from its double meaning. Not only was it highly applicabl...
the moment, but it allowed us to mock scripture that unfairly attributed
travails and whoredom to our fair sex.

showcased a hooka for transcendental ceremonial
school exploits could top this.
 "Innistock has been shut down," Robyn said. "...
We just found out."
 "Maybe we can get the land back." Nanc...
expectantly.
 "It's tied up in litigation," Robyn said. "...
maybe . . ."
 "We should get it," Christie stated, as if the feat only...
to the lost and found. She nodded at Nancy, alluding to...
ties to the old camp.
 "The guys' camp is safe for now," Robyn said, looking to...
He nodded, giving credence to her remark. Then he squint...
the sun and pointed to a distant puddle of blue, saying, "Mirr...
 "We camp there tomorrow night," Robyn interpreted.
Thaddeus hooked his canteen and led us away from the peak...
the main trail. The air cooled, the ground flattened, and a thick
forest closeted around us.
 "He's a wiry fella but he's fast and strong," Tori announced for...
benefit. "Just my type."
 "Tori!" I balked at her audacity. I couldn't believe she considered hi...
eligible let alone desirable. Obviously, the line had disappeared for her, but
it hadn't even blurred for me. And the more I learned about the other side
the less I wanted to cross it. Two nights before, my sister had cornered me
outside the Murphy. She had come from the upstairs office. Lou Ellen and
Robyn had scolded her for going bar hopping with Joanna on her day off.
 "You went bar hopping?" I had been shocked by her daring. Apparently
my good sister was not so angelic Up-North. The drinking age in Michigan
was still eighteen so her actions were not illegal. But according to Lou Ellen,
she and Joanna had put their safety and the camp's reputation at risk.
 "I want to chuck it all in and go home," Susan had moaned.
 "Oh, it can't be so bad," I had said, fearing she still had the power to
leave and take me with her. Her bouts of homesickness over the y...

FORTY-FIVE

REFLECTIONS AROUND THE FLAMES

WE POSITIONED FLAT rocks in the smoldering fire for trivets. They hissed from the extreme heat as their encapsulated moisture evaporated into steam.

"This pot needs to boil a long time," Susie said, inching forward, trying not to spill it.

"Wait," Lori said. "Not yet. The rock could explode."

"A rock explode?" Susie shot her a skeptical glance.

"I've seen 'em," Nancy said. "They fly off in pieces."

"The trip to Sandy Point!" Lori, Nancy, Mary, Robyn, and Cindy spoke as veteran comrades, citing one of the many trips the rest of us had declined. I wished I had gone along so I could belong to their memory. But the canoe trip loomed large, providing a dose of reality. Who knew what other catastrophes had occurred! It was tough to find out because they always relegated them to the colorful background of a humorous anecdote; as if the incorrect map, the unexpected storm, and swarms of mosquitoes were all part of the fun. It seemed a diabolical ploy to lure unsuspecting campers on at least one trip to round out their summer experience. Otherwise, who would ever go along? The alternative, which meant they actually enjoyed it, was beyond my belief.

"Okay," Susie gave in, resting the pot on the ground. "But no one kick dirt into it."

"We're having Chicken-à-la-king and raspberry cobbler," Robyn enticed, shaking a few shining packages of freeze-dried food.

"Yummy!" Tori gushed, clenching her back teeth through refined insincerity.

"Where's the latrine?" Cindy inquired.

Robyn laughed at the implication. "It won't be that bad!"

Nancy pointed. "Over behind that thicket."

"Okey-dokey!" Cindy speed-walked into the woods.

Our eyes followed her, taking careful notice for future reference. "Everyone look for a roll of TP on a forked stick," Nancy said. "There's a limb to grab and sway back, if you want. Scatter a layer of dirt after you use it."

"Last person in the morning has to carry the shovel," Lori added.

I perked up. This rule could determine the weight of my pack for days to come!

"So this is greasy, grimy, gopher guts," Tori scoffed, after we'd eaten the main course and started on the dessert. She raised a spoonful of raspberry cobbler, peppered in soot, and let it plop on her tin plate.

"I'll eat it," Sarah offered, reaching out. They stretched toward each other, struggling to make a connection and groaning against stiffening muscles. The sun had fallen behind the trees, dimming the woods beyond our circle of fire.

"Good plan." Robyn nodded her approval. "Leftovers will attract bears."

"Bears!" Susie choked.

I glanced at our flimsy nylon tents, then Mary. She had not been kidding!

"We'll hang our supplies from those branches." Thaddeus pointed overhead.

"Include everything, even chewing gum," Robyn said. "Unless you want to wake up and find your pack torn to shreds, or missing."

"Missing," I reconsidered, seeing a way out of the trip's future agonies.

"If you hear some strange noises, don't start messing around with the flaps to get a look," Robyn said. She snickered to herself as if this had happened on a previous CT trip. "Use the latrine before bed," she added.

"Oooh." Lori's eyes widened as she gazed into the shadowy woods. "A park ranger told me the last campers to visit here never returned to their van."

"You're not spooking me," Susie said. "I'm going to sleep like a baby."

"Me, too," I said, rubbing my shoulders. "I'm going to wake up every hour and cry."

"That's practically what I did my first night at camp," Christie whispered to the blazing fire, not meeting any of our stares. "I hadn't made any friends. I wondered how my mom could do this to me. To bring me all the way up here, to this strange place, then leave me for three weeks. I fretted and worried all night. The next morning after everyone had left for the flagpole I sat on the edge of my bed and simply said to myself, 'Christie, you can sit here and feel sorry for yourself, or you can make the best of it.'" A tight, determined grin tugged at the corners of her mouth. "And so I did."

Nancy's eyes met mine from across the flames. We'd never experienced Christie's sense of abandonment. From the first, we'd had each other. Our friendship had fanned out over the years, turning wide and encompassing toward others, yet it remained strong and familiar when life drew us near.

"Still," Lori said, "it's a whole lot easier to make friends here than back home. No one ever teases me about being flat-chested."

"You tease yourself," Nancy said. Thaddeus turned his head, as if trying not to laugh.

"You guys played so many tricks on me last year," Susie accused.

I gazed at the smoldering coals, wishing I had stood up for her more often.

"But some were kind of funny, and liberating." She fluffed the curls at the nape of her neck.

I studied her relaxed manner and realized our insecure camper from Sunblazer had grown some confidence.

"Not all of us played tricks on you," Christie said.

"Yeah," Sarah agreed.

"Just remember this when you have campers of your own next year," Robyn concluded.

My thoughts ventured ahead to next summer and hit a snag. Not because of the fatalistic doom I'd experienced on the summit, but from the exhilarating prospect of college. The thrill of a fresh start so inflated my mood I couldn't imagine ever saying good-bye to these friends. Wouldn't they always be around, offering caring support, staying exactly the same until we met again?

"There are dishes to scrub!" Robyn barked. She stifled a yawn halfway into her sentence.

The nine of us took ourselves to task. We had become too sedate and comfortable. Armed with a small bottle of soap, we gathered the cook pots, collected our individual tins, and headed for the lake. The utensils cleaned easily enough but blackened soot and crusty food clung to the pots. We took turns scouring with sand and soap, even using the knife and our fingers to pick away the burnt food. When our hands were dirtier than the pots, Mary said, "That's as good as it gets." She issued us a few drops of soap. We rubbed away the surface grime, picked some grunge from under our nails, then returned to the campsite.

We fed more logs to the fire and illumined the night. Thaddeus spread a tarp in the middle of the clearing and Robyn deposited numerous packets of freeze-dried food. "No peeking!" she snapped when we tried to read their generic imprinted labels. "Get your Gorp, and anything else that smells like food, even soap and toothpaste."

"I'm glad you put our names on the bags," Christie said, as the pile grew.

Thaddeus cinched the tarp and hurled the opposite end of the rope over a branch. He yanked the bundle into the air and tied it off. It dangled like a giant hornet's nest about twelve feet above us.

He and Robyn settled into their individual tents near the fire pit. The rest of us milled about and tripled up.

"Schmidty, sleep here with Lori and me," Christie said.

"I'll take the middle," I volunteered.

"I'm not taking the middle," Nancy laughed from the opposite side of the clearing, sizing up Cindy and Mary's layout. "You two flop around like fish out of water!"

"Roman, you snore," Cindy teased.

"I think I do," Mary said. "At least that's what my campers tell me."

"Sarah, you want the outside?" Susie offered through a sleepy yawn. Tori had already crawled inside. Ever cognizant of my friends' familiar presence, they transformed the campsite into a cozy place, safe as our cabin. As their voices turned to whispers, I squeezed between Christie and Lori and rumpled my sweatshirt for a pillow. The ground felt soft enough, mainly because my body had grown too tired to care. We zipped shut. Our shoulders touched, and the fire's crackling embers soothed us to sleep.

A light melody of songbirds penetrated abstract dreams and induced a gradual awareness of my surroundings. Christie's deep morning voice croaked in my ear, "I heard bears last night." I opened my eyes and blinked away some confusion about the bright orange nylon stretching over our heads. I am camping, I congratulated myself, inhaling deeply of the sluggish morning air tainted by the pungent scent of a newly kindled campfire.

"I slept like the dead," Lori said, trying to stretch.

"Wait." I scooted backward, inching out the opening to give them space to move around. I rubbed my eyes awake, slumped into a stagger, and headed for the latrine. When I returned, Christie and Lori had already rolled their sleeping bags. An undercurrent of impatience ran beneath the bustling activity. The tents went down, and we distributed their parts among our packs. Robyn had a pot of oatmeal ready, and she doled out generous spoonfuls while cautioning us to ration the small packages of brown sugar and raisins.

After rinsing our tins and giving our hands and faces a quick splash, we attempted to clean the pot. Since it required a good soak, and we hadn't the time, we left it crusty, shook away the water, and returned to the site. Our packs loomed large from their resting places against the perimeter of trees. The skin along my shoulders hurt to the touch, and every muscle in my back and neck had stiffened through the night. I wanted to run away like a newly broken horse, shying from the saddle.

"I got mine on by myself," Susie crowed triumphantly because Tori had just received help from Thaddeus.

"Oooh," Tori said, laying a finger on Susie's collar bone, "let me touch you!"

"Does anyone else need help?" Robyn wiggled into her straps. Her intense, roving stare spurred us on.

Bristling from her offer, I shouldered my weight, gaining courage from the others as we shared stoic, cheery smiles. I adjusted my straps into new grooves across my skin and wondered why it didn't feel lighter. I desperately hoped the burning sensation would fade once my feet started moving.

We picked up the trail on the opposite side of the clearing and resumed our lineup. A passing hiker would never guess we had just camped there. We had burned all the firewood, stashed the garbage in our packs, and doused the pit to eliminate any chance of sparking an underground root.

"Who's got the shovel?" Nancy called from up ahead.

"I do," Susie faintly replied.

FORTY-SIX

A NATURAL WONDER

TWO DAYS AND nights passed comparatively similar to the first except my tormented self-analysis quieted to a slow-motion drone, and one dull thought remained: follow the feet in front. I had become a mindless pack mule. I lived in the moment because it was all I could bear. I did not feel up to Robyn's standard, and never would. I wanted to change, but lacked the stamina and mental attitude to handle any more than my pack and one-ninth of the workload. Others besides me performed beyond their share to accommodate Robyn and Thaddeus and to improve the campsite. Increasingly, I did not feel equal to them either.

On the fourth day, after long hours of hiking and short evenings of unappetizing meals, a miracle occurred. The trail still unfolded beneath my plodding royal-blue Nikes, but my thighs did not jiggle. They rippled from toned, defined muscles.

"We are lean and mean!" Christie cheered.

"We are lean and mean," we repeated, loving the truth of it.

Suddenly everything improved. Especially the scenery. Most of our hiking had occurred inside the confining corridors of tightly knit trees. Now the sky opened, and we skirted the edge of a lazy river. When the sun reached its zenith, we diverged from the main body and ascended beside a bubbling tributary.

Conditioned to climbing, we balanced our packs and conquered the rocky passage like mountain goats. About an hour into it, Thaddeus halted for lunch. Few of us had any Gorp left. Cindy lamented wasting so many raisins on Nancy. Lori wished she hadn't dropped peanuts for the squirrels. I wished I hadn't eaten every last M&M.

Thaddeus called a halt anyway. He sat on a boulder beside the lively stream and eulogized, "Thousands of years ago, rock-slides, floods, and droughts forced the river to travel underground. A vast network of tributaries was formed, which in turn created caves and tunnels. Many of these caves are active copper mines."

We had gathered around, finding rocks to sit on and trees to lean against. We were a polite bunch, automatically intrigued and ready to listen because Thaddeus had never put so many words together at one time. I noted his glaring lack of accent and decided that even if he had come from Russia, as Tori insisted, he'd definitely grown up American.

His jet-black eyes focused upriver where sheets of water spilled over giant slabs of rock. "This particular stretch once flowed over a tunnel. From ages of heavy rains the water pressed its monumental force and caused it to collapse. These sandstone boulders are a by-product of the collapse and the tunnel opening is now in the middle of a cliff. Water pours over it, creating a waterfall."

"A waterfall!" we repeated as the distant roar made sense, along with the tumbling rapids.

"Can we see it?" a few of us asked.

"Better than that. We're camping here," Robyn said. "There's a site along the bank."

"It's so early!" I realized, speaking to my friends. We had covered half our regular distance.

"Tomorrow we reach the van," Thaddeus said. "This is our last night. You can drop your packs and take a swim." He got to his feet and ventured a reclusive path upriver.

We awaited Robyn's direction since she hadn't made a move to follow. "This way." She waved us on a different path. We jostled after in a flurry of silent enthusiasm, glancing at each other through restrained grins as if the whole plan would unravel if we showed too much excitement. We jogged only a short distance before the ground leveled out. A rock-lined fire pit resided near two picnic tables. This alone would have been a delicacy, to sit on a flat surface. But also having a chance to swim proved luxurious. On our second night we had reached Mirror Lake and bathed in a body of water ten times the size of Crooked Lake. Its firm bottom and clear water, free of minnows and muck, had been refreshing. The next day we had camped beside a rivulet so small we could barely wash our hands, faces, and utensils. Now we felt the accumulation of grime and could see it on our clothes.

We shed our packs, kicked aside shoes and socks, and stepped over rocks and sticks to aim for the sound of rushing water. When our dusty, blistered feet sank into a carpet of spongy moss, we stood on the brink of a twenty-foot drop into an elliptical pool. Bedrock rose twice that distance into the air to enclose it. And a sparkling ribbon spilled down its length to feed it. The basin overflowed its opposite end, draining across a maze of boulders, becoming the tributary we'd hiked along.

"This is sooo beautiful!" Christie said. We strained to hear above the rushing water.

"Let's jump!" Lori said.

"Is it safe?" Mary wondered.

"If there were hidden logs or rocks, we'd see whirlpools and eddies in the water," Lori said.

"There's a path leading down," I pointed out.

"Let's scale the cliff," Nancy interrupted. Our mouths dropped at this fantastical proposition. Sure enough, a horizontal ledge cut the cliff's midriff. It presented passage if someone wanted to reach the middle of the waterfall. Apparently Nancy did, because she sidestepped the bank to stand on par with this outcrop. We crowded next to her.

"I can see the cave!" Susie called above the din. The waterfall reflected a silvery sheen from the sun except mid-center where a faint, dark shape loomed behind the torrential curtain.

Nancy gripped Cindy and Lori's shoulders to stretch a foot. Sensing our reluctance, she said, "What's the worst that could happen?" Her hazel eyes enticed us. I sized up the narrow shelf, considering it equally treacherous as scaling the roofline of a two-story building. I doubted my willingness to follow until she said, "The price for falling will be a swim."

"Show us how, Roman," Cindy nudged, egging her on.

Facing the rock, Nancy planted both feet on the ledge and pressed her palms against the cliff. She inched along, her chest and cheek grazing the striated layers. At the culmination of each step, she brought her heels together and paused. Halfway there, she turned slightly to peer down at the elliptical pool. Eight, seven, six more steps, and she'd reach the end where the ridge tapered away to nothing from decades of pounding water. She would have to jump through midair and into the thundering flow, relying on faith alone for the cave's hospitable admittance. She craned her head our way and offered a resigned grimace.

I nibbled on my thumbnail from the suspense, smoothing a rough edge that had splintered on my sleeping bag's zipper.

At the water's thundering edge, she reached out with splayed fingers. The force dragged them downward. She inhaled sharply at being caught off balance. Her rib cage expanded beneath her T-shirt, and she aggressively steadied herself. A second later, she kicked a leg and catapulted sideways. The water bent into a million fragmented rainbows, and she disappeared behind it. Five seconds felt like an eternity until her hand poked out and the onslaught shoved it down. We laughed at its absurd presence.

"I'll go!" Lori declared. She duplicated Nancy's technique: crossing the rock face, leaping sideways, and disappearing into the falls.

One by one we ventured out until Mary and I remained. "We can do it," she said. "You go first."

Quite simply, I had grown accustomed to my friends' constant company and now wished to regain it, whatever the price. This alone motivated me from the safe moss to the narrow ledge.

Baked dry from constant sun, the rock solidly assured my toes as I shuffled sideways, touching my entire body against the cliff. My fingertips gripped protrusions, and I focused exclusively on the next hold. Upon reaching the raucous, racing water my feet fused into the rock, and I could not move or breathe. I had expected some sign of the cave, perhaps even a glimmer of my friends' presence inside. Even more so, I had not expected a gap of nothing between the hard rock where I stood and the hidden place I needed to reach.

"I'm coming!" Mary called. "Can you see them?"

Feeling pressured, and irritated, I started to back away. Then a hand darted from the confusing flood, gripped my wrist, and tugged me into the pounding flow. Thankfully, my legs acted independently of my brain. I leapt across nothingness. Liquid slammed solidly upon my head, as if to push me down. My body was drenched in one simultaneous slap and punch of stimulating shock, more powerful than a fire hose. Somehow, both feet found purchase and my toes squished into silted sand. Encouraging hands patted my arms and shoulders as I blindly stumbled. Mary bumped against me. We blinked water and adjusted to the dim interior.

FORTY-SEVEN

MOTHER NATURE'S THEME PARK

THE MAJESTIC WATERFALL served as an enchanted portal into another realm. We may have found Merlin's magical fortress, crossed through Alice's looking glass, or entered a tunnel leading down to a cavern full of gold and silver from a Grimm's fairy tale.

The walls shimmered in a coppery glow. We howled and shouted, but the thundering fall would not allow our voices to be heard. Its jealous volume dominated. We strained our diaphragms to the limit, but we couldn't even hear our own voices. Together, we experienced the strange and frightening isolation of the deaf and mute.

We danced, a circle of midsummer nymphs, weaving a silver cord of connectivity. Our feet skipped over silky golden silt, and we flung luminescent drops from the curtain holding back the outside world. Moisture dripped from the walls, and the back of the cave receded mysteriously. We wondered what might lie beyond the twenty feet or so of visibility, past the pile of rocks and into darkened depths. But none of us wanted to explore. Our interest held to the water. And through each turn of our circle we grew less intimidated by it. We kicked and punched the torrential veil until we had washed dirt from our ankles and grunge from our fingernails. In short spurts, we tackled our T-shirts, watching stains disappear while the fabric stretched hopelessly out of shape.

Eventually, our boldness extended to the pool below. Nancy, Cindy, and Lori hooked arms. They waltzed to the rear of the cave for a running start. The rest of us lined the seeping walls. They dashed by, pushed into the portal, and vanished. We felt a tug at their extraordinary departure, as if the silver cord joining us had grown taut. Fearing it might snap, leaving us alone in this netherworld, we rushed to follow.

Susie, Christie, and I linked arms, never doubting a safe splash down. We only delayed to give the others a chance to clear out below. When it seemed enough time had lapsed, Christie sprang forward. Her unexpected strength dragged us along. We squeezed our eyes shut, splashed through the deluge, and flew into the air, sprawling into a clumsy freefall. I saw the blinding sun for a few seconds before Susie landed on top and pushed me into liquid darkness. It stung on impact, and the cool submersion rendered me blind. I blew bubbles out my nose and pushed Susie away while trying to prevent my T-shirt from rising up and suffocating me.

"What a riot!" Susie exclaimed. I bobbed for air and flinched at the unexpected sound of human voices. We swam for the bank. As if on cue, Sarah, Tori, and Mary hovered overhead performing a flying kick-line, leaving a geyser in their wake.

We climbed the bank, dotted in tiny white flowers, and rushed to repeat the experience. The cliff's treacherous ledge faded to splendid amity. The cave became our secret bastion and the waterfall its guardian. We sprinted from it, hurtling into an unfathomable depth to produce cannonballs, one-knee tucks, and spreadeagles. Always, we returned to its coppery glow, mineral dampness, and jeweled facets of inner light.

"You're missing the best part," Robyn shouted from the woods. We sat along the bank wringing water from our shirts preparing for another launch. "Thaddeus went off to read his book, so you'll have privacy to change into your suits." We noticed she had changed into hers.

Since our clothing had stretched into cumbersome baggage, we trekked to the campsite. Pine needles and dirt clung to our feet as we ran. We flung our wet clothes across tree limbs then stretched stiff nylon over our cool, damp flesh. Tugging and adjusting along the way, we scurried back to the falls like little kids at an amusement park.

Everyone urged Robyn to experience the cave with us. They enjoyed her company while I tried not to think of her as an authoritative outsider. When she stepped into the cave, my reticence seemed justified as she severed that magical cord stringing us together by taking charge of who would jump next, and when. Our perfectly seamless necklace now had loose ends and needed a clasp to repair it. Robyn was this clasp; the new focal point to our otherwise plain and balanced arrangement.

She executed a perfect forward-one-and-a-half-somersault-pike through the waterfall, then sat along the bank under the afternoon sun and indulged our antics in the manner of a mother of nine at a playground. Christie performed flips, the only other precision diver among us, while the rest of us reverted to silly jumps.

When we had created every possible combination among the nine of us, Robyn hollered, "Enough jumping! Time for something new!"

We swam toward her. A devious grin plumped her cheeks. She hiked a short, muscular leg over the basin's lip and sat upon a watery slab. Maintaining a stiff back, straight legs, and toes pointed downstream, she raised her arms. "Ta da!" she sang, catching the current. She slipped away beneath lush trees and a sunny sky. "Come on!" she commanded over her shoulder.

We watched her plummet harmlessly, shrinking smaller and more distant until the river hooked left and she passed from sight.

"Holy smokes!" Lori exclaimed.

We lined up. When my turn came, I gripped the edge of the boulder. Liquid slithered beneath me like a magic carpet readying for flight. I let go, and the rivulet propelled me fast enough to be thrilled but slow enough to stop, if I wanted.

But I didn't want to. A stunned smile had plastered itself to my face. It seemed nothing could be better than the cave. In truth, I was sad to leave it behind; safe as childhood itself. But this wildly unpredictable ride satiated my thirst for adventure as our trail of speeding bodies gained velocity.

Just ahead, three slabs merged for a hairpin turn. My insides tensed for the inevitable sharp edge and uneven split. I dragged my fingers, trying to slow my speed, envisioning cuts and bruises. But hundreds of years of running water had polished and tamed every edge.

I focused on Christie's trailing blonde hair, finally understanding the wisdom of poets and philosophers who had likened life to a river. The rocks beneath were flawed as the earth, and the current sustaining us above was perfect as the heavens. For the moment, we were in heaven. But usually our life was in the river, bouncing over obstacles, moving slow then fast, always changing, facing fear at every turn, with faith determining our willingness to stay.

Around the fourth hairpin turn, the pace quickened. Cries of gaiety flew from the bank as if spectators lined the shore, cheering us on. I skimmed down a vertical slide and plopped beside Christie in the deep, subdued river.

Our feet touched small pebbles, and we waded for shore in the waist-high water, encircled by little whirlpools of our own making. Tori, Mary, then Susie splashed down behind us.

"Wasn't that cool?" Lori said. She sat in the sun, waiting for us to hike back. "You look good like this," she said, as we mounted the embankment.

"Who?" I asked.

"You," she said, "from four days without mascara."

"Yeah, right!" I huffed, admiring her freckled complexion and thick lashes sparkling like spun gold. I reached up and touched my own. "They do feel thicker."

"I'm telling you," she remarked, hooking her arm in mine to climb the steep trail. "You should try going without when we get back."

"Maybe less, but never none," I decided aloud.

"Speaking of getting back . . ." Christie leaned near and whispered intensely. "Can you believe we're nearly finished with our CT trip?" She took my other arm.

"I've had a really good time," I said, shocked by my own sincerity.

"I want to be the gymnastics counselor next summer," Christie stated.

"I want to be the canoeing counselor," Lori said. "If Nancy is the Trips Counselor we can take trips together."

"Aren't you scared of getting lost?" I balked at her willingness to assume such responsibility.

"Nope," she replied. "The key is not to get afraid. Like my granny always says . . ."

Christie and I sought eye contact, anticipating a ridiculous bit of lore.

"Animals have instinct, but we can reason. And God is the reason." As if to demonstrate the concept, a squirrel stood terrified in our path. "We're not gonna hurt you," she cajoled. It bolted around the base of a nearby tree.

"It's true," Christie said, her eyes glinting. "If I let my head get filled up with all the things that could go wrong, I'd never do a roundoff back handspring, or a backflip. Instead of giving in to those crazy doubts and fears, I start reasoning that God is taking care of me. I get all calm and relaxed. That's when I do my best stuff."

"So, ignorance is best," I concluded.

"Enlightened ignorance," Christie corrected.

"Get moving, you enlightened water-nymphs!" Tori padded behind us.

"Yeah," Susie piped up. "I want to do this a bunch more times."

FORTY-EIGHT

THE END OF THE TEST

THE SUN DIPPED behind the trees. We had purple lips, goose bumps, and waterlogged fingers. We slogged into our tennis shoes and foraged for firewood, still wearing our damp bathing suits. Thaddeus and Robyn sat at the picnic table while we assumed our routine, taking on the various chores and knowing instinctively whose turn it was to do them. The fire peaked large and bright before settling. The tents went up, we changed into dry clothes, and the food bubbled an aromatic cloud of homey comfort. Our final reconstituted packages of beef stroganoff and apple crisp disappeared in a noisy scrape of metal against metal.

We fell asleep early and woke at dawn, still entranced by the previous day's idyllic quality. After a cold breakfast of grape jelly, spread thinly over smashed pieces of white bread, we loaded up. Having no fire to douse, or dishes to clean, we broke camp in record time.

Thaddeus guided us away from the river and into a maze of foliage. The unmarked trail was little more than a deer path. Foot-long grass, shrubbery, and saplings grew to reclaim it. Our packs had lightened over the days, since most of our supplies had been eaten, but we hardly noticed. No one sang, and few of us spoke. The sun baked our heads for hours while we concentrated on avoiding thorny vines, spiderwebs, and branches.

Midmorning, we crossed a wooded mound, parted some bushes, and landed on the shoulder of a two-lane dirt road. Our trail legs hardly knew how to walk on the groomed surface. Like drunken, giddy fools we swaggered amid the wide-open space, unable to navigate a straight line. We faced possible traffic, though none appeared, and after less than a mile the parking lot came into view.

"There's the van!" Susie pointed. She rushed past, and we sprinted after her, our packs bouncing and shifting. We couldn't shed them fast enough. "Woman thou art loose!" we repeated over and over, heaping them outside the rear door, leaving just enough room for Thaddeus to unlock it.

"Waffles and butter," Tori said, her eyes wide at the prospect. "Pancakes and bacon," Mary added. Robyn had promised us a real breakfast at the Waffle House outside the state park's entrance.

"You have the keys?" Robyn asked Thaddeus, in a tone designed to torment us. He smiled and nodded reassuringly, reaching into one of his many pockets. He rounded the van and turned the locks. We tagged along and flung the doors wide while Thaddeus and Robyn tossed their packs in the back. We threw ours on top and poured into the seats, waving goodbye to the woods as Thaddeus peeled from the parking lot.

We stormed the Waffle House in hiking formation, beelining for the lady's room. We crammed inside a two-stall bath and took turns at the mirror.

"My eyebrows need plucking," Tori observed.

"Mine need mowing!" Susie gasped.

Sarah stuck her head between them. "I have new freckles on my nose."

"Oh, my hair is crazy!" I moaned, trying to run my fingers through it like a comb.

"It feels great to sit and pee," Mary said from inside the stall.

"I have pine needles in my unders," Cindy said from the other.

Nancy eased close for a glimpse at the mirror. "Is that a zit on my chin?"

"No," Christie said. "It's a mosquito bite. You never get zits."

Lori leaned against the wall, queuing up for Mary's stall and refusing to look. "We've been camping!" she proclaimed, exonerating all our perceived shortcomings as temporary anomalies.

"We are wild women," Tori said, swinging her unencumbered hips into Christie.

Christie bumped back. "And lean and mean!"

"Uh-oh," Susie warned as the restroom's door pushed into her. She jumped to make room, and an older woman entered. Quietly and efficiently, we formed proper lines to take care of matters.

Robyn had secured the largest booth in the diner. It filled an entire corner. We squeezed across the red vinyl, leaving a chair in the aisle for Thaddeus. Our greedy orders swamped the table with main dishes, side dishes, juices, milk, and extra butter and syrup. Camp would be picking up the tab, and food had never tasted so great.

Having our bellies full for the first time in days, we geared up for naps on the long drive back. "Wake us up at the Mack-in-naw bridge!" we correctly pronounced, collapsing head upon shoulder against each other.

Robyn roused us near St. Ignace. We rubbed our eyes and stretched awake. None of us wanted to miss a view of the Mackinac Bridge. This sleek feat of ingenuity was the longest suspension bridge in the world and would remain so for another twenty years. Concrete and metal shimmered five miles to link the Upper Peninsula to Lower Michigan and marking an otherwise indiscernible border between Lake Huron and Lake Michigan.

"The Golden Gate Bridge is nothing compared to this." Robyn's claim held the conviction of someone who'd actually seen it. "It's not even golden! This should be the Silver Gate Bridge."

Two white towers gleamed in the sunlight, serving as anchors for the wire cables spanning above our heads. We peered from side to side, admiring a splendid view of both lakes.

"On windy days you can feel it moving," Thaddeus said. "It took seven years to build, and five people died during its construction."

"Only five?" Christie whispered from the middle bench.

"Yeah," I agreed, unable to imagine anyone working from such heights. The lake's surface rippled far below, hard as glass.

We cleared the second tower and crossed another mile of its southern extension. Upon reaching land, we promptly resumed our sleeping positions.

Long past the hour of "Taps," Thaddeus pulled into the gravel lot.

We unfolded our bodies and extracted our personal items from the backpacks. Staring at Robyn through mute sleepiness, we waited for further direction. She waved us on, offering an excuse about helping Thaddeus return the gear. We headed into the woods, hearing the van grind loudly into the still night.

"She's probably meeting Luke," Tori whispered.

We nodded our silent agreement, stepping through the lonely woods. At the threshold of the bridge, Nancy's solemn voice rose into the night. "Guys," she said, bringing us to a slow pause. We shifted until facing her, each of us hugging our dirty clothes, toothbrushes, and canteens. "We did it."

Her words fell like a blanket of finality, covering us in the implied success of a graduation plus advance acceptance into the next phase. "Yup," Christie agreed, using the same somber tone. "We did it."

Under the faint light of a half moon and plenty of stars, we acknowledged our agreement through unified silence. It was settled. All our years of camp had come to this moment, and we'd passed with flying colors.

Or rather, they'd passed with flying colors. This trip may have been my watermark of personal accomplishment but it had also turned a spotlight on my mediocre position inside the group. My future at camp felt increasingly unsure and far from settled. Steeped in doubt and trepidation, I crossed the bridge beside my fellow CTs. Feeding off their proud, triumphant energy, I felt nourished but unsatisfied.

"The CTs are back!" Placid whispers floated through sleepy Wildwood as campers bestowed upon us an aura of mystery and a dash of awed respect. The counselors conveyed slight annoyance, since full-fledged disruptions never occurred after "Taps." But we had to enter our respective cabins so they made the best of it. I crept into Whippoorwill, poking about my cramped space while Joanna quieted the campers' sleepy greetings. I heard the Murphy door creaking as my friends took muted care, seeking hot showers. I headed for the lake. Alone in the darkness, I swam in the company of my inner turmoil, unable to name it or shake it. I longed for clarity. I prayed for direction.

FORTY-NINE

AN ATTITUDE ADJUSTMENT

"WHY?" MY DAUGHTER peered at me. She tilted into her pillow, pressing against the window. "Why did you feel like that?"

My mind grazed on several possibilities, searching for an insightful view tempered by time. "Change comes whether we want it or not," I said, "and I resisted. Naturally, I got hurt, which is usually what happens when a higher power is trying to gain our attention and we fail to listen." I laughed cynically. "After that, I still didn't listen." Under my breath, as Angela began to speak, I whispered, "It took two tornadoes to get the job done."

"It would be cool to just take off somewhere," Angela said. Her brown eyes glinted at the prospect. "Maybe not backpacking." She reached forward and jabbed KT. "Hey, maybe next summer after we graduate we can take a road trip, like this, only by ourselves." For my benefit, she added, "No offense, Mrs. Taylor."

"None taken," I replied, though the idea terrified me.

"My mom would never let me," the other Katie said.

I breathed a sigh of relief, absently studying the passing signs. Traffic had dissipated soon after the Michigan border. The speed limit jumped from 65 mph to 70, and everyone passed me at 80.

"What is the name of our exit?" I asked, stepping on the gas to join them.

KT grabbed Chip's directions and read the stages we'd already completed. "This is it!" she pointed excitedly. "Keep right."

"We're there?" Angela hunted around for her shoes.

"Almost," I preempted. We came to a screeching halt inside the ramp. Orange barrels blocked the turn lane so everyone waited for the red light at the top of the hill. I reached for my cell phone and punched Nanny's number.

"Hello."

"Nanny! It's Nancy!" I carefully enunciated, trying not to trip over the similarity of our names. "We're just getting off the interstate."

"All righty then," she said.

"See you in a bit." Sunlight cast a blinding glare across the dashboard as we traveled through intersection after intersection of chain stores and franchise restaurants.

"They have the same places we do," Katie remarked from the backseat, sounding disappointed and surprised, as if she'd expected some unique establishments to validate our extreme distance from home.

I turned from the main road. "We're looking for a stone entrance," KT read.

"There!" KT and Angela shouted.

I slowed for the turn, and a silver pickup whizzed around us in a blur of reckless impatience.

"That guy's crazy!" Katie huffed.

We counted houses and pulled into the cement driveway of a modest ranch. Overgrown flowers surrounded its small porch. Nanny descended the steps, gripping the rail. "Oh you darlings!" she called.

We stretched and yawned from the car. When she stood by my side, her head barely reached my bustline, despite her straight posture and trim figure. I wondered if she had shrunk below four feet. But for all her ninety-some years she looked great. Lipstick brightened her tiny lips, and she wore homemade earrings, remnants from some craft project my cousins had completed decades earlier.

KT introduced her friends, and they gave her a hug. Nanny's petite stature and caring smile invited nothing less. "So you are here for the night? Then off again early in the morning?" She stated her questions as facts.

"That's right. Katie's friends have never seen the lake. So we're excited to get Up-North."

"Well, as soon as you get inside, call Marie," she scowled. "She has dinner plans for us. Your girls and hers will see a movie at the mall." Despite her exasperated tone, I noted an air of critical acclaim. She secretly loved the busy lives my cousins orchestrated, though she'd never admit it. "Steve may go along when he gets off work," she added, shaking her head.

"Steve?" Angela coyly nudged my daughter.

"He's my cousin!" KT gasped. "He's in college, and has a girlfriend."

"Paula's girls will meet up with you also," Nanny said. "And Julia is driving up from Clarkston to have dinner with us."

"Wait!" Angela said. "Who are all these people?"

"Nanny is my mom's mother," I explained, placing an arm around Nanny. Then I faltered. I should have used the past tense. Nanny was my mother's mother. But, this would sadden Nanny, so I quickly explained the connection. "Nanny has another daughter, my Aunt Jean, and she has three daughters who I grew up with almost like sisters. Their kids are close to your ages. You are going to hang out with them tonight, if that's okay?"

All three assessed their unwashed hair looped in messy ponytails, the happenstance blemish calling out for makeup, and their sweatpants rolled low on their hips with the labels poking out like geometric plumes. Unmindful of their appearance all day, they whirled into action and darted for the house, hauling their plastic athletic bags from the trunk.

"Take the big bedroom," Nanny called. Her tiny voice carried far in its high range of nasal insistence.

The girls hustled up the front stoop. "I get the shower first!" KT pulled rank. "Second!" Angela shouted, gloating triumphantly. "Third," Katie groaned as the aluminum screened door flopped against her.

Nanny and I followed more slowly. I gathered trash, hunted for my purse, then rearranged the trunk.

"I'll take that!" Nanny plucked the trash from my hand, same as she'd once plucked shopping bags from my youthful grasp. She moved toward her house, energetically swinging her arms. She slowed when mounting the stairs. I caught up and held the door, pausing on the threshold to peer over her head. I breathed deeply of the old familiar mélange: coffee grounds, perfumed powder, and Oil of Olay. A wave of grief tightened my chest. I had never been to Nanny's house without my mother.

We cleared the small entry, and I turned left for the bedrooms, newly amazed that my mother should die at sixty-four while her mother remained so vibrant and healthy. It also bolstered me in a peculiar way by offering hope for my own longevity.

"KT, can I wear your brown corduroys?" Katie's voice bargained from the spacious master bedroom. Nanny had long ago given up this suite to guests, preferring instead to sleep in the tiniest room of her house, just across the hall. It wasn't much more than a walk-in closet and held a youth-sized bed salvaged from one of the great-grandchildren.

I tossed my luggage into the third bedroom.

"Let me wear your pink shirt," Angela's voice carried into the hall.

"I don't want to go out!" my daughter angrily exploded. "I don't want to put on makeup or fix my hair. I just want to get Up-North," she moaned, plopping down on the bed.

I darted inside and closed their door, hoping Nanny hadn't heard and misunderstood. Go as you are, I wanted to say. But I knew she couldn't.

"I'll get in the shower first," Angela offered, taking the outburst in stride.

I sought a distraction. My mom had taught me this trick when KT was an emotional two-year-old. It proved equally effective on teenagers, both being either too young or too old to discipline out of a bad mood. I knew KT loved shoes, all kinds. It had been hardwired into her personality. I slid the closet door. It wobbled heavily on its suspension until resting flush with its counterpart.

Just as I had hoped, my other Katie, as I now thought of her, eased near, and we gazed upon three tiers of pointed heels, elegant flats, and ornate sandals in a rainbow of colors. The dresses once worn to accompany them had disappeared long ago. Only these trophies of bygone days remained; each the memento of an occasion from Nanny's younger married life. I hadn't fit inside any of them since the age of eight.

"Check out this one." I held up an emerald green sandal covered in clusters of glass jewels.

"Gorgeous," my daughter muttered sarcastically, though her eyes followed its placement into the rack.

"These are soooo cute," Katie gushed, kneeling to examine a pair of silk fuchsia having pointed toes, silk flower appliqués, and tiny spiked heels. KT leaned across the bed, examining them closely.

We noted styles making a comeback and lamented our inability to try any of them on. Gradually, an atmosphere of geniality permeated the room. "Going out is no big deal," I tried again. "Just run through the shower and put on some jeans."

"Uhhhh," she groaned, placing a pillow over her head, bewailing my failure to get it.

I sighed because I had known the same anguish at her age, and my mom's advice had similarly fallen on deaf ears. I decided to let her friends deal with her. After all, this was why I had brought them along.

Nanny and I visited while they showered, blow-dried hair, and applied makeup. After an hour, I tapped on the door. Angela bade me enter, and I positioned myself in the twirly-chair. Its cream-colored fabric had yellowed, and its tiny roses had faded to gray, but the ballbearings still rolled solidly along a metal track beneath the pleated skirt. I imagined it could still twirl a kid into dizzying oblivion.

Wrapped in a towel, KT stood at the base of the bed gazing upon an array of options pooled from their bags. Her friends had already dressed. They cajoled and complimented, like salesclerks in a boutique, tiptoeing around her temper. I watched the process, utterly fascinated, knowing this occurred on Friday and Saturday nights behind her bedroom door. I faintly recalled Susan and I vented similar frustrations before going out. But KT didn't have a sister. So these friends, each having a sister, kindly filled the void, often dressing at our house on weekends for hours of what my generation called primping.

When the best outfit emerged after numerous tries, KT faced the mirror and donned the one thing I had been waiting for—her smile. "And guys think we dress for them," I murmured, spinning in little sideways spurts.

"Yeah," Angela agreed as she began stuffing clothes into her bag.

In truth, we dressed for ourselves. How could we offer a kind, generous expression to the outside world when we looked in the mirror and did not like what we saw? Whatever the standard, success or failure dictated the inner mood and its convergence on the outside world. The best we could do as parents was to help our daughters improve their physical appearance while downplaying its importance. A fine line indeed! How many times had I prevented my husband from coming down too hard as KT stomped and fumed around the house for no apparent reason? I knew she would have to beat the cycle by gaining a spiritual calm about her unique beauty. It would take time, patience, and consistency as we appreciated her inner strengths, took a healthy interest in her life, and praised her accomplishments, not just her looks.

I credited camp for allowing me to grow weary of this struggle long before my high school and college peers. Camp had isolated us from the pop culture and insulated us in a community that cultivated our unique qualities so we could learn to separate the mirror image from our true, inner selves. Perhaps this explained why my daughter had fallen apart when her friends had not. We were going camping, in her mind. She had already switched gears along the road, disengaging from concerns about clothes, hair, and makeup. But now, circumstances forced her to reverse.

FIFTY

THE TWO SIDES OF NANNY

IT WAS NEARLY ten o'clock and completely dark before I drove Nanny back to her house after meeting my cousins and Aunt Jean for dinner.

"How can you possibly know where you are going across so many states?" Nanny decried. "You'll get lost. I know it." She appeared especially tiny strapped into my front seat. The belt grazed her chin, and she sat at least two heads lower than my usual passenger.

On the way to the restaurant she had praised my driving ability and called me smart, capable, and brave. But the sun had set on Nanny's optimism for the day.

"Lordy." She hardly paused, waving her tiny hand for emphasis. "Your dad used to make you girls drive Up-North to that camp all by yourselves. What kind of father was that to leave you fending for yourselves? He should have driven you there, to make sure you arrived safely. You could have gotten lost, or met up with some bad people. And why did he send you for so many weeks? Your sister hated that camp and was terribly homesick."

"No," I objected. "We loved camp." I lowered my window. The night air streamed across my face offering a bit of relief from her old, stale grievances. "And being independent at an early age made us stronger," I added.

"I suppose," she said, drawing her words through a long moment of reconsideration. As a true child of the Depression she couldn't condemn this fact. She had been one of twelve, impossibly burdened by the responsibilities of raising younger siblings after her father had died. He had worked the coal mines of Pennsylvania in order to buy a farm and raise a family in St. Helen, Michigan. Then, barely into his fifties, and barely into the realization of his dream, he faced an agonizing death from black lung. Without medication and driven crazy by the pain, he hung himself in the barn when the youngest was only a few days old. Nanny's mother took control of the farm and left Nanny to run the household.

"But my husband would not have treated our daughters that way," she scolded, shaking a finger at me, perchance speaking of her father as well as mine. Her tiny rounded thumb bobbed along, smashed like a soupspoon from obsessive childhood thumb sucking. "My husband used to follow your mother everywhere to make sure she was safe," she proudly added.

Mom had always known Papa was out there, skulking nearby in their oversized Buick. "He just wanted an excuse to visit the tavern," I whispered under my breath, spouting another of my mom's recollections.

"And why isn't your husband with you?" Nanny viciously disapproved. "A woman should always travel with her man."

"He's with your great-grandson who is working to save money for college in the fall. They are content to be home. Neither of them is interested in my reunion."

"Your mother had so many problems finding directions," Nanny bemoaned. "I always told her she wasn't any good at driving. It was too difficult for her."

"Yes, you told her," I scoffed, wanting to add, and every day of her life she fought your words in her head wanting to prove you wrong. Mom had a college degree, the first in her family. Why wouldn't she be able to drive a car?

"She shouldn't have been driving that day," Nanny grieved. Tears rolled down her plump, wrinkled cheeks.

"It wasn't her fault," I said, knowing facts held no merit in this conversation. "The truck didn't see her merging." I took extra precaution just then, using my turn signal to enter her driveway.

"Look out for the drainage ditch!" she warned.

Mounting the curb, I laughed at the chance of me veering off her double-wide driveway into the small drainage ditch. But then, out of some hereditary flaw, or dutiful impulse, I actually envisioned the car tipping over. Nanny knew how to plant a seed and make it grow! I shrugged it off and quickly parked the car. I jumped out to help her. She had already opened the door and slid off the seat. I held her arm, and we advanced to the front porch and entered the house.

"Your poor mother." She paused in the hallway, standing before a child's portrait, painted in faded colors. The little girl had Mom's eyes and undeniable smile. "Isn't her hair beautiful?" Brown ringlets fell from a large blue bow. "I pinned it every night so she would have those curls in the morning. Little Dorothy was so afraid of everything, of heights, of swimming. But she always had a smile on her face."

I cherished the times that smile had been for me, alone. Dependable as the sun behind the clouds, despite inner pain and sorrow. Mom could always manifest the most brilliant smile. It lit her face, brightened everyone around her, and always seemed effortless and honest. Did it make her feel better? I wondered. Even at the end when morphine glazed her sight, her last breath had come from a calm, distant smile. But that smile had not been for me, or Susan, or Nanny as we gathered around her. It had been otherworldly, a greeting for the place we could not follow.

Nanny pressed a finger to her own wrinkled lips, then touched the same finger to the little girl's lips. "Your father took her from me and moved her to South Bend. A different state! I'll never forgive him for that," she vowed for the millionth time. "Maybe she would still be alive. Maybe you and Susan would be living here. I could have seen you every day when you were growing up instead of every few weeks."

I sighed, wanting to say the real reason we had moved when I was four. Everyone knew save Nanny. Her constant negativity and interference had taken an unhealthy toll. Mom's humble personality prevented speaking out so she had internalized every struggle until it ulcerated into full-blown colitis. When I was in high school, doctors at Mayo Clinic had removed her lower intestine. Nanny had literally worn out her daughter's intestinal fortitude. If we had stayed in Flint she may not have lived so long!

We didn't blame Nanny. At sixteen, she had left the farm for a factory job in Detroit. A Dickensian fate unfolded when she fell into a dodgy crowd and learned to shoplift. She'd return home bearing gifts impossible to acquire on a menial wage. Her siblings' grateful praise cemented her role as family benefactress and set the stage for her lifelong addiction. Not even Papa's generosity could prevent her from using my mother and aunt as shills to block the salesclerk's view while she stuffed merchandise into her purse, shopping bags, and even her daughters' clothing. She went to jail a few times under their innocent, watchful eyes. But Papa managed to keep it out of the papers and away from the rest of the family.

When Mom reached adulthood, she refused to shop. Even trips to the grocery store caused anxiety. Susan and I shopped for her at the corner grocer, and Mom ordered our clothes from catalogs.

Aunt Jean had fought back. She was the first to poke her head in the cellar when they returned from school just to be sure Nanny hadn't kept her promise. "You'll come home and find me hanging from the basement rafters," Nanny had relentlessly warned. Through each injustice, Aunt Jean grew more vocal, which only fanned Nanny's wrath. As an adult, she bore her scars in a very different way. She loved to shop. For as long as I can remember, Aunt Jean spent most of her time in upscale boutiques and high-end department stores, flaunting her husband's success and proclaiming her ability to pay honestly for her heart's desire. Her hair, makeup, jewelry, clothes, and matching shoes always displayed meticulous perfection. She often took us with her, setting a frivolous example in the extreme from our mom. The more Aunt Jean spent, the more Nanny complained. But it never bothered my uncle, so I could never figure out why it bothered Nanny. Now I could see, plainly and simply—Nanny was, and remained poisonously jealous of her own daughter.

Since Mom's accomplishments had nothing to do with shopping, Nanny found other ways to torment. She demeaned Mom's education and her subsequent career. And Dad would forever be the fall guy for providing an escape route.

"Your mother had to buy everything from catalogs instead of nice stores, because your dad wouldn't let her," Nanny griped. "I always told her to wear bright colors and new styles, not that L.L. Bean stuff."

Mentally I argued; our mom was stylish because she wore classics. And that L.L. Bean stuff had allowed me to have some camping equipment.

"And why go to that big lake when there are so many small lakes around here? For seven weeks!" she said, placing a tiny hand on her hip. "Your poor mother must have been so lonely."

"She kept busy," I protested, forsaking my usual litany of camp virtues. Instead, I defended Mom, not letting Nanny's seeds of guilt take root. "She had her bridge group, Lunch Bunch, AAUW, and PEO meetings." I paused to ponder these acronyms. I had no idea what they stood for, or what their membership represented.

"Now your Aunt Jean is always busy!" Nanny vigorously disapproved.

I puzzled her illogical tirades. In one broad swoop she had discounted my mom's entire life as "not busy enough" while managing to criticize Aunt Jean's life for being "too busy." How could both merit her disapproval? I supposed it was because neither of them had devoted themselves to family as she had. Her whole life, she had never joined a club, or cultivated a circle of friends, or instigated a social gathering outside of family. Entertaining Papa's business clients during his career proved her only exception. When her eleven brothers and sisters started passing on, Nanny's devotion shifted to my cousins and their children. She laundered their clothes, whether they wanted it or not, loaded dishwashers, brought in the mail, and fed their pets. She drove from house to house to perform these tasks, sitting on a cushion to reach the steering wheel while cleverly avoiding traffic.

She shot her hand as if swatting a fly. "Gad!" she wailed. "Jean is never home. Going here and there. Losing her husband last year didn't slow her down. Not one bit! She has her Junior League, her shopping friends." She practically hissed the latter. "And she is always doing nice things for that church."

I bit my lip in earnest, trying not to absorb her words as she began to criticize my aunt and cousins. Delving into Nanny's world could be a dangerous and misleading pastime. She spread just as many falsehoods about them as she did about us. And how ironic! She wanted her family to be close, yet in the mutterings of a few sentences she could drive a rift as deep as the Grand Canyon.

FIFTY-ONE

SPREADING THE SECRET

JUST BEFORE MIDNIGHT, a bass line boomed from the driveway, and car doors banged. KT, Katie, and Angela rushed into the house, giggling and whispering.

"What movie did you see?" I asked. They grinned in wide-eyed innocence. "What movie?" I persisted.

They grabbed my arms and tugged me away from Nanny's watchful eyes. "We didn't see a movie," they whispered, flouncing on the bed. "We went to a party!"

"So, you never made it to the mall?"

"No, no," my daughter clarified. "We went to the mall. We just didn't stay."

"Your cousins are so much fun," Angela declared.

KT hardly knew her generation of cousins apart from a handful of trips to Flint over her young life. However, I knew my generation very well, and they had been loads of fun. "You don't have to tell me any more," I said. "No one is going to be sick, though?"

"No." Angela's eyes flashed reassuringly. "We were good. Some of those parties were pretty wild, but when things got rough we left and went to another one."

"They knew of about seven parties!" KT exclaimed.

"I have to say," Katie primly spoke up. "The people around here spend a lot of money on their cars, but they drive like maniacs. I've seen some of the worst driving in my life. People don't stay in their lanes on these country roads. They don't even stop at stop signs!"

Angela and KT placed their arms around her, saying, "But . . . nothing happened."

"Thank goodness," I said, greatly relieved. "Let's get to bed."

They shuffled into the bathroom, and I returned to the narrow, carpeted hallway. Nanny stood where I'd left her, no doubt listening. She wore a hairnet over patches of dyed blonde hair. Her round, lined face glistened from Oil of Olay. My heart swelled for this enigmatic tower of strength who had always been in my life, just like a nanny. In Flint, or at the cottage, our parents would play golf, visit friends, or take in a show while Papa found his buddies. But Nanny always watched the children.

She kissed the tip of her finger and placed this same finger on Mom's portrait. "Goodnight, little Dorothy," she whispered.

I kissed Nanny's soft cheek, wishing she could embrace her living daughter with half the tenderness she bestowed upon this old picture. Aunt Jean's portrait hung a notch higher. A child's face, framed by blonde ringlets tied in a bow, gazed stoically past Nanny's head.

The next morning, deep voices beckoned from the sunken family room. "This warm front," the old console television boomed from its fabric speakers, "has moved across Lake Michigan bringing rain and low clouds to the northern part of the state. It will continue across the Upper Peninsula toward Ontario. . . ."

One by one, the girls filtered in, dressed in their travel clothes. "More rain," KT grumbled.

"No, this is perfect," I said. "The weather will be cruddy while we travel, but it will clear when we get there."

"All right then," Angela concluded, eyeing my pajamas. "Let's get going."

Needing no other hint, I spun around and headed for the bedrooms. In the stretch of a halfhour we had packed our bags and loaded them in the car.

"I can't believe these girls!" Nanny wore a wide, pleased grin. "They made the beds. They don't want any breakfast, and they are ready to go!"

She had awakened into a happy grandmother. I hunched down to wrap her in a hug, thinking this nanny would be difficult to leave. She waved from her porch as I coasted down her driveway at a snail's pace. Her insistent voice warned, "Watch out for the ditch!"

"She's so cute," Katie said. "And that ditch is so tiny."

"Bye, Nanny!" my daughter called from her lowered window. I leaned across her lap and hollered, "Bye! I love you!" just before accelerating from the neighborhood.

Angela blandly stated, "You'd never know she was a kleptomaniac."

I narrowed an accusing glare at my daughter.

"You were going to tell us anyway," she soothed. "Don't worry. No one heard me. I told Katie and Angela in the bathroom at one of the parties. I explained everything about the Depression, about how hard her life was."

"Did you ever see her in action?" Angela asked when we sat at a red light, waiting for a green arrow to enter the freeway.

"No, but I always wondered why Aunt Jean never lost sight of her when shopping, or why my mom never wanted to come along. When Paula got her driver's license, Nanny insisted on escorting us to the mall. She never bought anything and only stayed near until one of us made a purchase. Then, she'd pluck the shopping bag from our hands, as if we couldn't be trusted to keep track of it, and would sit on a bench outside the drugstore. We'd stop by often to unburden other bags. She wouldn't let go of them until we returned to her house. Sometimes they appeared bulkier. Once, while crammed into the backseat, I tried to get into my bag, and she turned vicious. It was really scary. She hissed at me and slapped my hand. When I mentioned this to my mom, she had a fit. When we were back in South Bend, she told me about her childhood. She made me promise not to tell Susan or my cousins. From then on, Nanny never shopped with us again." And I foolishly became enamored with the possibility of trying it for myself, I thought, shaking my head.

The light changed and I merged onto the freeway. A car sped past at nearly 90 mph loaded full of kids. They cut me off and made a hasty exit. "Did you see that?" I exclaimed, hoping for sympathy as I tamped the brakes. The girls mumbled incoherently from their reclined positions, and I realized our hasty departure had been engineered so they could return to sleep while I carried us to our destination.

FIFTY-TWO

A RACE AGAINST THE TRUTH

THE HIGHWAY'S RHYTHMIC seams created a hypnotic ride, and I slipped into a lethargic trance. Fighting the impulse to close my eyes and keep them shut, I grabbed Chip's directions from the glove box. His bullets of information directed me off the interstate. I merged from four lanes to two and came fully awake from the abrupt change to seamless asphalt.

Low clouds cast a blanket of tranquility upon the clusters of tidy farmhouses, silos and barns, cow pastures, and cornfields. When farmland gave way to dense, rolling forests, flashes of steely blue appeared at intervals between narrow driveways leading to hidden lakes and cottages.

I came upon an old Pontiac. Its chrome bumper exhibited a collection of stickers, and I squinted in vain to decipher them. My speedometer dropped lower, and lower. Hills and blind curves prevented me from passing, and the persistent solid yellow line forbade me to try.

After an hour, I decided to cross the line, whatever it took, to get around him. Luckily, a sign appeared, "Passing Lane Ahead." A mile further, a sign instructed, "Slow Traffic Move Right." I thrilled at the prospect, fully confident of my role in this unfolding drama. When the new lane surfaced, I anticipated the Pontiac's shift to the right. Inexplicably, it lurched ahead, hogging the main lane and becoming a hotrod. After forty miles of below-limit cruising, it sped up! The extra pavement slipped away at an alarming rate. I gritted my teeth and vowed this driver would no longer have the lead. I angled to the right, floored my accelerator, and passed from the slow lane.

Veering back to the main lane, I settled into a comfortable speed and tamed my heart to its normal pace. The sky misted, and I braked for a curve.

A red Chevy filled the road ahead, traveling far slower than the Pontiac. Eventually the Pontiac caught up and both of us submitted to the Chevy's dallying. Mile after mile the solid yellow line taunted us, demanding strict adherence. When it changed to a broken line, oncoming traffic barred the way. After fifteen miles a passing lane rose from the wilderness. The pavement widened, and I crept closer to the Chevy, trusting it would move over, hoping the Pontiac had been an anomaly.

The Chevy sped up! I growled at its rudeness. "Move over!" I grumbled, wondering if local drivers refused to share the road. Or were their motives more sinister? Did they take pleasure in taunting the foreign car with out-of-state plates?

I flicked my signal and peeked through the mirror. The Pontiac thundered toward me, heading for the right lane. "Oh, no you don't!" I said. If the Pontiac trapped me behind the Chevy, he would gain the lead. I cut in front of the Pontiac, speeding neck and neck beside the Chevy. The Pontiac fell back while I entered a drag race. I could see the end of the pavement just ahead.

"Hang on, girls!" I shouted, flooring the gas pedal. The speedometer spiked to 85 mph, and the pavement ran out. Tires ground along the shoulder, flipping gravel, and I gained the lead. Jerking to mount the asphalt, I swerved into the opposite lane. An onslaught of traffic rounded the curve just ahead. I jerked back and reentered our lane just in time. My palms sweat on the steering wheel and my shoulders tensed into my neck. We could have died.

The Chevy became a red blip in my mirror as I coasted into the speed limit. "Why the hurry?" I quietly admonished. There was no rush hour to keep ahead of, no bumper-to-bumper traffic to avoid. Better to arrive safely than not at all. Soon I would see the lake, and everything would be fine. An extra hour mattered little now. And hadn't there been a time when I enjoyed cruising along these country roads at a slower pace? Rude drivers existed everywhere, but I didn't have to join them. And I didn't need to prove anything to them, or to myself. What happened to my mom could not happen to me. I was stronger, faster, and more assertive.

She had always been too timid about merging into traffic, too reluctant to demand her place in the flow, and maybe if she had been a little more aggressive and accelerated more quickly, she could have sped ahead of that truck and would still be alive.

Perhaps her demise was my justification for conquering these roads like the Indianapolis Speedway. But it was better than facing reality. For deep down, I knew the wreck that had sent her to the hospital was not the reason she never came home. It had been something else; a fearful, unbearable word that happened to other people, not to my mother. But I could not say it. Neither could Nanny. We chose to blame the truck instead.

FIFTY-THREE

TRANSITION

"CAN WE HAVE breakfast?" the girls asked. My outburst had awakened them.

The road curved north, and we entered a small town. I slowed to the posted limit and admired the pine log exterior and red-checked curtains of a local restaurant. On impulse, I pulled in.

"Here?" all three gasped together.

"It must be good. There are lots of cars," I observed.

"Can't we find a Hardee's, or a McDonald's?" my daughter lamented.

"Come on, this won't be so bad," I coaxed, also trying to convince myself. "We're not complete strangers to these parts," I said, thinking of The Blue Bird in Fishtown. "Besides, when you were little we ate in homegrown places all the time." I grabbed my purse and stepped outside. The Chevy and the Pontiac rumbled past. My eyes followed their progress through the one-light town, cementing my decision. "We have plenty of time," I said, walking away, and raising the key to activate the car's remote lock.

They jogged to catch up, fussing to place their tangled manes into ponytails. I tried to exude an aura of self-confidence, to set them at ease. I pushed into the wooden door. It propelled far too easily and slammed loudly against the inside paneling. A few patrons stared. I stammered an apology and the girls eased past.

"Maybe you should lighten up on that weight lifting, Mrs. Taylor," Angela chuckled.

A waitress came around the other side of a bakery case. "Good morning, table for four?" She grabbed a stack of menus and ushered us to a booth near the kitchen.

"What's the special?" I inquired, hoping such a thing existed.

"The Wolverine Breakfast," she said, plopping down the menus. "Two eggs any style, hash browns, sausage, bacon, three pancakes, and your choice of juice."

"I'll have that," KT piped up. "Scrambled eggs, with orange juice," she added, almost in question.

The waitress gave a tidy nod.

"Me, too," Angela said. "I will, too," Katie agreed.

The waitress stared at me, pencil in hand. I panicked. My passengers were more experienced than I thought! And how could they eat so much and be so thin? "I'll have the same, but with apple juice," I heard myself order for the sake of speed and ease.

Our waitress reclaimed the menus and sauntered away.

KT gazed about, smiling genuinely. "This is like The Silver Diner," she observed. Angela cleared her throat and grunted a warning.

"How many first-period classes have you spent there?" I ventured, knowing I had never taken her.

KT inhaled sharply, preparing to object. But Katie effectively changed the subject by pointing to a wooden sign in the opposite corner. We stood at once, all having the same need to visit the bathroom. When we returned, the table held juices, milk, water, and small pitchers of syrup. We sat down, sipped our chosen beverage, and waited for our food.

"Mom," KT said, "I can't remember. Were you ever a counselor?"

"Would you like the short version or the long version?"

They snickered at me. "Somewhere in the middle," KT answered for them.

I smiled, wistfully counting their age, still unable to believe the impossible. They were the age I had been during my last year at camp. I wondered if they wrestled against internal challenges. Did they struggle to find themselves amid the confusion of their outside worlds? Would their current friendships help or hinder this quest?

"You stayed friends with Nancy, Christie, and the others?" KT prodded, sensing my sadness.

"Oh sure," I agreed. "After the CT trip, younger campers monopolized our time. But we squeezed in a few moments here and there. The sounds of construction crept closer, and we heard rumors of the girls' camp to be rebuilt along the river, having access to the beach. The boys' camp had adjusted. So, why couldn't we?" I sighed heavily, reliving my angst. "I had refused to think that far ahead. Mostly, I craved solitude on the end of the dock. I would stare out at the lake or back at the camp, feeling a deep, pensive melancholy. It had taken hold, and I couldn't shake it."

"I know how that feels," Katie said. She furtively tucked a blonde lock behind her ear and stared into the kitchen.

I nodded thoughtfully and added, "I think that was how Papa felt just before he died."

"Why?" Angela and Katie automatically replied. My daughter shot me a perplexed expression. Clearly, she could not fathom the comparison and was too embarrassed to try.

"He died the winter before my first summer at camp," I attempted to explain. "However, the doctors had told him months before that he was terminally ill."

"You weren't dying!" KT incredulously argued.

"No, but hear me out," I pleaded. "Papa spent long hours sitting in a lawn chair in the middle of his yard. And I don't mean on the patio near the house. I mean right smack in the middle of a half-acre lot. Sometimes he read but mostly he just gazed into the distance. Once in a while Nanny took him a pitcher of lemonade. The rest of us left him alone. The adults kept their distance out of respect. As kids, we didn't understand. Back and forth from the pool, the mall, or heading down the street to my cousins' house, we'd call, "Hi, Papa!" He'd smile and nod, wearing a patient expression. It softened his face, making him appear younger. This man who'd been bigger than life, jolly, raucous, caustic, but rarely quiet and thoughtful seemed wholly changed. I'd watch him from the glass door of Nanny's kitchen having a vague sense of the moment's magnitude, all the while wondering, 'What is he thinking?'

"I woke at twilight one weekend in August and saw he'd been there all night. He faced the house with his back against the north wind. A harvest moon hung low on the western horizon, amazingly beautiful, burnt orange and fully round. Equally magnificent to the east, the rising sun cast a crescent glow over the neighbor's garage and bathed his profile in golden light. His attention roved between the east and the west, between the setting moon and the rising sun. Literally, he sat in the middle of night and day. Figuratively, he sat in transition between one world and the next."

"Okay," my daughter sneered. "You just need to stick to the story and quit getting into these weird philosophical bents."

"Wait." I leaned into the table and whispered, "During my last ten days of camp, I understood Papa's solitude. He felt change coming."

Suddenly, the waitress appeared like a culinary genie, placing steaming plates of heaping food across the table. Her wiry arms crossed everywhere at once.

KT, Katie, and Angela smirked at me, noting the irony of her timing.

Angela grabbed a sausage and took a huge bite as the waitress walked away. "So," she mumbled, "tell us about the changes you felt coming."

"But stick to the story," my daughter added.

"My memories are thirty years old, and much of it has faded, but parts of it feel like they happened yesterday." I met their eyes, smiling warmly. "Thanks for listening. I'm a little nervous about this reunion." They casually nodded, munching their food, and I took advantage of the silence.

FIFTY-FOUR

A FATEFUL ACCIDENT

"COME ON," BETH pleaded, placing an impatient hand upon her twelve-year-old hip. Her sandaled foot propped the door. A hot breeze ruffled through the cabin's confining quarters. "Now mascara?" she protested. "And I hope you aren't going to change your top again!"

"I had to. It was wet. Why do you come to camp anyway?" I needled, knowing she could handle a bit of teasing.

She stifled a giggle and rolled her eyes toward the rafters.

I held a tube of mascara, a hand mirror, and twisted about, trying to find a streak of sunlight in the shaded cabin. Finally, a shaft illumined my face, and I spread the wand of mascara over my eyelashes for the first time since returning from our CT trip. It was a moment of pure pleasure to see stubby, blonde tips transform into lush, long lashes like a Cover Girl commercial. I admired the effect from every angle. "Don't your folks have a cottage around here?" I asked, returning the mirror to the window ledge, beside my collection of fossils from the lake.

"Yeah, on Glen Lake. But they want me to make friends my age," she said, flipping hair from under her collar.

I tossed the damp shirt over the open lid of my steamer trunk and said, "Then you should walk to meals with Elly, Annie, and Missy."

"They already left!" she huffed.

"We aren't late, you know. We have at least ten minutes from the time Lou Ellen rings the bell. It's only been five minutes." I maneuvered for the opposite windowsill to reach a pair of earrings. Whippoorwill had been designed to hold four regular cots plus the counselor's slightly larger bed. Having mine added to the mix meant our cots stood barely a foot apart and our trunks touched sides. Since August had arrived, bringing warm nights and still days, the cabin felt especially cramped.

"Actually, Joanna told me to get you to meals on time," Beth grinned, thinking she pulled rank.

"Ha! I don't believe that," I said. In fact, nothing about Joanna intimidated me anymore. Instead, she made me laugh. I had discovered her droll wisecracking extended to everyone, not just me. No matter how hilarious a situation, even if the entire camp howled from gut-splitting laughter, Joanna would simply crack her gum in the back of her molars and share a tight smile. It was the same smile she wore when killing spiders. The girls in Whippoorwill adored her because she never lectured on cleanliness or spiritual growth and allowed whispering and card games during the afternoon quiet hour. We'd huddle on her bed, and she'd tell me about my sister. It humbled me to learn of Susan's successes at camp from someone who valued her friendship.

"If you don't put your shoes on now, I won't wait any longer!" Beth interrupted my thoughts in a final ultimatum.

"Guess what! That's all I have left." I shared an overblown smile. Grabbing my sandals, I turned to sit on my trunk. I plopped down in a hefty force of habit, anticipating a rock-solid wooden lid beneath me. "Woaaaah." I realized too late that I'd left it open. Down I fell into my clothes, desperately trying to save myself. I flung my arms wide and leaned forward. The sandals weighted my left arm so it fell short, but my right arm violently struck the open lip. I recoiled from the sharp metal edge as if a bolt of electricity had shot through me. Then, gravity took me down anyway.

I heard Beth giggle as I sat in my clothes. What was I doing? No one ever fell into her trunk! Sensing damage, I tilted my arm in front of my face. Midway between elbow and wrist, a deep chasm of puckering disfigurement had appeared. Tiny white balls resembling fish eggs pushed to the surface of my pale forearm. "Wow," I marveled, profoundly amazed as my high school science book attained a whole new level of reliability. Who knew my body perfectly resembled one of its colorful illustrations! Mentally, I analyzed and cataloged the findings. "The round white balls are individual cells. And the black dots in the middle are their nuclei. All of this is sandwiched between pinkish layers of dermis and epidermis!"

I hung suspended in time, numbed by objectivity and the thrill of discovery. But then my heart galloped into a jump-start and ripped a jolt of pain down my arm. Dark blood flooded the gap, and my impersonal study came to a close.

I struggled to extract myself from the trunk. I grabbed a dark shirt to stave the flow. "Don't come near," I said, delicately lowering the lid, feeling like a wounded lion-tamer. I would never take this trunk for granted again, or view it as a friendly companion. "At least it happened to me," I concluded, peering at Beth, fearing the thought of her or someone else getting hurt on my trunk. I kicked into a pair of rubber thongs, abandoning the sandals.

My arm pulsed. And fear weakened my legs. Ever since the sixth grade when Susan had sliced the skin near her Achilles tendon on a crazy bicycle trip down Killer Hill, I had feared stitches above all else in life. I couldn't stomach the sight of black threads holding jagged, jaundiced, blood-encrusted skin. But most of all I feared the process; the needle and the tugging.

"What should we do?" Beth asked. Her frightened eyes shared my concern.

"We'll go to lunch," I declared, walking blindly out the door, nearly falling off the cement stoop.

I crooked my arm and pressed the shirt against the gash. Sticky blood saturated it, and the skin throbbed beneath my fingers. Beth jogged beside me, keeping to the sand, and I suspended all effort save holding my back straight and lifting my knees. Now would not be a good time to trip across the boardwalk!

A few campers hovered near on our climb to the dining hall, pestering to know, "What did you do?"

"Don't say it." I glared at Beth.

She kept quiet, looking stricken between hilarity and terror.

When my CT class gathered around on the wooden deck outside the double doors, I still could not get myself to say it. Instead, I answered their perplexed questions with a shake of my head.

"How bad is it?" Lori persisted. "Let me see."

I held the shirt tighter. "I just need a Band-Aid," I said at last.

"What happened?" My sister pressed through the crowd. I wavered at the sight of her, knowing how motherly she could be in a crisis.

Robyn emerged from the double doors. "What did you do?" she accused. Before I could answer she gently peeled away the blood-soaked shirt. After inhaling sharply, she composed herself. "This is deep," she said. I winced as she haphazardly tried to push the gap of skin together. Blood splattered the deck and everyone stepped back. "How did you do it?" she demanded. Her voice rose irritably from confusion as if unable to remember whether I'd answered or not.

"I fell into my trunk." There, I said it.

"I saw her," Beth confirmed.

"Not your trunk!" Nancy said, struggling to keep her balance because a camper tugged at her neck, trying to climb on her back.

Christie gave my shoulder an encouraging squeeze.

"Everyone go eat!" Robyn directed. "Nancy, come with me. We'll go to the guys' for first aid. It's closer," she thought aloud.

I berated myself for being so bent on reaching the dining hall and half-suspected Robyn of using me for a reason to see Luke. Bess had always kept gauze bandages and antiseptic in her office. I could have stayed in camp and sought Lou Ellen for these supplies. She often skipped lunch altogether.

Robyn ushered me through the atrium and out the other set of double doors. Tiers of decking descended toward the year-round school and its dormitories. The guys were assembling, and we jockeyed against their stream, brushing the outside rail and overhanging pine boughs. They no longer came to meals from the beach, having lost their cabins forever. They still had two embedded trampolines near the water, volleyball pits, gymnastic equipment, a covered boxing ring, two catamaran sail boats, a speedboat, and some new contraptions called windsurfs. But I think they would have traded it all just to have cabins on the beach once again.

"We need some first aid!" Robyn accosted Luke. His head towered above the crowd. His blasé attitude told me accidents like this occurred all the time in the guys' camp.

"It's just a little cut," I downplayed. "I'm sure I just need a tight bandage."

Robyn lifted my arm and exposed the wound. "She fell into her trunk." A wry smile of amusement rounded out her cheeks. "It's an old steamer with metal edges."

"I remember that one," he said, effectively completing my humiliation. "Rusty metal?"

They stared at me for the answer. I squirmed in place, warily noting the passing boys and their unabashed interest. Many of them had carried my trunk at the beginning and end of camp, cursing its size and weight. They probably thought I deserved it. "Maybe a little rusty," I said, wondering why this mattered.

"At the very least she'll need a tetanus shot," Luke remarked.

"A shot!" I moaned.

Luke leaned down to examine the wound more closely. "Oh, yeah, and stitches," he said.

"Stitches," I breathed, practically swooning.

Robyn sighed, "Someone will have to take her to the clinic in Traverse."

This meant over three hours, round trip, of drive time alone.

"I can't drive her," Luke preempted, determinedly shaking his head.

"Neither can I." Robyn defended her own busy routine, sounding stressed. "Maybe Lou Ellen, or Mr. Chinn."

I inhaled my shocked disbelief. I couldn't imagine spending so much time alone in a car with either of them. I widened my eyes against tears of self-pity, trying not to blink, wishing I hadn't put on mascara. "Maybe my sister could take me," I offered. "We have a car." I took a hopeful breath, deciding it would be nice if some CTs could come along.

"No," Robyn said. "Susan can't authorize treatment, and she wouldn't know where to go."

"I'll go," a deep voice heralded from outside our small circle.

My insides prickled. The possibilities had worsened.

The crowd parted, allowing Thaddeus to approach. "We'll have to leave now," he said, drawing near, speaking directly to me.

I glimpsed kindness in his dark eyes and a sincere desire for my approval. "All right," I heard myself say. My fingers moved of their own accord to gather the bloody shirt against my arm.

"Need anything from Traverse?" he offered the head counselors.

"No, thanks," Robyn and Luke replied together.

"Over here," Thaddeus directed me toward a white pickup. He opened the passenger door and laid out a first-aid kit. "This won't hurt," he advised, prying the bloody shirt from my grasp and tossing it on the truck's floor mat.

I stood with my arm bent, my fist brandished. He doused hydrogen peroxide into the open wound. It fizzled and dribbled off my elbow, forming a pink trail down my leg. He tore a wad of gauze and dabbed the wound until it stopped bleeding. The textbook view of my arm had vanished, but plenty of other fluids oozed forth as the healing process began in earnest. He tossed the gauze atop the bloody shirt, took the roll and wrapped it around and around my arm until it felt snug and secure. "Is that better?" he asked.

My stomach churned from missing lunch, and my arm pulsed in bursts of pain but I said, "Sure."

He replaced the kit and gestured for me to climb inside. He shut the door and walked around to his side. We rumbled from the parking lot.

FIFTY-FIVE

ONE STEP FORWARD, TWO STEPS BACK

I STARED AT the dashboard, needing to know if my sister's harrowing experience was normal. Fifteen stitches had been sewn into the back of her ankle. Nothing had killed the pain, and it took three nurses to hold her down during each puncture of the needle and tug of thread. She had cried and blubbered for each stitch to be the last while the doctor kept poking and jerking one sinewy cord after the other into a snug knot having stiff loose ends. These same loose ends had caused howls of pain during her recovery when they brushed up against blankets and pillows.

I glanced repeatedly at Thaddeus, wondering if he could separate Susan's fact from fiction. I finally worked up the courage to ask when my stomach growled unbelievably loud. I laughed uncomfortably and wrapped my good arm over my waist so he wouldn't think some other part of my body had made that noise.

Keeping his left hand on the wheel and his eye on the road, he reached into a brown paper bag and handed me a peanut butter and jelly sandwich enrobed in waxed paper.

"Thankyou," I whispered. The bag resided between us, on top of two leather journals, worn from use. Had he intended to find a secluded spot with his picnic lunch to pen a story or poem? What work of art would never be recorded because he had driven me to Traverse City? I munched on his sandwich and swallowed a heap of guilt with every bite. Surely, the kindest favor I could offer right now would be to remain silent. Then, he could at least be alone with his thoughts instead of my fears.

After a while, I blamed everyone I'd ever known for ill-equipping me to handle this emergency. I blamed my sister for her anecdotal account of barbarism, and I blamed Thaddeus for not letting me talk about it! I blamed the church and camp for believing all troubles could be handled by prayer. I blamed my parents for thinking all ailments could be remedied with a glass of Vernor's ginger ale, though they would seek medical treatment if it was serious. But even then, God received more credit than the doctors. Mom rarely spoke of her hospital stays and never let us come visit her. Lastly, I blamed God for making me so darn healthy because this ensured I knew practically nothing about the craft of physicians. Nor could I muster a single prayer to calm myself down!

Perhaps my healthy life thus far had been a function of my mom's daily diligence. Even if she couldn't always get it to work for herself, her prayers had kept me safe. It made sense, and I grudgingly assumed full responsibility for my current lapse in coverage. But did it have to be so terrifying?

Thaddeus drove to a small medical building. He placed the truck in park. I made a move for the door handle.

"Wait," he said, closing his eyes and bowing his head. "Lord, we ask for your wisdom and power to be made manifest through your servants in this clinic to bring a speedy and harmonious healing."

I exhaled a long-suffering breath. Obviously, Thaddeus knew nothing about stitches either.

He looked right at me and said, "You seem worried."

"No, I'm not," I quickly argued. Hadn't I been a great passenger, quiet and peaceful for the entire drive? I deserved praise, not criticism. I proudly raised my chin and bore my spite like a badge of honor.

He pointedly stared at my right leg.

I followed his gaze and watched in horror as it bobbed up and down. My rubber footwear slapped a rhythmic beat against the floor mat. I firmly planted my heel along the floorboard. The truck grew eerily quiet. Had I done this the entire way?

"You've never had stitches," he guessed.

"I've never really been hurt or sick. I'm terrified of doctors! My sister once had stitches and—"

"Here's what will happen," he cut me short. "They will clean the wound by irrigating it with antiseptic. It will probably sting a little. But this is good. You don't want them sewing it up before getting it really clean. It could get infected."

"Infected? How will I know?" I whispered.

"You'd know," he dismissed my concern. "After this, they'll give you two shots. One in your left arm to prevent tetanus, the other in your wounded arm to numb it. The shots are quick. The medical staff will wait for the numbing to take effect. Just like being at the dentist." He paused to see if this sprang a connection.

"I've never had a cavity!"

He sighed. "By all means, if you feel anything beyond a little pressure, make them stop. You can always have another shot of Novocain. Of course, you may not be able to use your arm until tomorrow." He chuckled. I frowned. "You'll be numb for a while," he explained. "It's a strange sensation."

"So, I won't feel the stitches?" I clarified.

"You will not feel the stitches," he promised. "There will be papers to fill out, and I need to get gas in the truck. But I'll be in the waiting room when you're finished." His voice dropped to a serious, confidential tone. "Don't worry about what comes next. Think of what you know about God's infinite goodness. Believe you are meant to receive these blessings, now and always. Then you will see His love for you in action. When the present moment becomes unbearable, take your thoughts to a pleasant place. Feel His presence. This is praying. It's very simple."

I sat perfectly still, absorbing his words, greatly relieved I hadn't cracked a smart-aleck reply like, "Oh yeah, well what if God is a woman?" His faith had been expressed so honestly I respected him for it, and I believed it. "It's simple," I repeated, calmly reassured and almost giddy.

Thaddeus removed the key from the ignition, took his wallet from the dash, and stuck it into his back pocket. I realized the error of my preconceived notions. I had misjudged these church guys. For the first time I imagined a man of faith could be liberating, rather than stifling. Suddenly, I wanted to look for more in the guys I met. And I wanted to ask for more from the ones I already knew.

I had rebuffed Thaddeus as a judgmental adult, arrogant and condescending. In reality I had been the judgmental one, locked inside my own insecurities. I hadn't seen him clearly at all. He was just a nice guy who wanted to help. "Thanks," I said, "for driving me here on your day off and for sharing your lunch. And, I've been meaning to thank you for saving me from falling off that cliff."

"Don't worry about it." He gave me a reassuring wink. "Sometimes the unexpected happens. It's how we react when it does that matters." He came around to my door and walked me into the clinic. I held my head high to prove I could handle it. He had treated me like an adult so I intended to act like one because suddenly I felt like one.

Less than an hour later we walked back to the truck. Thaddeus whistled a jaunty, nameless tune, and I scuffed alongside feeling off balance and detached from my arm.

"How was it?" he asked, opening the passenger door.

"I didn't watch."

He gave a satisfied nod.

I planted my feet on the floorboard for the long drive back. Plenty of sparkling revelations danced about in my head. How friendly the medical staff had been! The needles had only stung for a second. The stitches didn't hurt! I would have shared this, and more, if he'd shown any interest. Instead, he turned on the radio and never said another word until we reached the camp parking lot.

"I'll let you off here," he said, coming to a halt near the dining hall. About four hours of sunlight remained for him to enjoy the rest of his day off.

My arm had slowly come back to life and so had my temper. I'd forgotten his kindness and had grown impatient with his self-absorbed company. I opened the door and stepped outside. "I'm going to throw this away," I said, reaching for the bloody shirt.

"One last piece of advice." His words seemed to draw back like the pull of a bow before the arrow's release. Now what? I fumed defensively. Couldn't he make conversation? Did it always have to be advice? I was quite sure he'd found some glaring fault and wished to share it. After all, I had plenty to choose from.

Thankfully, he spoke ahead of my transmutation into an irrational victim. His dark eyes penetrated mine, and his gentle expression conveyed amiability. "Don't let this stop you from doing everything you want."

"Oh." I quickly clamped my mouth shut. A pang of remorse pummeled my breath away. Another second, and I would have blown it. I forced a grateful smile. I was still misjudging him. I held up a generous supply of oversized waterproof bandages. "I'm all set," I said, beginning to shut the door.

"I'll get it," he offered, reaching across and grabbing the handle. I stepped back and the door slammed. I waved. He gave a little salute.

In that moment it occurred to me that I did not deserve a church guy. When times got tough, people like Thaddeus reached for a higher power, found it, and then relied on it. I, on the other hand, wallowed in my own worrisome self-pity and filled the silence with negativity. Here was an opportunity to take one step forward on the road to inner growth, and I had just taken two steps back. Hopefully, Thaddeus hadn't noticed. When his truck disappeared behind the wooded curve, I turned toward the dining hall.

Ironic laughter rumbled from my chest. I had arrived early for the first time in my life! The boys' camp was already eating, and the girls' camp straggled in. I was picking up where I'd left off, minus an afternoon of sailing.

FIFTY-SIX

A NEW AWARENESS

I STUFFED THE crusty shirt into a wooden trash can near the boys' dormitories.

"Did you get stitches?" Joanna called.

"Five!" I shouted, mounting the wide, tiered decking.

She rocked against the door's metal release bar. "When do they come out?" I puzzled this new obstacle. No one at the clinic had mentioned it. "Oh, don't worry." She beckoned me inside. "They're easy to snip out, anyone can do it."

I cringed at the prospect.

"Come on, we're having lasagna!" Beth lured us into the cafeteria.

I picked at my food, grateful to be back among my friends. They seemed especially entertaining and attentive.

"So, how was your date?" Tori's voice tickled my ear as she returned from the soft-serve machine wielding a vanilla cone.

"You can have a date, too, if you fall in a trunk," I said, completely enchanted.

"That will never happen!" She laughed heartily all the way back to her seat.

"Does it hurt?" Christie inquired from the opposite table.

"A little," I admitted, turning to face her. "The numbness is wearing off."

Nancy passed between us, clearing her tray, and gave me a sideways hug. "So," she instructed and deduced, "let's try not to blame the trunk!"

"Too late," I smirked.

"Was there a moment of pride before this fall?" Lori inquired, standing over me.

"Yes, mascara!"

"Ah, the dreaded mascara," Cindy said, scooting everyone along.

Lori called over her shoulder, "Told you not to wear any!"

"CTs!" Robyn announced. We obediently spun our heads until locating her near the windows. She presented a stack of folded papers. "Don't let anyone outside your cabin see these."

"Mystery skits," Joanna said for my benefit. "Counselors have a meeting. CTs will lead the activity. Be sure to come up with something entertaining. I'll be a judge." She slid the pepper shaker to Linda. It stalled in the middle of the table.

Linda wrapped her fingers around the shaker and slid it back. "I'll open the arts and crafts shed if anyone needs supplies." She tried to project her melodic voice beyond our table's scope of hearing.

"Oh, just for us?" Elly begged.

"Have you forgotten Stardust's motto already?" Linda gently chastised.

"Stardust has a motto?" Joanna said, as if turning the idea over in her mind.

Elly offered, "Let go and let God."

Beth said, "You can't climb uphill when you're thinking downhill thoughts."

"Oh, you tease me," Linda laughed, capturing the pepper shaker then sending it back to Joanna.

"I know," Annie decided. "It's not you. It's God shining through."

"Girls," Linda scolded her former campers. "Stardust's motto is 'Grace for one must come at the request of grace for all.'"

"How does that apply to opening the arts and crafts shed?" I wondered.

"It's a promise and a warning," Linda said. "It promises everyone the blessings of prosperity. But it warns that such prosperity will not be granted if it is asked at the expense of others." She flicked her wrist, taking aim for Joanna. "In other words, life is not a competition having a limited number of prizes. To prosper, we must desire blessings for everyone, as well as for ourselves. Specifics are not necessary. Just having a sense of God's infinite benevolence will do." The shaker slid smoothly across the Formica. Our eyes followed its progress.

Pithy words of wisdom, akin to those she had just uttered, floated around all summer. We felt their influence in every activity. They came from hymns, the twenty minutes of Bible study before cleanup, quotes in the Murphy, and Sunday School. They surfaced as often as the lakeshore breeze, on a low-key level, and bathed us in an optimistic euphoria. In essence, our greatest camp duty was to overcome limitations. We did this by conquering challenges with brash, fearless ease. Ancient Greeks believed anyone who wished to evade their duty could summon an illness to their assistance. Quite simply, we refused to summon anything but health, harmony, and progress. The resulting mind-set was so uplifting and prevalent I took it for granted and never delved too deeply and never internalized any bit of wisdom for very long. I didn't need to. It was spoon-fed daily.

Now I wanted more than snippets. They didn't get the job done when tragedy struck. And they provided only enough nourishment to last the summer. In fact, they always wore off inside a month of my returning home.

"So, it's kind of like the Golden Rule," I mused, staring at Linda, realizing she had been my Sunday School teacher for most of that summer, and I could not remember any of her lessons.

"Ohhh!" Our entire table gawked at the pepper shaker. It hung halfway over the edge of the table defying gravity. Linda had executed the perfect play. Her tranquil smile, directed at me, implied this little demonstration had been for my benefit, so I could see her lively faith was grounded by works. I wanted to ask her a million questions.

"Whippoorwill!" Robyn called near our table. Just the sound of her voice caused every question in my head to evaporate. "Here!" I jerked my arm upward, and Robyn deposited a folded paper into my hand.

"Gull's Nest!" Robyn called next.

Hutch announced something unintelligible about the guys' evening activity, and Missy bounded into our little circle, taking a newly emptied seat. Having all of Whippoorwill present, I recited the contents of the piece of paper.

"Quiet!" Annie hissed, pressing the note to my chest.

My sister had come to stand behind me.

"She's a counselor!" I laughed.

"She's a judge. She'll have to guess along with everyone else," Beth said.

"How'd it go?" Susan asked.

I puzzled her meaning. Then, I remembered. "Five stitches, and I didn't feel anything." I proudly sent sunlight into the attic of my childhood fears.

"Good," she said, a little taken aback but openly relieved.

Jenny pushed her head between us and whispered succinctly, "Put some vitamin E on it, and you won't have a scar." Her blonde, silky hair momentarily swung across my shoulder.

"Where will I get vitamin E?" I asked, but she had moved on to the next table.

"Were you afraid?" Elly asked.

Before I could answer, Linda's pleasant voice sprinkled over us. "Let us put a conclusion to the entire matter; fear God, and keep His commandments."

"That's kind of off the wall," Joanna said. She and my sister shared cheeky surprise.

"It's from the last chapter of Ecclesiastes," Linda said. "Solomon had struggled an entire lifetime through success and failure, then he makes this conclusion." Her gaze locked onto me, challenging me to think and respond.

"I've never liked that passage," I said, surprised by my honesty. "It's so harsh. Especially when everyone preaches that God is Love. The two seem to contradict each other. You can't have love and fear at the same time."

Our campers paused from their conspiring whispers, anticipating Linda's rebuttal.

"Exactly," Linda said. "God is Love, yet we are instructed to fear God. So, take the next logical step. If we fear God alone, all the while knowing God is Love and God is all, then what is there to fear?"

"Nothing!" The four campers danced in place, hee-hawing their delight. Linda smiled approvingly at them.

"Unless you forget there's nothing to fear," I sagely retorted, in light of my recent challenge.

"That is the secret," Linda said. "We must store up prayers through daily study so we'll have the right frame of mind when we need it."

I admired her conviction. But it was easy to be a prophet on the top of a mountain. What risk or challenge could be found in arts and crafts? Such rigors paled beside those of sailing, waterskiing, or even soccer. On what occasions did Linda apply this wisdom? She never seemed to have a voice in camp leadership. She had been a counselor for as long as Robyn, but she never organized Cedar-Dune competitions, led an evening activity, or headed up a trip. If camp could be stereotyped into high school clubs, Linda would have been captain of the chess team while Robyn coached every single athletic event.

"Sounds like a Stardust thing," Joanna said, popping a stick of gum into her mouth. "You four have been in the same cabins for a long time. What motto would you suggest for Whippoorwill?"

"Killing spiders!" they jeered together.

"Great," Joanna cracked. She stood to leave, and we joined her, meshing into the flood of humanity passing through the double doors to the atrium.

To my great relief, not a single camper or counselor, including my sister, requested a view of the wound or a replay of the gory details. They only wanted to offer a kind smile or a tender remark to show they cared. Back home I might have moped and babied myself to solicit sympathy. Here, I didn't want or need it. I only wanted to return to my activities.

FIFTY-SEVEN

AN UNFULFILLED PROMISE

"CHECK OUT THE sky," Nancy said. We leaned against the back wall of the Hylton. Windows on both sides of the fireplace revealed a fiery blaze over the lake. Striated, milky clouds and a patch of blue perfected the oblique image of an American flag.

"It would have been a nice backdrop for Whippoorwill's Olympic victory against the Soviets," I mused. "Instead of Puccoon's Day at the Circus."

"Is that what this is?"

"That's my guess," I said, feeling warmed by her indulgent laughter.

"Where are you going for Cabin Day tomorrow?" she asked.

I bristled at the question because she'd never had to ask it. We'd always been together. "Waterskiing," I said, "and it's going to be weird."

"It is," she agreed, keeping her eyes focused on the raised platform we used as a stage. She seemed older and wiser, and I imagined a small gulf between us. She'd already experienced a Cabin Day with her campers while I had attended my college orientation. "By the way," she said, "tell Joanna it's your turn for hymn sing."

"Tonight?"

She nodded and clapped as Puccoon left the stage. I couldn't fathom how she knew, but it had been this way since the beginning. She kept abreast of camp's inner workings, and I bumbled along. Try as I might, I could not feel bad about this any longer. Instead, I felt a calm acceptance and deep gratitude for our friendship. She had taken care of me, making sure I hadn't missed the one thing I'd wanted to join since my first night of camp.

"The nine of us have been going in order," she said. "You missed a turn when you went to I.U. and the backpacking trip threw us off."

"This is my only chance?"

"Yup." She avoided my eyes, and we maintained a portentous silence, unable to bear the inevitability of Wildwood's demise.

Campers called out their favorites while counselors reviewed their notes toward an arbitrary judgment. I restrained myself from shouting for Whippoorwill. After all, I was not a camper. I knew this now because Nancy continued to remind me. I felt no resentment or jealousy because grace for one must come at the request of grace for all. Linda's words had never felt more appropriate. I wanted Nancy to be the best counselor she could be, to prosper wherever the camp moved, while I only wanted to sing "Taps" here at Wildwood before it disappeared completely.

A winner was chosen, and campers rushed from the Hylton. The Murphy door banged a steady beat while everyone readied for bed. Robyn yelled, "Lights out!" from the office window. I stood inside the cabin, beside Joanna, as the bugle played its lonely rendition of "Taps." When silence filled the night, we padded across the cement stoop in our slippers and cotton nightgowns, crossed the sand, and gathered near the flagpole. I stared into the darkened screens of Sandpiper imagining a bunk bed and two young girls whispering. When all of us stood in a circle, I was thrilled to see that Lou Ellen and Robyn had remained upstairs.

"What should we sing?" Theresa asked. She smiled at me to acknowledge my presence.

"How 'bout 276?" Sue Reilley rattled off the page number of a favorite. "And 412," Linda said. "We haven't done either of those in a while," Bobbi confirmed.

Amazingly, their furtive whisperings did not include a discussion of their days off, or plans to sneak out later. And their choice of hymns did not spring from the pages of a master register. Had I known this, I would have accosted our counselor with my own suggestion every night, through the years.

"Sue Reilley and I will sing the harmony on 'Taps,'" Jenny instructed.

"I can do the harmony!" I blurted.

"We only need two," Jenny said with the authority of a choir director. "Or we'll drown out the melody."

I grunted at this flare of dictatorship. My sister offered a grim smile of understanding. I had spent years preparing. She and I would serenade our folks before bed. Mom would hum along while Dad stretched beside her, absorbed in a book, his reading glasses propped on the end of his nose. Susan would plug her ears and skip around, jumping into my part, finally getting it right on our third try. Now the moment had arrived to sing for real, and Jenny wouldn't let me!

"Create in me a clean heart, O Lord," Theresa led. We cranked out this hymn, and the next, stiff as metronomes. When we transitioned to "Taps" our style relaxed.

Sing the harmony anyway, a small voice urged me to rebel. Why did Jenny have to be so selfish? She sang the variation every night like a small pig gorging on truffles.

My sister plugged her ears and furrowed her brow in order to stay on key while Sue Reilley and Jenny overlaid a stepped-up chord. I watched Susan, tenderly amused, without a bit of my old embarrassment. At least I could sing either part and enjoy it without having to struggle to produce it. Feeling a swell of gratefulness, I decided to perform my best. Maybe Jenny would lighten up and allow me to sing the harmony when we repeated it for the older campers.

I reached down into my diaphragm for a clear, strong tone. Our voices wove a cocoon of comfort and safety about the camp, enhancing nature's peace and beauty. A warm breeze tugged on our pajamas, and I breathed in the lake's scent, cherishing the thought of eight more days at Wildwood.

"From the lake, from the hills, from the sky . . ." We held the note on "sky," presenting a solid pitch for Sue Reilley and Jenny to modulate.

"All is well," we sang, preparing for the last two phrases and a feast of blends. "Safely rest. God is nigh." I closed my eyes to savor it. When finished, I decided the harmony had been lacking, especially at the end.

Jenny cast me a wry look of "I told you so."

"Next time, sing a little softer," Maggie said, laughing tenderly. She crossed the sand toward Beacon and Sunblazer.

I hung back to digest my mistake, absently watching as Joanna lightly tapped the screen of our cabin. "Goodnight, Whippoorwill," she whispered.

I had blown it by drowning out their part! Jenny would never trust me to sing the harmony now. I couldn't blame her. If I had earned the right to enrich our song like a symphony orchestra, beneath this sky, beside this lake, I would have guarded the privilege with equal vigor.

We struck into the sand and paused on a small bluff having an equal range between the two cabins. I spun around, fascinated and intrigued to see camp from a new perspective. After so many summers it amazed me to stumble upon a new vantage. The lake triggered a moment of awed inspiration.

"Create in me a clean heart," Theresa led. Our voices expanded into hers.

I lowered my volume, becoming the faintest among us. And when we sang "Taps," I hummed. I also did the harmony, just loud enough to hear it resonating between Linda and Maggie on either side of me. It was about as perfect as it could be, and ever would be. The water shimmered from starlight and I willed myself to savor it, to memorize it.

Forever afterward this memory would belong to "Taps." And "Taps" would belong to Wildwood, evoking an image of waves, pines, and sands, so potent it would overshadow my disappointment and carry me through the coming years.

Back in the cabin, Beth whispered, "We heard you."

"You weren't supposed to hear me," I snorted, scooting between beds.

"But you sounded good," she said, rolling on her stomach and burying her head in a fluffy pillow.

I folded my quilt and crawled between the sheets. Elly breathed, "Cabin Day tomorrow." This incited further whispery comments from bed to bed. I hushed them, recalling a time when I was so thrilled I could hardly sleep.

I fell on my pillow, flung my arm above my heart to ease the throbbing, and closed my eyes. It had been a really long day. I heard nothing until Reveille and awakened in the exact position in which I had fallen asleep.

FIFTY-EIGHT

A PEEK BEHIND THE SCENES

THE WOODEN CHRIS-CRAFT floated on Big Glen Lake beneath a blistering sky. We ate our lunch, lounging on boat cushions amid the scent of hot vinyl, fumes from the gasoline tanks, and a twinge of mustiness from the stack of life vests.

"You have a mosquito on your shoulder," Annie said.

"It hitched a ride from the marina," Joanna said between nibbles on her chicken-salad sandwich.

Beth raised her hand to smash it.

"No," Joanna said. "Once it gets full, it will take off. They only itch if you interrupt them."

"Right," I grunted.

"It's true," she claimed, watching its belly turn crimson.

"Kill it! Kill it!" the girls chanted.

"I can't watch." I stood up to untangle the ropes. "Who's doing what?"

"Missy has to cross the wake on two skis, Annie on one," Joanna outlined. "Elly and Beth need to ski double for ten minutes and criss-cross each other's ropes three times."

"I want the shorter rope." Elly poked a finger at Beth. "You lift while I duck under."

"Okay, but you better go low as you can," Beth warned. "I'm tired of wiping out every time we try it."

Missy stood in front of me to eclipse her friends. Folding her arms she bemoaned, "This boat makes the biggest wake in the world!"

I rapped my knuckles on the wooden cabinet that housed the inboard motor. "Yeah, this beast has quite a draw. But you can do it," I said. "On my Cabin Days we had ten of us, including the counselor, to weight the boat down." I pictured my friends sprawled about, filling all the seats. "It will be much lighter today."

I reached into the pile of life preservers for a hardened Styrofoam doughnut covered in red-checked fabric. It was Christie's favorite. Missy took it from me and slung it over her shoulder. "I need to start from the dock," she said.

"That means heading over to the narrows." Joanna plopped the rest of her sandwich into her brown bag and turned the key. "Grab a seat!" She tilted her shoulder to display a mounded mosquito bite. "See, it's gone and it doesn't itch." The motor roared to life, raised us up, and we glided across the lake in a welcome breeze.

Through the course of the afternoon Joanna and I combined our expertise to facilitate our campers' needs. Having a two-to-four ratio ensured they accomplished a week's worth of activity in one afternoon. It wasn't Susan's fault the weekdays were less productive. As the waterskiing counselor, she had twice as many campers, which forced her to be more of a timekeeper than an instructor.

Beth and Elly floated inside an entanglement of towropes, having successfully conquered the nuances of skiing double. They clowned around while I gathered the shorter rope into the boat. My shoulders ached from the prior day's shots, and a pink circle seeped through my Band-Aid. Worst than this, a lonely ache filled the pit of my stomach and would not go away. "Do you miss being a camper?" I asked Joanna.

"You bet," she said, snapping her gum. "But I'd rather be here than anywhere else. Have you ever been to Florida in the summer?"

"Hot?" I ventured.

"Humid, sticky, smelly, buggy, you name it," she confirmed, checking her watch. "We have a halfhour left."

"You take a turn. I'll drive," I offered, thinking it couldn't be too difficult. I was sure she hadn't skied all summer.

"Can't," she said. "Not allowed to let anyone else drive the boat."

"But Susan drove as a CT."

"New rules this summer. Something about insurance. Looks like you get a turn."

I eagerly sorted through our life vests for a dry one, until Joanna cautioned, "Better check the gas tanks."

"Good idea," I agreed. There could be no greater humiliation than running out of gas in the middle of the lake. On the Monday before last, during the morning activity, the disgraceful event had occurred. Susan remained onboard in the middle of the lake, protecting the campers, while Christie, her CT, swam a halfmile to shore. She had knocked on the door of a random cottage and used their phone to reach camp. Hours later, the guys' boat had towed them in.

"Your sister took the heat for that one," Joanna confided, as if reading my mind. "And it wasn't her fault." She snapped her gum and smiled, daring me to ask for the full scoop. Obviously, another counselor on Cabin Day had failed to fill the tanks. But I didn't want to pull aside the curtain of my mirage world and peer into the greasy, inner gears of camp politics. Instead, I opened the motor's cabinet and studied the round gauge on the primary tank.

"It's almost empty," I interpreted the needle. Planning to switch tanks, I crouched near the other bright red container. "Oh no, this one is really empty!"

"Then, we have to gas up. Can't leave Susan with empty tanks on Monday!"

Suddenly, we were pressed for time. The pumps resided on the opposite shore from our marina. We hauled in the ropes, took our seats, and skimmed across the lake. Joanna greeted the attendant who secured the stern while the girls ran inside to buy candy. Torn between the two, I stood on the dock to watch the mysterious process since, of course, on previous trips I'd been inside buying candy.

"Fill both tanks," Joanna advised. "And don't drip on the carpet," she chastised while the attendant switched the nozzle between tanks. When he presented a bill, she signed the bottom and stipulated, "Charge it to the camp's account."

How casually Joanna wielded her power! I couldn't imagine duplicating her air of authority. Not with a straight face, anyway. And my sister had been doing this all summer.

We journeyed back to our marina. Mr. Chinn had parked the van and waited by the boat slip. Under his watchful eye, we cinched the nylon ropes, gathered our towels and trash, stowed the life vests, and locked up the ski equipment. I lagged behind to admire the Chris-Craft's wooden grains and sleek bow. This had been my first time on Glen Lake without skiing. I feared it would also be my last time on Glen Lake, skiing or not.

Mr. Chinn stopped by the Manitou Market. Susan, Christie, and their campers crammed into the bench seats hauling bags of cherries, blueberries, and candy.

"Woo-hoo! Cedars are going to win beach volleyball tonight!" Beth exploded, thrusting her arms into the air, grinning at Susan. When she remembered Susan was a counselor, and no longer her captain, she redirected her enthusiasm on me. "Go Cedars!" she hollered.

"Go Cedars," I repeated. Competitions remained close that summer, but we usually lost in the very last second of the game. As our new captain, Susie devoted all her spare time, including those moments previously spent on hair-styling and boys, toward devising a winning strategy. With only one week left, I doubted our ability to overcome the accumulation of defeats. We'd have to win the Talent Show, the highest-scoring event of the summer and the most celebrated because we used the school's auditorium.

"It's my night off," Joanna reminded me.

"Mine, too," Susan crowed, giving me a look that said, Ha ha, you have to go to bed after "Taps."

Joanna sighed, "I'm not rubbing it in. I just want to know if she can get the sweet rolls and juice in the morning so I can sleep in."

"Oh goody, we get to sleep in!" Eight ecstatic voices chirped. "Yummy, sweet rolls!"

"Of course," I replied uncertainly. Here was another new counselor duty I'd missed by leaving for a few days.

"Just go to the Hylton when everyone else does," Christie said. "The cooks bring the buns right from the oven. You'll probably smell them from Whippoorwill."

The van ground to a stop beside a convoy of construction vehicles. We fled for the woods amid the deafening pounding of hammers, the high-pitched screech of a circular saw, and the scent of freshly cut cedar. I aimed for the beach with the instincts of a newly hatched turtle escaping predators.

Perched on the end of the L-shaped dock, I swung my legs over the water and leaned against my palms, luxuriating in the steady breeze that ensured the construction noises remained inland. After a while, I shifted to face camp, committing every detail to memory from the grains of sand embedded into my palms to the Hylton's roofline and the faint creaking of trampoline springs. I willed it to last.

When the bell rang for dinner, Nancy beckoned me from Beacon's front stoop. On the way to the dining hall, we shared the day's highlights while her campers hovered about, interjecting comments. I still wore my suit under my clothes. It was a slovenly, disrespectful statement of apathy, almost as forbidden as wearing pajamas to breakfast. I wanted to ask Nancy in a breathless whisper, Does camp feel different? Hours passed by, choppy and cumbersome. They used to run seamlessly, bathing me in a blissful euphoria. Instead, I felt bogged down by details. Every activity glared in face value alone, having only a sliver of intrinsic worth as old motivations melted away and new ones failed to materialize.

Our evening activity pitted me against Christie and Mary. The volleyball net stretched between us, and I feared their spikes. Luckily, I had Cindy by my side. She could cover the entire front line. I only needed to step clear, as Susie often reminded me from the sidelines. I smiled and laughed in a desperate race to maintain an enthusiastic attitude. There was no place else I'd rather be. So, why did I need to work so hard to show it?

I should have been riding high on adrenaline as we filtered back to our cabins, not wanting the evening to end, since we'd won three out of five games. Instead, I visited the Murphy, chalked up the victory as a nice boost to morale, then climbed into my cot.

FIFTY-NINE

A LASTING IMPRESSION

"WE STILL HAVE six days!" Susie called from Gull's Nest the next morning. We swept sand from our respective stoops and no longer counted the weeks. We had regular activities to attend, a talent show to rehearse for, and our final Banquet and Council Fire to plan. I knew the hours would drag, but the days would fly.

"Am I supposed to clean the sweet roll tray?" I warily considered.

"No," Susie said. "Just take it back to the Hylton."

"Did you hear that?" I pressed my face into the screen, squinting inside to solicit help.

"Six days until we win the banner!" Beth shouted.

"Go Cedars!" Susie automatically responded, still hoarse from the evening before.

I stifled a laugh and addressed the screen once more. "I'm talking about the tray. Someone please bring it out to me."

The door creaked, and Annie emerged. "I'll take it to the Hylton," she volunteered, sauntering away, picking at the remains of frosting.

"Hey, guys!" Christie shouted from the back of the Hylton. "Pass the word. We're taking a CT picture on the log after cleanup. Wear something goofy."

"Don't forget, we have an hour before church!" Mary called from Sandpiper. I laughed at her predictable caution, usually aimed at every excuse we invented to be together. Though she sought to minimize Robyn's criticism, she only managed to ensure the rarity of our stolen moments.

I ducked inside Whippoorwill for a change of clothes. "Beth," I said, "can you go to Beacon and Sunblazer? Tell Nancy and Sarah to dress goofy for a CT picture on the log before church."

"Can do!" She bounded from the cabin. I watched her run past the flagpole, flinging sand as she stretched her agile legs. Perhaps she planned to steal a jump on the tramp. "She runs everywhere," I observed to Joanna. Then, I tried to remember when I had stopped.

My fellow CTs and I formed a long procession for the beach wearing an odd assortment of pajamas and street clothes. Our campers traipsed along, skipping around us, carrying cameras and chanting our names: "Nancy, Nancy, Lori, Tori, Cindy, Christie, Mary, Sarah, and Sue!"

Josie mimicked an orchestra conductor demanding a staccato beat.

"Golly it's hot." Cindy fanned a floppy hat. "I'm going to need another shower."

Instinctively, we searched the lake for a rippling breeze. "I wish we'd get a storm or something." Lori waved a bonnet to cool her face.

"Yeah, these tights are a little warm," Nancy said. In aqua-and-white-striped leggings and heavy long sleeves, she wore far more clothing than the rest of us. We laughed at this typical understatement of her plight.

"For sure, I'm wearing a tanktop to church," Susie said. "If I can find a clean one."

"Has anyone ever had Sunday School on the dock?" Sarah wondered.

"Too hot," Nancy advised. "No shade."

"Oh, the trampoline," Christie realized. "It's in the shade right now."

"What color do you think Lou Ellen will wear?" Lori said, since our campers had run ahead.

"Doesn't she know she's supposed to wear white to church?" I exclaimed, enjoying the privacy, as if we still resided in Sunblazer or Whitecap.

"She wears white," Nancy said. "She just likes to add some trim."

Tori uniquely predicted, "Simon says . . . hot pink and polkadots for today."

"And matching dingle-balls on her necklace and earrings," Mary added.

"How 'bout that lime green ensemble," Lori said. "That's my favorite."

"So who will lip sync in the Talent Show with me?" Tori lunged ahead, stretching her arms and pointing her toes. "I found the perfect song. It's a tango!" She pivoted in the sand.

"Hush," Sarah warned. "There are Cedars among us!"

"I'll do it," Christie said.

"Good, you can be the guy." Tori spun her around.

"You're leading," Christie said.

"Hurry up!" Josie had run back, waving her arms, wildly impatient. "Give us your cameras." We stacked them into her arms. She doled them out while we took our places on the driftwood log. Polished and smoothed by years of wind, rain, and winter waves, it spanned about ten feet wide and three feet tall, presenting the perfect place to sit for a sailing lesson.

"Pull together," Mary said. "I'm hanging off the end." We wrapped our arms about each other's shoulders and tightened the line.

"Cindy should be in the middle," a few campers suggested, because of her height. We agreed by traipsing across the log in a high-wire act.

When we had realigned, Susie shrieked between peals of laughter, tipping backwards, "Who is pulling on my shorts?" Linked like a Mardi Gras dragon, the waver traveled down the line. A loopy struggle ensued as we tried to disentangle before tumbling into the shrubs. Our laughter effervesced like bubbles in a newly poured glass of soda pop. Contagious and expansive, its familial sound lifted my spirits and filled the empty pit in my stomach like nothing else could do.

"Roman!" Cindy guffawed as we remounted. "If you're going to shove peace signs behind our heads, at least don't lean back while you're doing it."

Nancy gasped in a wounded tone, "They were bunny ears!"

"No bunny ears!" Christie said.

"Do this," Tori said. She bent her leg and pointed her toe, placing the ball of her foot against her opposite knee.

"Do I look like a Rockette?" Lori objected just before Christie yelled, "Cheese!"

Our renegade fan club went to work beneath a bright blue sky capturing our final photo together. Tori held a coquettish pose on the end, impishly grinning. Lori smiled angelically beneath ginger bangs and a baby doll bonnet tied in a bow at her chin. Nancy thrust a hip against her. She also held bunny ears behind Lori and Susie's heads and managed a sophisticated expression despite the unconventional leggings, sunglasses, and low visor that made her look like a racetrack bookie. Susie was captured mouth open, mid-whoop, with a beach towel around her neck. Cindy wore a floppy hat that hid her face in shadow, but her long tanned legs, as well as Christie's, filled the center, accentuated by their shortshorts. Sarah and I crossed ankles in tandem, wearing baby-doll smocks, next to Mary who wore two different sandals and a bandanna in milkmaid fashion. Sarah's timing fell short for bunny ears, with a half-opened fist behind my head and two closed fingers behind Christie's sticking up like an antenna.

The weight of my arms is connecting me to the line. I feel myself falling backwards. My eyes are shut, and I am supremely content and happily frozen in time.

"One more!" The row of campers called in vain as we collapsed into a jumble of resigned laughter. "That's all you're getting from this group!" Mary declared, striding forth to claim her camera. Her voice of authority scattered our fickle groupies. They returned our cameras and bolted for their cabins to change into whites for church. We followed more slowly, prolonging our connection until we neared our different cabins.

SIXTY

TWO CREATIONS

SCATTERED AMONG THE rows of benches, the nine of us could barely keep straight faces as Lou Ellen delivered a tidy sermon wearing pink polka dots, bauble earrings, and a matching necklace.

We sang a couple of hymns then disbanded for Sunday School. My group of six remained in the Hylton. We ranged from eleven years old to my seventeen, headed by Linda at twenty-three. I straddled the end of a bench, grateful to discover that the Hylton retained a bit of coolness, despite the lingering aroma of charred smoke from the fireplace.

We opened our King James Bibles to Genesis. Linda read, "And God said, Let us make man in our image, after our likeness: and let them have dominion over the fish of the sea, and over the fowl of the air . . ."

A flock of seagulls cried overhead, sounding alarmed. I stared at the ceiling beams and envisioned their passage.

" . . . In the image of God created he him; male and female created he them." Linda snapped her fingers for emphasis. "Just like that, God's word created male and female. No mist was needed, no ribs from Adam." Turning her blue eyes on each of us, her lilting voice declared, "God blessed us and commanded, 'Be fruitful and multiply, and replenish the earth, and subdue it . . .'"

I stared glassy-eyed at my Bible's ultrathin pages and tiny print, following along as she read, "And God saw every thing that he had made, and, behold, it was very good."

She paused. " So, why isn't everything in our world still good?"

A thick, humid breeze squeezed through the windows on both sides of the brick chimney, temporarily dissipating the pungent odor of stale smoke. I gazed out at the lake and shrugged, unable to respond. Who could possibly know the answer to such a question?

"Why do we have wars?" Josie said. "One of my brother's friends died in Vietnam."

For a few seconds we simply stared at her. The conflict had ended three years earlier with only a few of us personally knowing anyone called up, let alone lost. "I'm sorry," I said. "I can't imagine what that must be like." But Josie was young and I grew skeptical. "Did you know him?"

"Not really." Her eyes strayed down to the floorboards painted gray to match the benches.

I cast Linda a triumphant glance, as if Josie's distant connection absolved us from feeling sorrow. But Linda's eyes held tears, and I regretted my callousness. She was exactly the right age to have lost boyfriends and classmates.

"Why do we have to lose our camp?" Shane asked, mentioning the one thing we could all relate to.

Linda swallowed hard then took a deep breath. "You don't think these things are good?" Smiling kindly, she patted Josie's knee. "Well, sometimes we have to wait to see the good in a situation. Right now our view of the world is like an ant staring up at a lion. The ant would only see a paw and never understand the lion's full majesty. But, nevertheless, there are many things in our world that are not good. And the rest of the Bible is full of examples as man forgets that God has already created us. Instead, we believe Genesis 2 and '. . . the generations of the heavens and of the earth . . .'"

She pointed around the circle. "What are generations?" Our vacant stares proved we hadn't a clue. "They are a less direct form of creation, made by the offspring of the original. For instance, suddenly man is made from dust and woman of a rib. This is a secondary creation sprung from the earth, quite inferior to the more perfect original. It is the reason women have sorrow in labor, and men till the ground with sweat in their faces. These are not God's blessings," she said.

"Maybe God wants us to experience some pain and sorrow before we receive blessings?" I ventured.

"Poppycock," she said. "We created pain and sorrow, not God. The dust and rib story is our human dream. When God made us in His image, we were perfect and complete. When we understand the difference, we see the material world is an outer picture of our thoughts. And we can change this picture by allowing God's thoughts to be our thoughts. It won't solve our problems. It will make them disappear."

I leaned forward, interested and engaged.

"In the second chapter of Genesis, and every page after, we rarely hear God's word. It is man's word and his creation. It's what people say and do while figuring out God's relationship to us. It's our struggle against the power of our words, our earthly concepts, our bodies, and the results of our choices. We have forgotten that God is not the creator of evil, we are. We discovered toil and sorrow in the mist. But we can rise above it when we remember the truth; we are God's perfect image and likeness."

"But the mist is very real," I objected. The other girls had been peering about, daydreaming, and now brought their attention back to the circle.

"Nan," she said, pleased by my comment, "this is why we must guard our daily thoughts. We can't allow fear, hatred, jealousy, or anger to take hold, not even for an instant. The Bible is full of stories about men and women who do, and they face awful consequences. But God is always there for them in the end."

I leaned back and crossed my arms. "If these are human traits, why is the Old Testament full of references to God as being jealous and vengeful?"

"So we can understand difficult concepts on our terms. It can seem like God is jealous when we don't love Him, alone, as we were created to do. And we experience longing and strife when we disconnect ourselves from Him, which can seem like vengeance. Again, God did not create evil. We did, as we live this earthly existence according to our will. Evil spelled backwards is live." She paused for each of us to spell out the letters. "God gave us Life, and we must live it according to His will, by thinking and speaking His words, or evil will result."

She closed her book and rested her hands on the cover. "Let us keep our minds filled with the good news that the first creation still stands. If only we believe it."

The back door banged, and a few classes returned.

"Moses understood the power of the spoken word," she concluded. "When you get a chance, look in chapter 30 of Deuteronomy, verses 10 through 14." She glanced about the room. "Well, that hour sure passed quickly."

The younger ones in our group made polite efforts of turning the benches before extracting themselves.

"Yes, it did pass quickly," I agreed, closing my small red Bible. I fanned my face with a bookmark. More and more campers filed in, adding to the stifling, unbearable heat.

"I've enjoyed having you in my class," Linda said.

"Thanks," I said. "I've enjoyed having you as a teacher." I basked in her glow as it landed fully upon me, as if she saw something she might take some credit for. How sad, here at the very end, I finally saw her as my favorite. And I wanted to be like her. Perhaps if I had swallowed my pride and taken some interest in arts and crafts I would be an easy hire for next summer. Linda had made it clear she would not be returning. She had finished her graduate schooling and was engaged to be married. I didn't know where she came from or where she would go. I only knew she would be leaving an opening and I would miss her.

We slid our benches to fill the rows facing the fireplace. Linda left for the back while Nancy and Christie joined me in the front.

SIXTY-ONE

STANDING FOR THE TEST OF TIME

"IT'S REALLY HUMID, like southern Indiana," Christie said, flapping a piece of paper folded into a fan.

Nancy exhaled, shooing air from her face. "It's definitely not normal for northern Michigan."

We squeezed together, making room for others. Moisture beaded on our faces. Our arms grazed, sticky and warm. Lou Ellen read a benediction and Bobbi's fingers came down on the musty upright piano. She slowed the tempo of our closing hymn to drive the point home. None of us would ever again gather to worship in the Hylton.

"The heavens declare the glory of God and be not far from me. For I shall exalt in thy strength, O Lord, and place my trust in thee."

My heart fluttered strangely, as if missing a few beats. A tingling sensation prickled my scalp, spread down my arms, to my feet, creating a perception of heightened awareness. Despite the sweltering heat, chill bumps raised on my skin as if this feeling could not be contained and must drift beyond my body, touching and blending into the other forty-eight souls in the Hylton, who also expanded beyond their limits. It seemed our spirits emblazoned a powerful imprint on this spot, strong enough to outlast a sand dune, a wooden structure, the surrounding trees, or even the passage of time. I wanted to believe a casual stranger, thirty years hence, wandering where the Hylton's foundation used to be, where our cabins once stood, even our trampoline and flagpole, would know a girls' camp had resided here, housing our adventures, hopes, and dreams from a charmed moment in time. Perhaps they might even hear the echo of our voices singing in the bright sunlight, sounding like a peculiar whistle on the wind.

When the hymn ended, no one moved to leave. The sky appeared a strange pale green. Our tallest pine tree bowled over from a burst of wind. Wooden rafters creaked overhead, and the walls yawned, making cracking sounds. Air rushed through the open windows, rustling our hair and clothing. The back door burst open, straining against its spring. Bang! It slammed in release. I heard someone pounding upstairs to Bess's office, Lou Ellen's now.

We recognized the first signs of a storm, and almost everyone ran to secure the cabins. The wooden shutters needed to be lifted from their props then lowered against the screens, a feat best accomplished before the rain started since it had to be done outside. Cabins having taller foundations, like Stardust and Puccoon, required broom handles.

Shutters dropped all around the camp, slamming against their wooden sills, echoing loudly through the still air. Nancy, Christie, and I collected hymnals from the benches and stacked them beside the piano.

Robyn and Lou Ellen's feet shuffled above us, anxiously unsettled. Their agitated voices traveled easily from the knotty pine stairwell.

"They are just water spouts," Lou Ellen said. "I've seen them in fair weather when it's warm and humid. They rise from the water then fizzle out after an impressive show. They are harmless. They will never reach the shore."

"These did not come from the water," Robyn argued. "I saw them drop from the clouds. I think they formed over the Manitous. And if they did, we're in trouble." She pounded down the stairs and leveled a serious gaze on us. "Seek shelter. Not in the cabins!"

"You can see them?" Linda's tone sounded dubious.

"From up there," Robyn ground impatiently. "And they're headed for shore."

"Should I call the rangers or the police?" Lou Ellen called down.

"There isn't time!" Robyn said. She pushed the screen door and hustled along the boardwalk, walking as fast as she could in an effort to appear calm as she pushed open doors and called inside, "Come to the Hylton's basement! It's a tornado!"

"There's barely enough room for fifteen people down there," Nancy said. I hadn't even known the Hylton had a basement! And she had been down in it.

"I'll take a group to the resort," she said, slapping the door open and running toward the flagpole. "Listen up!" she called. "Get out of the cabins! Come with me!"

Christie caught the door midslam, and muttered upon exiting, "Someone should be using the megaphone."

Bobbi methodically placed the master hymnal in the piano bench, giving Linda a relaxed smile. I glimpsed an island of calm between them while chaos and tension billowed around us. "Ready to go to work?" Linda asked. Bobbi nodded, and they strolled from the Hylton.

I leaned against the wooden paneling, having an inexplicable urge to bolt for shore to see this spectacle, quickly, before anyone could object. I held my breath, wondering if I dared carry it out. I could see Whip-poorwill from where I stood. The shutters had been secured.

"No, Margie, you can't bring your trunk!" Mary called to her younger sister as a group ran past. "We're heading for the river to lie down around the bank!"

"Do we have everyone?" Nancy rounded the Murphy, counting her charges. Sand whipped about, and her campers shrieked from its stinging, blinding swirl.

"Is it really two tornadoes?" one of them gasped, covering her eyes.

"They won't harm us," Nancy declared. She paused at the door and squinted inside. Her worried expression belied her words. "Nancy, come with us to the resort." She didn't wait for my answer and moved out of sight. Her campers bunched around her, willing to follow wherever she led.

"What are you going to do?" Maggie asked.

I jumped in place, completely unaware of her standing there. "I don't know. I usually follow my friends," I said, bewildered by my own candor. "What are you going to do?"

She smiled mischievously. "Probably take cover somewhere. But a waterspout is a once-in-a-lifetime thing. And there are two of them." She stepped around me. "Someone should witness this." The wind whipped her voice as she crossed the sand. The walls of the Hylton strained as if they would burst apart.

"How do you know they're waterspouts and not tornadoes?" I called through the screen, but she hadn't heard. Whippoorwill's door flapped against a passing gust. I rushed to secure it. A rectangle of sunlight filtered in upon our empty, buttoned-up cabin. Sparkling bits of dust floated wildly about, trying to settle on the neatly made beds. I slid my Bible across the floor, gripped the latch, and shut it tight. Cleared of my duties as Whippoorwill's CT, I hopped off the stoop and aimed for the lake. My heart pumped so forcefully, veins pulsated along the gums of my teeth. Like the final dash from school grounds when skipping out, I didn't dare look back. When I cleared the last cabin, a gust slowed my progress to a cumbersome trudge. The giant pine prostrated, creaking and moaning. Its stubby needles quivered. Sand swirled into my face.

I squeezed my eyes shut. I didn't need to see the way. I knew it by heart. Ten more paces, and the chute would widen into our beach. The L-shaped dock and the schoolyard slide would be standing firmly in the water. I'd see six surfboards stacked against wooden posts near the driftwood log and two sailboats grounded nearby, their masts poking up like giant toothpicks. Our floating dock would be rocking wildly on its barrels amid opalescent whitecaps, sparkling in the sun, meshing seamlessly into a crown of puffy white clouds. It was the typical windy-day scene I expected to see as I peeked through my fingers.

Nothing could have prepared me for the extraordinary spectacle before my eyes.

Foaming crests submerged the dock at intervals and rushed up the slide in a fountain of spray. The sailboats and surfboards were missing. Our floating dock had spiked to a forty-five degree angle and stayed there. Whitecaps buried the shore. And two spiraling funnels dominated the sky.

SIXTY-TWO

SUSPENDED DISBELIEFS

"You stood on the shore and watched?" my daughter interrupted, drawing me back to the diner.

Katie said, "That was kind of crazy."

"Obviously, nothing happened." Angela gestured for my apparent lack of scars or disabilities.

"I didn't get hurt, if that's what you mean. But plenty happened."

"Like what?" Angela prompted.

"Well," I began, wanting to justify my impetuousness. "I wasn't the only one who had come down to the beach."

"Let me guess," KT said, beginning to giggle. "Linda was there, and because of her shocking Bible lesson she held up her arms like Moses and sent those tornadoes packing." Her tone carried a hint of mocking and an underpinning of wishful thinking.

"Oooh." Angela's eyes widened, and her voice lowered seductively as she ventured into further speculation. "I know, Linda was really a white witch, and she summoned her coven to the beach where they conjured a circle of power, chanted some camp songs, and waved pine boughs until the tornadoes came ashore, jumping over the camp but completely demolishing the evil resort!"

"You've seen too many movies." I reached for the pitcher of syrup to drizzle dark lines across my stack of pancakes. "None of us has the power to bend the laws of nature," I said, wiping my fingers on my napkin, "unless credit is given where credit is due."

KT choked on her orange juice. "What does that mean?" she spewed.

"It means . . ." I caught myself midsentence because I didn't really know. My gut told me something miraculous had occurred, and that it had changed me. But I couldn't say how. The event to which I had alluded was encapsulated inside a vault of memories too fantastic to be believed. On its surface was the vague impression of huddling on the beach in a group, shrouded by a vaporous mist. Beneath its surface was the certainty of facing danger and escaping harm.

I squinted at the blurry memory, wishing it into focus. My entire camp story had been leading up to it. Surely it deserved to be recollected! I closed my eyes and tunneled down into the foundation of my life, down to bedrock, where it lay dormant and hidden by subsequent layers of experience, doubt, and neglect.

"You are right about one thing," I whispered. "Linda is the key." This tiny fragment of illumination created a fissure that cracked my geode-encrusted memory wide open and caused it to sparkle. The mind can know such things in the blink of an eye, if the timing is right.

SIXTY-THREE

THE TRUTH MADE CLEAR

THEY DANCED A spectral duet. An island of clouds tethered their lasso tops to the sky, and their blue, wiry tails lashed the water like giant whips cracking a sleepy beast. The lake seethed and boiled on contact. The sun cast rainbows in their mist.

My world had turned upside down. Clouds were not supposed to reach down like destructive fingers from a cloudy fist. They were supposed to be sideways, parallel to shore, benign and harmless to enhance the water's beauty.

"Up here!" My sister's voice beckoned from the sweeping edge of the chute.

I could not believe she had been drawn to the beach by the same urge! She reached down. I took her hand and climbed the bluff. The sailboats and surfboards had been lifted to safety amid the dune grass. It was something Robyn would do, but I saw only Susan, Linda, Bobbi, Shane, and Maggie.

Like birds flying a V formation, Linda commanded the lead position and we gathered behind her. Spray lashed our skin and subdued the sand, preventing it from blowing in our eyes. I didn't blink. I didn't move. A swishing hum vibrated on the wind and a high-pitched whistle rose above it as the two cyclones alternated away then near each other, as if they knew it would be disastrous to touch. They also appeared to spin one way, then another, as if defying the laws of physics, when in reality they spun like tops, in one direction, and their outer edges whirled like the blades of a circular saw heading straight for camp.

"Are you afraid?" Linda sternly challenged.

"No!" we shouted. Incredulous laughter bubbled inside me, amazed to find I spoke the truth. I had never seen a real tornado, let alone two at once, and both rivaled massive oak trees. How could I feel happy in the face of such danger? How could stitches have caused terror, but not these?

"Good! We have no room for fear. If you feel afraid, leave!"

She meant it. I glanced at the others. Their eyes glinted at the challenge.

"Join hands!" Linda's blonde curls whipped about as she boldly faced the water. "Let us recite Psalm 46, 27, and 19," she demanded, having changed into that Scandinavian Goddess I'd so often imagined.

I leaned toward Susan, stunned by the absurdity of the moment, and said, "Who has that memorized?"

"She writes the sayings in the Murphy," Susan spoke directly in my ear.

I stared at Linda, newly impressed. I had always assumed Jenny crafted those inspirational verses. "Offer up your fearless revelry," Linda shouted, "for He has already saved us."

The funnels now equaled the height of skyscrapers. Their piercing cries ratcheted to an ominous roar. The northern one remained lithe and willowy. She touched lightly and sparingly upon the lake's surface, progressing in continuous sweeps. But her southern sister spun more laboriously, in clumsy jerks and starts. Each time she hit the surface she gained mass. When she could no longer lift her weight, the lake fought back by hurling streaks of water. A whirlpool lifted into the sky. Her lasso top thrashed angrily and she issued a low-pitched growl.

"God is our refuge and strength, a very present help in trouble," Linda said. "Therefore will not we fear, though the earth be removed, and the waters thereof roar and be troubled. . . . God is in the midst of her, we shall not be moved. God shall help her, and that right early!"

Her top snapped loose of the clouds and her body slogged in the deep. Just past our sandbar, she whipped a raging fury, filling with water and foam in the same way a tornado could fill with dirt, boards, and trees when traveling across land. Like a giant blue leg stuck in a tar pit, she sank into the turbulent water, mired in a watery grave.

The other danced a solo effort, spinning in a roiling tempest. She had the fierce intensity of a runner darting for shore to demolish the finish line. If a straight attack had been possible, she would have already achieved her goal. Instead, she spun about, teasing and cavorting. Her midriff sashayed, and her tail skimmed the surface, creating great swirling intakes of sucking pressure.

Our hair flew outward toward the cyclone, then slicked back from an onslaught of moisture. My ears popped, and I swallowed repeatedly while our charging foe towered above us, spindly and wicked, widening as she neared.

We'd heard stories of destruction from tornadoes traveling across water reaching speeds of over a hundred miles per hour. They rarely ventured far inland, but their annihilation of the immediate shore could be fatal and absolute, ripping up trees, throwing boats and houses about like matchsticks, sometimes with people inside.

Linda's cadence rose above the wind, strong and determined. I focused completely on her words, harnessing the carefree trusting youth of summers gone by, before the confusion of growing up had settled upon my shoulders. I held adrift in an acute state of wonder expecting something glorious to happen, never once thinking of the danger as we stood in the cyclone's path.

"God is our Hightower!" Linda declared. "Say it with me," she pressed and we hollered the same, elevating God to a greater force than this violent offspring of nature.

"The Lord brought me forth also into a large place . . ." Linda called out.

The twister had gained a misty translucency, and her leading edge enveloped us in hissing vapors. This ethereal substance blasted our bodies, blinding us to the lake, though we knew it was still there, large as ever. Its presence could not be denied. Through fog, wind, and rain, over many summers the lake had proved its reliable sameness, even when we couldn't see it.

Suddenly, my teenage accumulation of half-formed thoughts regarding the lake, the camp, and my relationship to both clicked into shape. Here was the reason I was so drawn to the lake. It was the "large place," the dwelling of the most high. And when I sat along the beach or dangled my feet from the dock, I felt its connection to me.

"He delivered me," Linda called out, "because He delighted in me. And now shall mine head be lifted up above mine enemies round about me: therefore will I offer in His tabernacle sacrifices of joy; I will sing, yea, I will sing praises unto the Lord."

Laughter rumbled in my chest. Not jeering and challenging, but amazed and delighted. The cyclone stretched from the shoreline up to the clouds. Her whirling force, so real and threatening, held a transparent haze of incorporeal moisture. I barely heard Linda singing though I joined her. Bobbi flung her arm toward me. I reached out to her and felt myself rising inside the tornado's velocity like a wing lifting into the air. My sister pulled me to her chest, and Bobbi caught my wayward arm to close our circle. Shane likewise started to liftoff and we hauled her in, linking arms around her shoulders.

"There is no speech or language where our voices are not heard!" Linda declared.

Maggie ordered, "Go away!"

"Yeah, go away!" Shane and Susan joined in.

We huddled low on the track of an invisible train. Our limbs vibrated from its imminent bellow as it bore down upon us. The temperature dropped. A deluge saturated us, and the funnel tried to rip us apart. We held fast, hugging close, remaining grounded, despite the tempest spinning at our backs, tugging us upward. We stared into each other's dripping faces, grinning and laughing at this unlikely situation, feeling the beauty of our connection.

At the pinnacle of its upsurge, when it seemed we couldn't hold any longer, the roar ebbed to a shrill hiss, and the turbulence diminished to a balmy swirl. We sensed the cyclone's top half mounting above us, escalating back into the clouds. Her lower half dissipated through us, heading inland as feathery wisps.

A hush fell upon us. The wind ceased to blow. The sun reemerged, bringing startling rays of golden warmth.

We let go and squinted up at the sun. The oppressive, humid morning had cleared into a dry, pleasant afternoon.

The cloudbank passed beyond Council Fire Point, into obscurity. Already its danger felt dreamlike and hazy but the large, thunderous waves, without a hint of wind, proved it had really happened.

"I wish the whole camp had seen this!" I spoke over the colossal swells covering the beach and tearing away the edge of our dune.

"They'd think we were crazy," Maggie said.

"People will say they were waterspouts," Bobbi decided, staring out at the lake, almost in a trance. "And not tornadoes. Meaning we never stood in the way of any real danger. So, I'm not telling anyone."

"You were all very brave." Linda smiled, giving Shane a sideways hug.

"We were lucky," I sighed.

"Lucky?" Linda's quizzical expression confronted me. "Save that for a disbelieving crowd. You know better. Miracles are not a random bit of luck. They are the operation of a Higher Law."

Shane blustered, "We are the ants who have just seen the majesty of the lion!" Her dark, youthful eyes sparkled, and we laughed at the beauty of Linda's lesson coming full circle.

As last I understood Linda's contribution to camp's harmonious existence. Her prayers were the glue that held us together. I also realized my rebellious nature, which often landed me in trouble, had brought me to the lake. So, instead of shepherding a few campers to safety, like the rest of the crowd, I had added my prayers to save them all.

"This is my last year," Maggie said. "My parents don't know it yet," she added, in response to our gasps of surprise. Her family provided active support to the camp. We assumed she'd return year after year like the rest of them.

"Me, too," my sister agreed. "I'm done."

At any other time, Susan's conviction would have caused me to hyperventilate. Instead, I accepted it. "They probably won't ask me back as a counselor," I said, staring at Linda, supposing she would know.

"You don't need to come back," she said. "There are so many wonderful things you've never done, places you've never been. I may not see the lake again for many, many years."

We held a respectful silence, facing the surf and the horizon. I wondered if the same would hold true for me. "Most people have a place where they feel the Lord dwells," Linda said. "This will always be mine. And I will carry it here." She pressed a hand against her chest. "Decide what you want out of life, speak the words, and then let it happen. Creation happens by letting."

"That's right," Maggie agreed. "Let there be light.'"

"Oh, yeah," I whispered. By letting myself be different, I had found the strength to break free from my friends, to create a new path for myself. At the beginning of every summer I had plopped down on my cot and sensed camp's fleeting existence in my life. Now I recognized its lasting presence. These time-outs from the distractions of home had helped me formulate who I wanted to be. Though still fuzzy and out of focus, the view had just grown clearer. I had the right tools for me. I only needed to enter the world and learn to use them in a productive manner. Let the bulldozers come. Let the camp move. My friends could return as counselors, but I would move on.

"I'm returning," Shane said.

"We'll be counting on you to carry on our fearless revelry." Linda smiled.

"You have many years of fun ahead," Maggie predicted.

"Even if I don't get awards?" Shane asked.

"Who cares," I said. "You're funny, practical, and honest. We love this about you."

"Thanks," Shane said, drinking it in.

Susan gushed bombastically, "Let's go swimming!"

"Oh!" Bobbi laughed, shaking droplets from her hair. "I feel like I already have."

I grabbed Susan's arm, full of gratitude to have her for a sister, and tugged her from the bluff. "What a great idea!"

SIXTY-FOUR

RAYS OF THE RISING SUN

"Mom!" KT said, pinching my arm. "So, what happened?"

Blinded by the unexpected clarity of this long-forgotten episode, I took a deep breath and said, "We watched the tornadoes disappear."

"That's it?" Angela accused.

"Maybe." I smiled through an aura of mystery. "And maybe not."

"Just tell us," KT pestered.

"The lake brought them down to size, and camp returned to normal." I felt their curious stares. "Okay, one other thing." They leaned near, expecting a juicy secret. "When I broke free from my friends that morning to face those funnels, I let go of my agonizing self-analysis and desire to please the crowd. Plus, I had discovered the lake's hidden meaning. Its calm feeling, reliable sameness, enduring strength, and wide-open beauty matched my perception of a higher power. The prospect of spending summers away from camp no longer terrified me. I could take the lake's 'large feeling' with me."

Setting down my fork, I crossed my arms, and said, "Now, I'm heading back because I need a refill."

"That's not exactly a news flash," KT said, eyeing her friends for their reaction.

"How big were the waves?" Angela asked.

"Probably eight feet at the sandbar."

"That's decent," Katie said. "Like the ocean after a storm."

"Better!" I exclaimed. "No salt. We spent the day body-surfing, coming in just long enough for a hot dog at the cookout. Right up to the sun's colorful setting, after everyone had called it quits, Nancy and I swam, side by side. It was our last adventure together as carefree, fearless campers."

"Who won the banner?" KT asked.

"Cedars."

"All right," she said, presenting a fist for me to pound.

"Christie and Tori's Tango was the hit of the Talent Show, but we scored the most points. At the final banquet, they announced the winner. Through all the screaming and clapping, I watched Susie's reaction. She just nodded her head, real slow, as if thinking, 'I did it. Look what I am capable of.' It was huge because I'd always thought of Susie and me as the ditzy ones. With that victory, all her airhead moments seemed to disappear. As well as mine. We had each found an inner confidence. I imagine it changed her life, but I don't know for sure because I never saw her, or heard from her again."

"Then you took that picture from the dock?" KT prompted.

"Yes." I smiled because she remembered it. An afternoon shower had deposited beads of water, like tiny mirrors, across every surface to amplify the sun's golden rays. The beach, the Hylton, and its prominent brick chimney, the driftwood log, and the giant pine tree all retained a honey glow, like a pleasantly yellowed photograph. "I used the dock as a dividing line and pieced the pictures together after they were developed. We didn't have panorama cameras back then."

"You did a good job. I hardly noticed it was two pictures," KT said. "Well, except for the tape."

I took a bite of my pancakes and imagined its exact placement inside my photo album. It had been the night I planned my future. Darkness had fallen on Wildwood, and I had vowed to hold firm when returning home. I would break up with my boyfriend and stop experimenting with a lifestyle that didn't suit me. Never again would I get lost in the mind-altering fog of social pressure. I wanted to be a college graduate, to have a serious profession, and to share my life with someone I could love and respect on all levels, and who would provide the same in return. I also wanted to live in interesting places and have a family. I whispered those goals on the wind, to the lake and the clouds, to where my future would come.

"So, the next summer they moved the camp along the river?" KT said.

I stared at her. Here was the living proof of my success. My daughter. "That's right." I paused, allowing the past to fold into the present. "The camp changed locations a few more times until they acquired the old land."

"And you never were a counselor," Angela concluded. She leaned back from the table, signaling the meal's conclusion. Katie and my daughter pushed their plates away, suddenly disgusted by their leftovers.

"I was never offered the job," I said, wiping syrup from my elbow. "I might have turned it down. But I still wanted to be asked. Rejection is never easy!"

"Will you be happy to see Robyn, if she's there?" KT wondered.

"Sure," I said, though a flutter of anxiety caused me to doubt my own sincerity. I wondered if she'd be happy to see me. "I mean, I hope so," I added, seeing their perplexed expressions. "It was her job to be critical, I realize now. And when I attended I.U.'s registration, she thought I was more interested in college. I probably was. That trip ruined my perform-ance review. I had no idea we were under such scrutiny!"

"Have you seen any of your friends since then?" Katie asked, perhaps imagining a time when she, too, might lose contact with these close friends.

"Not really. I met up with Christie a few times when I visited Indiana. I talked to Nancy on the phone after her husband died, very tragically. Other than writing once in a while, we haven't really connected until now." I felt a pang of worry, second-guessing my reasons for attending, sensing my link in the chain had been replaced. Lori, Nancy, Mary, Cindy, and Christie had met Robyn's high standards and become veterans of the inner circle. "I might be the only one attending who was never a counselor," I realized, a bit fearfully.

"When I was a camper, I never wanted to be a counselor," KT said.

My insides jolted from motherly guilt. My camp days were gone, but hers could still be here! Had I limited her opportunities? The longest she'd ever stayed at camp was four weeks during the second session. Should I have pushed a little harder? Should I have forced her to try the full seven weeks? It was a startling summation, and it melted my smile. I should be taking her to be a CT instead of going to a silly reunion!

"Nancy is staying with us at your dad's, right?" Angela interrupted.

"Oh," I groaned, "I forgot to tell him about that. But, yes, Nancy called me right before we left, desperate for a place to crash with her three girls. Their other plans had fallen through and every B&B and hotel is packed this time of year."

"Her girls are a few years younger than us," KT said. "I went to camp with them my last year." She tossed her crumpled napkin on the table and cast me a sly grin. "Did you find any petoskeys after those tornadoes?"

"Tons of them." Angela and Katie shared puzzled expressions, so I explained, "They are the state stone. Actually, they are fossils. All of Michigan was once a shallow sea, before the Ice Age, and the Great Lakes were a giant coral reef. Petoskeys are basically petrified coral." I used the outer tine of my fork to draw interlocking pentagons on my napkin, fanning tiny lines inside each one. "Petoskey means, 'Rays of the Rising Sun.'"

"We need to look for those," Angela said.

"They're kind of hard to find," KT said, wearing a thoughtful scowl. "But we can try! We'll be there in a couple of hours. Right?"

"Right," I confirmed, unable to believe it. Finally, I would see the lake. And if the reunion turned out to be a disappointment, I would always have that.

The waitress strolled by and slapped our bill on the edge of the table. I reached for it. The girls rummaged through their tiny purses for some cash. "This is my treat," I insisted, standing up.

They smiled energetically. "Thanks, Mrs. Taylor!"

At the cash register I handed my daughter some bills. "Run this back to the table and slip it under the sugar shaker," I whispered, in penance for all those times I had never thought to leave a tip at The Blue Bird. Some things change for the better, I congratulated myself as we settled into the car and drove away under a low sky. And some things change for the worse, I worried, as the unhurried miles unfolded.

SIXTY-FIVE

CONNECTING THE DOTS

"TURN LEFT AT that red barn." KT pointed. We followed the same instructions I'd followed five years earlier when bringing KT and her brother to camp. They had been unable to offer any navigational help that afternoon, sitting in the backseat, leery of their impending adventure while I struggled to interpret landmarks because few signs existed.

"We're looking for a fork in the road," KT alerted.

"Shouldn't a fork have equal splits?" Katie said, peering past my head as we descended into a valley. At the bottom, a bald road cut away from the main.

"It's a fork," Angela said.

"Take it," my daughter decided before the opportunity coasted away.

Two stressful miles later, an old clapboard schoolhouse rewarded our decision. "Now we're looking for a graveyard," KT said.

"There!" Angela announced at the first sight of a tombstone.

Winding through the countryside I lost all sense of the familiar until we reached a low bridge. "This is Glen Lake! We're almost there," I promised, perceiving restlessness from the backseat. It had been two hours since we left the diner.

KT narrated like a tour guide, "Big Glen is on the right side of the narrows. Little Glen is on the left. Ski boats can pass under in search of smooth water. Usually when Big Glen is choppy, Little Glen is not."

I slowed to absorb the view, searching for a familiar dock or a distant marina, feeling like a returning camper rather than a fortysomething mom. Too quickly we entered the woods. An embankment rose on our left. Steps had been cut at intervals for unseen homes to access the lake. On our right, gated entrances led to three-car garages and manicured lawns sloped toward a field of blue. The cottage-like structures of my childhood memory were now year-round estates. Sophisticated and forbidding, they clearly illustrated the passage of time and the influx of upscale civilization. If Christie had to swim ashore now because the boat ran out of gas she'd probably have a guard dog nipping at her heels.

"I don't remember these mansions being here when I brought you to camp," I grappled confusedly.

"They were," KT replied.

"I guess I was preoccupied," I said. She and her brother had bristled at the idea of spending three weeks away from home in a distant state. Since none of their friends attended overnight camp, they had no frame of reference except the camp brochure, my old photos, and promises of fun. Basically, I forced them to attend, taking complete control during their father's remote military assignment. During days of driving, I had pumped them full of encouragement, telling them how much they'd enjoy it. On my solitary drive home I had feared they wouldn't. Would they be homesick? Would they feel abandoned? I had fretted especially about my son, Andrew. The boys' camp remained a mystery.

When the counselor's weekly reports arrived in my mailbox, news about KT had been positive. News about Andrew had been disheartening. Penciled in a tight, crooked cursive, his letters home narrated a profound desire to escape. He'd felt abandoned through trickery upon realizing the camp I'd described, having breakfast in bed on Sundays and movies when it rained, was actually a mild version of boot camp for the boys. He'd been subjected to mandatory dips, military-style inspections, hikes in the rain, little privacy, and an absentee counselor having little patience for homesickness. Plus, he hadn't made any friends. Of course he chose to stay home the next two summers when KT begged to return! I had toned down my insistence after that, letting her make the decisions about when she would attend and the length she would stay.

"You only came Up-North my first year," KT reminded me. "After that I flew to Indiana and everyone took turns getting me up here; Gramsy and Chip, Gramps and Barbara, Aunt Sue and Uncle Kevin . . ." Even my husband's family had climbed into the act, timing their vacations to coincide with KT's schedule to help with the driving.

"Good thing, too!" I exclaimed. "Could you imagine making this round trip twice in three weeks?" I solicited sympathy from Angela and Katie, glancing back to see their reaction.

"No," Angela firmly agreed.

The two-lane highway wove beside rivers and lakes until we climbed a mile-long slope. We ascended so quickly it was like becoming airborne in a small aircraft. "Can you see the lake behind us?" I asked.

My passengers craned around and peered into open sky. Ribbons of clouds unfurled above the landscape. Their ruffled pinnacles shone from the hidden sun like the pearly insides of an oyster. Their navy and charcoal base meshed into the horizon, obscuring and camouflaging the lake.

"I don't see it," Angela said.

"It's there," I promised.

"Isn't this a sand dune?" KT asked.

"Sure is," I eagerly validated her memory. "Under this greenery is a mountain of sand."

We entered a neighborhood of wooded lots. The chosen driveway held mature cedars inside its gravelly path. I steered through this obstacle course of sentries, passing mere inches from their red crinkled bark.

Dad was outside splitting wood, surrounded by a carpet of heart-shaped leaves glistening from drops of rain. He stowed the axe, and when I hopped from the car, he gave me an athletic hug honed from years of rigorous training.

"We have a window of sunshine and better get some exercise while we can," he advised, glancing into the backseat. "Who's up for a hike across the dunes to the lake?"

The girls yawned, preening for an extraction from the vehicle. "We're in," KT replied.

"Super!" Dad declared. "Barbara and I are training for a triathlon. It's been raining steadily in South Bend so we came here in search of some better weather to work out."

"And to see us?" I teased.

"Of course." Dad laughed a bit sheepishly.

Barbara assigned rooms inside the chalet, so christened by a little plaque near the main entry. I deposited my suitcase in a bedroom on the main floor then dashed upstairs to check on the girls. Two more bedrooms and another full bath filled the second floor of the triangular roof.

"How exactly will you sleep in twin beds?" I stood in their doorway checking on their progress.

"I don't know," Angela said, tossing clothes from her bag. "Maybe one of us will sleep on the floor. Or two of us will share a bed."

"Mom!" KT said. She straightened from her plastic duffel. "Don't worry, we'll handle it!" She waved me away and pulled the door shut.

I inhaled sharply, feeling the teenage barrier rise against me. I glanced into the smaller bedroom. Twin beds had been squeezed beneath the slanted ceilings. Somehow, Nancy and her girls would have to share this room and the sofa downstairs.

"I thought we'd drive to the national park," Barbara suggested upon our reassembly outside.

"National park?" I started to ask. I knew of few state parks.

"Great idea!" Dad said. His coach's eye scrutinized the girls' attire and turned critical at the sight of their flip-flops.

Barbara calmly interpreted, "Running shoes are easier to hike over the sand." Her professional manner, always in gear, contrasted nicely against Dad's unpredictable bursts of energy and emotion.

"We'll go barefoot," KT said. Angela and Katie shrugged, not caring either way.

"It's three miles round trip, and quite a workout over the soft sand," Barbara cautioned. "It spends muscles you don't normally use. But the morning rain has firmed it up, so it will be a bit easier."

"These fine, healthy girls can handle anything!" Dad passionately asserted. The girls questioned his sincerity through embarrassed looks. "Here's what we'll do," he narrated. "We'll come upon the lake unexpectedly, just like the first explorers. The area looks much the same as it did then, except the woods are not as mature. Early settlers and the lumber industry darn near wiped out all the trees! Plus, wood-burning sailing ships in the 1800s needed fuel as they traveled back and forth from Chicago and Cleveland to bring supplies. The winters are real tough up here, especially if the lake freezes over. When the ships couldn't get through, settlers died for lack of food. You had to be hardy stock to survive up here!"

"Dad!" I cut short his history lesson, knowing his urge to enlighten. I had inherited it. "How far is the walk? These girls may not have as much stamina as you two jocks."

"We can do it!" the girls said.

"Great!" I smirked. They'd soon learn the competitive pleasure he took in pushing others' limits.

"Can I drive?" KT presented her open palm for the keys.

SIXTY-SIX

TORTOISES AND HARES

"Dad," I alerted, "don't lose sight of them. His expression begged credit for having had a role in teaching me to drive.

"I'll pay for the car behind us," he offered at the park entrance. As we rolled away, I watched from my open window to be sure KT got the message.

We pulled into a parking lot at the base of a mammoth dune.

"Now, this is familiar!" I stepped from the car and envisioned young girls pouring from a bus. Its national park status still confused me, but I had rarely paid attention back then. We boarded the white van or the blue bus, sang songs, and arrived at our destination. We could have been anywhere, and I would never know by what route we had arrived, or how we would return.

Katie, KT, and Angela ran ahead, eager to join the handful of tourists. "The keys!" I shouted.

KT ran back and tossed me the ring. I tucked it deeply into my front pocket and patted it into place. Of this I could be certain, if something fell into a dune it would be lost forever.

Dad loaded his fannypack while Barbara and I crossed the grassy area, passing through rows of picnic tables to the edge of brown-sugar sand. It rose eighty feet from level ground as if thousands of dump trucks had arrived in grand procession and plopped it there. Hundreds of windblown footprints, encrusted by the morning rain, peppered its vertical surface. More recent prints had cut holes to expose pale sand below.

Barbara and I ceased our social visiting to climb. My thighs burned, but a happy smile had frozen to my face.

"The barn!" my daughter called from the halfway point. In a meadow below, a classic dairy barn resembled an ornate loaf of bread with its gambrel roof, dormers, and ornate ventilators.

"It's been there forever," I exclaimed, sharing my daughter's amazement.

"It is part of the Historic Lake Shore," Barbara remarked.

I cast her a quizzical look, having always thought it was privately owned.

"Take a picture!" Katie tossed her disposable camera, and I cupped my hands for an easy catch. A skein of sunlight burst from the sky and lit random sparkles upon the sand. We watched the cumulus mass move east, casting a line of shade across the countryside. Overhead, one puffball remained. Outlined in gray, it scudded though the air like a fat wayward sheep seeking its herd. The air grew steamy and the sand started to bake. Birch trees bleached before our eyes amid the carpet of cedars, pines, maples, beech, and poplar.

"Race you to the top!" Dad announced, gyrating past.

We giggled at his sudden appearance, and the girls took the bait. They waddled laboriously, sinking to their ankles as they tried to run. Dad held the lead with his waffle treads and pumping technique as if riding a bike.

We basked in a sense of accomplishment upon reaching the top and paused to admire the view. The girls and Dad bent from their waists, gripping their sides and heaving for air. At this dizzying height, the equivalent of a seven-story building, we could see for miles. Big Glen and Little Glen formed giant blue puddles amid the rolling forests. Cars in the parking lot resembled colorful toys.

"Off we go," Dad said, taking a trail of old and new footprints. We funneled past two untouched craters and into an immature stand of poplars. Their circular leaves fluttered in the breeze like wind chimes. They seemed out of place in this desert-like setting.

"Stay along the path," Dad called as the girls darted ahead, flinging sand. They leapt off an abrupt edge, and we lost sight of them.

Plain logic suggested we would now descend a similar mound to the lake's edge, or at least see water in the distance from our elevated vantage. But we had just mounted the elemental equivalent of a glacier. This body of living, moving sand encompassed miles of craters, ravines, and ridges precariously held in place by the fragile plant life.

"I hope the girls get exhausted," I confided. "So they'll be mellow when I have to leave at six o'clock to register at the camp." Sensing the perfect moment to broach the subject of houseguests, I outlined my dilemma to Barbara.

"We have plenty of room," she reassured. "We're just a little short on hot water. The chalet has a very small tank."

Raucous laughter pierced the breeze. We paused at the edge of a ravine. A near-vertical trough fell fifteen feet, then rose up again to an even greater height. The girls had tried to make their own way, off the trail, by cutting a sharp angle up the backside. Buried to their knees, they perched along the abrupt incline, unable to move.

Dad leapt below to offer some guidance. "Best to stay on the path. You made a common mistake thinking the untried sand would be firmer and easier."

"Don't push me!" KT threatened, and she grabbed a fistful of Angela's shirt.

"Don't you!" Angela shrieked.

"Let go!" Katie demanded, pushing Angela and KT away.

They reached for each other, all at once, in blind hopes of at least one of them holding steady. They failed miserably and rolled into a heap at the bottom, laughing incredulously.

"There's another reason to stay on the path," Dad said. "You'll disturb the dune. See these blades of grass? They built the dune. They hold the sand in place until a juniper takes hold . . ." The girls brushed sand from their limbs and faces, while he explained the process as Jenny had once done.

His voice faded. Barbara and I ascended the ravine and crossed an elongated plateau. Wildflowers provided a splash of color in an otherwise barren landscape. A wall of dunes hemmed us in on our left and a vast sea of sand stretched below on our right, eerily resembling the lake on a blustery day, except that the wind had chopped away every crest and etched rippling lines along every trough.

"Look at the pretty white flowers," Barbara said.

I was surprised she didn't know their name. Then I realized she had not grown up here. I grew up here. I know this land. I willed myself to believe it. Over the past three decades, military assignments had landed me near mountains, deserts, rivers, forests, and the ocean. Lovely as they were, they belonged to others whose memories were longer than mine. Finally, I could assume this enviable position. I furrowed my brow and studied the white flower. "They could be wind anemone."

"Let's see," Barbara surmised, walking away. "You left Virginia on Tuesday?"

Obviously, I lacked Mr. Chinn's conviction. "Yes," I agreed, moving along, searching for a plant I could name with more authority.

"And you have until Sunday," she said.

"Three whole days," I sighed. A purple, brushlike flower on needled spikes grazed my leg. "This is pitcher's thistle, and these are puccoons." I pointed to a small yellow flower. Barbara paused to study them further, and to my delight she repeated their names. I squinted at the pockets of vegetation, searching for another snippet of botany. "There's a kind of reed," I explained. "Some call it horsetail, others call it snake grass. It's hollow, jointed, and tapers to a cone. It grew in patches near the old camp. You could remove the stalks at each joint, reattach them, and they would still grow and thrive. They were great for straws, wind pipes, and fake cigarettes."

"I've never seen anything like that. And your dad and I have walked all over these parts."

Her tone remained polite, and she had not disputed my memory, but I felt a stab of panic. Perhaps I no longer knew this place! Worse yet, what if the plants hadn't grown and thrived? The urge gripped me to scour the entire shore until I found one, so I could grasp a piece of my youth.

"Maybe they grow on the Manitous," she offered. "Most of this vegetation gets eaten by deer, but the islands retain many of the endangered plants."

I nodded, wanting to believe her.

The girls shot past, sprinting toward the end of our plateau. In rapid succession, they sprang from view. Dad let them go and remained with us.

We crossed three more level segments and two crevasses before the girls emerged on the opposite side of a deep chasm. Out of breath, their faces beaded and flushed, they stood in accusation. "How many more of these things?" KT addressed her Gramps, expecting he'd have the answer.

"We're 'bouts halfway," he said.

"Halfway!" they groaned. When we caught sight of them again, they scuffled inside a large blowout, attempting to write their names. The pallet proved tempting, but I turned my back on their riotous mess and caught up to Barbara. A refreshing breeze sliced through the warmth and hinted at the water's existence.

Dad stood at the top of the next ravine and shouted, "Here it is!"

A seagull soared overhead. My gaze followed it across the lake's sparkling luster. In the distance, gray clouds gathered, adding depth and contrast to the distant horizon.

In this heartbeat of initial contact, a magnificent symphony seemed to vibrate on the air. The endless water, open sky, fresh air, and inviting sand revived a flood of memories so captivating and haunting that if my daughter spoke, I did not hear her. I had fully succumbed to the lake's hypnotic effect. She pointed to the Manitou Islands, representing the two baby bears, miles across the lake. But I gazed up at the Mother Bear. Her legend and the bond of motherhood had been a distant concept the last time I stood so near. Now I understood why she would wait forever, watching and hoping her cubs would reach safety.

A patch of shaggy forest held vigil at the edge of a tall dune, representing the Mother Bear's head. The sand continued to rise, ever higher, to the south. Its tallest point vaulted at over five hundred feet above the lake's surface; the equivalent of a forty-five story building. If thousands of dump trucks had been needed to replicate the first dune we had climbed, this one would require tens of millions.

"The Sleeping Bear Dunes," Barbara narrated into my reflective silence.

"I raced up that tallest part many years ago," Dad mused. "Took me twelve minutes. Don't think I could do that now."

"We can drive up there before we head back," Barbara said. "They've constructed an overreaching deck. The wind is so strong it practically blows you over, but the view is spectacular."

"We can run down it, if you like," Dad offered, cleverly disguising his dare. The girls sized up the enormous wall of sand, envisioning the feat.

"No!" I blurted, practically celebrating my ability to finally say "no" to him. "I'm amazed they let people climb down! The rocks and gravel are really slippery."

"They have warning signs posted everywhere." Dad's smile of perilous fascination suggested this made the prospect even more alluring. "We came one day," he chuckled, getting ahead of himself, "and they had to send a rescue party down for a woman who couldn't get back up!"

"That would be embarrassing," Angela laughed.

Opting for a compromise I searched for the spine of sand I had climbed with my friends as the sky revolved above us and the lake shimmered below. I trailed my sight across the vista and met empty space. The great sleeping bear no longer had a spine. A cliff stretched up to her shaggy head, and we stood hundreds of feet below it. Intellectually, I knew the nature of a dune was to change and reshape from westerly winds. Every summer we had noted its effect through gently creeping degrees. But now I feared too much time had passed. I couldn't reasonably expect it to look the same.

The girls and Dad bolted for the lake. Barbara remained at my side.

"There used to be so much more sand!" I insisted, searching for the remnants of a deep blowout and the lingering shadow of an Arabian tent. "We camped over there." I squinted into the sea of sculpted sand, envisioning that sunny day and the undulating golden hills. "We pitched a tent. We climbed to the Mother Bear, following a peak all the way up there." I traced my finger across the sky, increasingly perplexed by the sand's deficiency.

"Oh, they don't allow camping," Barbara said, shaking her head. "This is protected beachfront. You couldn't have been here."

I studied the shore and wondered if she had hit upon the reason everything appeared so different. I felt my connection slipping away like quicksand. "We hiked in and never met another living soul." I struggled to speak through a befuddled grimace. Had I confused the facts down the years? By my own admission I remained ignorant of specific locations. I looked to the Manitous, then back to the Sleeping Bear, willing myself to see a trail of girls hiking a peak of sand that no longer existed, if it ever had existed.

Suddenly, Barbara tilted near. She wore a compelling expression. "How long ago was that?"

"Well, I was a teenager. It's been nearly thirty years."

She began to nod, thoughtfully reconsidering. "I suppose that long ago you could very well have camped here." She nodded more definitively, adding emphasis to her decision. "This shoreline didn't fall under the Dune Protection Law until 1976 as part of the preservations initiated by Lady Bird Johnson. It took many years to change local policy, transferring from state to national jurisdiction, and acquiring private lands through eminent domain."

"That would explain a lot," I said, as my memory shifted back to a secure, unchallenged state.

"However . . ." She gazed upon the flat landscape. "Not even a governmental edict can halt the shifting sands. You were lucky to have had that experience."

"Let's run!" I heard myself say. Barbara's steady laugh joined mine as we launched out of control, right to the water's edge.

KT had already stripped down to her Speedo. "I'm going in!" she announced.

"Is it cold?" Katie begged for an honest answer.

The lake reflected a powdery blue sky, and the breeze barely disturbed its surface. It could have been a backyard pond, except for its scope. However, because it was Lake Michigan, I folded my clothes on top of my shoes, adjusted my suit, and prepared for the likelihood of some sort of shock.

Angela and Katie hovered between us, wondering which of us to follow. They gravitated toward me when KT drew breaths, stretched her arms, and touched her toes as if readying for battle. When she charged into the glassy water, I shrieked on her behalf, enjoying the sight as she dove under.

"Such bravery!" Dad said, wading to his knees.

"I did win the Polar Award every year," she shouted.

"Well, here goes," I said. Liquid ice numbed my toes. I took a few steps, dipped low until the chill reached my shoulders, then popped up like a jack-in-the-box and ran for shore.

Angela allowed the tiny waves to lap her feet. "It's freezing!" She leapt back and said, "You're all freaking crazy!"

"You'll get used to it," KT called, shaking water from her hair and showering them in droplets. "Both of you are going to swim with me before the end of this trip! I mean, going under and actually swimming."

"Spoken like a true Deena-hahna camper," I sighed.

"Let's head back!" Dad announced. Never able to stay in one place for very long, he'd already donned his shoes.

"I'm going barefoot," I decided. "The sand will fall off as it dries." I stuffed my socks into my shoes, tied the laces, and flung them over my shoulder with a certainty of purpose. The girls remained in their bathing suits and dressed in stages on the way back.

"We timed that just right," Barbara said when we faced the final drop to the parking lot. She pointed to a cloudbank building in the distance. "Another front."

"That looks serious," Dad observed. "We should get moving."

"I sure hope this reunion is inside," I said, beginning to run.

SIXTY-SEVEN

WEAVING A NEW CHAIN

AN UNCERTAIN MOOD entangled me as I struck out under gray skies. I found the camp's entrance and followed a narrow two-lane road. Deserted farmhouses stood back from the road, well preserved and suspended in time as part of the Historic National Lakeshore. When the pavement turned to dirt, I recalled the first time I'd brought my kids to camp. The farmhouses had been occupied, yet I had met no other vehicles along the way, same as now, and received no reassurance of what lay ahead. "Are you sure this is it?" Andrew's youthful voice had worried from the backseat. The morning had been crisp, and the wind had blustered from a blue sky, sweeping over bountiful greenery. It had been the quintessential northern Michigan summer day.

The road curved near an old farmhouse converted into a camp office. Two wooden signs announced, "Camp Shenahwau for Boys and Camp Deena-hahna for Girls." That morning, counselors had swarmed the lawn dressed in white shorts and shirts. They had consulted clipboards, greeted campers, and loaded trunks and duffels into a green pickup for transport to the cabins. We had been directed down the road, toward a gravel lot. Andrew openly fretted the whereabouts of his belongings.

Now that uncertain middle-school student was heading off for college in the fall. Age had mellowed his initial camp experience enough to return for another try as a rising junior in high school. Too young to gain employment and weary of joining the swim team, he had willingly attended the second session of camp along with KT. It had been their final adventure together in Michigan. But I had been vindicated.

He had thrived. Chosen to represent his team in a nonstop Capture the Flag game hailed as the Banner Trip, he'd endured three days of survival in the wilderness. He'd slept in a ditch, ate food tasting like dirt, and learned to appreciate the cleansing effect of a warm, gentle rain.

Tonight the camp office was closed. The lawn was empty. I scrutinized their signs. "Camp Shenahwau for Boys," I read aloud, envisioning another sign suspended from a chain in some hidden, far-off woods, emblazoned with the single word: "Wildwood." These had been the names of my camp. For a split second I harkened back to the anticipation of choosing a bed, finding my friends, and embarking on an idyllic summer.

"Deena-hahna for Girls," I read aloud, and was instantly restored to a sedate, responsible adult. This was my daughter's camp. I drove on, aiming for the gravel lot. It was almost as full this evening as it had been that sunny day, with cars and vans from Michigan, Ohio, Pennsylvania, Wisconsin, Indiana, New Hampshire, and Missouri. Now, Virginia has arrived, I thought, choosing a gap between two vans. Gripping the keys in my hand, I continued to sit. My kids no longer attended. I felt like an intruder. So why have you come all this way? I asked myself, tentatively opening the door. My feet moved, but my torso felt like it stood still. When I cleared the trees, a heavy breeze augmented the sensation. I pulled my jacket close and headed for the lawn. It sloped toward a grassy knoll where a lodge, built of painted logs stacked horizontally, rose from a stone foundation. Hewn rock steps of fine craftsmanship led to a generous verandah.

Near the road, a giant oak spread gnarled roots along the lawn. Its thick branches bulged from leaves and acorns. An awning had been erected beside it. A congregation of women barred my way.

This was the reunion. My mood deflated further as the sky spit and the wind blew it sideways. The awning provided little shelter, and I had not dressed warmly enough. Somehow, I doubted the weather had ever been this cold and bleak.

Fortunately, the faces behind the sign-in table were warm and friendly. One of them flipped through pages on a clipboard. "What is your maiden name?" she asked, after not finding my married name.

"Schmidty," a voice called. My head jerked around, still responding to this name. And of course, I recognized the voice. A pair of soulful eyes greeted me from a heart-shaped face framed by reddish brown hair. Her presence immediately elevated me from trespasser to welcomed guest.

"Roman," I sighed, and the most wonderful laughter resonated from her chest. It still comes to me in a recurring dream so joyous it startles me awake from the answer of my own laughter. We are always running! Crashing through the woods, across the soccer field, along the river toward Wildwood. Clearing logs, leaping over bushes and rocks, we are swift and fearless. Though I fall behind she always turns to be sure I'm there, thrilled by the race, chuckling fiendishly. How well I know this laugh! It erupts from her diaphragm, between breaths, rippling back to me as a rich, woodsy cascade of energy. And now as I hear it once again, I am speechless.

"We've been waiting for you!" She exhaled, utterly relieved, and reached over the table to give me a hug. A crease of worry furrowed her brow. "Are you still willing to put us up? My mom, and my two girls?"

"Yes!" I reassured and quickly recalculated. Nancy and her mom could use the twin beds in the remaining bedroom. Her girls could sleep on sofas in the great room.

"You don't have Haley?" I asked about her youngest daughter. She had been a baby, less than a year old when Nancy's husband passed away.

"She's with my sister, Amy." The name rolled off her tongue as an outpouring of pure affection, same as the day I'd met her, denoting intense family devotion. "Haley's very happy in the company of her cousins, much happier than traveling in the car."

I returned her smile, and we shared a moment of nostalgic disbelief. I noticed new lines around her eyes; the same lines that greeted my own reflection in the mirror.

The woman holding the clipboard chirped, "You registered and paid for two."

"Oh, Susan is unable to come," I replied. The woman immediately pulled out a calculator to cipher my refund. "That's fine," I reassured. I could have used the money, but suddenly it seemed unimportant. She pocketed the calculator, appearing very pleased.

Nancy handed me a boxed dinner. "I'll be right there," she said, launching me in the direction of a rectangular table under the awning's far cover. I wandered over, bracing myself for introductions. This may have been a reunion, but I didn't expect to recognize anyone. My life since camp had spawned hundreds of new faces and only a handful of renewals. After the fifth military relocation I had given up trying to place them. Embarrassing mistakes had taught me the person I thought I'd met before was only a resemblance. Consecutive moves solidified my role as newcomer among old friends.

I tugged on a metal chair and dragged it over blades of grass and a tree root. When I sat down, the shock of cool metal sent shivers up my legs. I inched forward, preparing to give a polite nod for the ladies on either side of me and a vague smile for the rest of the table. Instead, my eyes lingered on the woman at my right. My guard slipped, and for the first time in decades I allowed myself to believe I had recognized a familiar face.

"Josie," I said. "Or is it Sue?" I floundered, thinking of her older sister.

"Josie," she happily whispered.

I reached out to embrace this adult who still bore freckles and sandy red bangs. I held my gaze much longer than etiquette would allow and returned to my cold chair. Cognizant of other eyes staring at me from around the table, I turned to my left. "Robyn!" I gasped.

She greeted me through a hoarse melody of laughter, as if she'd been shouting directions to her family all morning. We leaned into each other, touching shoulders in the facsimile of a hug, and I melted inside. "You have a bunch of sons," I said, latching on to this equalizing topic. "My son went to camp with some of them."

"That's right," she affirmed, straightening in her chair. "Luke and I have five boys. No girls, though."

"You married Luke," I realized, envisioning her as the supreme ruler of a household of men, engaged in daily battles of wits and always winning. "Does he play the guitar for you?"

She tilted her head and laughed. "When is there any time!"

I nodded while shifting a smile about the table. They all seemed younger, more Josie's age, until the very end. Two faces quietly waited for me to notice them. I bounded to my feet, as did they, and we met in the middle. Despite the lack of emotional screams and wild ferocious embraces, a low-key, surreal contentment kindled inside me.

Christie and I hugged. Mary chastised warmly, "It's about time you got here!"

In the back of my mind Mary's words took hold. "Am I late?" I said, realizing I had been the last to arrive. Everyone else had eaten. I glanced across the gathering, toward Nancy, and scowled. Had I been the root cause of our lateness to every meal?

Mary spoke to Robyn. Christie and I inched closer as if from the pull of magnets. Having nothing to say, and everything to say, I began to laugh. Her grin twisted into fierce dimples, and she stifled a husky rumble. In that moment, I remembered the times I'd felt my life crumbling around me and Christie's laughter had brought it back.

"Its official," Nancy said, filling the last empty chair. Her tone meant adult business.

Our mirth dissipated. We cleared our throats, wiped our eyes, and took our seats.

"We have the most in attendance from one CT class," Nancy outlined. "Now, if we can only find Lori." Her eyes narrowed slyly. "Then we'd have five of us."

"How will you do that?" Christie inquired. "She didn't sign up for the reunion."

I tore open my boxed dinner and stared at Nancy. Everyone awaited her reply. Her sundry expressions outlined the formulation of a strategy. I knew every nuance of this transformation. Confusion solidified to determination. Then, determination softened into clarity. When she finally shared the plan, which would in all probability lead us from our comfort zones, I listened more to the sound of her voice, rather than her actual words, amazed by its enduring imprint upon my memory.

"Lori always comes Up-North this time of year, and her family always rents the same place." She took a large bite of an apple. "I think I can find it," she gabbled.

"Ha," I burst aloud, envisioning a camper hiding under the old bridge. "I've heard that before!"

Christie chuckled, and Mary smiled.

Robyn grinned. "Me, too. I heard those words on every trip we took as counselors!" Here was the dreaded reference. They had become Skys while I remained a Cedar. A deep curiosity plagued me about their accumulated memories after I'd left.

"I'm game," Christie said. "Let's blow this pop-stand and go hunt for Lori."

"Want to?" Mary nudged my shoulder, letting me know their plans included me. The old chain was linking us together, and I needed no other invitation as I nodded my consent.

"After you find her, meet us over at Sue Reilley's," Robyn said. "She lives along the frontage road in Glen Arbor."

"Was she the riding instructor?" I whispered to Josie between bites of my cold sandwich.

Josie nodded then laughed. "Yeah, another Susan."

"First," Nancy added through a painful grimace, "I have to get my mother settled. She's been up since four this morning."

Feeling responsible, I chucked my box into the nearby trash and said, "It's not far." Inwardly, I girded myself for our entrance into the chalet. My insides churned nervously, and I hoped Dad wouldn't mind the intrusion.

SIXTY-EIGHT

NOT SO FAST . . .

CHRISTIE STOOD UP. "Meet my mother first." An attractive silver-haired lady beckoned us over. Familiar dimples outlined her smile. A dark-haired woman stood beside her, resembling Nancy's older sister, Theresa, and I realized she was Nancy's mom.

Introductions rounded the table, including a few titles belonging to the board of directors. My professional career had prepared me to ask all sorts of intelligent questions about their endowment fund and its related investments, but a dense fog had descended on that part of my brain.

"We saved some of the original signs from our old cabins," a trim, elderly lady boasted.

I glanced excitedly at Christie. She shook her head to rein me in. "They didn't save any of our signs." Sensing my disappointment, Christie's mom gently squeezed my wrist.

"We even kept The Ritz!" The same lady exclaimed, capturing the approval of her peers.

"We called ours The Murphy," I whispered, recalling my daughter's frustration when she had returned home buzzing with stories of traditions, dating way back, that held no meaning for me. I'd had to reexplain Wildwood's intermediary existence.

"Before you go," Christie's mom said, "sign up for tomorrow's activities."

"Activities?" I snorted. How far would they carry this?

"Come on," Christie said, tugging me toward the registration table.

"Take sailing tomorrow afternoon," Mary said.

"All right," Nancy agreed, picking up a pencil and writing in our names.

"What else?" Christie prompted. "Tennis, a nature hike, arts and crafts?"

"Is there waterskiing?" I teased, wondering if I could still get up.

"No," Mary seriously answered. "Right now it's the slow time between sessions. We're lucky to have these."

In the distance a horse neighed. Two dappled grays stretched their necks over the fence contemplating the grass they could not reach. "Are you up for that?" Nancy grinned.

"No! I'm sure there's some mucking involved."

"Did KT take riding lessons when she went to camp?" Christie asked.

I tilted my head, flattered by her question. I had completely forgotten my daughter's existence! "I think so," I decided. "But you know, she's a water person. So, camp was all about the lake."

The four of us instinctively faced west, knowing it was there though we could not see it. Two girls emerged from the woods beyond the tennis courts wearing bathing suits and towels cinched around their waists. One of them resembled KT at a younger age. She would have traipsed across this lawn when going to meals, coming from the row of pines along the bluff where cabins nestled cozily for a bird's-eye view of the lake. My son would have come from beyond the soccer fields and basketball courts where cabins towered on stilts inside the woods.

"Did they really swim in this weather?" I wondered aloud.

"Yup," Mary affirmed. She stuffed fingertips into the front of her blue jeans. Her bland expression turned to roiled chastisement. "We used to go out in all kinds of conditions! Remember?"

I knew the truth of it, but the air felt freezing. The sun had all but disappeared, and the rain drizzled sporadically. "But do they skinny-dip?" I asked.

"Now that, I do not know." Mary pursed her lips and raised her eyebrows.

"My girls are up in the lodge," Nancy said. "If we're ready, I'll go and fetch them." She paused, taking a slow appraisal. "Anyone want to come?"

"I'll wait here," Christie said.

"Me, too," I decided. The lodge failed to muster any nostalgic curiosity for me, especially because I had heard the original one did not survive Innistock's debauchery.

"I'll come," Mary said. "I need to check on something for tomorrow."

"Are your kids here?" I asked Christie as they walked away.

"Yes. At the cabins we rented, with my husband and my dad." She inched closer, turning serious. "This is our family vacation. It's difficult to do anything with three boys under the age of seven. And Maribeth is not yet two."

I smiled at the memory of such challenges, and we quietly pondered each other's stages in life. "Who have you heard from?" I asked.

"Well," she began, "Cindy and her husband live in St. Louis. They are crazy about baseball. Their daughter is in high school and pitches on a boys' team. She's even been featured on the news a few times. I'll send you the link. She's really good. And their son received a baseball scholarship."

"Baseball," I repeated, envisioning Cindy's blue eyes in challenge as she balanced a flat rock in the palm of her hand then skipped it across the lake.

"And Cindy is a language specialist."

"No kidding." I giggled, recalling her penchant for idioms like "hold your horsies," "shilly-shallying," "super duper," and "muchly obliged."

"I've also been exchanging e-mails with Sarah." Her mention brought to mind a green-eyed, freckled-face girl, curled up on her cot in Sunblazer, discreetly reading a letter from a boyfriend. "She got married right after college, just like you, and has two boys who are close to college age. She's living in Ohio and would have loved to come, but she couldn't get away. She runs a small company."

"So, she went into business, like me," I realized.

Christie inhaled sharply as if recalling some earth-shattering news. "Bess died about five years ago."

"Oh no," I sighed, wondering if my last year might have turned out differently under her guidance.

"I wrote her, and told her how much we adored and missed her." She raised her chin into a somber smile.

"Thank you," I said, and we shared a volume of understanding silence. Finally, I asked about Tori.

Christie smiled mischievously. "Mary and Victoria have been corresponding." She held perfectly still.

"Tell me!" I prodded.

"No, Mary needs to be the one."

I would have pestered until she relented, but her tone held unyielding strength. For decades she had been a high school English teacher, a cheerleading coach, and now she carried the additional responsibilities of a mother of four. Her natural discipline had turned to tempered steel.

"Nancy," she confided, "did you know my middle son was diagnosed with autism when he was three?"

"No," I gasped, unable to hide my concern.

"He's a perfect angel," she whispered, tenderly. "But I worry about how to protect him from the world. It's like someone once told me . . ." Her eyes strayed to the clouds above, searching for the right words. "It's like he is playing a game. A game in which everyone knows the rules except him." Her eyes returned to me. "And he is so trusting. He would go along with anyone."

"I remember those fears when mine were little. But once they understand the concept of strangers, those fears slip away."

"Exactly." she nodded. "He may never understand that concept." Her careworn expression lifted into a tight shrug. "It used to bother me what other people thought. Everyone wants to change people with disabilities to be more like us. But my son is who he is. I've learned more from him than any college textbook. In fact, I don't even like to say, 'he is autistic.' Rather, he is someone living with the difference of autism, because he's our son first." She softened upon saying this, melting from a teacher to a mother, and I knew she was opening a private window for me. "It's amazing," she said, "how this one little boy has taught my family to be compassionate for those who struggle."

I nodded along, thinking I'd never completely understand.

Her eyes widened in alarm. "You know, I'll be nearing sixty when my youngest graduates from high school. What if I'm not there for her?"

"You will be," I said. "Heck, you'll be showing her how to do a roundoff back handspring! Her energy will rub off and keep you young. Besides, there is no situation too great for God to handle." A spasm of laughter caught in my throat.

"What's the matter?" she said, beginning to do the same.

Sensing the years had not lessened our ability to crack each other up, I quickly explained, "Thaddeus said that to me once. When he took me to Traverse City for stitches."

"He did?" She emitted a throaty laugh. "Why?"

"Because of that time I fell into my trunk!"

"Oh, that!" Her eyes penetrated mine, serious and intense, despite her tight smile. It was the same combination I had always found intriguing. "But you know our fears can become so gnawing and real at times."

"Yes, they can," I agreed, reviewing a few of my own. A long journey awaited me in getting back to Virginia. After that, a long life of celebrations and challenges lay ahead, none of which I would ever again share with my mom. Without her guidance, how could I be brave enough to send my kids into the unknown with an energetic smile? And what if I grew old like Nanny, full of debilitating worries and bitter regrets? Even worse, what if I didn't grow old at all? One moment Mom had been merging into the freeway, and the next moment she was rolling and spinning beneath a semitractor trailer like a wind-up toy. Three days later she was gone.

"Christie! Do you need to drive your mom back to your cottage?" Mary called.

Caught unaware, we turned to smile at her. Instantly, my mind heralded back to a time before any of these worries ever existed.

"No." Christie smiled bemusedly, as if she, too, had just shed the last thirty years. "Mom has her car, and she knows the way!"

"I'll meet you at Sue Reilley's," Mary said. "I have a carload." She wagged a finger and added, "Don't take too long!"

"I'll ride with you," Christie said, turning stiffly from her waist to face me. "Nancy can follow us."

SIXTY-NINE

REDACTED IMPRESSIONS

A FIRE CRACKLED in the wood stove, drying the damp night air, and Dad sat in a recliner with his glasses propped on the end of his nose. He peered up from his newspaper as I rushed into the great room just ahead of my guests, hoping to have it settled before they came in. I felt seventeen again, coming in too late, spouting a stream of excuses and trying not to appear loaded. Such episodes had defined my last year at home, and I dreaded the look of disappointment on his face. But these were not my controversial friends from high school. These were the friends who had helped guide me toward responsible adulthood.

"My friends are in a bind," I said, not wanting to let Nancy down. "The girls only need a floor to lie on, and Nancy and her mom could have the last bedroom." I sensed Barbara standing in the hall, ready to jump in if needed.

"We'd be happy to help out," Dad said, putting aside his newspaper and rising to his feet.

I took a step back, surprised at how easy this had been. Was this the same Dad who had never let my friends come over because they made noises and messes? Admittedly, his divorce from Mom had left a gulf between us, as divorces will do when time is unequally delineated between parents. I had expended far more effort on seeing Mom, which left us little time to replace those old patterns with new ones. Luckily, I was heading into a phase of my life when I could do something about it.

Nancy's mother entered the sliding-glass door clutching a pillow and a small suitcase. She smiled wearily, grateful to be done traveling for the day. Dad offered help and a greeting, becoming the gracious host offering a port in the storm.

Nancy, her daughters, and Christie floated in. I stood immobile, unable to move or speak as if stuck in the hallway between two rooms. One held the ever-increasing challenges of adulthood while the other remained untouched in adolescence. Nancy stood beside me holding an armload of belongings. I took her suitcase and leapt into the adolescent room. Cabin mates once again! I smiled, feeling like a conspiring teenager.

"Mrs. Taylor!" Angela's voice alerted me from across the room. "We took camper showers!"

I glanced at Dad. His helpless frustration sent me back to the days when he had tended my childhood shenanigans.

"You should have heard them," Barbara said.

"After we got out," KT explained, turning a bit embarrassed, "I remembered that a real camper shower is when you turn off the water between lathering and rinsing, not squeezing everyone into the same shower!"

"Ah," Nancy sighed, droll and contemplative, "good old camper showers." She paused at the base of the open stairway. Her declaration mesmerized me because of its adult implications. My camping days had ended with the Marriott Rewards Card, but she spoke with the authority of someone still capable of roughing it. "Remember camper showers?" Her eyes begged me to recall a distant and irrelevant memory.

I shook my head in denial. Then, ever so slightly, an image flashed of the cramped, dingy shower in the Murphy. It provided thirty seconds, tops, of hot water, and you never knew when the stream of mineral-laden, iron-rich liquid would turn icy upon you. It was a stressful, infuriating experience. "Yes," I said slowly. "That's why I chose to dip in the lake."

"And dragged us with you," Christie said.

"Really? I thought you dragged us out there." Christie laughed at my denial.

"And, Mom!" KT proudly stated, "Angela, Katie, and I walked to the lake after you left."

"How far was that?" I asked.

All three of them swung about to face Barbara. "Almost three miles round trip," she answered, giving the girls a professional nod of approval. "They struck out by themselves."

"You live in South Bend," Christie addressed my Dad, effectively releasing the girls from adult conversation. I breathed a sigh of relief, sensing the room's atmosphere had become friendly and relaxed.

At the top of the steps, Nancy, her mother, and I stood outside the small remaining bedroom, looking in on the twin beds. "Is this all right?" I inquired.

"It's perfect, dear." Nancy's mom smiled appreciably. "I am looking forward to lying down."

"We won't be gone long, Mom," Nancy said, dropping her things.

"We are heading out to meet some people," I explained when we had returned downstairs.

Christie waited by the sliding-glass door. Barbara and Dad reclined in their easy chairs, and KT raided the silverware drawer of spoons, dumping them in a pile in the middle of the table. Dad focused a skeptical eye on his granddaughter, wary of the raucous game to follow. This had been a familiar scene at Papa's cottage. However, Dad would have been long gone with the other adults, leaving Nanny in charge. My cousins and I would have spent noisy hours shifting cards around the table, trying not to be the last to reach for a spoon while Nanny fed us popcorn and lemonade.

I wavered in my resolve, knowing how much he valued peace and quiet.

"Go on!" he urged, sensing my hesitancy.

Marveling at the role reversal, I thrilled at the exit. We walked through the patio doors and across the deck. "I hope the girls will be quiet enough so the adults can sleep," I added as my final thought on their behalf.

"It will be fine." Nancy jingled her car keys. "I'll drive."

SEVENTY

MOTHER HENS

SHE DROVE DETERMINEDLY toward Glen Lake. Christie sat in front to help navigate the dark, winding roads. The sky had cleared, the wind had died, and the night air felt warm and exhilarating. We could have been teenagers out for adventure on a summer night. Though I had never done this at camp, I imagined they had spent some evenings this way as counselors. It seemed natural and exciting to be with them, and we shared snippets of our lives, throwing them into the mix, maintaining a thread of continuity.

Embarking on our second tour of the lake, Nancy maintained, "I'm sure I can find that little cottage."

"It's nice to know some cottages still exist," I said.

"Everything looks so different in the dark," Nancy bemoaned. She leaned into the dashboard and slowed to a stop. "I wish there was a way to shine my headlights sideways."

"Was it along that inlet road?" Christie suggested.

"Okay, we'll try that," she muttered, making a U-turn. Light posts illumined an open lawn encircled by small bungalows. She placed the van in park, hopped out, and crossed the lawn. Christie and I watched her enter a screened porch. A solitary table lamp defined her profile as she peeked inside the main door. After a moment, she ran back to us.

"Does anyone have paper?" she asked. "And something to write with?"

I dove into my purse, grappling among its contents.

"Maybe this isn't the right cottage," Christie said.

My hand clutched a pen as I waited for her answer. Nancy gave a non-committal shrug. "What will you write?" I asked. She inhaled abruptly, as if she hadn't thought about this yet.

"You want to leave a note anyway?" Christie asked.

"Sure," Nancy said, puzzled by our laborious stalling.

I thrust my hand between the front seats, presenting the pen.

"I don't have any paper," Christie curtly announced, closing her purse and crossing her arms.

Nancy took the pen and walked back to the cottage. When she entered the house, its front room flooded in light.

"Someone is there!" Christie said. "What if it's not Lori?"

"Oh no." I gleefully imagined Nancy trying to explain her uninvited entry. I gripped my door latch, ready to provide reinforcement.

We heard the inner door slam, and she rushed through the porch wearing an unreadable expression.

"What happened?" We asked as she opened the van's door and slid inside.

"I found a napkin and wrote a note." She stared at us as if we'd gone mad.

"No one is home?" Christie attempted to clarify.

"No," Nancy said, still perplexed. "That's why I left a note."

"Oh," I sighed. Christie explained, "You left the light on."

"Shoot!" Nancy hissed. "Oh well." she gave a small laugh. "It will be another surprise. They have a cake sitting out with candles. They are probably coming back to celebrate after a late dinner."

"Is there a name on the cake?" Christie asked.

"I think it's her husband's. Or maybe a nephew? Anyway, it's a guy's name. So, it's not one of her daughters."

We sat for a spell, curious voyeurs into Lori's life. She had not married anyone from Shenahwau, and her children had not yet attended camp. In fact, none of my fellow CTs had married from that pool of bachelors.

"Let's stay for the party," I said.

Nancy appraised me in the dark. "But we'd be intruding into a family thing."

"I'm only kidding," I said, a bit embarrassed. I hadn't thought she would take me seriously. Our friendships had always held boundaries, and the rest of the world existed outside of them. Not many people understood why we turned introspective and blissful at the mere mention of camp. Either they believed the lampooned versions in movies or thought of it as a one-week excursion into cheerleading, band, scouting, or sports. Perhaps those bands of brothers who had experienced combat together could understand it best, though the military men in my life resented the comparison. I had suggested it once at an Officer's Club in Minot, North Dakota, being a newly married transplant aching for my summer friends. I had been informed ours was a country club existence made possible by the service of those brave soldiers. How could I argue this? Ever since, I had taken my memories underground.

I expected my camp friends had done the same, which made our reminiscing so precious. Finally, we were sharing closely guarded memories among those who had made them. But we could not deny the boundaries. Our husbands and children belonged on the inside now.

"Do you know how to get to Sue Reilley's?" Christie asked.

"Oh, I know the road," Nancy said.

I had no inkling of our whereabouts.

"But you don't know the house address," Christie said fifteen minutes later. We cruised past double garages belonging to cookie-cutter condominiums.

"No," Nancy said, turning around at the deadend. "But I really think it's only about the fourth house in. Mary, what are you driving?" she whispered. The driveways were full of similar minivans. Then, it seemed Mary answered, because the garage door opened and Mary walked out.

Christie and I shared crooked grins, sensing it had been more than just coincidence.

"Did you find Lori?" Mary peered into the open window.

"We think we found her cottage," Christie said, "but we're not sure."

"Nancy left a note," I said.

"What did you write?" Mary asked.

Nancy opened her door and raised her arms into a catlike stretch.

"What did you write?" I tried to decide what I'd write to Lori after so much time.

Nancy sized us up. "When did all of you turn into such clucking hens?"

"The moment we all hatched eggs," Mary said.

Congenial laughter filled the air as we headed into the garage. Two golden retrievers sniffed our legs. "Jake and Amos, back off!" Sue Reilley reprimanded from the doorway. "Come on in. There are some people waiting to see you." She led us toward the front of the house. A wall of windows faced the lake and enclosed a year-round sunroom. In the vast darkness, water lay black as onyx under a moonless sky. In winter, I imagined this glass room would turn frigid as slushy waves pummeled the shore. But now it felt warm and cheery. Plus, a few new faces had shown up.

"Beth!" Her name flew from my lips.

"I just hopped over from my parents' place on Glen Lake," she said.

"You're tall!" I exclaimed and she hunched over to give me a hug.

Beth and I squeezed hands, then Christie grabbed my arm. "Sit here, Schmidty." She indicated some kitchen chairs set between the sofas. I plopped down and draped my sweater, unable to keep my eyes off the faces around me. One woman in particular, having dark wavy hair and piercing black eyes, looked stunningly familiar. "Shane?" I asked.

"Kappy!" she corrected. "Shane's little sister."

Robyn took center stage. "Let's go around the room! Everyone tell one thing you remember most." Her finger landed on Beth.

Beth's eyes widened, and she whispered, "The water spouts." A heavy silence fell upon the circle. "I was terrified," she added before clasping a hand over her mouth, as if she had confessed something unforgivable. Her eyes darted about begging for agreement.

Then, everyone spoke at once.

SEVENTY-ONE

MUDDLED MEMORIES

I SAT UPRIGHT, keenly interested in the rush of comments. They had all been afraid, and sounded relieved to admit it, as if this had been a secret bottled up for decades. In a way it had, because we had pushed the event behind us and entered our last week of camp as if nothing extraordinary had occurred.

"It was right after church. I was in a full-fledged panic," Robyn said, openly amazed and freshly stunned.

Sue Reilley tapped her chin. "A bunch of us ran to the dining hall, but it was locked."

"Good thing. The glass windows," Robyn said, as if she, too, had once considered that option and found it lacking.

"We huddled in that dingy basement in the Hylton," Beth sneered.

"We stayed inside Stardust," Kappy said. "We crammed under our counselor's bed, fearing how much our cabin resembled the house in *The Wizard of Oz*. The wind was brutal. The rafters creaked as if the roof would lift off. Then it just stopped. We didn't move until Lou Ellen got on the megaphone and called off the afternoon activity."

"Didn't you hear me shouting, 'don't stay in the cabins'?" Robyn asked through a wide concerned smile.

"No," Kappy laughed, shaking her head. "I don't even think our counselor was with us."

She innocently validated my memory; Linda had been her counselor.

"I led a group downriver," Mary said. "Thank goodness those darn things went into the water before we had to hunker into leeches!"

"I was with you!" Christie turned to face Nancy.

Nancy folded her arms, thoughtfully confused. "Well, I vaguely remember rounding up a group of campers to go to the resort. I can't tell you how far we got." She laughed uncomfortably.

"We took the back road." Christie nodded decisively. "We both had a group."

"I remember how big those waves got!" Annie said.

I perceived a chance to speak up. My heart thumped wildly, same as that morning though now I feared ridicule instead of detection. As if from very far away I heard myself say, "A group of us stood on the shore and watched and prayed. I wasn't afraid. One of the funnels went into the water, and the other passed right through us."

My statement hung out there, hovering conspicuously, perhaps too crazy to be believed.

"We swam in those waves all afternoon!" Annie continued.

"It was a blast," Beth agreed.

"Shopping bags washed ashore from Chicago," Sue Reilley said. "And we found tons of petoskeys."

I stared at the carpet feeling invisible.

"A giant limb fell near Stardust," Kappy added, "but it didn't hurt anything, and we used it for the bonfire."

"We took those surfboards out," Mary said. "I actually rode a wave into shore, standing up!"

My eyes latched on to Kappy. "Your sister was with us," I said. "Has she ever talked about it?"

"No." Kappy shook her head. "She doesn't even remember having a cabin named Puccoon! She cracks up every time I say it."

"Is Maggie coming to the reunion?" I leaned across the circle to gain Sue Reilley's attention. For some reason, I thought she might know.

"She lives out of the country." Her pale blue eyes examined mine, thoughtfully sincere, and my mind raced as I studied the freckles on her nose.

"Has anyone kept in touch with Linda?" I asked next, scanning the room. Their expressions turned to confusion as if she'd never existed. I pronounced her last name. Still, no one recollected. Robyn appeared to try. "She was your counselor," I addressed Kappy. She tilted her head in listless puzzlement. "What about Bobbi?" I stubbornly persisted. More blank stares met mine. "She played the piano?"

"Who has another striking memory?" Robyn cut me short and pointed to Mary.

My mental image of that day melted like film on a projection reel, burning along the edges until it turned cloudy and indistinct, no clearer than it had been at the beginning of the trip.

"I remember sneaking over to the boys' camp to steal their bell," Mary said. "It was about three times the size of ours and weighed a ton!"

"You went to the guys' camp?" I choked, glancing at Nancy and Christie to see if they had known. Nancy appeared truly confused, and Christie shrugged. "We stole their bell?" I reiterated unable to believe they'd had the guts to do it.

"We played so many pranks on them," Mary said.

"Did they retaliate?" I asked, suspiciously.

Robyn, Mary, and Sue Reilley looked at each other, then smiled. Robyn said at last, "Maybe a few panty raids."

"They came into our cabins and rifled through our trunks?" I protested, feeling violated thirty years overdue. I glanced at Nancy to see her reaction. She listened intently, showing no sign of emotion.

"They put your trunk in the trampoline pit!" Annie shrieked, pointing at Mary.

"The guys did that?" I challenged.

"Did they?" Mary laughed, staring at Annie, and they burst into cryptic hilarity.

Deciding to get to the bottom of it, I confronted Nancy. "Did you hide Susie's curling iron and hair dryer?"

She rubbed her forehead, and her eyes grew distant. "I honestly can't remember. It's quite possible. I remember being the victim of some good ones. I suppose I gave as well as I got."

Stories flew around the circle, mostly from the younger women who had never attended Wildwood and only knew of Shenahwau's existence beside the river.

"We were counselors," Christie said, half-listening.

"Could you hear the lake from the cabins?" I wondered. "And weren't there mosquitoes?"

"We missed the lake. But we had fun," she said. "These girls were so precocious and witty. We introduced old traditions from our mothers' era, and they updated them."

"Like the ending to the canoe song?"

"Exactly." She grinned. "You know, Schmidty," she added, inching closer to me, "You can't miss what you don't have."

My own words had doubled back to me, and I reconsidered my daughter's experience. I had no cause to disparage hers, or anyone else's. I listened to their antics through a prism of fresh delight. It was their camp, their memories, and their time. How could I feel sorry for them or think my memories were better?

I leaned back and watched Christie and Mary recall events that had occurred after I'd left. Nancy listened, smiling incredulously. Mary's sharp, practical memory kept them focused, and Robyn remained in the center of every story. She had been at Wildwood and along the river. Everyone wanted to hear her words and share her robust laughter. We still craved her approval. She had become our Bess.

Robyn and Mary cited numerous trips, and Nancy figured into every adventure. She listened to their tales of woe and worry as if they'd happened to someone else. I drew on my knowledge of her personality to inject color and depth to the narration. She would have been fearless as a counselor, never letting the details of planning and execution bog her down. She would have weathered torrential rains, soggy sleeping bags, unruly winds tossing sailboats off course, missed pickup points, and portages to wrong locations through a tight smile and a sardonic laugh. No wonder she grew increasingly perplexed by their stories! She remembered them differently. In her mind they had not been catastrophes. They had been fun.

When the conversation slipped to events beyond Nancy and Christie's tenure, when Mary ran things with Robyn, I slouched toward Nancy in search of a commonality. "Remember the sunsets?"

Her eyes appeared distant. "We'd sneak away from the Council Fires."

"Remember that snake grass that grew between the two camps? We would take them apart and pretend they were cigarettes?" She nodded along, clearly onboard.

"Nancy!" Robyn's voice cut us short.

"Yes!" we answered together, placing the burden of choosing on her.

"Either of you!" she choked on an exasperated laugh. "What do you remember most?"

Nancy's face scrunched into a helpless grimace. "Everyone has named most everything," she said. "I guess the trips. Getting lost, yet always finding the way somehow."

Robyn approved and turned her eyes on me.

"That time we moved your bed on the dock." I anticipated an explosion of jocular agreement.

Robyn's brow furrowed. "I don't remember that," she reluctantly admitted.

My mouth formed a wordless "Oh." I looked to my friends for corroboration.

"Don't look at me," Nancy cautioned.

"I sort of remember that," Christie said, more patronizing than sincere.

"It was our CT year?" I begged. "All nine of us carried the bed with her in it? We took her trunk and all her clothes." I rolled my hands like a frustrated coach, urging them to join me on the same mental journey. All the while my confidence shrank, and I began to sweat, fearing I'd also jumbled this memory into something it never was.

"Are you sure it was me?" Robyn insisted, trying to be kind.

"Wait!" Mary took charge. "I remember the morning you guys came to the flagpole in your bathrobes with pillows stuffed inside."

"I have a picture of that!" Christie confirmed.

"Someone must remember Robyn's bed on the end of the dock," I stubbornly endured. "Josie!" I begged. "Don't you remember any of this?"

"Maybe," she ventured. Her expression proved otherwise.

"I couldn't have imagined it," I said.

"No," Christie sympathized. "We just remember things differently." She poked Nancy. "If we remember at all!"

"I can't argue that," Nancy said.

Christie stated for all to hear, "Theresa married Jay Clarkston, right?"

Nancy brightened at this. "Yes, they have a great marriage."

"And he's the reason Theresa always sneaked out," Christie said.

"She did?" Robyn exclaimed.

"I suppose you never snuck out and met Luke?" Mary deadpanned.

"We had to meet as head counselors for official reasons," Robyn said.

"You're not fooling us," Mary chuckled. "You had so many lame excuses for visiting the guys' camp."

"Yeah," Sue Reilley agreed, and she proceeded to list them.

"You know," Christie said, speaking directly to me. "They're lucky. They get to talk about Shenahwau every time someone asks, 'How did you two meet?' Camp is hard to explain, especially to my husband. I don't want to bore the poor guy, but I need him to understand so he'll be willing to send our kids in a few years. It was the one time in my life when I got along with nine girls who actually respected me and loved me for who I was. No strings attached."

"And we were all very different," I said.

"How else to explain the discrepancies in what we remember?" she said. "I wish my co-workers and neighbors could be so generous. Why do women have to be so backbiting and nasty?"

Beth reached out and swatted the air next to my arm. "Where is your sister?"

"Oh, Susan wanted to come, but she had a chance to go to Mexico with her husband." I glanced at Christie. "Did you know she owns a preschool for needy kids? Many of them have learning disabilities."

"I bet she's really good with them," Christie decided.

"She never let that dyslexia beat her," I said, crossing my arms. "She would devise all sorts of little tricks to cope, fooling everyone, even me."

"Guys," Mary interrupted. "Tori and I have been swapping e-mails." Christie started to laugh and I shifted in my seat, overcome by curiosity.

"She has a son, and is interested in sending him to camp." Mary looked around, speaking to everyone. "She's been asking about the stables, the soccer fields, the basketball courts, gymnastic equipment and trampolines. I told her we couldn't fit any embedded tramps along the beach, because it was too narrow. She wrote me back and said, 'Mary, my love, no matter how narrow the beach, I'm quite sure embedded tramps have no business at a summer camp!'"

"She hasn't changed," I mused.

"Still," Mary said, "camp is a long way off because her son is just a baby." I pictured Tori juggling the unpredictable routine of motherhood in her forties until Mary added, "She and her husband split their time between Chicago and Phoenix, and they have a nanny who travels with them!"

"Of course," I said, recalling Tori's self-assured presence. Even as a teenager, she had known exactly what she wanted out of life while the rest of us spun in circles about what earrings to wear.

"Speaking of babies . . ." Christie stood to put on her sweater. "My three little guys and one little girl will be getting up pretty early tomorrow morning."

"Christie, wait," Robyn said. "You're the last one. Tell us your favorite memory."

"That's easy." Her voice lowered into a mystical range. "The camping trip with Jenny."

"Ah." Nancy and I sang the same low note. "The tent," we said together, and I thanked Christie for ending the evening on this common ground.

Christie explained to the group, "Quite simply, it was the perfect day." She slung her purse over her shoulder and exited the room. Nancy and I understood the loving tug of family responsibility and dispelled our good-byes in favor of the reunion activities.

SEVENTY-TWO

NANCY'S SACRIFICE

"So how did you end up in New Hampshire?" I asked Nancy after we'd dropped off Christie. Draped in the cloak of confidential shadows, we sped along the country road and relaxed into comfortable honesty.

"After college, Warren and I took out an atlas. We decided we wanted to be so many minutes from skiing, canoeing, and hiking, so many miles from the ocean, and so many hours from a major city. Then we just put a dot on the map and moved there."

"That was very brave," I said, unable to imagine placing roots without connections or jobs lined up ahead of time. She laughed in the self-deprecating way I knew so well, sputtering for an instant as if many other attributes besides bravery fought for prominence. Giving up, she stared at the road, and her mournful eyes softened into sadness. Suddenly it occurred to me, she knew they had been brave. Her laughter did not spring from modesty. It carried the full import of incredulous disbelief.

"But this isn't what I signed up for," she said through a forced, hurt groan. "Warren wasn't supposed to die. We were a team, and he was supposed to stay with me. When he died, I learned to worry."

To me, she remained the carefree camper and confident trips counselor, the one who always bolstered others and rarely needed encouragement. I stared straight ahead and didn't know how to respond.

"I want to feel light again," she yearned. "I want that back."

Her depth of longing crushed my insides. More than anything, I wanted it for her. I wished words could provide swift and immediate results, like the words Linda had spoken in the face of two tornadoes. I could have repeated Thaddeus's bit of wisdom or Nancy's own words to me on the CT hike, "We endure for growth." But these rang hollow. Surely, she'd heard such proselytizing in all its forms and deserved more. I could only imagine the extent of her concerns about money, household repairs, and a male role model for her girls. Similar worries had plagued me, at one time or another, especially the year of my husband's remote tour. But I had always known he would return to ease the burden.

"You were fearless," I said at last, trying to convey my admiration. "To me, you still are. With all you've been through, you are still laughing, and smiling, and driving cross-country to take your girls to camp."

"I'm trying to be happy. But it's tough putting on the outside what you don't completely feel on the inside. Every day, every hour, I throw my smile into the thick of it, offering those sacrifices of joy."

I stopped short of blurting, "me, too." The grief I felt for my mom paled before hers and the uncanny coincidence of us both relying on the same bit of wisdom seemed hardly worth mentioning. So, I ditched my empathy because it bordered on pity, and turned to objective analysis. Decidedly, Warren had augmented her natural bravery and catapulted it to new heights. When he'd left unexpectedly, she'd fallen from the blow and landed lower than she'd ever been in her life. She'd forgotten how to be brave without him. "It will come," I said, holding fast to an image of her being courageous and free. The image felt so secure and correct that my insides lightened for her. "God shall help her, and that right early," I prayed. Then, speaking from a level of certainty, I said, "You will be happy again." I trusted my faith would help in the same way hers had once helped me.

"Ya think?" she speculated, offering a sly grin.

"Yeah," I promised, reading a flicker of teasing optimism in her tone.

"There is something," she said. "My kids want me to start dating again."

"Oh?" I raised my eyebrows. "Do you have anyone in mind?"

"No." She cringed. "Maybe," she added, as if wanting to say more, yet we knew she wouldn't. I had seen that expression, long ago, when the prospect of another romance took place along the wooden deck of the dining hall. Whoever she had in mind, I hoped it would be the start of something sweet and lasting.

"It's strange," she said, as if reading my mind. "But my daughter and I will begin dating at the same time."

"That would be weird," I agreed. We laughed, contented and relaxed, until we had to sneak back into the chalet.

SEVENTY-THREE

IT'S ALL ABOUT THE LAKE

THE NEXT MORNING I woke to the fuzzy awareness of preparations: muted footfalls, doors and cupboards cautiously opened and closed, things being carried from the bedroom to the outside. When I emerged from my room, Barbara and Dad had loaded up and were ready to return to South Bend.

I panicked as if he still held the authority to halt my fun and take me with him.

Barbara whispered insistently, "Please let your friends know it has nothing to do with them. It's the weather. You know your dad. He will go stir crazy if he can't get out and exercise. They are predicting overcast and rainy all weekend. But it's sunny in South Bend. We can get in some training, which is usually the reason we come up here."

We stood in the kitchen. I was alarmed and confounded. How would I explain this?

"Don't worry," she said. "This is for the best. Now everyone can have a bed."

"We've changed the sheets," Dad whispered, emerging from around the corner.

"But we only just got here," I protested.

Dad gave a helpless sigh, and his hands supplicated heaven as if he was caught in a snare. This had always been his reply to our little-girl pleas when we wanted to stay at Papa's cottage and he wanted to leave. Now I gave him credit, and my mom, for lasting as long as they had through Nanny and Papa's dysfunctional aggravation. They had stuck it out so Susan and I could know our cousins. Perhaps this cottage, now filled with five girls, skirted the edge of things he'd rather forget.

"It's okay," I absolved his guilt. "I understand," I added, meaning I understood him. He needed his space.

"We'll see you again soon," Dad promised, giving me a firm hug.

Barbara handed me a list. "You must follow these directions exactly before you leave on Monday." The septic tank needed treating. The garbage had to be placed a certain way along the curb. The doors had to be locked in sequence, and the kitchen needed to be pristine to deter bugs. Dad gave instructions for the wood stove while Nancy's girls slept soundly: one on the sofa, the other on the floor. Within five minutes they had left. I stood motionless in the kitchen trying to digest it all.

Nancy treaded downstairs. I waved her into the newly vacated bedroom and explained.

"It's true," I maintained, as her confused expression deepened into worry. "They took off because of the weather. They would have left anyway. Having you here makes it less awkward." For them, I wanted to add, but not for me. I rambled on about their habitual training. "So, you and your mom can share this bed." I placed my palm on the double mattress. "And Lindsay and Kelsie can move from the floor to the twins upstairs."

"I need coffee," she breathed into a great, heaving exhale.

I clamped my mouth shut, hearing instead a young girl's croaking response to Reveille, "I hate to get up, I hate to get up, I hate to get up in the morning!" Pursing my lips against laughter, I waited for her to speak.

She stared at the carpet. After a few moments her voice sauntered into some planning. "I need to take my girls shopping for a few things. We are not due back at the camp until five o'clock."

"Can I ride with you?" I spoke in a slow, metered drone. "KT wants to use my car to visit Fishtown. Your girls could go along."

"Or," she stated realistically, "my girls could remain happily out there in front of the television. We don't have cable or satellite at home, and they are about to go to camp for four weeks."

"Primitive as can be," I quoted, having also allowed my kids to gorge on lazy entertainment before the fast. The sizeable array of games and music available to this generation had been ruled out by the camp. Unbelievably, few kids, including my own, complained for very long because the camp kept them busy and fulfilled. They soon learned to appreciate the distinction of having a life instead of watching one.

"Tomorrow night we have a banquet inside the lodge."

"No kidding," I mused, wondering how she knew this. "Did I miss a brochure at the sign-up table?"

She smiled ambiguously. "It should be nice, the camp has a wonderful chef. And there is a sort of Council Fire tonight."

My stomach contracted from nervous energy. I placed a hand across my midriff, experiencing the same sort of panic I felt in the workplace when called upon to perform a task long forgotten, or never quite mastered. Reminiscing about Council Fires was one thing, but reenacting one did not sound appealing. "I can't remember," I asked, just to be certain. "What did we do at Council Fires besides sing songs, watch me get passed over for beads, and run back to see the sunset?"

Nancy chuckled. "You'll remember. And there won't be any beads."

I squinted out the window. Raindrops plopped upon wilted leaves. "I hope the weather clears."

"I know," she agreed. "I'd really like to go sailing tomorrow."

I conjured an image of her in a purple two-piece suit hauling the sail against a forceful wind. We'd sit along the gunwales and hike out until our backs skimmed the lake's surface. When the wind fell off and the boat hit the skids, we'd topple backwards. Still hanging by our legs, we'd capsize the boat on top of us. I cleared my throat, having second thoughts about this, too, as I envisioned water in my ears and up my nose.

Mrs. Roman emerged from upstairs, fully dressed and groomed for the day. I repeated my story, speaking slowly because she also appeared to need coffee. When all were ready, they headed out the glass door in pursuit of java. Kelsie and Lindsay walked sluggishly behind, sleepy and obedient.

I ran up stairs to check on my girls. One of the twin mattresses had been stripped from its box springs and resided on the floor. Angela and KT sprawled upon it while Katie lay like a regal princess on the undisturbed bed.

"Guys!" I whispered, giving them a few seconds to open their eyes. "Let's go see the lake!"

"Now?" Angela moaned.

"Sure!" I offered my daughter a hand as she struggled to stand.

"I just need a minute," she said, shuffling to the bathroom, taking my eccentric proposal in stride.

"It's all about seeing the lake as much as possible, in every kind of weather," I explained to Angela and Katie.

"If you say so," Katie whispered in a trusting voice.

They hastily donned sweatshirts and sweatpants. We piled into my car and sped downhill to the access road. A quarter-mile corridor of overhanging branches fell away to a panorama of agitated waves roaring toward shore. The lake lured us from the car to stand along its edge and feel its power.

"Is this the same lake?" Angela called over the rush of wind.

"Yes," KT shouted, and the air tumbled her words toward the parking lot.

Multidimensional clouds of gray, white, and navy puffballs marched toward us, funneling into a narrow contrail. Rows of dark, severe waves burst from the lake, foaming and curling. They rolled across the sand in staggered arrival, spending every last effort to reach us. We stood at the nexus where sky and water converged in a race with the wind.

"I mean, is this the same lake we hiked to last night?" Angela insisted.

"Yes!" my daughter and I hollered together, nodding our heads, trying to convince her this was the sleepy pond from the day before.

"Wow!" Katie gasped, uttering her first word thus far. She thrust her camera into my hands. "Take pictures of us!"

They ditched their flip-flops and danced in the wind and kicked in the spray. Their robust energy and the grays, white, and blues of their athletic clothing fused into the vista as the sun painted an opalescent sheen on the cresting waves and a silvery outline upon the dark clouds.

When a ribbon of blue appeared along the furthest edge of visibility, my intuition roamed the miles of water, assessing the lake's disposition and the sky's pattern to form a prediction of my own, quite contrary to the weather channel. I felt entirely qualified since my friends hadn't changed in any way that mattered. I supposed the lake hadn't either. "It will be clearing this afternoon," I ventured. "There will be scattered sunshine and more beautiful waves."

"Okay," KT said. "We need to buy some tanning oil. Forget that sunscreen. We'll hit the grocery store, then get cleaned up. We'll take our suits and towels to Fishtown. If the sun comes out, we'll lay out on the beach. If it doesn't, we'll shop and have dinner."

SEVENTY-FOUR

THE SPIRIT OF DEENA-HAHNA

WE APPROACHED THE giant oak, and Mary admonished, "There you are! We saw your van in the parking lot. Where were you?"

How could I explain our disappearance? Mere words seemed inadequate. The last hour had been more refreshing and relaxing than a week's vacation in a posh spa, pampered by an eager, flattering staff. My soul felt renewed and pleasantly at peace.

"We took a walk on the beach," Nancy said.

I glanced at Mary. She smiled. I should have known she'd understand.

"Come on," Nancy said, aiming for the parking lot. "Let's ditch the rocks."

Mary tagged along, and we sidestepped the groups of older ladies. They conversed vivaciously, pausing midsentence to greet us through bright lipstick smiles.

"The campers have left for their Council Fire on the overlook," Mary said. "First session ends in the morning. The seven-weekers have a field trip in the afternoon. So, we'll have the beach to ourselves."

"The day after, I bring my girls to camp." Nancy released the handle then swooshed the cargo door back on its rails. "Then, I head back to New Hampshire."

"Let's not think that far ahead," I begged as we dropped our rocks on the floorboard.

Mary wet her finger and brushed the edge of a pale, dry stone. The telltale webbing appeared. "A coat of clear nail polish will show that off real nice. You know, even a small petoskey like that would cost you around eight dollars in one of those gift shops in Glen Arbor."

"It's only partially covered," Nancy argued.

"Doesn't matter," Mary said.

"Really?" We voiced unanimous skepticism as Nancy shut the door.

Cars overflowed the lot and spilled beside the road. "Where did all of them come from?" I gaped at the generous attendance of ladies gathered across the spacious lawn.

"Many live in the local area, or spend their summers up here," Mary said. "Some can't come to the banquet so they're here for the Council Fire. And, of course, others will attend the banquet who aren't here now."

Christie emerged from the crowd wearing a short raincoat. Her thick blonde hair lay neatly across her shoulders. "Hi, guys!" She smiled brightly.

"What did you do today?" I asked, grinning to see her.

She composed a thoughtful expression. "We took a walk across the dunes. My kids are worn out."

A woman hollered from the top of the hill, cutting her short. "Line up, everyone!" Her voice carried the same authority as Bess, though she stood five or six inches taller. The ladies formed a twisting, turning line, two by two, from the lodge to the awning. Robyn stood near the front. Josie and Kappy gathered there as well. Except for this handful, the ladies belonged to older generations. The four of us hung together beneath the awning and watched them, as if their orderly conduct had nothing to do with us.

Christie's mom spoke to the woman beside her, "Doesn't Joan remind you of CJ? No one could line us up the way she used to!" They shared proud, inspired smiles.

I inched closer to Christie, wishing to escape their conformity. I could not believe they waxed sentimental for a cattle call!

"You never heard from Lori?" Mary asked. She folded her arms and waited for Nancy's answer.

"Nope. And I kept my cell phone with me all day."

Christie's mom glared at us. "Come on, you four! Line up now!"

We could not escape her motherly attention. She paired Christie and me in front of Nancy and Mary. We stared at the faces in line, baffled by their solemn comportment. I wanted to laugh. Did they think we took part in a meaningful act of historical significance? Did they expect a new bead, or world peace? "They are so serious!" I whispered to Christie, hoping she would agree or at least offer some insight.

"Shhhhh!" Christie's mom placed a rigid finger across her lips and whirled to face us.

Laughter bubbled in my chest, and I bit my lip against an audible eruption. Her chastisement held a surreal charm, especially at our age, and only added to my sense of the absurd. The entire occasion felt ripe for satire. I dared not look at Christie. If she registered a flicker of humor, I would come undone. After all, it was her mother! Water formed in my eyes from the agony of holding it in. I glanced at Nancy, who continued to visit softly with Mary.

Christie gripped my arm. Our eyes met, and we stifled a cascade of chuckling snorts. Audible gasps of intolerant surprise rippled down the line, directed at us! We drew apart, presenting hasty, contrite smiles. Nancy and Mary stopped visiting and eased closer.

Perhaps being children in the sixties among liberal-minded adults had doomed us from the start. Our parents scoffed at the trappings of conventional, organized religion. Our classmates sneered at the American dream of becoming president. Our nation's flag morphed into something to wear or to burn. And the summer President Nixon resigned, all politicians became crooks. We attended Bible-based churches, void of ceremony and guilt, with simple messages of unconditional love. God was our personal friend, formless and divine, yet very effective if given a chance. We didn't require an intermediary pastor, a confessional, or a ritualistic ceremony to find Him. So, who or what on earth deserved our respect and reverence? Even our patriotism remained guarded. Mostly, we resented forced solemnity. So when Nancy said, "Look in the trees," I choked.

A pixie-like wood nymph stood in shadow at the edge of the woods. Spun of forest-green cloth, her native outfit melted into her olive skin splattered with golden sparkles. Her augmented eyes shone dark, youthful, and mysterious. A golden leaf crown adorned her long black hair.

"The spirit of Deena-hahna!" the ladies whispered. Their singsong cadence carried down the line, echoing worshipful wonder. They tried not to stare, as if an apparition had truly appeared and would disappear if given too much notice.

Christie's fingers wrapped tightly around my arm and we stiffened against each other, pursing our lips. "Remember that movie, *A League of Their Own?*" I managed to whisper. Christie squeezed her eyes in recognition, adding, "And that corny song they sang." We could appreciate the story, but its characters belonged to a generation far removed from ours; when gals were gals and darn proud of it. Whereas, we deposed girlhood and all its weak symbolism to break professional barriers. At every turn, we insisted, "We are women." A boundary of obscured femininity stood between us. The waning values of their day seemed trite against our turbulent quests for equality. And now they surrounded us, imposing their old-fashioned values. We could only laugh.

Then again, the girl dressed as the spirit of Deena-hahna hailed from this time and place. Her willing participation intrigued us. "Is she a camper, or someone's granddaughter?" I whispered.

Christie's mom whirled around. Her eyes pleaded for us not to break the spell. Quick dimples appeared at the corners of her mouth, relaxing the severity of her expression.

We turned to see if Mary and Nancy shared our disbelief. "Are they doing a onetime reenactment for our moms?" Christie asked. "Or have they revised this tradition for the new campers?"

"They do it once in a while for the young ones," Mary said, pleasantly indifferent. "It adds an imaginative twist to an otherwise responsible occasion, like Santa Claus to Christmas." She held her head high and hadn't even tried to whisper. Her matronly attitude and rational explanation swept away the sugary coating and tethered a serious expression to our faces, more befitting to our age and experience. After all, hadn't we traveled a long way to partake in just such an event?

We picked up our pace. The spirit of Deena-hahna melted into the woods, and the first half of the line disappeared behind the lodge.

"Is there a fire pit 'round back?" I asked Christie. She shrugged, and it comforted me to learn she was equally as clueless as I, despite her mother's connections.

Passing the edge of shadowy woods, we reached the spot where the little wood nymph had briefly materialized. We rounded the eastern corner of the lodge, and a faint timbre of song winged toward us. At first vague, the tune gained distinction as more voices added volume and harmony. I leaned toward the front of the line and listened. Over the years, I had occasionally hummed its haunting melody to myself but I had not heard it for nearly thirty years.

SEVENTY-FIVE

PRUNING AWAY MISCONCEPTIONS

"WE CLIMB, WE cliiiiiimb, to Council Fire with open, ameeeenable hearts. . . ."

Christie's stunned expression reflected mine, and a startling transformation occurred between us. Intellect alone had guided us thus far, erecting a fence between generations. But now the familiar melody loosened a layer of buried emotion. We melted from its touch and changed from icy onlookers to smoldering participants. We had been as two grounded sailors, stranded along a deserted shore stalled in our sailboat waiting for a breeze. Now our sail opened, and the once familiar song hit us like a blast of wind and scooted us toward the water's edge so we could join the armada. Words erupted from our mouths with astonishing ease. Even if our minds could not yet conceive of it, our voices knew the way.

"To light the fire of living hope . . ."

We blended our voices with Mary and Nancy. Their patient, indulgent smiles proved they'd been waiting for us to catch up.

"To light the fire of Wildwoooooood, Wildwoooood, Wildwoooood."

In a mismatch of tangled linguistics we had sung "Wildwood." They sang "Deena-hahna." We shared a moment of sad resignation. When the melody doubled back upon itself in a three-way round, we sang Deena-hahna.

Christie's mom slowed her pace to measured steps, and I nearly stomped the back of her heels. The grass gave way to uneven paving stones. The line bunched, and the singing stopped. We had reached a bottleneck. Christie's mom turned to face me. Tears formed in her eyes.

"This same walk. These same steps." she pointed to a modest back porch. "Fifty years ago my camp friends and I came this way to Council Fires."

"You had it inside?" I glanced at my friends. "All the time? Even when it wasn't raining?" I pressed. She nodded, and I realized the implications. "But wasn't this lodge destroyed?"

"No, they saved most of it," Christie lightly responded.

"It's the same foundation, front and back, and the same stone fireplace." her mom proudly raised her chin.

I reconsidered the faces of the women crowding toward the entry and imagined a different path and a different lodge. How would we react if suddenly all of us from Wildwood shuffled along the boardwalk past Whippoorwill and the Murphy, heading for the Hylton? Or, more fittingly, what if we climbed the old path leading up to the Point?

I critically revised my first impression. These were not dutiful cows, reenacting a mundane activity from a bygone era. They were sane adults, crashing headlong into the manifestation of a deeply personal memory, and they were stunned.

When my turn came to stand at the threshold, I gazed into a vaulted space. Streams of light cast a honey gleam upon the oaken floors, knotty pine walls, and mahogany beams. It smelled of cool dampness and the charred remains of old, smoky fires. Four summers in a row I had delivered my daughter to this camp—two of them included her brother—and I had never walked up the hill and entered this lodge. Pure ambivalence had kept me away. I had only wanted to see my kids' cabins, to help them carve a cozy niche, and meet their counselors. After that I had deemed it best to leave and not draw out the good-byes.

As if drawn by force, my eyes found a single banner tacked upon the far wall. Handmade letters and numbers of white felt stood against a field of green. The left column ascended from 1970 to 1979. The right column hailed DUNE as the winner of every year, except 1975 and 1976; the seasons my sister and Susie had been captains.

"They hung our banner?" I said, teetering between affronted surprise and flattered humility. "Nancy," I whispered, sensing her beside me. "Our first year at Shenahwau was 1971. Why is 1970 there?"

"They were here," she said.

"But . . ." I could not put my confusion into words. I had never imagined the transition from Deena-hahna to Shenahwau occurring so fast. One summer on this land, the next at the boys' school. I had expected some kind of a line drawn between their Deena-hahna and our Wildwood. At the very least, I had expected different pennants.

Nancy wore an equally puzzled expression. "I'm quite sure ours started in 1971. They probably added it later," she said.

"Or made a new one?" I suggested.

"No. This is ours."

I didn't argue, figuring she would know. That contentious year, 1970, proclaimed another Cedar victory. Though pleased to see it, I could not envision a Cedar victory occurring on these grounds. Nor could I mount sympathy for those campers who had lost their land. Instead, I noticed other banners evenly spaced across two walls. I sought my daughter's banner from the nineties. Cedars had won all four years she'd attended. She had left her mark.

The new millennium hung beside it, kellygreen and bearing four years of the new decade. The present year's winner remained blank, still to be decided as the competition unfolded. Taking it all in, my gaze spanned the decades, past the seventies, the sixties, fifties, and forties. The fabric lost more and more of its brilliance as two more banners turned the corner. The thirties and twenties had faded to mottled gray. Each held a decade. Each announced either DUNE or CEDAR all the way back to 1916.

"This is remarkable," I whispered, sizing up the women who had placed them there. They had incorporated Wildwood and the turbulent eighties into their legacy. I folded my arms and enjoyed a moment of notability. They needed us. Otherwise, the chain would have been broken. My daughter had told me so, many times over, but I had never understood. Maybe because Bess had made us feel special and new. She had never mentioned Deena-hahna, or drawn comparisons, or linked us to its history. Suddenly, I wondered why.

"The guys have their banners here, too." Christie nudged me toward the opposite wall where an equal number of blue pennants depicted North and South, spanning back to 1912. Their earlier decades had likewise faded to mottled gray. Ashes to ashes, I thought, instinctively backing away, feeling less of a connection. We had shared a dining room and our camp's name with the guys, but little else.

"What years did Andrew come to camp?" Nancy asked.

"My son," I said, proudly stepping forward. For two years he had been part of the North team. "Look" I pointed to 1996 and 1999. Both declared NORTH as the winner. I lowered my arm and realized Andrew had contributed to those victories. He had breached this unfamiliar territory.

"Check this out." Nancy steered us toward a collection of old photos from both camps. They hung haphazardly on the walls, bereft of any chronological order. "That's my mother."

A black and white photo presented six young women in calf-length skirts, bobby socks, and saddle shoes, dressed for a Cabin Day. It could have been a snapshot from my mom's high school yearbook.

"Second from the right," she said.

I noted the resemblance to Theresa and a quaint, homey feeling overtook me as if we visited the family homestead of a long-deceased relative to whom we could all trace our genealogy.

"There aren't any pictures from Wildwood," Christie said.

"I brought my photo albums," Robyn's voice answered from across the hall. "We can look at them later. I'll bring them to the banquet."

"Robyn is the only counselor from both Wildwood and Deena-hahna," Christie said.

"What about Bess?" I stuck to my deeply rooted assumption.

"Oh no," Christie corrected though she looked pained to admit it. "They hired Bess just for Wildwood. She never went to Deena-hahna."

"You mean like Lou Ellen?" I blustered, completely aghast. "No, no, forget that." I waved the comparison away. Bess may not have attended Deena-hahna, but she had always embodied the essence of Wildwood.

"Robyn is the only one here who has memories of all the locations," Nancy said.

My eyes sought Christie, and she confirmed it. Robyn moved near, and we stepped aside for her to study the next photo. Numerous girls of graduated heights posed along the front staircase of this lodge. A cute little girl with short spiky hair, very young and tomboyish, sat in front with her arms tucked around her knees, grinning excitedly.

I inched closer, staring at the likeness until it came alive for me. I recognized Robyn at about ten years old. This undeniable proof of her longevity expanded my view of her importance. Our petite, formidable redhead, always a powerhouse of loyalty and conviction, had exemplified her own standard. Plus, her resilience through difficult circumstances had played a huge part in keeping Deena-hahna alive. Sure, they needed fundraisers and influential people behind the scenes who knew the system. But if campers did not return year after year seeking and finding something they couldn't find back home, there wouldn't be a camp. Robyn had single-handedly doled this out, summer after summer, during the most troublesome years of the camp's history.

"You should feel proud," I said, unable to believe a solid line of age and authority had once existed between us!

"What did you say?" Robyn asked, somewhat distracted, as if still trying to associate names and memories with the other faces in the picture.

"You kept this going," I said. "You should feel proud."

Perplexed wonder furrowed her brow beneath her tussled bangs. "Thank you," she whispered. Then she smiled.

I smiled back, hoping she'd notice my unqualified approval. I wanted to reverse anything negative I had ever said or thought about her.

Nancy treaded lightly beside us and asked, "Do you still have the wind to play the bugle?"

"You?" I asked, facing Robyn.

"Yes." She grinned, mildly amused. "You didn't know that?"

My mouth had fallen open and stayed there as I sought a reply. I had never thought about the person behind the bugle. Each night, I had imagined its perfectly executed melody descended upon us from another realm. And in the morning, well, the shock of waking up eclipsed any curiosity about the source. "Apparently I did not know a great many things," I said, having squelched my naïve bewilderment in favor of self-effacing candor. "And I wish I'd worked harder to become a counselor."

"Weren't you a counselor?" She balked, through a look of penetrating disbelief.

A little "ha" gurgled in my chest and exploded from my lips as a gasp. Her sincerity could not be doubted. In a flood of affection, I reached out and hugged her. Had she changed her mind about me over the years, and now saw me as counselor material? I decided then and there, our human dream could be cruel or majestic depending upon our memories. Truth stood solid as an oak, but our minds could alter its appearance. Bitter emotions wrought gnarled, twisted branches, while compassionate optimism allowed straight limbs to reach new sunlight. Forgetfulness caused them to die and rot on the trunk. Robyn was allowing me to sprout sideways branches of superfluous confusion. "No! I wasn't a counselor," I declared, pruning away any misconceptions.

"You would have made a good one," she said.

A crooked smile pasted itself to my face and would not leave, even as we took our seats around the fireplace. I had not been a counselor, and it didn't matter. We were all alumni now.

SEVENTY-SIX

A RESILIENT HISTORY

WE SAT ON stiff, wooden chairs, and I braced myself for more surprises. As if not to disappoint, Mary donned her Pioneer Camper hat. Thick brown hair poked out beneath the rim of this tattered fisherman's cap. Supporting a menagerie of lapel pins, felt patches, and wilted feathers, it had seen better days. But when an affable grin spread across Mary's face, it seemed to glow like a faded green halo.

My initial shock produced a spontaneous chuckle. When Robyn, Josie, and a few others also produced hats out of thin air and plopped them on their heads, I marveled at their ability to smuggle them in without notice. And bracelets! Many more of them wore their faded, wooden beads strung together with fresh jute.

Christie shifted toward me, emitting a small mirthful moan. I forced myself not to look at her. Instead, I looked at Nancy. She could be similarly adorned. As if in answer, our eyes met, and she shrugged. Either her life had moved beyond keeping track of such things, or they had never really mattered, as she had always insisted when we sat along the beach to watch the sunset.

So why did it matter to the others? Certainly not to boast or solicit compliments; the hats were too ugly. And despite my inner amusement, I knew it wasn't a joke. These ladies had accomplished challenging feats by expressing the seven camper qualities. Perhaps the hats served as visual reminders to keep these qualities alive in their daily lives. And perhaps Nancy hadn't kept hers because she needed no reminder. They were ingrained in her personality.

Recessed spotlights highlighted the grand fireplace and its puzzle of round, fist-sized rocks, harvested from the lake, and stacked artistically up to the beamed ceiling. The lights clicked off, and the fading sun cast shadows across the floor. A teepee of logs filled the hearth, and Joan squatted beside it, athletically at ease. Her lean fingers lit a match and kindled the flame.

A woman rose from a nearby chair. Her silver hair glinted from the blazing fire and her dark eyes roamed our semicircle. "Near the beginning of the last century," she narrated, "a woman named Caroline Jeanne, or CJ, as we would know her, dreamed of teaching young women outdoor skills along the shores of Lake Michigan. Fully reliant upon her faith in one abiding God, she surmounted many obstacles to attain this parcel of land."

Obviously money was not one of the obstacles, I thought, as a financial mind-set governed my outlook. I imagined a wealthy family from Chicago searching for a land investment and a tax write-off to justify an indulgent gift to their daughter.

"Surrounded by the lake, hills, and trees, Deena-hahna resided within ten miles of where CJ's brother had started a school for boys. By word of mouth the invitation spread."

What source of wealth had funded a boys' school and a girls' camp? I wondered. Had CJ's father been a railroad baron? Was the family heavily invested in steel, or coal mines? I craved such details and felt disappointed when the answers did not come.

Another woman rose from the group. In an unsettling way, she resembled my mom. Thin and petite, having auburn hair and lightly freckled cheeks, her energetic smile produced breathy excitement when she spoke. By virtue of this uncanny likeness, she squelched my financial analysis and softened my perspective.

"Young women found their way to northern Michigan, eager to escape the city heat and the boundaries of a rigid society just beginning to relax its hold," she said, her eyes bright and engaging. "They came in their long dresses, weighty hairstyles, and large hats held in place with sharp pins, all in search of a less constricting setting. They traveled on dirt roads, often times taking days to get here. They also took the train from Chicago, meeting in small groups at the station, riding in sleeping cars. And while they learned about nature and athletics, they formed a sisterhood beneath these pines in view of this same lake."

I grinned at her contagious smile and undertone of perpetual cheerfulness. I found myself wishing my mom had been a camper. If she had come to Deena-hahna during her teenage years these women would have been her friends. They would have played tennis together, learned to ride, swim, and camp. Their influence would have strengthened her natural faith to overcome a fear of water and heights, to undo Nanny's negativity.

However, my mom had not been born until 1936, and this narrative began when Nanny was a child. I recalled the earliest photo of her—a wedding portrait. Sleek and shining, her bleached blonde hair had been tucked to the side by a large white flower. A ruffled chiffon collar, glamorous and divine, floated near her daring neckline, and she smiled seductively, holding a bouquet of white daisies. If she had attended camp among such kind, generous women, they would have taught her charity, empathy, and the joys of sisterhood outside of family ties. Perhaps she would have gained enough optimism to last a lifetime, to rise above her real or invented sense of doom and worry.

But Nanny had been poor. When the stock market crashed in 1929, she had been sixteen. CJ and all the early families must have been filthy rich to send their daughters and sons to camp during the Great Depression! How frivolous to be learning tennis when fathers stood in bread lines or hung themselves in barns! I could just picture Nanny waving her hand at such nonsense. "Gad!" she would say. "Why travel Up-North to play games when there are chickens to feed, cows to milk, and fields to plant?" Suddenly, it seemed the only difference between Nanny and these women was a birthright into money. I folded my arms and slumped forward. A heavy chip of envy and suspicion tainted the camp's history like poison ink dripping down a wet page.

The story moved into World War II. My mom had been five when

Japan bombed Pearl Harbor and our country joined the war. Fuel, butter, and sugar had been rationed. Children collected old tires and scraps of metal for the war effort. Moms worked in factories to relieve dads of eighteen-hour shifts, seven days a week. Despite these hardships, young girls continued to find their way to summer camp in northern Michigan. They wore victory colors, wrote letters to boys heading overseas, and stomached an artificial butter called Oleo.

Rapidly, the story headed into the fifties, my mom's teenage years. She'd worn calf-length skirts, bobby socks, and saddle shoes while smiling happily for the camera in her high school yearbook. A few years later, this same smile appeared beneath black horn-rimmed glasses in my baby pictures. She had been twenty-three. I mentally flipped through our family photos as years sped ahead and Susan and I grew. An errant voice popped into my head like water pushing through oil. My family wasn't rich. The seventies had given us double-digit inflation, high unemployment rates, and exorbitant fuel costs. Despite all this, my parents had found the means to send Susan and me to camp.

And none of my camp friends came from wealthy families. I sat a little taller, wondering if I had been wrong about those early campers. Perhaps they had not come from wealthy families either.

What, exactly, had prompted our mom to pack us up for seven weeks? Supposedly, the sole recommendation of a woman from church who had advised, "Shenahwau is a nice place for young girls to grow over the summer." Mom had admired this woman. And she had wanted us to have something she alone couldn't give. Had this also motivated Christie and Nancy's grandmothers to send their daughters to camp? Was this the reason I'd sent mine? Perhaps we all shared a certain mind-set, rather than a certain sum of money. And maybe CJ really had started this thing with more faith than funds. Add to this the camp's struggle to survive a depression and war years, then its unbroken existence deserved my admiration, rather than my ridicule.

"CJ passed away in 1969," a different woman carried the story. "Her son was not interested in running the camp so he gave it to his daughter.

Regretfully, this grown woman did not treasure her grandmother's legacy and a few years later she sold the land. Because bloodlines do not always produce kindred spirits and kinship is no guarantee of a like mind, for over a decade, this site became home for something very different and a new generation of Deena-hahna campers headed south, taken in by the boys' camp."

Only, we didn't know we were Deena-hahna campers, I thought.

Her eyes widened in suspense. "Behind the scenes our efforts grew. Deena-hahna alumni raised funds, hoping and praying the land would come back to us. As fate would have it, CJ's son outlived his own daughter, the very one who had sold the land. As he lay on his deathbed in 1989, he heard news of our efforts to reclaim the land. He had always regretted his daughter's actions and vowed to make it right. His estate bought the land and signed it over to the newly rejuvenated Deena-hahna Foundation. From there, a mad fund-raising dash ensued and word quickly spread."

This part I remembered. Susan had telephoned me in North Dakota. She had been so excited, imagining Wildwood's return. Condominiums surrounded our old stretch of beach, but none had been built directly upon it. We thought the old place had been secured. However, further inquiries revealed this dream would never be realized. In its place, an even older dream would be fulfilled, though we hardly understood its significance.

"While the history of the boys' camp is not intended for this presentation," the woman continued, "I will say they encountered similar land issues. Therefore, when the foundation brought Deena-hahna back to life, it was only natural the boys' camp join us. Now we share a restrictive land-use clause and shall remain here, preserving our memories and our faith, as long as campers continue to come."

Joan returned to the head of our circle. She reached into a pile of pine clippings and extracted a tiny bough, shaking away a few hitchhikers. She turned to face us. "I am thankful for every moment I can spend here. For the friendships I have made and for the omnipotent bounty pouring into my life, seeming to spring from this place." She placed the needles upon a crimson log.

I could almost see Bess standing in this woman's place at my first Council Fire. "I hope each camper strives to achieve her goals this summer," she had said. "And if the way becomes difficult, look around at God's beauty and know that such power is near." Bright orange and red heat petals licked upward. The branch fought hard to stay green, wafting its essence of pine, sparking and crackling in defiance. I had once rooted for the bough to fight harder, to resist, forming my own barrier to growth. It had taken many Council Fires for Bess's words of wisdom to sink in.

"We all look for petoskeys," the next speaker said. She twirled the bough, staring down at the wooden floor. "We walk with our heads down, combing the beach, searching for the little fossils. Our belief is solid. We are quite positive the petoskeys are small and we must look very hard to find them. But one day," she said, raising her eyes to gaze out the window, "I found a boulder half-buried in the sand. I can't explain what drew me near. But as I stood over it, confused by its markings, I saw a petoskey! Instead of pea-sized pentagons, they were the size of a child's footprint."

We shared looks of surprise, never imagining the ancient coral had once grown so large.

"This is true," she said. "And it is also an analogy for our goals in life. Think of it, most people spend their lives trying to attain small ones when they could set their sights higher." Her words rippled around the circle in a tremor of truth. "This is what binds us together, everyone in this room, and everyone who stuck it out. Camp set our goals higher." She set the pine needles upon a crackling log. "And gave us the faith to achieve them."

We breathed in the smoky air, richly laden by the fire's transformation, and lent our silent agreement. She had named the one thing none of us could explain outside this setting. For all of us from different times and places, we had found our faith along the shores of Lake Michigan. The woman at church who recommended Shenahwau to my mom had known camp would do this. This is why Robyn, and all the women back to CJ, kept it running. And this is why I had sent my kids.

Through my teenage years, I was searching for a power beyond the physical world to rely on when life became either too bleak or too intense to handle on my own. Camp and church had told me it was out there. During the school year, friends, teachers, books, and pop icons told me it was not, declaring the most I could ever rely on was the echo of my own mind. So, drinking and drugs became a tool of discovery as I sought the answers from within. Back and forth, from summer to winter, I believed one way, then the other. Finally, when I could no longer tolerate the regurgitated echoes of my own frustrated mind, I gave up trying. In that quiet, still moment something real and powerful had reached me, giving me the evidence I needed.

Surely, this sort of faith could be realized elsewhere by anyone, at any time, without attending camp. But I would always be grateful to have found it at Wildwood under the stars, on the backpacking trip, and while facing two tornadoes. My friends had taught me to put on a smile despite an aching heart or body. The spiritual atmosphere had armed me to beat back the tides of cynical skepticism always lying in wait to engulf me.

This foundation of courage and confidence allowed me to achieve goals away from camp. In college, I ran on the women's cross-country team. I still tripped, but I had learned to fall without injury. As a new-lywed, I took flying lessons so I could better understand my husband's career. On level with the clouds, performing stalls and spins in the vast blue sky, I had discovered another large place. Yet, somehow between babies, military reassignments, and professional advancements, the concerns of motherhood had taken root and crowded out that carefree camper and fearless pilot. My faith had thinned, and I had grown lax in its replenishment.

I studied the women as they told what camp had meant to them—pranks, activities, personal achievements, and always an appreciation for the lake. Had they arrived at their current ages with their fearless natures intact? Had frequent reunions made a difference? Many of them were committed and involved like Robyn and Mary. For them, camp had always been more than just a summer job. However, many more were like me. They had only been campers.

Participation weaved a sporadic pattern around the circle. No one kept track though it seemed like we did. So, when my turn came I knew it. I walked toward the pile, plucked a cluster of needles, and faced the circle. "I want to thank the reunion committee," I heard myself say as the sticky pine resin coated my fingertips. "And the women who have kept the camp alive, safeguarding our banners and traditions." There, I admitted it. "I have to say, I never understood how Shenahwau was a part of Deena-hahna, or what it meant to reacquire this specific piece of land. When I first came to Shenahwau for Girls, to Wildwood, I thought I had joined something new. This reunion has opened my eyes. And thanks to everyone in this room, I have passed it along to my son and my daughter."

Turning toward the fire, I heard gasps of disbelief. Considering why, I peered over my shoulder. Many faces appeared puzzled by my remarks. Their eyes pierced me like daggers, and I sensed palatable annoyance at my ignorance. One of the ladies, perhaps having the distinction of being the oldest among us, walked beneath the mottled gray banner from the twenties and pumped her arm upward. Strong, worn fingers pointed emphatically, and her wounded expression beseeched me. Had I caused her fleeting, fragile memories to melt on the projection reel?

Seriously, what could I say? Did she really believe every person who had ever attended camp knew of its heritage? I had been a kid, fully centered on my time to the exclusion of all else. I hadn't known or cared about these ladies. And when my time had ended, I had moved on to other adventures. Hadn't camp aligned me to do just this? Such tunnel vision went hand in hand with youth. Even my own daughter categorized a five-year-old song as an oldie!

A few of the women smiled, showering goodwill and approval upon me. I whispered, "Thankyou," and placed the needles into the flames.

Returning to my seat, I decided it required an adult's perspective to really appreciate the longevity of Deena-hahna. Our numbers seemed large, but we represented only a handful of the generations of women. Most likely ignorance carried the day among those absent. They would never attend a reunion and never send their kids to camp. Perhaps this bothered these ladies the most. Maybe they worried about the future. Times could change. Schools could operate year-round. Too many of us could forget.

"Way to go, Schmidty," Christie said. And just like that we were campers again.

Mary sent me a crooked grin from beneath her jaunty fisherman's hat, and Nancy stared out the windows in search of a sunset. A few more ladies placed pine boughs upon the fire, but I did not hear them. I saw only my friends.

Lastly, we stood in a circle and joined hands. Joan led us into an unfamiliar song. Christie, Nancy, and I held our heads high in silent defiance while Robyn and Mary sang it for us. At the end, Joan announced, "Time for a bedtime snack!"

The Deena-hahna ladies squealed while lining up for Graham Crackers and Dixie cups full of cold milk. Two by two, they faced the kitchen like orphans in a workhouse.

"Girls," Christie's mom beckoned us, "there is plenty to go around."

"No thanks, Mom," Christie said, hooking her arm in mine, trying not to laugh. "Don't take too long," she called over her shoulder. "I want to say goodnight to Maribeth and the boys. I'll meet you at the car." She propelled me out the double screen doors.

We stepped on the wide stone verandah and burst into laughter. The air felt warm. A refreshing breeze blustered from the north.

Nancy came through next, followed by her mother. "We're ready," she declared.

"Now, don't forget," Mary called, pressing her face against the screen. "Sailing tomorrow at one o'clock sharp. Meet down at the beach. Rain or shine."

SEVENTY-SEVEN

DECIDING TO BREAK A RULE

GOLDEN SUNLIGHT PENETRATED the deep woods and filtered through the chalet's face of windows. Precocious and insistent, the rays demanded notice, creeping into every bedroom and waking us at the crack of dawn.

We had lingered in bed too long anyway, or so it seemed, and bolted awake as if having slept in shadow for days. Either real or imagined, the sunlight smelled of coconut oil, baking sand, and musty beach towels.

"We're ready!" KT announced. She and her friends rushed downstairs wearing bikinis. They carried towels and tanning oil.

"It's only seven o'clock," I said, rummaging around in the kitchen for some breakfast.

"We need to get a decent spot," Angela said.

"We're not in Virginia Beach, you know!" I laughed at the idea of Lake Michigan resembling the East Coast beaches paved in humanity.

The girls plopped upon the sofa, and KT raised the remote. They intended to wait me out. I dumped some cereal into a bowl and reached for the milk. As the TV came to life I paused midair, recalling my sister's warning. The campground filled up fast. It was extremely popular as the only protected lakeshore where tourists could sleep on the beach and build campfires. It was first-come, first-serve at the ranger station. There were no advance reservations. Not even a telephone.

"We need to get a campsite!" I said. "That is, if you still want to camp out tonight."

"Oh, yeah!" They spoke as one, voicing a drawn-out affirmation of remembered enthusiasm.

"We should do that now." I dumped the cereal back in the box.

"I'll drive," KT said. Leaning across the kitchen table, she cupped her hand over my keys. Scrunching her sunburned nose, she impishly dared me to stop her. I noticed peeling skin from the previous day and worried about sunscreen.

Nancy emerged from the bathroom. She peered into the small kitchen, and I told her our plan. She nodded silently and waved us on.

All the way to the campground, I bit my tongue against criticism. I wanted to say, "Don't drive so close to that car," or, "Don't take this curve so fast," or, "See, if you'd been driving slower you wouldn't have to brake so hard." But she performed within tolerable limits, and we arrived at the ranger station unharmed.

Inside the newly constructed cabin, we stood before a bare, wooden desk and a tall, imposing ranger. Official badges covered his forest-green coat. The strap of his wide brimmed Stetson cut into his chin and his riding breeches buttoned at the knees, just above his full-length boots.

"We'd like a campsite for tonight. Please," I added, gazing up at his nose, cleverly avoiding full eye contact.

An eyebrow raised slightly. "Take your pick."

I puzzled how to do this since the desk lay empty. Not a chair or trash can accompanied it.

He shifted his broad shoulders to reveal a detailed map burned into the cedar wall. "Oh," I said, and the four of us leaned in to decipher its layout. A thick, squiggly line represented the lake. A meandering maze delineated the campground and two rectangles designated the latrines. Numbers stood for each campsite, and hooks had been screwed below them. Round circles of occupancy hung from every site.

Angela tugged on the edge of my shirt. "They're all taken," she whispered.

"No!" the ranger boomed loudly. We jumped in place. "There are two left!" He slapped a pointer on space 82. A circumspect smile tugged at the corner of his mouth as he paused for our consideration. "This is near Latrine One," he clarified. "And this," he projected his stick toward space 34, "is near the ranger station." A series of dots, supposedly trees, separated it from our current location in the cedar hut.

Both sites had been rejected by everyone before us. No doubt, close proximity to the latrine had been judged equally undesirable as close proximity to the ranger station. I glanced up, wondering if he slept on the desk. He raised his chin and peered down his nose at me.

The girls beckoned me into a tight huddle. We had become quiz-show contestants, fearful of choosing a horribly wrong answer. The girls whispered a rush of pros and cons. "There will be traffic all night near the latrine . . . it could stink . . . but we wouldn't have far to go in the middle of the night . . . the other is closer to the beach . . . but do we really want to be near the ranger station?"

"Take this one," the ranger interrupted, tapping the wall. Before any of us could object, he placed a marker on 34. He folded his hands behind his back, rocked forward on his toes, and began to recite the rules. "No alcohol or firearms permitted. No littering. No propane. Quiet hours are from ten p.m. to six a.m. Fire is allowed only in the metal rings located at each site. Twelve dollars for the campsite. Five dollars for a bundle of wood. Pay here. Pick it up near the beach."

I dug into my wallet and paid for one night and two bundles of wood. He accepted the wad of folded bills, inspected each one, fixed creases in their corners, and arranged them faceup. Handing me a cardboard number and two tickets he said, "Have a nice day."

"Thank you," I responded, noticing all the rules he'd just recited were burned into permanence beside the exit. First and foremost, it read, "Must be eighteen or older." The girls hustled past like students fleeing the principal's office. But I worried about this rule. The girls were barely seventeen, and I did not intend to stay with them. Obviously, the ranger had skipped over it making certain assumptions.

Beyond earshot, the girls spoke as one, "Maybe we won't like the one he picked? Why did he want us near the ranger station? We should tell him we want to switch . . . let's see where the firewood is . . . let's check out the beach . . . we need stuff for s'mores."

I hovered near, biting my tongue, wanting this to be their adventure, despite the rules.

"Let's drive past both sites," KT concluded, handing me the keys. "You drive, so we can decide."

We crunched through the woodsy setting past tents and pop-up campers. Our open windows captured the heady scent of dew, decomposing leaves, and newly kindled fires mingling into the aroma of coffee and bacon. "There!" They pointed. I stopped at 82, and they spilled out, leaving the doors wide open. They discussed where to put the tent and park the car. They ran over to the latrine and quickly returned, sharing pleased smiles at finding it clean.

On our way to 34, we cruised past the woodpile and a few enviable spaces having views of the lake. A cool breeze swirled into the car, clearing out the morning smells of humanity, and we spied a wide sandy beach, blue water, and a clear sky. The road turned shadowy once again as we circled back toward the entry. The girls jumped from the car to examine 34. Surrounded by woods, it had no view of the ranger station and proved pleasantly inviting. The girls admitted he had been correct.

"Want to set up the tent?" Katie offered.

"No, someone might mess with it," Angela decided.

"Then, let's hit the beach," my daughter declared, leading them back to the car.

SEVENTY-EIGHT

AN UNEXPECTED ARRIVAL

I POUNDED DOWN the last flight of steps. The heavy cover of trees gave way to a refreshing breeze and I glimpsed long waves rolling across the beach. I leapt off the one-hundredth step, sinking into sand. Squinting across the beach, I saw Mary and Nancy sitting on a log.

"Schmidty!" Mary called.

"Are we the only ones signed up?" I asked, out of breath. I had run the entire way from the parking lot, fretting I might be late.

"This wind may have spooked the Deena-hahna ladies from joining us," Mary said, gazing at the lake.

We quietly assessed its sparkling surface and rows of dark water that occasionally peaked into white crests.

"This isn't bad," I said, sitting in the sand.

"No. It will be perfect," Nancy said.

"So, where's Christie?" I asked. "She's always on time."

"She needs to be with her family," Mary said. "But she is coming to the banquet."

Nancy stared past me toward the sound of footfalls on the final landing. Mary and I turned to follow her gaze.

"Lori!" I exclaimed. Flaxen red hair fell in waves past her shoulders, and her slim figure was draped in a white cover-up. "You look exactly the same!" I declared.

She paused to slap her hands against toned thighs. "Oh, there's a little more of me here than there was back then," she said. "Unfortunately," she raised a honeyed eyebrow and glanced at her chest, "it's still in the wrong places!"

"How did you know we would be here?" I pried for details.

She narrowed her eyes toward Nancy. "We talked on the phone this morning."

"And you didn't tell us," Mary chided.

Nancy bit her lip, clearly delighted by her ploy.

"The banquet!" I blurted, fearful of our waning time together. I hadn't seen Lori since our CT year. Finally, she stood before me, and I wanted it to last. "You have to come to the banquet tonight," I pleaded. "It will be the only way you can see Christie. Then all five of us can be together!"

She turned skeptical. "But I haven't officially signed up for the reunion. I haven't paid for anything."

"I paid for my sister, and she couldn't come. The Reunion Committee offered to refund it, but I told them to keep it. You can take her place."

"We'll see," she promised, too hastily, as if intending to say no at a later time.

I imagined her harboring misgivings about any official involvement because she did not need a reunion to lure her back Up-North. She visited often, during all four seasons. Since Nancy had convinced her to come this far, I plotted for her to come a bit further. "There are so many people you know," I insisted.

"Told you," Nancy said.

"They will love to see you," Mary added.

Lori slowly shook her head, painfully refusing.

As a camper, she had always been a bit of a rebel, though a perfectly acceptable rebel for camp, because she loved trips. And she had become the canoeing counselor after our CT year. "Heck, you'll know more of these people than I!"

She smiled at me, visibly relenting. I'd finally said the right thing. "Well, I suppose my family can entertain themselves for one evening," she yielded. "They can eat leftover birthday cake!"

"You have two girls, right?" Mary prompted.

"They are in middle school," Lori said. "Doing great. But we have our challenges, you know, typical worries about the quality of education

they're getting and who they're hanging out with, all that. Our neighborhood is a regular melting pot. It's a blast. Never a dull moment. Get
this," she said, striking the pose of a stand-up comic. "We get these new
neighbors, behind us. You have to know my husband loves his grape vines.
He's been trying to grow them along the back fence for three years now.
Finally, they are about to have these cute little grapes all over the place.
So, we're sitting down at the kitchen table, having coffee, and admiring
them out the back window when we see this old lady, completely covered
in black robes, stooping along the back fence in our neighbor's yard. She's
hugging a big bowl and has plucked nearly all the leaves off the vines!
'Do something!' my husband says. Well, what can I do?" Lori asked us.
"This lady keeps plucking and plucking and we're just staring through
the window. 'Lori, do something!' my husband insists. So, I go out to the
backyard and say, 'Hey, lady.' When I get to the fence, she starts spitting on
me, over and over, like some exotic black lizard. So I back away, thinking
she's possessed or something, when her son comes out yelling and cursing
at her. He shoos her into the house and apologizes to me over and over."

"Did you get any of whatever she was making with the leaves?"
Nancy asked.

"Well, at that point, who cares?" She shrugged. "Hey, they don't have a
dock," she said, as if just noticing the water.

"Yeah, the current along this point is too rough to hold one in place,"
Mary said.

We stared at the water. I envisioned the kind of waves generated by
two tornadoes, and decided if it ever happened again they'd lose the
entire beach and part of the cliff.

"At least they have three sailboats, five windsurfs, volleyball-nets, and
a motorboat," Lori said, gazing about at their equipment. Down shore,
we noticed a male and female preparing the beached motorboat for entry
into the water. Mary waved at them.

"Who are they?" I asked.

"Oh, the camp has a few new rules," Mary said. "There has to be a
guard-boat while we're in the water."

Lori tossed her shoes upon the sand and said, "I'll go with Roman!" I had been enthralled by her melodic voice while the lake, the beach, and the log blurred into an old familiar time and place. From the moment Lori had entered our cabin and my life decades earlier, the two of us had been in a relay race with Nancy as the baton. Lori always arrived just in time for me to hand her off. She would appease Nancy's daring nature. Together they could be as bold as they wanted. If they chose to heel the boat and capsize, they were welcome to it. I would have my own adventure at my own comfort level because, same as then, camp provided numerous friends to turn to. Its atmosphere had taught us certain activities remained better suited to different friends. So, instead of competing for attention among a small clique, we created new friendships along the road to personal achievement. And today, my achievement level meant I would sail with Mary.

SEVENTY-NINE

IN SEARCH OF A FAMILIAR SHORE

"I'LL HANDLE THE boom and the sail," Mary said. Our skiff was cradled in the sand about twelve feet from the water's edge. "You do the rudder and the daggerboard."

"Okay," I played along. My eyes blurred at the jumble of rigging.

Nancy and Lori had taken control of the furthest boat. The rich hum of their familiar bantering convinced me I had done this many times before, though I could not remember what to do.

"Ready?" Mary gripped the sides of the boat. The mainsail, stiffened by wooden battens, had already been threaded into the boom. It lay unfurled inside the boat. The wind toyed with its leading edge, flapping it about like a bird longing for flight.

"Ready," I replied, taking hold. We dug our feet and dragged the fiberglass tub. Its hull grated roughly. At the water's edge, it rose up from the onslaught of waves, and the wind doubled its force, like always, as if by magic, whenever a sailboat made contact with Lake Michigan.

"Slide the pintle in the gudgeon," Mary hollered, planting her feet and holding the boat steady.

Impressed by Mary's recall, I waded toward the stern. Cool water fell away and I felt very tall. Which was the pintle and which was the gudgeon? I wondered. And why were they called this? Water splashed my knees as I reached into the helm and lifted the wooden rudder. Crouching down, I aimed for a track of metal along the boat's transom. The skiff moved four directions at once and knocked me off kilter each time I lined it up. The rudder weighed a ton, my arms and back ached, and the waves kept lifting the stern away from me. I swallowed an irritated expletive. At last, six inches of what I assumed to be the pintle slid into the supposed gudgeon.

"Got it!" I yelled, loosening my hold and letting gravity take control. The rudder ground into the lakebed. Mary allowed the boat to drift into deeper water. I wrapped my fingers around the stern and hopped along, planting my feet beneath the rudder, despite an internal warning telling me not to do this. Sure enough, the boat floated upward, and the rudder fell along the rest of its track like a guillotine, landing squarely upon my big toe and a protruding bunion. Excruciating pain doubled me over. I held my breath, unable to cry or laugh. A twinge of adolescent pride prevented me from admitting such a stupid mistake. I jerked my foot free, swallowed the pain, and stepped back as the rudder embedded its tip.

Mary noticed the snag and pushed the boat deeper. She flung a leg over and climbed aboard, saying, "Hold it steady!"

I dug my feet into the lakebed, gripped the stern, and pitted my muscles against each new wave. I endured banged knees and bruised shins while Mary secured the boom then tugged the halyard and raised the sail for a snug fit at the tip of the mast. Bright nylon gleamed in the sun. Its loose edge flapped chaotically.

Taking a seat at the helm, she hollered, "Hop in!" The boom swung into the boat, and the sail harnessed the wind.

I clung to the port side, hopping along as water rose to my waist and the boat thrust forward. Catapulting over the edge, I fell inward.

Mary gripped the rudder in one hand, the main sheet in the other, and smiled as we glided on a swift, sharp angle from shore. I lowered the daggerboard and tried not to notice every bruised part of my body.

Instantly, it grew quiet. We no longer fought the wind's elemental force. We had joined it. Lori and Nancy skimmed across the water off our starboard side.

"Do you sail very often?" I asked, admiring her expertise.

"We have a boat like this at my parents' lake house," she said, concentrating on the water. "They have a place outside Indianapolis. My kids love to sail." She smiled. "It's one of the few things small children can safely do on the water. Claire sits next to me and holds the tiller while Timmy handles the sail. They feel so proud of themselves, like they're doing something really important."

"I bet they're cute," I gushed, recalling mine at the same age.

"Oh, they're a handful." She smiled and I knew she enjoyed them immensely. Her keen blue eyes looked sharp upon the water and the breeze tussled her thick layers of brown hair. Hadn't she always been like this?

"Do you want to take the sail?" she offered.

I perched on the windward side, chilled by my wet suit and the sail's shadow. "Actually, I'd love to sit on the bow," I said, staring longingly at the triangle of sun.

"Go ahead," she said.

Warmth radiated from the fiberglass and reflected off the sail as I leaned on my palms and stretched my legs. I closed my eyes and thought of all the years ahead for Mary as her children headed into middle school, then high school. The inevitable mantra flowed from my lips and carried to the helm, "They grow up so fast."

"They sure do," she agreed. "And it's tough to watch sometimes! I see Claire out my kitchen window as she jumps on the trampoline. She is eager to try all the tricks and flips we did as kids, but I can't watch! I start imagining all the different ways she can fall and get hurt!" A smirk of wonder crossed her face. "Where did these fears come from?"

"It gets harder," I said, recalling my son's dangerous skateboard tricks followed overnight, or so it seemed, by driver's education.

"I never knew such fears before having kids," Mary said. "And I don't want to impose them upon Claire. So, I go to another part of the house and busy myself. But I worry the whole time." She laughed. "Why can't I watch her like I used to watch Shane or Debbie?" Her question hung unanswered while we assessed our distance from shore. We had just sailed beyond that indefinable boundary of "far enough." Nancy and Lori already angled back. "Let's come about," Mary said, beckoning me to the seating area.

She tossed me the gray rope attached to the mainsail. I fingered its silky, intricate weave and recalled having once thought of it as elfish rope.

"Prepare to come about," she said. "Ready about? Hard-a-lee!" She shifted the bow abeam, and the wind fell off, leaving us in a void. The sail rippled, and the boom crossed over our heads. We ducked low. From this crouched position, she shifted across the little bench to sit on the opposite side of the tiller. I pulled on the mainsheet. It wound through two sets of pulleys and coiled at my feet. We waited for the wind. In this quiet oasis, Mary said, "Did you know my brother's wife died last year?"

"David is a widower?" I gasped, just as the wind found us. Snap! The sail caught the new direction. We lurched forward.

"It was sudden and very sad. He's bringing his boys to camp this weekend for their first time."

Having the same thought, we turned to watch Nancy. She and Lori scrambled beneath their boom, switching places at the tiller for about the fifth time. They laughed through rusty clumsiness.

"Does she know?" I fished for the possibility of a rekindled romance.

"Yes. She's known for a while about his wife. I called her at the time, hoping she could help since she'd already been through it. But I only just told her about David bringing his kids to camp tomorrow."

We studied the shoreline. Deena-hahna remained hidden atop its bluff, and the beach below barely hinted at either camp's existence. A few wooden lifeguard chairs, a couple of volleyball nets, and some buoys bobbed in the waves. The rest of the protected shoreline appeared pristine.

"Let's head south," Mary decided, and we set a new tack. The shoreline resembled a ribbon of sandy brown topped by green fringe. It jutted outward, like fingers, creating dimensional layers of increasing length.

"Can we see it from here?" I asked.

"Just barely," she answered my reference to the old camp. "It's in the bay beyond that second point."

I squinted across the shimmering water to see Nancy and Lori fleeing on a slightly different tack. How many times had I watched them from a different boat, admiring their prowess, entertained by their antics? They had become engrossed in conversation, unmindful of us, and we swept past, stealing their wind, smiling and waving. They quickly returned to nautical concerns, discussing their strategy and how to recover.

I squinted into brightness. Sunlight sparkled on my lashes and created luminescent circles around Nancy and Lori's boat. Time sped backwards. The breeze fluttered through Nancy's loose layered hair. She shifted the tiller wearing her purple-flowered two-piece suit. Her deeply tanned arms and legs flexed in muscular grace. Lori's pale orange bikini matched her flowing hair as it wrapped around her shoulders. She pointed toward the horizon, offering an urgent appeal while grinning through delicious anticipation.

My eyes followed to where she pointed. A row of whitecaps frothed on the surface. "A gust is coming!" I warned Mary.

She chuckled at the prospect, and I let the sail have more reach, to slow us down.

"They are going to hike out," I realized as Lori tightened their sail to harness more of the wind.

"I don't feel like taking a dip. Do you?"

"No," I laughed. "I'd rather watch them!"

"Me, too!"

They scrambled to the windward side, sat along the gunnels, and leaned out to balance the wind's force upon the sail. Nancy used her bare feet to maneuver the tiller and Lori hauled the sail taut as a drum. The boat spiked upward, racing away from us. "Woo-hoo!" they hollered, bouncing across the choppy water. Their backsides skimmed the surface, and they grew wet from the spray. Predictably, the wind fell off just as quickly as it had risen. "Woah!" Their virulent cries carried on the wind as their bottoms dipped into the lake and the boat nearly capsized. They leaned forward, sprawling inside, and the craft reached an even keel for an abrupt stall. We sped by, laughing.

Mary pointed toward shore and suspended our competition to gain a closer proximity. I searched for a familiar landmark, fully expecting a white L-shaped dock to come into focus beside a gray metal slide and a dock floating on barrels. A group of swimmers would be practicing their technique inside buoyed lanes. Heads would be bobbing up and down behind a row of junipers from a hidden trampoline. Red shingled roofs, hinting at the location of dark cozy cabins, would appear among mature stands of cedars, birch, and poplars. And rising above them all, one pine would figure prominently, foreshadowing a wooden lodge, painted deep red and boasting a brick chimney, bleached by the afternoon sun.

I imagined we could sail right through Beach Time and head for shore just in time to change clothes and race to dinner. All preparations would take care of themselves, and we only needed to show up at the dining hall. We could eat as much as we wanted because an evening of running, jumping, and playing would follow, and we'd fall into bed satiated, happy, and exhausted. No purses, no keys, no credit cards, no bills. No danger lurking in hidden places, or heavy responsibilities, no setbacks to progress, no fear. Only one carefree moment stretching into the next surrounded by beauty and friendship.

"You guys should head back now!" a deep male voice called out of nowhere. A sleek speedboat idled upwind on our port side. A young woman stood beside him at the windscreen.

Mary reached over to direct my release of the sail, and we glided to a near stop. She read the time on her waterproof watch and strenuously objected, "We have until three!"

"We need to be somewhere, though," the young man replied, and the young woman smiled grimly, as if it could not be helped.

Mary squinted, sizing up their authority.

Lori and Nancy eased alongside, steering clear of the speedboat's churning motor. "What's up?" Lori called.

Stark reality cut through the swirling mists of my illusion, and I saw us from their teenage perspective. Our sensible one-piece suits, uneven tans, practical hairstyles, and seasoned faces would seem out of place in their summer mirage. Did they think us inconsequential? Did they think they could easily manipulate us, cutting short our afternoon of reliving the past? Maybe so, but I could not ignore the sparkling water, the soothing breeze, and the sun's embracing warmth. I did not want to leave.

Thankfully, Mary refused to give it up. "We have until three," she snapped. "The camp directors and the counselor staff have known of this day since the beginning of camp." She wielded a presumption of authority just like those mysterious older Deena-hahna ladies who ran the show behind the scenes. In fact, her stature grew so exponentially by this exchange I started to believe she was one of them.

Both co-eds, especially the young man, stared speechlessly as if shocked to discover we would not obey.

I took advantage of the standoff to peer closely at our adversaries. Their ages and mannerisms seemed familiar. Instinctively, I turned on the motherly charm. "It is so beautiful out here," I sighed, focusing my energy on the young woman. "You are so lucky to be near this lake all summer. Couldn't we please have just a little longer?"

"We'll wait," she decided, facing the young man. Her compassion caused him to reconsider. He revved the motor and left us rocking in their wake. "This is ridiculous," Mary fumed. She shifted the tiller and yanked the boom back into the boat. I tightened the slack, and we cruised away in the opposite direction. Nancy and Lori shot ahead of us. "They have known for days, even weeks, that our time on the beach ran until three. It's barely two-thirty!"

I questioned her quibbling over a halfhour when she had a boat at her disposal any time she wanted. But then, this wasn't really about sailing. It was about the four of us recapturing something we had forgotten, something we needed to remember.

I shuttered my eyes against the sun and basked in the serenity of the lake. When our time wore down and we could put them off no longer, we headed for shore. I raised the daggerboard. Our bow hit the beach. The rudder scraped aground. I scrambled out to detach it while Mary lowered the sail. Side by side, we dragged our boats inland, removed the battens and sails, and coiled the lines. Mary directed us toward an equipment shed embedded in the sandy bluff, and we stowed the rigging. Our conversation rolled easily, and it seemed we had never been apart. We didn't look ahead, and we didn't look behind. We brushed sand from our feet and placed shorts and shirts over our suits. Combing fingers through our windblown hair, we climbed the hundred steps together, pausing often to stare back at the lake and admire the slightly different view from each landing. At the top, Lori promised to attend the banquet.

We paused at the sloping hill leading to the lodge. "I need to find my mom," Nancy said, staring up at the stone verandah.

"I'll come with you," Lori decided.

"I need to find Robyn," Mary said.

"Then, I'll see you guys later," I concluded, waving casually. Hardly breaking stride, I aimed for the parking lot. I had something to do, though I had forgotten what. I fished for my keys, climbed into the driver's seat, and turned the ignition. The tires stirred up white dust as I drove away. Upon reaching the main road, a pall of responsible concern attacked my blissful amnesia and wrestled it to the ground. "I have kids," I said aloud, and the youthful abandon I had recaptured vanished into a load of fresh worries.

An old Cadillac, rusty and scarred from dents, emerged from an obscure side road and darted in front of me. My pulse quickened. What if the girls decided to wander back to the chalet and got hit by this monstrosity? I drove like a maniac, unable to squelch this irrational fear. Mary's voice spoke in my head, where do all these fears come from? I did not know and I could not shake it off.

At four o'clock I reached the end of the access road. All the cars were gone. The beach was deserted except for three empty towels, some collapsed beach chairs, and a pile of shoes and clothes. I plodded through the sand, almost running, until I saw them frolicking in the lake, fully acclimated to its temperature. Bright carefree smiles greeted me from the water. They had written messages in the sand, built some desolate structures resembling sandcastles, and piled rocks along the edges of their towels as keepsakes and anchors against the wind.

I could only stand and smile, feeling contrite and foolish. What an extraordinary amount of energy I had wasted!

EIGHTY

A ROLE REVERSAL

"MRS. TAYLOR!" ANGELA beckoned from the outside deck. They had showered, changed clothes, and loaded the car.

I stood in the kitchen, dressed for the evening, watching Lindsay and Kelsie as they fixed a dinner of salad and warmed-up lasagna.

"Mom!" KT called more loudly.

I leaned out the sliding glass-door. Angela held the tent, still in its original box, and asked, "How do we set this up?"

I charged forth, fully prepared to study the directions, perhaps even assemble it along the deck so they could see how it's done. "It's never been out of the box," I said, reaching out. I paused, reconsidering. "You'll figure it out," I said, to impart self-reliance, the way Bess and Robyn had done for me.

"Oh, great!" Angela chuckled.

"We can do it," KT affirmed, and I glimpsed the same determination I'd once seen in Jenny. She slammed the lid and dug into her pocket for the car keys. "Bye," she said, reaching out for a hug. "Wait." she critically appraised my dark pants and red shirt. "Is that what you're wearing to your banquet?"

Angela swatted her arm. "Don't say that to your mom!"

"What's wrong?" I fretted.

"It's a banquet, Mom," she moaned. "I guarantee Nancy and her mom will be wearing whites."

I placed a hand on my hip and playfully argued, "Maybe I want to be different."

"Yeah," Angela agreed.

"Not for this," KT said.

The other Katie's eyes shifted between us, considering both points of view.

"I don't have any whites," I said.

"I'll be right back," KT said. She gripped my arm and tugged me into the chalet. It felt like Susan had a hold of me and I was twelve again. We passed Mrs. Roman and Nancy's bedroom. Faint rustlings of formidable harmony issued from behind their closed door, proving they dressed without any doubts of what to wear. KT lured me into my bedroom and quietly shut the door. "Okay, do you have any white shorts?" she asked.

"No, who does?" I snorted, sitting on the edge of the bed and crossing my arms.

She dug through my folded clothes and tossed them all around. I caught them midair to retain their ordered state. "These khakis will work," she said, plucking them from the pile. "How 'bout a white shirt?"

"No," I repeated, feeling a stab of panic.

"Wait here," she said, leaving the door open to dash upstairs. She returned seconds later, out of breath, and tossed me a white T-shirt.

"It's see-through!" I gasped, placing it across my chest.

"You're supposed to wear a bra-top, or a tank top underneath," she whispered, closing the door.

"I didn't bring one. Did you?"

"No." She flung my clothes across the carpet. "Wear this." She held up a white jog-bra.

"Won't that look funny?" I considered whether a bad attempt at wearing white was better than none at all.

"Try it," she insisted, waving it like a flag. Her extra pair of hands duplicated those hurried moments in changing rooms when I had helped her search for the perfect prom dress.

"There, you look cute." She smiled her approval. "Wait," she added, removing her white sweatshirt and placing it over my shoulders. "This will help hide the bra if it bothers you."

I crossed the sleeves and looped them. "Is this weird for you?" I asked. "Not even visiting camp? I could take you over in the morning when Nancy takes her girls?"

"No," she reassured. "I'm having lots of fun being able to drive around and take some time. It would be fun to see some camp people. But I may not know anyone." She echoed my concern from two days before. "I just want to remember everything as it was."

"I doesn't matter that we weren't counselors," I ventured. "We were part of the camp. Even if you've already found what you need, it's nice to go back."

"Maybe someday." She smiled. "If it makes you feel any better, I was the same person at camp as I am at home."

I nodded, knowing the truth of it. She reminded me more of Nancy at this age, than myself. And, thanks to Christie, I could appreciate her as an individual separate and different from me.

Soon, I would have to let her go completely. No more hovering about, my arms wide-open, issuing gentle warnings and ultimatums. And hopefully this kind, compassionate adult would return to stay, and we would be the best of friends, as I had been with my mother.

She stretched across the bed to grab my red sweatshirt. "You're wearing mine, so I'll wear yours."

"That's fair," I agreed. She kicked my clothes clear of the door. I surveyed the mess around me. "How ever did you earn a cleanliness bead?"

She tugged me from the bedroom, forcing me to leave the mess behind.

I trotted along, thinking of some last-minute advice. "Don't go wandering off," I warned, speaking through the open window as KT settled into the driver's seat. Angela strapped on her seat belt and Katie rested an elbow out the backseat window. "If anyone asks your age at the campground, you're all eighteen."

"Why?" they said together.

"It was one of the rules at the ranger's station." I explained its placement near the door.

"That's just for the person who's renting the space," Angela guessed. "That doesn't mean you have to be with us the whole time. Does it?" She glanced at both Katies for reinforcement.

"Let's tell anyone who asks that my mom went out for a bit," KT said. "That's not lying."

"Good." I nodded. Satisfied by her solution, I stepped away from the car. "See you in the morning."

"Wait." KT hesitated, casting me a timorous smile. "Can you come out later and check on us?"

"But how will I get there?" Her instant look of anguish, a holdover from childhood, begged me to find a way. Inwardly, I treasured it. "I'm sure Nancy will take me." I offered a promising smile.

She placed the car in drive and maneuvered through the staggering pine trees. I watched until she turned the corner, all the while thinking fondly of the disciplined park ranger, hoping he really did sleep on his desk.

EIGHTY-ONE

SUSAN'S PRACTICAL ADVICE

NANCY EMERGED FROM the bedroom wearing lipstick, a newly pressed pair of khakis, and a white shirt. I flushed embarrassingly, like that inadequate and tumultuous CT who had wanted desperately to become a counselor but couldn't express the needed qualities. Nancy peered distractedly about the room, lighting on her girls, then me, before she took a seat on the ottoman. She strapped her sandals while studying the choice of entertainment.

The moment reminded me of our first day at camp. We had returned from dinner, changing from sandals to sneakers, and I had dug through my trunk feeling confused and uncertain. Then I had followed her lead, forming the pattern of days, weeks, and years to come. How well she had understood camp's philosophy and requirements. "How do you know?" I had queried. "My mom went to camp," she had replied, defining an intriguing connection, which had aroused in me a genealogical sense of inadequacy. It dared me to imagine life with a different sort of family.

Mrs. Roman appeared in the hallway, also wearing beige shorts and a white shirt. I smiled, feeling a swell of affection. There she stood. The living embodiment of this connection, the source of Nancy's knowledge and nurturing that had filtered down to me through her friendship and guidance.

I opened my mouth to speak, wanting to tell Mrs. Roman how acutely I had felt her presence all those summers, long ago. But I couldn't find the words. Especially since to all outward appearances we had only just met.

Nancy's girls laughed at the movie, and Mrs. Roman peered over Nancy's shoulder to scrutinize the source of their hilarity. I gazed upon this family portrait, imagining how it would look if Nancy's sisters and their daughters were here as well, further expanding their ties to camp. Even her younger sister, Amy, had experienced Shenahwau during its sojourn along the river.

I felt the loss of my mother and everything she might have been. Grief mingled into a twinge of jealousy. But I refused to give it life. I pushed it away, actually taking a step backward, and my foot landed on Dad's leather work gloves. The afternoon sun warmed my legs, and I felt his presence hovering about, urging me to notice my own familial connection. It lay about me like a comforting blanket.

It resided in my daughter, from her burst of nurturing energy that had seen me dressed appropriately and delivered me from a potentially awkward situation. And how agonizing that first day of camp would have been without my sister! All told, I had fared better having her along instead of a maternal legacy back home. She had been willing to be my friend if no one else had, ultimately preventing the sort of anxiety Christie had faced alone. Susan had always been there to offer a motherly comment, a helping hand, never demanding anything from me in return, not even my respect.

When the two of us had reached our twenties and thirties, she had understood my longing. Season after season, when the days turned warm and I thought of camp, she knew I was waiting for my kids to be old enough. When the time arrived, she had been my strongest backer. She had insisted on riding with me from Indiana.

Once again, I pictured navigating the winding roads Up-North with my kids in the backseat, visibly leery and reticent of their impending adventure. But now, Susan materialized beside me. Like a radio droning contentedly in the background, she had filled the car with her genial, talkative presence. She had poured joy into the empty spaces, same as when we were kids, and bolstered us so effectively I'd forgotten she was even there! But I could not have done it without her. She had become an extension of me, a second mother, and a source of knowledge and strength.

While I had concentrated on the road, her spontaneous laughter and quirky remarks had relaxed and reassured my son, even as he watched his trunk and duffel drive away. And finally, just before leaving, she had gathered KT in a dark, cool corner of her cabin. Smaller than Whippoorwill, it had held four single beds including the counselor's. I was stuffing spare sheets into a duffel, uselessly gazing through the screens at the pine-rimmed bluff, yearning for the old camp. But Susan was huddling on KT's newly made bed whispering advice. I tilted my head as if I could just now hear her practical tips on earning beads, winning morning inspections, how to keep a bed warm at night, and when to find a hot shower.

KT had absorbed every word. In this way, she had started camp knowing what to expect. She had made instant friends and adored her counselor the way Nancy or Mary would have, instead of considering her an authority figure to be avoided, the way I had. My obedient sister, who had been a successful camper, CT, and counselor, despite homesickness, had passed her knowledge to my daughter. As a result, KT had embraced the camp spirit wholeheartedly.

Mrs. Roman backed away from the television, signaling our time to leave. My sense of inadequacy vanished. I tied KT's sweatshirt about my neck.

"Ready?" Nancy asked. Instantly, an aura of formality pervaded the room, bringing to mind other final banquets and the excitement and sadness they had generated. More than ever, I vowed to make the most of our last night.

EIGHTY-TWO

A FEAST OF VALIDATION

WE MOUNTED THE generous staircase, beautifully crafted from asymmetrical chunks of rock and blending artistically into the verandah. Two screened doors beckoned at the top. Mrs. Roman headed for them, but Nancy tugged me aside. She leaned a hip against the stone wall and adjusted a looming bough. "I bet you could see a heck of a sunset from here."

The scent of pine mingled into an easterly current, newly crossed over from Wisconsin. Feminine voices floated to us from inside and I reveled in the smells and sounds of camp. Simultaneously, an old excitement stirred of youthful abandon. I peered through the tree limbs, past the grassy lawn, over the tennis courts, across the cabin roofs, and beyond the pines anchoring the bluff. A thin blue line delineated sky from lake. The golden sun, partly veiled by flimsy clouds, hovered above the treetops about two hours away from the promise of a vibrant sunset.

I smiled and nodded. Granted, this camp may not have easy access to the beach, but they could see it from here. Perhaps over the decades a few other like-minded girls had discovered a safe spot along the bluff to glimpse an endless horizon awash in a blaze of color, ever mindful of the megaphone's warning or the bugle's finality.

"It was too cloudy last night," Nancy said.

I had left the porch immersed in conversation with Christie, not even glancing west. I studied Nancy's profile, watching her as she watched the lake, and wondered how many sunsets I would have missed without her influence.

Voices beckoned us inside. The wooden floors gleamed from a buffed shine. Long tables covered in white linen fanned out from the stone fireplace. Their benches remained neatly tucked, and stainless-steel utensils and cloth napkins marked each place setting. Aromas of buttery bread and savory herbs wafted from the kitchen.

Robyn presided over her photo albums at the nearest table. We all had similar albums back home, though not nearly as comprehensive in the years they spanned. Mine were committed to memory, like a classic silent movie. But now I viewed an alternate version, shot from different angles, bearing slightly different subjects and backgrounds. The main stars of my photos held bit parts while hers filled the spotlight. It was refreshing, but also startling.

Glossy black-and-white squares, neatly trimmed in white borders, covered the early years. Forthright poses depicted campers and counselors in front of the Hylton, the cabins, the flagpole, and the beach. Everyone wore long, straight hair, parted down the middle, tucked behind ears or tied into a ponytail; except Robyn. She had always worn hers cropped short, framing a wholesome smile.

There was a snapshot of two swans floating near a wall of fog, and many others of Cedar and Dunes in action. I laughed to see the end of the relay race on the river. Joanna stood on the bank, in the foreground, while I remained in the water tugging on my suit. The colors of those days lay buried in our memories. Then, quite suddenly, in the summer of 1972 they changed to living color.

Harvest tones and grainy images revealed horse shows, dune walks, and skits from the psychedelic seventies. Two more albums cataloged Shenahwau's stint along the river. I politely skipped through these unfamiliar campers and located a photo of eight CTs on Whitecap's front porch. It was opening day, and Mary stood in the doorway with a foot on her trunk. That very afternoon, Robyn had moved her from Sunblazer to Whitecap, making her a CT. We had welcomed her and never questioned the move.

The double-screened doors slammed at intervals, announcing each new arrival into the lodge. Crowds of older ladies milled past to join their circles of friends. Christie eased closer to me. I flipped pages, hoping to find Robyn in her bed on the end of the dock.

We smiled at bras in unlikely places and registered awed respect for the image of a large brass bell setting triumphantly on some cabin's wooden floor. We knew its sound, having heard it three times a day, but we had never seen it. Morbidly fascinated, we studied the boys' bell as if viewing a corpse in a crime scene photo.

The next page over, beside a picture of us wearing overstuffed bathrobes, cold cream, and curlers on Whitecap's verandah, was a blurry photo of Robyn in a flannel nightgown. She squinted into the sun through a pinched face and a tight smile. A shirt dangled from her clenched teeth, and blue ripples filled the background.

My heart beat faster, and I studied it further. She was standing on the dock. The sun's angle confirmed it was morning. I lifted the next page, scanning for more, but it moved on to the backpacking trip and the final banquet. "Wait a second," I said to Christie, taking the album in hand. I balanced it beneath my palm and reached for Robyn. "Look at this picture." I pointed, laughing lightly, as if driven by casual amusement rather than a dire need to prove a point.

She took a glance. "Eeew, not a very good pose."

"You're in your pajamas," I said, trying to control my excitement. "You're getting dressed on the end of the dock."

"Could be." She shrugged, returning her attention to Josie.

Christie lifted the next page. She held it midair, expecting me to take it. "Oh, I remember those biting fish!" She pointed to a photo of her and Susie in thigh-deep water holding aluminum pots.

I held fast and would not turn the page. I wanted someone to agree we had moved Robyn's bed in the middle of the night. But Nancy, Mary, and Lori were engrossed in other albums. My attempts to make eye contact had failed. Robyn's attention turned to another year, and Christie lifted the next page. Oh, what's the use, I thought, letting it drop. Why argue with someone who thought I was a counselor?

"Here's our last official photo," Christie whispered reverently, staring at an eleven-by-fourteen blowup. She turned the album sideways. Decked out in Sunday whites, our entire camp was lined up between the tallest pine tree and the Hylton. Christie's finger pressed each face, one by one, trying to say their names. I helped when I could. Some rolled effortlessly off our tongues, others could not be recalled. And when we came to Tori, Susie, Cindy, and Sarah, we hummed a longing sigh.

"I wish they could be here," I said, lifting my eyes from the picture, trying to imagine them lingering among us and sharing our stories.

"They may not be thinking of this place at all," Christie said. "I wonder what they are doing at this exact moment. No one has heard from Susie in years."

Mary lifted the album's back cover. "I love this picture," she announced, grabbing everyone's attention. She extracted the album from us and held it up for all to see. A panorama photo pasted inside the back cover had been spliced together along the middle of the dock and looked back at the camp, regaling Wildwood's past glory. Muted and golden, it reflected the passing storm and the passing years. Wet sand remained dark and rich. Our towering pine dwarfed the distant Hylton, and a few rustic cabins poked through shades of green.

"Just the way I remember it," Josie concluded.

"That's the picture you sent me," Robyn said. "It's the only one we have showing the entire camp." She stared at me, wearing a sad, grateful expression.

I frowned through a daze of confusion. She meant me. I had never sent her one. In fact, I may have gone out of my way to exclude her! I had made numerous copies at the Photo Hut, pieced them together with Scotch-tape, then tucked them in envelopes and mailed them to my fellow CTs. Lori's had come back to me right away stamped "address unknown." This, strangely enough, allowed me to have a copy because I had forgotten to hold one back. And I would not have taken time to duplicate the process because directly afterwards I had packed up my things and moved to college. It had been my final act of devotion to

camp. Still, I could not recall having sent one to Robyn. I peered suspiciously at Mary. Had she given hers away?

Mary's dubious smile formed a voluminous reply of silence. For many years
I'd held a grudge against Robyn, one she didn't deserve. And somehow Mary
had known. Long past those years when the rest of us had moved on, Mary
had remained at camp working alongside Robyn. They had become peers. And
she had paved the way for me to move on, to break free from an old wound,
by ensuring Robyn never knew.

"Guess who!" Cool, slender fingers wrapped around my eyes.

I gripped them gently and plied them away. "Beth," I said, not having
to see her face. I had recognized her bubbly voice from summers past
and her tall stature from two nights ago.

"Great picture," she said, taking the album from Mary. Lori moved
near, and they flipped the pages. "This reminds me of that time we
moved Robyn's bed on the end of the dock," Lori said, tapping the picture
of Robyn squinting into sunlight.

"You remember that?" I raised my voice, hoping Robyn would hear.

"Sure," Lori said.

"No one believed me last night," I said, thinking what a difference it
made to have one more of us around!

"We did some wild stuff that summer," Lori said, and Beth turned
more pages.

"I have something you will be interested to read," Robyn interrupted,
waving a FedEx envelope. "It arrived this morning. A Saturday delivery
from Los Angeles," she added impressively.

Reaching inside, she removed a page from a magazine and held
up an article with the photo of an attractive woman having short hair
and warm brown eyes. When I looked into her smile, seeing past the
business suit and professionally styled hair, I could hear the echoes of
an uncertain giggle. A pink Post-It note contained a scrawling cursive
message, "To the CT class of '76. I wish I could be there. I think of you
often. You believed in me, long before I believed in myself. Thank-you
for the wonderful memories! Love, Susie."

"What is the article about?" I said, trying to read a key passage underlined in red.

"She has become the vice president of a major corporation," Robyn said. "This is the news release. But what's really cool is that inside the article she credits camp for changing the direction of her life."

I thought back to the moment it had happened. I had seen it on her face. It was the night we had won the banner. In her own way, it was the night Susie had set her sights on the large petoskeys.

"Time to wrap it up," Robyn said, plucking the article from my grasp. The lodge was packed to capacity.

Thoroughly pleased and vindicated, I helped collect the albums. My version of the tornadoes remained unverified, but every other memory had settled neatly into place.

We fit together at one table, all of us from Wildwood. As we rose for the invocation, I noticed the entire assemblage of women wore light pants and white shirts. If I hadn't changed, I would have stood out like a frilly bra on a flagpole. Thankfully, my daughter had saved me. And if she hadn't come to my rescue, Nancy would have. I felt certain of this, enough to relax and settle in beside dear friends.

EIGHTY-THREE

A DIFFERENT SORT OF SUNSET

A PARADE OF young women streamed from the kitchen bearing plat-
ters of crispy trout, smoked chicken, buttery beans, savory potatoes,
warm rolls, and a tangy tossed salad. We served ourselves family-style
while our conversation flowed. Questions and answers touched lightly on
husbands, children, and careers, steering clear of possessions. We skirted
the edge of dream and reality, mentioning the outside world only to help
define the women we'd become. No one wanted to dwell too long on
anything outside of camp, as if our entire setting would dissolve into a
fine Michigan mist if we tried. So, we paused, oftentimes midsentence,
to nip these lapses.

"Ladies, ladies," Joan announced when our young servers had
whisked all away but the drinking glasses. "Let me acknowledge
some special people who have been faithfully behind the scenes year
after year, heading up our fund-raising . . ."

"Ah," I sighed, feeling the dream dissolve. "It's the money part."

"They're pretty relaxed about it," Christie replied, having heard
me. "They put their wish list into a newsletter and mail it off to
alumni. They usually get what they want. It's kind of amazing,
really."

"And they have never even been campers!" Joan concluded. "They
simply love the place." We clapped as a woman in a gray shirt and
green tie approached the podium. "Now, instead of a homegrown skit,"
Joan said, "it is my pleasure to introduce a water quality specialist from
Traverse City to share some alarming trends."

Our key speaker stared at us over the top of wire-rimmed bifocals. The lights dimmed, and our far wall became the backdrop of a slide-show. "The lake is cleaner than it's ever been," she began. "And this presents a problem. These are zebra mussels." A striped, shelled parasite filled the wall. "They are not indigenous to these parts. They have been imported into our waters on the bottoms of boats. They feed on suspended particles in the lake, making the lake cleaner than it should be." She clicked a button, and we viewed a mass of green algae. "When the water is too clean, sunlight reaches the lowest depths of the lake and promotes the growth of algae."

She outlined a trend of increased phosphorus levels, sewage dumping from across the lake in Wisconsin, and a cycle of harm culminated by putrid clumps of Cladophora washing ashore. She targeted boat owners as contributors to the problem then provided an e-mail address and Web sites. Many of us dug into our purses for pens and pencils, jotting along the margins of our printed programs.

Christie nudged my shoulder. "We were so lucky."

"We were," I whispered back.

Nancy squirmed, itching to leave, as golden rays streaked the front windows and flared toward the back wall.

The speaker and the fund-raisers exited. The room became a sea of orderly movement. Tables and benches were pushed aside to clear an opening near the fireplace. The lights dimmed, and Christie beckoned me to stand beside her. We faced the banners, having our backs to the kitchen, and everyone filled the gaps to form a circle. Christie's mom stood next to me.

"Remember how to hold hands," Joan directed, crossing one arm over the other, forming a link between the two women on either side of her.

Nancy backed toward the double doors. Our eyes locked, and she tilted her head. Her adventurous smile beckoned me to join her. I shook my head, ever so slightly. My feet had rooted to the floor. Her expression tugged at my heart yet I held fast, amazed to realize I actually wanted to stay.

Nancy gripped Lori's shirt instead.

Lori shuffled backward, bearing wide-eyed surprise. They slipped through the screened door, and I watched them go, remaining secure in my choice.

The circle turned silent. A few of the ladies twittered.

"Who dropped the ball?" Joan solicited, gazing to her right. "Come on, ladies, liven up! Let's get it all the way around."

Christie clued me in. "It's the friendship squeeze. It only made it halfway around."

The friendship squeeze? I could not enlist a single memory of having done this among my Wildwood friends. Joan began again, squeezing with exaggerated gusto. Robyn passed it to Josie. It spread over three ladies I didn't know, to Mrs. Roman, past a few more, then Beth. I felt Christie's squeeze and stopped to think, this is it. The entire circle honed in on me. I squeezed my opposite hand, passing it to Christie's mom. All eyes moved along until Joan signaled completion by solemnly bowing her head. Most of the circle did the same, but I kept my eye on her, wondering what she had planned. From deep inside her chest she uttered a single consonant. The letter "D." It became a note, suspended for the mere wisp of a moment.

"Day is done . . ."

Their deep voices stuttered on cue, as did mine, and we sang the first line. A chill traveled down my spine. For over a decade I had sung 'Taps' to my children as a lullaby, oftentimes coaxing my husband's deep baritone to hold steady against my starving harmony. Mom had also succumbed to this yearning, making it her own. Why else had she strained against the morphine after it had glazed her sight and numbed her speech, to make this final request? Susan had cried at the foot of her hospital bed, and Nanny had held her hand as I choked on the melody, hearing the offsetting harmony in my head. Her life had rapidly extinguished while I took myself to that rise of sand, near a lake of midnight blue, trying not to face the truth. She was dying of cancer. Ovarian. The swiftest and deadliest kind. Her stomach bloated from a petite size four to a size ten and stayed there for weeks. They never considered her ovaries because of her chronic intestinal problems. Despite annual pap smears, it took a near-fatal car wreck and a search for internal injuries to find it. And now, years later, it still felt as if she'd died from a sudden and tragic car wreck.

"Gone the sun . . ."

My voice rang out, propelled from my chest by an unseen force. Everyone held steady on "sun," but I climbed higher, singing the two contrasting notes. It was the experience I had always longed for. We gathered beneath a vaulted ceiling, but I stood on that rise of dune, near the lake bathed in starlight, creating a wellspring of song among my peers. I looked up and out, staring at the banners, vaguely aware of curious eyes roving about in search of the lone singer who transformed their unified voices into a rich blend.

"From the lake, from the hills, from the sky . . ." I drew "sky" into a stepped-up chord, easily matching their volume. We created an elixir of sound, perfectly proportioned, and I gained confidence from the absolute clarity of my voice.

I could not see Nancy, but I sensed her presence just beyond, leaning against the wall, viewing the sunset, and listening. I did not need a visual confirmation of this sunset. I felt it symbolically setting on parts of my life, transitioning into a fresh, unique sunrise.

Every face in the circle blurred, except one. Ever so briefly, Robyn and I connected. Her startled recognition seemed to justify my old grudge. She appeared truly baffled. Among such distinguished counselors, how could I be the only one to remember the harmony? But before I looked away, I saw a proud smile as if she had just witnessed a second-string player emerging from the pack to score a winning goal for her team.

"All is well," we sang together. "Safely rest. God is nigh."

These phrases contained a feast of blends, and I savored every morsel. Their deep voices filled the cavernous space, and I placed mine on top, reso-nating high and clear. I vaguely wondered why no one else joined me. Had they forgotten the harmony? Did they no longer trust their voices to hit the high notes? Regardless, if I ever sang "Taps" again, it could never duplicate the perfection of that moment. It was everything I needed it to be. A child-hood wish had been fulfilled, and my mother's passing had become final.

I no longer faced the future empty and rudderless from a precipice of fear and grief. I had closed the door on adolescence and crossed the chasm into a new phase of adulthood because my cubs were heading for shore. Soon they would enter the woods without me. I needed to take the path my mother had blazed. I would send them off into a dangerous world with an encouraging smile lit by faith.

We fell silent, and no one moved. Our song had become a tangible prayer. We awaited its passage upward and outward into the world. Then, we dropped our hands and milled about. Since no one ever flattered the bugler, no one flattered me. Our voices had been otherworldly together, and we needed no earthly praise.

The five of us gathered on the rock-hewn steps, saying good-bye, and preparing for our separate ways. We lived in different parts of the country, knew little of each other's families, and many years might pass before we ever saw each other again. Our time together had been a gift. And when our bodies tugged hardest against vitality and old memories faded further away, hopefully the nine of us would find each other in some distant future to dip into the lake to refill our vessels.

"Wait, wait," Christie said. "I have something serious to say. It's a famous quote. Well, sort of."

"Not the Beach Boys," Lori said.

Christie shot her a devilish smile. "No, it's an excerpt from one of my favorite poems. I stumbled upon it in an old textbook." She cleared her throat.

> Heaven gives our years of fading strength indemnifying
> fleetness;
> and those of youth, a seeming length, proportion'd to their
> sweetness.

We paused to consider this. Nancy alone seemed not to hear. Her focus held to the lake. "Our English teacher," I sighed, noting how Christie's simplistic observations from younger days had grown profound.

"It's called 'The River of Life' by Thomas Campbell," she credited.

"I'm thinking," Lori said, "there's a better word for that 'fading strength.'" She raised her eyebrows. "It is called dementia."

Mary shook her head from side to side, avidly disagreeing. "We don't have to grow old like that. Let's not limit ourselves."

"Those were sweet years," Christie reiterated defensively.

"Life was sweet because we didn't fear anything," Nancy said. "We didn't know how."

This aspect of her personality had always startled me. She would appear disengaged, and right when you thought she wasn't listening she'd strike at the heart of the matter, leaping far ahead of the rest of us. Even if she didn't remember the day-to-day details of camp, at least she remembered this.

"I never expected bad things to happen," she continued, "but the world taught me differently. This is growing old. I refuse to give it power. I want to be strong again, fearless, always expecting something good to happen. I want to feel happy every day. And I want to know, to really know, that my children are cradled in the same loving hands we were."

I, too, did not want to imagine danger and failure where none existed. How many times did I have to learn this lesson? I still considered what might be, instead of taking notice of what was. Linda had said it wouldn't be easy as life offered increasing challenges. We had to watch our daily thoughts and not let negative concepts take hold, even for an instant.

I studied their faces, memorizing their smiles. "Y'all must be doing something right," I observed in my adopted southern drawl. "Because y'all have more wrinkles from smiling than worrying!"

"Guys," Christie said, "I need to go. My kids will want me to say goodnight."

"Yes," Lori agreed. "Mine, too."

"Come on, Schmidty," Nancy said. "Let's take my mom back. Then, I'll swing you by that campsite to check on your girls."

EIGHTY-FOUR

GOODNIGHT, SUNBLAZER

UNDER COVER OF darkness we discussed the books we had read and the places we loved. We wanted to share as much honesty as possible in the time left to us, to learn what brought each other joy and sustenance. Neither of us attended church anymore, yet our faith remained strong.

Nancy turned off her headlights, and we pulled into site 34.

"Are you in there?" We stood beside the tent.

"We're really tired," a sleepy voice groaned, and I recognized my daughter. "We built a fire and ate hot dogs and s'mores."

I partially unzipped the opening and peeked inside. They had layered two sleeping bags and piled the third on top, turning the space into one large bed.

"We figured out the tent," Angela proudly croaked.

"It was easy," Katie said.

"Can you sing us a hymn?" KT asked.

"Sure." I glanced at Nancy.

"How 'bout 412?" She named a page from the old hymnal. I nodded, knowing it well.

"I think we'll be getting up early," KT warned, closing her eyes. "We'll see you at the chalet."

"Okay," I agreed, zipping the tent against wayward mosquitoes.

Nancy and I began to sing. At the very end, without prompting, we both whispered together, "Goodnight, Sunblazer."

"Goodnight," the girls echoed.

EIGHTY-FIVE

TAKING OFF

NANCY AND HER family vacated the chalet in a whirl of efficiency. They would go for coffee and breakfast before heading for camp. Our good-byes were brief. We knew, no matter how much time might lapse before seeing each other again, we would not change; at least not in any way that mattered.

No sooner had they turned from the driveway when my car turned in. The doors flung open, and all three flew out.

"Look at my skin!" Angela demanded. "I never get sunburned, and I have little water blisters everywhere!"

She appeared beautiful as ever, but I took a closer look anyway, respecting her concern. "It's not bad," I said. "Does it hurt?"

"No. But I can't be out in the sun anymore!"

"It must be those skin care products you use," Katie interjected, as if she'd offered this possibility many times over but had not received the satisfaction of being heard.

"Mom," KT concluded, "we want to go home. We've had a great time, but there is this party tomorrow night . . ."

"Really?" I replied, unable to believe it. I would have loved to see the lake once more, but I was also ready to leave. I had accomplished more than I'd expected and was content to know my kids, my sister, and I were links in the camp's chain of memories and traditions.

"Okay," I agreed, "let's pack up."

The girls emptied the car, vacuumed the sand, and repacked while I meticulously followed Barbara's written instructions. By nine a.m. I was maneuvering down the driveway. At the bottom of the long hill I paused. "Sure you don't want to visit the camp?" I asked KT. The way home required a left. Camp required a right.

"Naw," she whispered. "What would Angela and Katie do? I'm ready to go."

I turned left.

As we headed east on the highway, somewhere not too far away, another Nancy headed for her van. She activated the remote lock, ready to leave her girls behind, when a tall blond man stepped into view.

"How's it going?" He smiled, and her heart melted.

WE STOPPED FOR the night outside Cleveland, Ohio, favoring a more direct route back to Virginia, requiring only two days of travel, rather than three. In a land of cement, neon lights, and franchised restaurants, we shared two double beds in a chain hotel and watched a movie we'd all seen numerous times.

That night, I dreamed of Wildwood. I ran by myself now, down the steps of the dining hall, over the bridge, and along the river. I passed under the Wildwood sign and veered toward Whitecap. It stood boarded and bolted. The shutters had been nailed closed. The door held a rusty lock, and I could not peek inside. I knew my name, all of our names, remained etched along the rafters next to the names of every girl who had ever been a CT at Shenahwau.

I wanted to rip the lock from the door, but an ethereal boardwalk beckoned, blazing a trail along the sand where Driftwood and Gull's Nest used to be. I floated toward the Hylton and its memory of a brick foundation. Our structures appeared as gossamer outlines. Only our tallest pine vibrated from living brilliance. It stretched toward the sky, healthy and strong. Dunes had sculpted and reshaped around it. The hollowed trench once leading from the bridge to the dock had filled in with sand and clumps of dune grass. The driftwood log had long since washed away.

I felt the presence of my camp friends. We flew separately now, in different flocks, but we could still come together and rest for a spell upon the same imaginary log. Nancy would find peace, happiness, and the rekindling of an old love. Christie would meet the challenges ahead. Lori would always have a ready laugh and a generous outlook. Mary would remain steady as a pine. I wished for Cindy, Sarah, Susie, and Tori to know how much they meant to me.

I saw them arm in arm, making room. I joined the line, and we faced the lake. It shimmered in an electric shade of aqua, teaming with life and the shifting currents of change. Puffy white clouds formed on the horizon. Some of them held gray outlines heralding rough weather. Others held an opalescent brilliance, surreal and beautiful. 365. The number popped into my head, and I knew it was the vista of a coming year.

I stepped away from the log and hovered above the turbulent waves. A single cloud, streaked by the rising sun, spiraled downward, becoming a white dock for passage. I landed on its planks and entered a new day while a voice whispered, "Let us hear a conclusion to the matter. Look up and see Thy Countenance through the mist."

The phone rang on the bedside table. I listened to the wake-up message, recalling the clarity of my dream. It would stay with me.

My face felt wet. Tears had leaked, unbidden, just like this, for weeks after Mom had died. Only this time, the overflow sprang from joy, rather than sorrow.

Within a halfhour we were in the car, and the girls had gone back to sleep. As the miles sped onward, I realized I was leaving camp with a replenished and satisfied spirit. I "felt jazzed," as Nancy had once described it. Even the freeway, so crowded and dangerous, could not wreck my calm. I had cleansed away regrets about the past and swelled optimistically about the future. For the first time, I was leaving camp as the same person I had been going in.

EIGHTY-SIX

LESSONS OF THE LAKE

LAKE MICHIGAN HAD faded to a pleasant summer memory. I stood in my kitchen with the phone pressed against my ear. It was sore from the wait. Finally, "Ma'am?"

"Yes?"

"There isn't anyone here that can pick you up this morning. But we're open until four o'clock."

I sighed. My breath whistled against the phone's mouthpiece. An engine light had appeared on the dashboard, necessitating a visit to the dealer. Now it was repaired, and I had no way to pick it up. KT was lifeguarding. Andrew was out of town. My husband worked too far away, and my closest friends attended a funeral. Three miles of pavement separated me from the dealership.

"Thank you," I said as another call cut in, making intermittent clicking sounds. "I'll find a way." I forced myself to sound cheerful.

I hung up, and the phone rang from the incoming call. "Hi. I'm on my way to work." My sister's hurried voice carried across three states. "I just wanted to hear about the reunion."

"And I want to hear about Mexico."

"I'm glad to be home," she laughed, condensing her entire trip into this solitary remark.

"One quick thing," I said. "Do you remember the waterspouts?" My question flickered among the fiber optics. I had never asked this. Not in thirty years. I even cringed a little to say it, like Beth at the reunion, as if the topic was somehow forbidden.

"Sure." Her voice went down on the end.

"What do you remember?" I prodded.

She responded easily, as if reciting a well-known event of international scope. "We watched them coming. We were not afraid. One sank into the lake, and the other turned to mist."

"So, it really happened."

"Yes. It was a miracle."

I hustled over to the bookshelf, amazed by the technology of cordless phones. "Let me give you Webster's definition." I fumbled for the book then flipped through the pages. "Here! 'Ordinary rules of nature are set aside in an extraordinary event manifesting divine intervention in human affairs.'"

She held silent on the other end, and I expected her to deny it, as I had.

"That's right," she replied. "We sent those waterspouts packing."

"We?" My heart thumped wildly.

"Maggie, Bobbi, Linda, Shane, you and me," she said. "But we had help. And that's what counts."

"But Maggie lives out of the country. No one has heard from Linda or Bobbi. And, apparently, Shane doesn't remember."

"That doesn't mean it didn't happen. We remember."

I wanted to believe her, as my wise, older sister. "So, the ordinary rules of nature were set aside that day."

"Yeah." Her voice returned to its lighthearted impatience. "The rules as our continents know them, anyway."

Her credibility crumbled around me. "You mean our consciousness?"

"Take your pick!" she guffawed. "Either way a higher rule took over when we asked and expected the ordinary ones to move aside. Call me later."

"Have a good day," I said automatically.

"And if it's not, I'll make it one," she laughed.

The line clicked dead. My house was quiet and empty except for our aging cocker spaniel, who snored a steady vibration along the wooden floors. I closed the blinds against the rising sun that would heat my kitchen like an oven on this hot August day. I tucked some money and my license into my pocket and headed for the door. I could be home in forty-five minutes and have my workout for the day. Skipping down the driveway, I held my back straight. Despite the trees, hills, and houses hemming me in, I sensed the stir of a breeze, the largess of the sky, and the wide expanse of a distant lake beckoning me to recall its lessons. Waterspouts or tornadoes, miracles or doubts, results are what mattered. I would walk the three miles to the body shop, I would cross heavy lanes of traffic, and I would be safe.

SOURCES

AMERICAN HERITAGE DICTIONARY of the English Language, 4th ed. Boston: Houghton Mifflin Company, 2000.

ANSWERS.COM, "TYPES OF Dune," http://www.ask.com/web?qsrc=2417&o=10260 4&l=dir&q=types+of+dunes.

HOLY BIBLE, KING James Version.

BRINKMANN, PAUL, "FOX River fuels Lake Michigan algae outbreaks, Phosphorus output into lake surpasses Milwaukee." Press-Gazette Door County bureau, September 6, 2004.

CAMPBELL, THOMAS "THE River of Life." www.bartleby.com.

EDDY, MARY BAKER. Various works.

FOX, EMMET. VARIOUS works.

"GREAT LAKES SHORELINE Geology." www.great-lakes.net/teach/geog/shoreline/shore.

HARRIS, VICTORIA A. "Nuisance Algae on Lake Michigan Shores," University of Wisconsin Sea Grant Institute.

INDIANA DEPARTMENT OF Natural Resources, DNR—Division of Historic Preservation and Archeology.

LELAND MICHIGAN CHAMBER of Commerce. "A Brief History of Leland." www.lelandmi.com.

LETTERS TO THE Editor (various). "Northern Express," August 29, 2002, www.northernexpress.com., "Dismay over swap plan," by Michael Huey, Vienna Austria

NATIONAL PARK SERVICE, U.S. Department of the Interior. "National Lakeshore Michigan, Sleeping Bear Dunes."

NOAA's NATIONAL WEATHER Service, Gaylord, MI Weather Forecast Office. APX Webmaster.

"SAILBOATSTUFF MARINE PARTS & Supplies—Glossary." Special to the *San Diego Daily Transcript.* http://www.sailboatstuff.com/glos_a_c.html.

"WATERSPOUTS ARE TORNADOES over water." *USA Today.* http://www.usatoday.com/weather/wspouts.htm.

ACKNOWLEDGMENTS

CREDIT FOR INSPIRATION must be given to F.M.G., Dorothy Ann Lincoln, the legacy of William M. "Skipper" Beals, Cora Mautz Beals, Helen M. Huey, Arthur S. "Major" Huey, Paul Hufstader, Marcia Schaberg Hufstader, Marilyn Rinker, and the written works of Emmet Fox and Mary Baker Eddy.

Thanks to my family: John, Andrew, Katharine (my K-girl), and David. Susan, you rock. Katie and Angela, you are the most beautiful muses. To Linda's family, wherever you are, her memory lives on. The CT class of 1976, and our counselor, deserve praise for their unconditional support and generosity of spirit. Thank you to my book group: Misty Watkins, Susie Parker, Sue Demeria, Melanie Wagner, Micki Turner, and Katharine Nace Taylor, for sharing your beautiful minds. Jerome Holton, you set me in the right direction. Thanks for seeing what I could not. Marsie Frost and Linda Whitlock, you arrived just in time! Thank you for sharing your wisdom.

These individuals kept me going, with suggestions and encouragement, whether they realize it or not: S. S. Peters, Marlin F. Schmidt, Pemberton H. Lincoln Jr., Mary R. Mason, A. Demas, K. M. Jones, Beverly J. Shomsky, Barbara Walsh, Patricia Kyme Kerr, N. G. Brook Heckel, D. Heckel, Susan L. Timoner, C. E. Sears, M. H. Thompson, C. M. Marston, S. W. Coté, S. K. Huscroft, V. C. Moore, L. M. Moffatt, S. Freund Blatt, Shannon Hall, Eric Mazzacone, Kyme Nygard, Kim Winston, Kimberlee Bowles Hahn, Debbie Beach, Felicia Mingione-Buzan, Cyndi Kane, Lisa Peters Owen, Jill S. Goss, Peter Phinney, Pamela S. Feurt, Maribeth S. Shaheen, Molly Goss, Mary H. Sisson, Minerva Moy, Tami Gladstone, Ted and Teresa Timmerman, Janice McLaulin, Paul and Lynn Green, Dr. Rob and Marci Waldman.

Thank you Michelle Gillette, Nina Ryan, and Jay Boggis for your insightful editing.

A special thanks to David Lamb and Joseph Pittman, and all the kind folks at Vantage Press, and Vantage Point.

Lastly, to camp alumni, thank you for making a difference.